# Pie in the Sky

## Other books by Susan G. Purdy

*The Perfect Cake*

*The Perfect Pie*

*The Family Baker*

*Let Them Eat Cake*

*Have Your Cake and Eat It, Too*

*A Piece of Cake*

*As Easy as Pie*

*Christmas Cooking Around the World*

*Christmas Gifts Good Enough to Eat*

*Jewish Holiday Cookbook*

*Christmas Cookbook*

*Let's Give a Party*

*Christmas Gifts for You to Make*

*Books for You to Make*

*Jewish Holidays*

*Festivals for You to Celebrate*

*Holiday Cards for You to Make*

*If You Have a Yellow Lion*

*Be My Valentine*

*Christmas Decorations for You to Make*

*My Little Cabbage*

# Pie in the Sky

## Successful Baking at High Altitudes

100 Cakes, Pies, Cookies, Breads, and Pastries

Home-Tested for Baking at Sea Level, 3,000, 5,000, 7,000, and 10,000 Feet

(and Anywhere in Between)

## Susan G. Purdy

*Illustrations by the Author*
*Photography by Dennis Gottlieb*

WILLIAM MORROW
*An Imprint of* HarperCollins*Publishers*

*This book is dedicated with love*

*to my friend and mentor*

*Hila Colman*

HarperCollins books may be purchased for educational, business, or sales promotional use. For information, please write: Special Markets Department, HarperCollins Publishers Inc., 10 East 53rd Street, New York, NY 10022.

*Designed by rlf design*

Library of Congress Cataloging-in-Publication Data

Purdy, Susan Gold
    Pie in the sky: successful baking at high altitudes: 100 cakes, pies, cookies, breads, and pastries home-tested for baking at sea level, 3,000, 5,000, 7,000, and 10,000 feet (and anywhere in between) / Susan G. Purdy.—1st ed.
        p.   cm.
    Includes index.
    ISBN 0-06-052258-5
    1. Baking.  2. Sea level.  I. Title.

TX763.P9624   2005
641.8'15—dc22                             2004053930

12 13 SCP 10 9

# Contents

# Acknowledgments

I offer this book to the memory of my mother, Frances Joslin Gold, who didn't live to see it completed but never doubted that I could do it. She always believed in me, cheered me on, and loved to see me baking her delicious recipes, especially apple pie. My greatest thanks go to my husband, Geoffrey, and our daughter, Cassandra, who offered encouragement throughout this project, and even baked their own pies while I was so often away from home. Special thanks are due my lovely Cassandra for her skill in testing my bread recipes, her editorial eye, and her help in styling the photographs. For reading my travel sections with loving yet critical eyes, I thank my favorite writers, Hila Colman and my aunt, Sesyle Joslin Hine.

A work of this scope involves nearly everyone who crossed my path during the time of my research and travel, from family to friends, neighbors, and professional colleagues. To all who visited our Connecticut home, to those who shared their high altitude homes with me or visited my homes-away-from-home, to all who tasted my desserts or tried out my recipes, to those who told me their high altitude baking stories or listened (interminably) to mine, to anyone inadvertently omitted from the following lists, I say a grateful thank you.

## On the home front, at sea level

For answering frantic mountaintop phone calls with calm and reassuring advice, I thank the eternally wise and patient Atlanta food scientist Shirley Corriher and her husband, Arch (research engineer, Georgia Institute of Technology), who cheerfully responded to more than his share of my technical queries and contributed heroically to my "high altitude science" chapter. They held my hand on the peaks and in the valleys. I know I would have fallen (or jumped) off more than one mountain without their help.

I am indebted to Florence and Wendell Minor for introducing my book to astronaut Buzz Aldrin, whom I thank for his gracious jacket quote. For being there when I needed help, I thank my attorney–literary agent, Arthur Klebanoff. For her belief in this book and incisive editorial skill, I thank Harriet Bell, as well as copyeditor Judith Sutton, rlf design, production editor Mareike Paessler, and editorial assistant Lucy Baker. For their enthusiasm, creativity, and technical skill, I want to thank photographer Dennis Gottlieb and retoucher Paternostro, Inc. For her generous food styling consultation, I am grateful to Delores Custer; for food styling, I thank Lynn Miller.

For reviewing the technical aspects of high altitude baking science, I thank good friends (and engineers), Seth Bredbury (MIT) and Jan Piet Hoekstra (IBM). For 24/7 computer assistance, technical wizardry, cyber-miracles, and patient encouragement, I again thank Jan, as well as David DeJean, my nephew David

Lieberman, Mark Devine, Ed Clark, Bob Flavin, and Donald Whittaker.

For introducing me to Sandy and Skip Porterfield in Breckenridge, Colorado, I thank my friend Mari Frohne and her sister, Kit Johnson. For travel information, baking help, recipe sharing, taste-testing, editorial advice, and general cheerleading, thanks go to Boston pastry chef Kristin Eycleshymer (who also developed recipes with me in Breckenridge), Carol Hook, Elizabeth and Pirie MacDonald, Joan Moore, Jane Hornung, Edna Alvarez, my students at Cambridge School of Culinary Arts, Susan (Charley) Kanas, Simone Demers Collins (Industry Development Officer, Alberta, Canada, Canola Producers), Janice Cole and Kathy Childers (*Cooking Pleasures* magazine), Kathy Fleeger, Patricia and Richard Abrams, Marcia and Barry Soloff, Stephan Chodorov, and Steve, Elsa, and Rachel Reiss. For a fantastic road trip from Santa Fe to Phoenix via the Grand Canyon and Mesa Verde, I thank Olivia and Willy Blumer. For information about mountain areas in New York State, I thank Penny Preston (Lake Placid), Peter and Elaine Pratt, Victoria Ward, and Rosemary Montague-Tiesler.

I am indebted to Justin Newby (Managing Director, KitchenAid, Saatchi & Saatchi) for supplying me with a KitchenAid mixer, and to Mary Rogers, Director of Marketing Communications, Cuisinart, for providing me with a Cuisinart food processor so I could have my favorite appliances with me out west.

For sharing personal high altitude stories for use in this book, I thank cookbook authors and chefs Letty Flatt, Joyce Goldstein, Elaine Gonzales, James McNair, Russ Parsons, Greg Patent, Jacques Pépin, Rick Rodgers, and Martha Rose Shulman.

*In New Mexico and Arizona*

After nearly five years of baking on mountaintops around the country, I have many friends in high places to whom I owe thanks. Nevertheless, it is easy to know where my list, and my story, begins: in the Santa Fe kitchen of Marilyn Abraham and her husband, Sandy MacGregor, where the idea for this book originated. They have never wavered in their enthusiasm for—and belief in—this book. They have always been willing to test a recipe, taste a cake, read a manuscript, and offer thoughtful advice on a moment's notice. To the generous "godparents" of this project, I say, "Toques off!" and offer my grateful thanks, and the highest pie in the sky!

Also in Santa Fe, I offer a celebratory laurel wreath to my capable baking assistant Stacy Pearl, whose common sense and creativity helped me through high and low times and greatly enhanced the recipes in this book; my students and the staff at Cookworks Cooking School, as well as Mary and Chuck Kehoe and Ann Lowry; and the helpful staff at Los Cosas Cookware and Cooking School. For being family when and where I needed it, I thank my cousin Bessy Berman. For insight into professional baking techniques, I thank Donna Brand and Maggie Faralla. For recipe tasting and testing, general help, encouragement, and travel adventures, I thank friends Nanscy Neiman and Bernie LeGette, Anney Levy, Lorraine Schechter, Jane Reid, Carol Anthony, Virginia Grey, David Jenness and Ken Collins, Mark Hopkins, Peter and Deborah Buehner, Linda Mason Hunter, Walter Cooper, Douglas Bland, Peyton Young and Harry Shapiro; "The Gardening Angels": Linda Rice, Nancy Helle, and Lindsey Caviness; Katherine Huelster, Olivia Ogorek, Katherine Peck, and Lupe and Sarah Baca. For publicizing my books and high altitude baking classes, I thank Patricia West-Barker, food editor of the *Santa Fe New Mexican,* and John Vollertson, food writer and cooking teacher. For testing last-minute recipes, I thank pastry chef Mary Cech. For reviewing my recipes when I was spokesperson for Softasilk

Cake Flour, I thank the staff at General Mills High Altitude Test Laboratory in Albuquerque.

For help researching test locations in Arizona, I thank Barbara Pool Fenzl, Regina Campbell, Miriam Youmans, Barbara Clarihew, Ann Marchiony, and Pete Arnold.

## In North Carolina and Virginia

A huge hug and grateful thanks to my cousin Stacey Seigle Carson and her husband, Jim Carson, for the generous loan of their vacation home in Grassy Creek, North Carolina. Thanks to their friends, including Helga and Jack Carpenter, who taught me about pound cake and raspberry cultivation; and Gayle Winston, owner of River House Country Inn (Grassy Creek), chef Bill Klein, and the inn staff and friends, including Jan, John, Brenda, and Warren. For enthusiastic daily recipe tasting, I send special kudos to Highland Builder Steven Greif and his helpers Juan Naum and Todd Melesco. Thanks to Jim Wooten, Soil Scientist (Ashe County) for help with maps and elevations and introductions. Thanks also to Jeannie Daubar; caterer Niki Weir; the Accidental Baker, Jacky Brown; Carolyn Goodman Shepherd, Associate Extension Agent (Ashe County Center, North Carolina State University); and Chris, Heather, and Cypress Taylor.

In Trout Dale, Virginia, I am indebted to my generous new friend Cynthia Moore, who (without a moment's hesitation) invited me into her life and allowed me to turn her kitchen into a two-week test site.

## In the Denver, Colorado, area

Thanks to Tracy and Randy Spalding who helped me in a million ways, including the generous loan of their home on several occasions; thanks, also, to Emma and Preston Spalding and their classmates at the Stargate School, who ate Tracy's test cookies. Thanks to pie aficionado and writer John Lehndorf and to Marty Meitus, food editor of the *Rocky Mountain News*. For testing recipes, I thank Tracy Spalding, Melissa Hornung, Mary Cech and Elizabeth Perrault, and Barbara Hann. For a fabulous weekend taste-testing at their Glenwood Springs home, I thank Marianne O'Carroll and Timm Fautsko.

## In Breckenridge, Colorado

For the gracious loan of their Breckenridge mountain chalet, I am indebted to Sandy and Skip Porterfield, who welcomed this friend-of-a-friend as if I were family and introduced me to an embracing community including Suzanne Pedersen, Pat and Wiley DeCarli, Judy and Tom Scollard, and Joanna and Lenny Wellington. For gracious advice on everything from pecan pies to night-roaming bears, I thank my next-door neighbors, The Reverend Ron and Charlotte Griffin, as well as Nathan Griffin and the young people at the Red Door Christian Ministry Center, who were the appreciative recipients of most of my test baking.

For their advice and help, I thank local professional bakers Laura Komeshian of Clint's Bakery in Breckenridge, David Fair of Mollie MacDuff's in Fairplay; Victor of Butterhorn Bakery in Frisco; Janet Crispell, former owner, Blue Moose Restaurant; Kevin Clarke of Colorado Mountain Culinary Institute in Dillon; and Ned Archibald, executive pastry chef of Keystone Resorts in Keystone, Colorado.

In Vail, I thank Nancy Hassett, owner of the Savory Inn and Cooking School, and her then-executive chef, Deanna Scimio, who shared baking tips and biscotti. Just a week after my visit, Deanna turned into my guardian angel when she drove me (with all my equipment) to Denver, helped me test a couple of bread recipes, and then rushed me to the airport when I had to make an emergency departure to come home. For offering me her home in Telluride (though I never got there), I thank Nancy Bynum and her parents and my friends Maggie Burke Snyder and the late Arthur Snyder.

## In Idaho

For inviting me to share their McCall, Idaho, home for three weeks while I transformed their impeccable dining room and kitchen into a sugary test studio, I am indebted to friends Ann and Dan Endresen. Thanks also to Gail Delp for her hospitality to me in Boise; and to the Endresens' family, friends, and neighbors who loaned me their baking equipment and showed me around, including their daughter Linda Pierson, her adorable son Zane (who helped me bake a soufflé), Donna and Ken Harjung, Maureen and Craig Perseo, Doris and Dave Early, and George Holloway, enthusiastic taste-tester and, with Dan, great tour guide. I appreciate the thoughtful notes written by doctors and nurses in the staff lounge at McCall Memorial Hospital, where I took the majority of my test samples with comment sheets attached. Thanks to professional bakers Corey McDonald (Evening Rise Bread Company, McCall), and Susan and George Dorris (Flight of Fancy Bake Shop, Donnelly, Idaho).

## In Utah

For generously sharing her specialized knowledge of altituding recipes at 8,000 feet and above, I am indebted to executive pastry chef Letty Flatt (Deer Valley Resort, Park City).

# Introduction

Crestfallen cakes? Miserable muffins? Pathetic pies? Not in my kitchen! Catastrophes are not my style—at least they weren't until I began traveling across the United States to teach baking. Before that, I blithely assumed that the recipes I had so carefully developed in my Connecticut kitchen (elevation 540 feet) would work everywhere else. When they did not, my frustration level quickly reached the boiling point (199.8°F at an altitude of 7,000 feet). At first, like everyone else, I followed standard high altitude "recipe adjustment guides" to make my cakes rise. To my surprise, many of the guidelines did not work. To remove the guesswork, I decided to bake a group of my favorite (sea-level) recipes over and over again at different altitudes, repeating the tests until I understood what was happening.

One of my first baking disasters occurred quite a few years ago, when I tried to bake a chocolate buttermilk cake in Santa Fe (7,000 feet). I flew in a day early to prepare for a demonstration baking class in town. Fortunately, I was at the home of some understanding friends. I whipped up my favorite chocolate buttermilk cake, smiled with confidence as the two layers rose in the oven, and then watched with morbid fascination as they cooled and crashed. I scooped up the mess, topped it with whipped cream, and served it to our assembled friends as pudding cake, but I knew I couldn't teach such a recipe to students without making serious adjustments.

What happened? Between the dry atmosphere and the high altitude, dramatic forces were trying to get my attention.

Soon thereafter, I discovered that a sea-level recipe for lemon meringue pie worked well in Denver (5,000 feet) and only needed a few changes in Santa Fe, but its well-whipped, mile-high meringue crashed and dripped onto the floor when I tried to serve it in Breckenridge, Colorado (10,000 feet).

In one of its early years, when the contest was located in Boulder, Colorado (5,000 feet), I was a judge for the All-American Pie Bake-Off sponsored by the American Pie Council. I was also scheduled to demonstrate both cake and pie baking there as the national spokesperson for General Mills Softasilk Cake Flour. Since my recipes had been developed at sea level, the General Mills High Altitude Test Laboratory in Albuquerque, New Mexico, wanted to take a look at them to make sure they would work in Boulder. Their results were instructive: only small adjustments were needed for cookies and piecrusts, but cakes required complete makeovers, with alterations in sugar-flour ratios, liquid and leavening amounts, baking temperatures, and times.

As I continued to travel and tinker, worrying about whether my recipes would rise or fall, changing ingredients with changes in elevation, I became more and more intrigued with the details and complexity of high altitude baking. It was a puzzle I wanted to solve.

My research started with baking colleagues, libraries, high altitude websites (few and far between and with a great deal of inaccurate but well-intentioned information), university extension services (especially in Colorado, New Mexico, and Utah), cookware shops, and bookstores in high altitude towns. Yet I found little information or help beyond a couple of books and a colorful plasticized bookmark with a finger-length list of hints and tips. Most general cookbooks ignored high altitudes completely or repeated the same incorrect timeworn tips. Others relied upon tables of altitude adjustment calculations, devised by computers or calculators, "above 3,500 feet use 29 percent less leavening and 5.5 percent more eggs," which were at best awkward and impractical to use.

To get a better grasp of the physics involved in the altitude versus air pressure story, I spoke with three engineers, Seth Bredbury, Jan Piet Hoekstra, and Arch Corriher, all patient good friends willing to explain theoretical complexities so that I could grasp them. A computer-savvy friend, Mark Devine, devised a computer solution based on our compilation of the tips we found in "expert" tables. Mark built these calculations into colored columns that he spread neatly across my laptop screen. All I had to do was type in a sea-level recipe and the adjusted ingredients list magically popped up, changing for use at 3,000, 5,000, or 7,000 feet. It was a brilliant (we even thought marketable) idea until I found—in my mountain test kitchens—that the rules were wrong most of the time. One size did not fit all.

Just when I was wishing I had a place to try out all my theoretical knowledge, the phone rang. "Would you consider coming out to Santa Fe for a month to cat-sit for Pete and Norman while we travel?" asked my friend Marilyn. Consider? It didn't take a proverbial New York

minute for me to realize my friends Marilyn Abraham and Sandy MacGregor, cookbook authors and publishing professionals, were offering me the chance of a lifetime to develop recipes at 7,000 feet in their wonderfully equipped kitchen.

I was scheduled to teach a dessert class at Cookworks, a Santa Fe cooking school, later that spring, so I devoted most of my trip to working on a group of cakes specifically designed for that altitude. I baked them over and over until Pete, Norman, and a few other, less furry, friends loved every crumb.

My class was billed as an interactive, problem-solving workshop in high altitude baking. It was standing room only as enthusiastic home cooks crowded into the kitchen with notebooks of family recipes they could not reproduce at 7,000 feet. A few were longtime New Mexico residents, but the majority of students had moved there from sea level in the previous ten years. All had nearly given up on baking at home. During the class, they took painstaking notes on their hand-out recipes, trying to record every tip I could offer. And they volunteered to be testers if I promised to take on the challenge and bring them a cookbook of fail-safe recipes . . . including a heavenly homemade pie in the sky!

I soon learned that baking was only one aspect of the high altitude story. Not long after I'd returned from New Mexico, I was at a dinner party when someone asked me what I was working on. Rather reluctantly, I mentioned my fascination with high altitude. To my delight, this led to a lively discussion, as several guests were interested in sports or had traveled across the country by car or RV. Everyone had heard of trekkers developing extreme high altitude sickness when climbing to high elevations; some had even felt common symptoms, like dizziness, shortness of breath, or headaches, while hiking in the Grand Canyon or riding horseback in the High Sierras. A backpacker, Hilary, said she never went climbing without a special finely tuned high altitude camp stove. Richard, a golfer, informed us that in New Mexico his golf balls went about 5 percent farther, due to less air resistance, changing his game slightly. Tennis-playing George noted that in Aspen, Colorado, he only used "high altitude" tennis balls.

I may have learned more than I needed to know at that party, since I don't play high altitude tennis or golf (I once asked for "cookie baking" sneakers in a Nike store), but the conversation made me realize how many people work and play at high altitudes. In fact, more than thirty-four of the fifty states and a large part of Canada have populations living at or above 2,500 feet in elevation. Newspaper reports frequently refer to the large recent immigration of Americans from the Midwestern and central states to the Mountain West. I have family living in the mountains of North Carolina and Virginia, which is a rapidly growing region. Increasingly, it seems, people are living the high life.

## Getting High Is Half the Fun!

When I began this journey, I had what I thought was a very simple plan: select about 100 favorite old-fashioned sea-level recipes, take them to kitchens in major high altitude locations, and bake them repeatedly until I understood why and how to adjust them. That done, I could publish foolproof, fully realized formulas, eliminating the need for altitude adjustment tables (or at least for these major sites). It sounded feasible. How many tests? How long would it take? What about ingredients and equipment? And where should I go?

I was able to locate most ingredients I needed wherever I went, although I carried an emergency pack of crystallized ginger, poppy seeds, and matzoh meal in my suitcase. Finding equipment became a more formidable logistical exercise. I had a six-page list of essentials, because many recipes needed different pans (9-inch round cake pans, 2½-inch muffin tins) and/or special utensils (pastry brushes, Silpat baking mats, and baking parchment). In the end, I solved the problem by begging and borrowing some items, shipping many cartons to each location from my Connecticut home, and then stuffing nearly my entire home pantry into my Subaru station wagon for the two locations within driving distance.

I wanted test locations in the eastern as well as the western part of the country, and I wanted places that would be fun to stay in. I guessed (underestimating every time) how long I would need in each place. I selected the elevations on the basis of my culinary research, but I also considered where the largest high altitude populations were located. Cooking authorities seemed to agree that 2,000 to 3,000 feet above sea level is (more or less) the point where cooking, and especially baking, begins to be noticeably affected by changes in atmosphere and humidity. I also wanted to push the envelope, baking at 10,000 feet in ski resort country, where, I had been told, home baking is simply impossible.

I'd originally planned to rent living space in each location, but the more people I talked to about my idea, the more opportunities presented themselves. Ultimately, I found many amazingly generous friends and relatives who were intrigued by the project, wanted to be involved, and offered to share their homes, cars, even their friends. Because of these opportunities, I settled on locations in Grassy Creek, North Carolina (2,850 feet); Trout Dale, Virginia (3,500 feet); McCall, Idaho (5,023 feet); Denver, Colorado (5,280 feet), Santa Fe, New Mexico (7,000 feet); and Breckenridge, Colorado (10,000 feet).

I was used to being a traveling teacher but not a traveling kitchen. My greatest worry was that I would leave behind some essential like my altimeter and compass, my rolling pin, or my recipe files. Fortunately, I kept it all together, never fell off a mountain, and only occasionally lost my place, both geographically and in my baking progression.

# Friends in High Places

—⁓—

## North Carolina • Virginia

"We live in the mountains, you know, why don't you come down to visit us?" my cousins Stacey and Jim Carson asked, inviting me to their North Carolina vacation home. Mountains? High altitude mountains? This could be a great opportunity to be with family and, coincidentally, perhaps be the answer to my search for a recipe-testing location at between 2,500 and 3,500 feet and east of the Rockies. "We're not exactly sure of our elevation. We'll figure it out once you get here, but we're near Boone [3,300 feet] and Blowing Rock [4,000 feet]," they assured me. "We're at the end of a dirt road, quiet, and private, and if you want to work here, it's all yours except when we come for weekend tastings."

*Grassy Creek, NC*

How could I refuse? I immediately began to gather my recipes and make lists. Stacey and Jim, both good cooks, had carefully designed a well-equipped kitchen, but I knew I'd have to bring my own gear, from springform pans, whisks, and icing spatulas to digital timers and oven thermometers. My lists grew with my enthusiasm. By the time I packed my car with books, Bundt pans, recipe files, laptop, compass, camera, and dried mango snacks, there was barely room for me to squeeze into the driver's seat with my road map.

I started out on a sunny May morning, filled with optimism and a sense of adventure. As I drove across Virginia to the southwestern corner where the Appalachian Mountains meet the Blue Ridge in Ashe County, North Carolina, the hills got steeper, the valleys deeper, and the towns had more colorful names: Mouth-of-Wilson was my first landmark, not far from Trout Dale, en route to Grassy Creek and my new home on the north fork of the New River, a curling bronze ribbon that wound languorously through flatlands of tall emerald and ochre grass.

I followed the river road as Stacey had directed until I turned into their drive and began to climb into the woods. In a clearing at the top, I came to their gray clapboard loft-house nestled cozily into the wooded hillside. It reminded me a little of a chalet, with a side deck overlooking the terraced vegetable garden and lawn sloping down to the overflowing creek.

I spent the first morning organizing my clutter of cake pans and unpacking my suitcase office. In the afternoon on the deck, we caught up on Stacey's work as executive director of the Art Alliance of Greensboro, admired her beautifully hand-crafted pottery, and talked about Jim's projects as an educator and musician/leader of a popular swing band. The next day, they gave me a scenic tour of the town, the farmers' market, and the best local supermarket—soon to become my primary destination.

My first job was to find out exactly where I was in terms of elevation. If my cousins' house turned out to be below 2,000 feet, I would have to rent a test kitchen in a higher spot. I went first to the local chamber of commerce. "Would you have any maps showing the elevation of the mountains in this area?" I asked. "You mean altitude? Nope," said the young attendant, "folks around here don't bother measuring their mountains, they just enjoy 'em. Can I rent you a canoe?" Smiling and shaking my head, I walked across the street to city hall. "Altitude?

Why do you care? No one here's interested in that, try the Ashe County Court House." I did. I worked my way laboriously through the departments of deeds and records, taxes, and the (woefully misnamed) mapping office. It was hard to believe: I was in the mountains, but I couldn't find anyone who knew the altitude (let alone who would admit to having baking problems attributed to it). In mounting despair, I told my story to yet another office manager. "What you need, honey," she said, "is to meet 'The Accidental Baker.'" She sent me a few miles down the road to an old high school converted into offices, where, in the revamped cafeteria kitchen under the sign "The Accidental Baker," I found Jacky Brown, a friendly young woman wrapped in a chocolate-spattered apron.

"Glad to meet you. Sure, I can answer your questions, but I have to keep moving here," she laughed. "Why the name? I guess I'm an accidental baker because I was a psychologist until four years ago, when I decided to do this instead." I could feel the rush of purposeful energy as she moved swiftly from a whirling Hobart mixer to a glass case of warm muffins and a cash register facing a line of hungry customers. At the first break, she handed me a big lemon–poppy seed muffin. "Try it," she said with a confident smile.

"Sorry I don't know our exact altitude, but it's a good question. That's certainly what caused all my trouble. My old recipes just don't work up here." (Bingo! My luck had finally turned!) "After lots of experiments, I've finally figured it out and now I can bake anything. I do all the breads and desserts for Sweet Aromas Bakery in town. When I adjust a recipe, I start small, but the changes I make are really important. Breads are easy. I just punch 'em down more often, because they rise too fast. I add a little extra flour to cookie dough, cut a bit of sugar or leavening from muffins, and tinker with oven temperatures. Have you talked to Carolyn Shepherd, our county cooperative extension service agent? She's in Jefferson, at the Agricultural Services building."

Another lead . . . I was on my way. When I saw the pressure cooker in Carolyn's bookcase, I knew I was in the right place. "Glad to meet you, maybe I *can* help," she said. "The topography here is so up and down, you'll find homes at anywhere from 2,500 to 4,000 feet. Your book would be a great help. I wish we had it now to give out to newcomers who move here from the flatlands. When their baking gets bad enough, they end up in here asking me for help and all I have is a pamphlet with some tables and tips. You know what you need?" she asked. "If you want to talk elevation, you want a soil scientist. The office is downstairs."

The first man I met said, "Altitude's not my thing," and pointed me down the hall toward the Farm Soil Conservation Office. It was nearly closing time when, exhausted, I stumbled into the cubicle of soil conservationist Jim Wooten. Wearing a windbreaker, with a baseball cap on his head, he was hunched over his computer, surrounded by stacks of U.S. Geological Survey topographical maps (the ones I'd been dreaming of). "I can't believe I found you," I laughed. He looked up quizzically. "I usually help farmers, not bakers," he said. The notion that I needed to find a precise location in which to bake cakes clearly amused him. "Sure the oddest request I've heard. Of course I can help." He unfurled a map, spread it across his desk, and in a minute had easily pinpointed my cousins' house at 2,750 to 2,800 feet (perfect!), their neighbors between 3,000 and 3,500 feet, and other local attractions at 4,000 to 4,500 feet.

"I know someone else who likes to bake," Jim said. "You should meet her. She's on my way home, come on." Afraid I'd get lost on my own, he led me to the real estate office of his cake-baking realtor friend Jeannie Daubar.

Jim had hardly introduced us and slipped out the door before Jeannie and I were talking cakes. "I'm from Florida, and I always loved to bake. North Carolina is fine," she glanced up at me ruefully, "but I haven't been able to bake a good pound cake since I moved here fifteen years ago. They just sag in the center and stick in the pan, especially on rainy days. I don't know why. Those recipes worked great before I came here. Breads are easier. I punch 'em down again if they rise too fast. I have to get things right because I sell most of what I bake, along with the vegetables I grow, at the West Jefferson Farmers' Market." "What's your altitude?" I asked. "Oh, I know that. We live at precisely 3,600 feet, on a hill just outside town. I have an altimeter on the dashboard of my car for my real estate business." My obvious delight and endless questions were interrupted by her next appointment. "Look, why don't you just come on over to my house next Sunday and bake with my mother and me?" she urged, holding out her hand to say goodbye.

Early the next morning, I began my own baking at Stacey's house. I decided to start with muffins, thinking success or failure would be relatively easy to spot, manipulate, and correct. My first effort, standard sea-level blueberry muffins, looked pretty good coming out of the oven. Could have risen more, but their taste and texture were fine. Test #2: I decided not to change the ingredients, but I raised the oven temperature 25 degrees and added a few minutes to the baking time. Result: good rise, fine texture, a keeper. After that relative success (only two tests), bran muffins, with their much heavier batter, were a big surprise. Test #1 (sea-level recipe) were flat on top, with a heavy, gummy crumb. I began to tinker, taking care not to make too many changes at one time. Test #2: Cut a little sugar and added a little more flour, hoping for more structural strength. Result: still flat. Test #3: Cut out the baking soda (it is there to neutralize the acidity of the brown sugar and molasses, but acidity is good at high altitudes because it helps batter set quickly) and reduced the baking powder by one-quarter (less is more: let the altitude do its work). Result: better, but still not enough rise. Test #4: Reduced the heavy All-Bran by ⅓ cup and added ⅓ cup lighter-weight flour, switched from ½ cup dark brown sugar to ½ cup minus 1 tablespoon white (again to lighten the load), and added a tablespoon of milk. Result: almost there. Test #5: Kept all the other changes and raised the oven temperatures 25 degrees. Result: perfect rise with rounded top, good texture. Five tests . . . it was clear that this project would be slow going, with many trips to the market, and plenty of muffins to share with neighbors.

Would my muffin experiences apply to cakes? I began with a sea-level recipe for butter cake, which sank as it cooled, stuck to the greased pan, and had a coarse, heavy crumb. Next, a pound cake that emerged flat on top, dense, and nearly wet inside. It was clear that I needed to "altitude" all my sea-level recipes, adjusting each one with small steps as I had done with the muffins.

Most recipes needed a little more flour and less sugar; and in some cases, but not all, it helped to increase the oven temperature and/or baking time. Each recipe presented different problems. I had to make some recipes seven or eight, or more, times until I got the texture and flavor right by sea-level standards. When I finally figured out a working formula and baked a perfect muffin or cake, I was so excited I might as well have won the grand prize at the Pillsbury Bake-Off!

For butter, sponge, and chiffon cakes, using tube pans, which allowed heat to reach the center of the batter instead of round cake pans resulted in success (most of the time). Heavy fruit-filled or oil-based batters, for some reason, rose beautifully with little change required except for an increase in oven temperature.

Pound cake gave me the most trouble. When I baked it in a loaf pan, the sides, which became hot faster, rose before the center (which stayed flat), and the texture was too coarse. When I raised the oven temperature a little, the top crusted into cardboard while the batter below remained gooey. But after five or six tests, several adjustments, and the use of a tube pan, I had a winner.

To solve the pan-sticking problem, I used different ingredients and techniques: Crisco, nonstick vegetable spray, or butter; greasing and flouring the pans, greasing the pans plus a parchment paper liner, and, finally, greasing plus paper liner, then regreasing and flour dusting again. The last method, which took more effort, worked reliably every time.

That Sunday morning, I had no trouble navigating the mountain road up to Jeannie's neat white hundred-year-old farmhouse ringed with bright flower beds. I found her with her mother, Ruth, in an immaculate pine-paneled kitchen removing jars of just-put-up pickles from the counter and setting out mixing bowls.

We began by comparing their Florida (sea-level) pound cake recipe with my brand-new Blue Ridge version. Neither were "true" pound cakes, and both used baking powder. "My favorite is called Five Flavors," Ruth said. "It's made with extracts of coconut, rum, butter, lemon, and vanilla, and it still tastes good when I make it here, but it sinks and sticks." We checked ingredients lists: both recipes used 1 cup sour cream and 3 cups flour, but my version used ¼ cup less sugar (to strengthen the batter structure) and added 2 extra eggs, separated, with the whites softly whipped, plus a tiny bit of cream of tartar (for stability) and baking powder (to guarantee a good rise, previously dependent only upon egg foam). I also raised the baking temperature 25 degrees. "No baking soda?" Ruth asked. "No," I explained, "we have enough leavening already and soda would neutralize the sour cream's acidity. At altitude, acidity helps batter to set quickly." Together, we measured, mixed, underwhipped the egg whites, and folded. Ruth was quickly restoring order at the sink as Jeannie hovered, distractedly drying bowls while peeking anxiously through the oven's glass window. "Cake's up okay, but it looks like it might overbrown," she observed. We covered it lightly with a foil tent for the last ten minutes of baking time, then tested the doneness and set it to cool on a wire rack.

By the time we had measured out flour and chopped apples for our second cake, the pound cake had cooled. As I unmolded it easily onto the serving platter, there was sigh of relief. "You got it," they exclaimed. "It didn't fall, it didn't stick, it looks, well, just like it should. Let's have a taste."

The sweet scent of our baking had reached the barn, and the coffee was brewing when Jeannie's husband, Armando, and his father stopped chores to join us. We sampled slices, picked at crumbs, and talked cakes and barbecue. I had been a stranger just one week ago, but now I felt right at home. "Don't forget to call me. Let's keep this going," Jeannie said, helping me out the door with a hefty slice of cake.

After studying the adjustments I made to Jeannie's recipes, I went back to work on the rest of my cake chapter. My life developed a serene rhythm: Each night I'd plan the next day's recipes. In the morning, after a steaming mug of Earl Grey and a walk to the creek, I'd start measuring and mixing. I made notes on a butter-splotched pad beside me, or at the laptop on the dining room table buried under test sheets, books, and recipes, while Miles Davis, Thelonius Monk, or Jim's swing band played in the background. In spite of my daily frustration with difficult recipes, I was totally at peace, alone in my own world. I happily baked late into the night, sometimes forgetting to eat anything but taste-bites of cake.

My biggest problem became what to do with the growing pile of baked goods. I was glad to be able to turn a couple of chocolate buttermilk layers into a birthday cake for ballet-dancing five-year-old neighbor, Cypress Taylor, and I wrapped up a mocha chiffon cake as a thank-you gift for my elevation hero, Jim Wooten. "Honey, you should have brought steak, not cake," laughed his secretary when I delivered it. "Jim's on Atkins, but I'll eat it."

My dining room table was covered with Stacey's pottery, piled high with test muffins, quick breads, cookies, and layer cakes. When she and Jim arrived home for the weekend, in a swirl of barking dogs and armloads of groceries, I was thrilled to see them both for their company and for their comments. "I love all this stuff," said Jim, tasting a brownie, "but we need to spread the wealth. It won't all fit in our freezer." "Delicious, but it shouldn't be around our waistlines," Stacey added. "Lets go see Gayle."

Their nearest neighbor, Gayle Winston, owned River House Country Inn, a lovely restored 1870 farmhouse in Grassy Creek. Despite its apparent isolation, it had become a destination, celebrated for its cuisine and romantic atmosphere. I looked forward to meeting Gayle, and I already knew she loved to bake.

Graceful and elegant, Gayle met us at the door with a radiant smile and welcomed me at once into the "family" of regulars at the inn. "Bring your desserts down to River House for us to taste anytime," she offered.

After that generous invitation, I regularly carted my accumulated goodies to the inn, knowing I would get an honest critique from Gayle and her colleagues, friends, and staff.

Yet I still had more baked goods than I knew what to do with. Although each recipe required many tests to reach perfection, the in-between stages were certainly good enough to eat, and I didn't want to throw them away. I worried about how I was going to get rid of them until the morning Steve Greif dropped in. Steve was a transplanted New Yorker, with an easy grin and smiling brown eyes, his face framed by a trim black mustache and beard. When I saw him admiring all the cakes, I offered him a bite. "Would you and your crew like to be taste-testers?" "Would we? Just try us! In fact the building inspector comes by tomorrow, so pile it on!" Steve and his "Highland Builders" were working on a project just down the road. That afternoon I brought the first of my daily deliveries: paper plates piled with samples of sour cream coffee cake, orange cheesecake, and brownies. "Are you real?" Steve's boys laughed. "Steve told us there was a lady in the woods who would bring us cake every day but we didn't believe him. We thought he made you up just to make us work harder."

Soon they couldn't get enough. When they heard my car on the gravel road, the guys would drop their hammers, shout "Cake break!" and shinny down the scaffolding to a rough board-and-sawhorse table. "Mmm, still warm, I like this one, not too sweet," mumbled Juan, biting into a square of gingerbread. Though tattooed, pierced, and bearded, with a red bandana tied over black dreadlocks and black cowboy boots on his feet, Juan had a quiet gentle manner. Originally from Argentina, he loved his country's specialty, maté tea, and carried a gourd, the tea leaves, a *bombilla* (silver mouthpiece), and a Thermos of boiling water in his red lunch box. By the time I unpacked my cakes, his brew would be steeping, ready for a seriously high tea in a very rustic setting.

In contrast, Todd, the second member of the crew, looked like a strapping college quarterback. He adored sweets and tried to cajole me into bringing cold beer to go with dessert.

One afternoon I was telling Steve the story of my first week's altitude quest. I mentioned that I had hoped to bake for a while in a kitchen a little higher than my cousin's, say at around 3,500 feet. His face lit up. "Of course! Why didn't I think of that, you and Cynthia need to meet each other. I built her a house in Virginia, just a few miles from here on top of a mountain at exactly 3,475 feet. I'll call her."

The next afternoon I followed Steve's directions, past hills covered with neat green patchwork squares of farmed Christmas trees, climbing into the slightly higher hills, then mountains just a few miles across the North Carolina border into Grayson County, Virginia. After I passed the intimidating "Road Ends Here" sign that was my landmark, I nervously turned onto a half-mile-long gravel drive, passing fenced fields of horses, donkeys, and pigs. I felt as if I were driving up a purely vertical incline, though the house turned out to be only about 200 feet above the 3,300 foot state highway elevation, according to my new dashboard altimeter.

Cynthia was waiting for me on the deck of her house, perched just below the peak of the mountain. The cedar-sided house stood tall, its three levels broken by broad picture windows and a plant-filled, covered deck that wrapped around its waist. A tall, slender young woman

Trout Dale, VA

with masses of long wavy salt-and-pepper hair, she leaned over the railing, a cat in her arms and a bunch of Jack Russell terriers bouncing around her feet. They watched me climb up the steep path from the car. "Glad you could come," Cynthia called out with a wave. "I'm so glad to meet you," she said, "Steve told me all about your work. Here's the thing. I leave at 7:30 a.m. come back around 6, and the house is empty all day. I want you to make yourself at home. Use my kitchen whenever you like." She showed me around and took me up to her aerie under the eaves to see her favorite view, a breath-catching sweep across the top of the maple forest to the Razor Ridge Mountains. "I'd love you to be here," she assured me. I could hardly believe the total ease with which she turned over her home to me, as if she'd known me all her life. The house was filled with light. The sun reflected off the white pine walls, beamed cathedral ceiling, polished cherry floor, and the kitchen island topped with bright blue tiles. I stood at the stove and was—surprisingly—eye to eye with three (seemingly) smiling prairie dogs in a cage on other side of the window.

I couldn't wait to start. I planned to continue staying at my cousins' house for another week, but I'd move out of their kitchen and drive up to Cynthia's each day. We passed each other on the driveway and talked on the phone, and although we never spent much time together, Cynthia and I felt as if we had been friends forever. "I knew as soon as I saw you that we'd be friends," she said. "Steve was right." She lived in what looked like perfect harmony with twenty-three animals, including six dogs, eight cats, three recently adopted Arizona prairie dogs, and the donkeys, pigs, and horses I'd seen from the driveway. I made friends with most of them as I hauled up my daily groceries.

I baked each day from morning to late afternoon, repeating my earlier efforts to see if there were any differences in baking between the elevations (none). The days flew by. When I cleaned up each evening, I wrapped and labeled the day's haul for Cynthia to sample and to share with her students. When she had a cold, I baked her a chocolate espresso cake, writing on top with white chocolate: "Rx. one slice/day, for Cynthia." The chocolate cure worked.

It was hard to leave the magic of the place—Stacey and Jim's wooded hideaway, Cynthia's

> Once during my early days of living near Lake Tahoe (6,250 feet), the brownies that had smelled and looked great while baking turned out so crumbly that they couldn't be cut. Due to show up shortly with dessert for a neighborhood party, I quickly whipped some cream, layered it in a pretty bowl alternately with the crumbled brownies moistened with coffee liqueur, and proudly presented my "Brownie Trifle" as though it were planned all along.
>
> —James McNair, cookbook author, *Afternoon Delights*

peaceable kingdom—and to say goodbye to all my new friends, but I was eager to return to my family. I planned a circuitous return route via a few famous sites I didn't want to miss, including Blowing Rock, the celebrated cliff where "swirling winds make the snow appear to fall upside down," and Grandfather Mountain (at 5,964 feet, the highest peak in the Blue Ridge). I roller-coastered through the spectacular Great Smoky Mountains to Franklin, North Carolina, for another family visit before turning northeast to Connecticut.

## McCall, Idaho • Denver, Colorado

McCall, ID

Dan picked up the phone on the first ring. "Susan, hello. It's great to hear from you. You need what? A place to bake at 5,000 feet? Well . . . okay. . . . No problem. How does 5,023 sound?" "Come on, Dan," I started to laugh. "No, I'm not kidding. Don't even think of renting. We live near McCall, Idaho, with a gorgeous lake, all the mountains you want, and an extra car for you to borrow." Absolutely too good to be true. It felt like a huge imposition to use their house while they were in it, especially since we hadn't seen each other since they had retired out west and we'd lost touch. When I called, all I had had was a phone number and the hope that Dan, a retired commercial airline captain, would know the altitude of towns where I might go and bake.

Ten minutes later, Dan called me back. "You really should come," he said. "We hardly use the house, let alone the kitchen. I play golf all the time and Ann's out a lot." "Now listen," said Ann, "aren't you just glad you have friends in high places?" (Offering me a chapter title as well as a home.) "Come on. You can stay with us until we close the house for the season." Born in Dublin, full of charm and wit, with a voice that still held a trace of lilting Irish brogue, she was hard to resist. In a few days, Idaho road maps and travel booklets began arriving in the mail. Their enthusiasm won me over, and I began to make an elaborate equipment list.

"What do you need?" Dan e-mailed. "I'll see what I can find out here." Before I knew it, he'd mailed back my list. With an attention to detail that only a pilot could muster, he had measured every pie plate and color-coded each item to show which ones his daughter Linda had in her kitchen and which a neighbor owned. "Easy as pie!" he laughed, when I thanked him for his efficiency. "But what I couldn't find, you better ship." So I packed up all the extra items I needed: soufflé dishes, popover pans, my favorite whisks.

Ann met me at the Boise airport in her little fire-engine-red convertible. "Glad to see you. Here's our plan," she said, as attractive and in-charge as I remembered her. "We're going to spend tonight near here with my friend Gail Delp, then tomorrow morning we'll shop for all your staples at the biggest market in the capital before starting our two-hour drive up to the mountains."

The next morning, we overloaded two carts with chocolate (bittersweet, semisweet, and white), flavoring extracts (pure vanilla, almond, and lemon), sugar (brown, white, and powdered), flour (high-protein, all-purpose, and cake), unsalted butter, and eggs by the three dozen. Roaring with laughter, we tried to cram everything into her little car, but even with the top down, it looked like a circus trick.

The drive up Route 55 was spectacular, a winding highway tight beside the wild, rushing Payette River. We followed it through the hamlet of Horseshoe Bend and up into the forested canyon, where we leaned into terrifying edgeless switchbacks that wound through the gorge. When the roller-coaster ride ended, we found ourselves entering a grassy plateau dotted with black cattle. The sign said "Welcome to McCall." A rustic nineteenth-century sawmill town now being quaintly "restored," McCall grew up around the banks of deep blue Payette Lake, sheltered by powdered sugar–topped mountains.

Dan met us at the house. He still had his Brooklyn accent, friendly manner, and brushy mustache, but he had traded his formal pilot's uniform for sweats and a baseball cap. Their trim clapboard Craft-style home was part of a new community. "Come on in," Dan said, "we have a surprise for you. This is all yours now." In the dining room, beneath a mule-deer horn chandelier, the oak table was covered with neat stacks of borrowed baking pans. Ann beckoned me into the adjacent white-tiled kitchen. "Come on in," she laughed, "I relinquish this to you too." I was completely overwhelmed. They had gone to a huge amount of trouble, but they both seemed genuinely glad to have me, and all of my stuff.

The spacious living room opened onto a broad deck literally touching the golf course fairway. Looking up, I could see Brundage Mountain. Closer to the house, towering blue-black pines and yellow-gold aspens shared the green turf with strolling golfers. "I've been worried about what to do with all my test cakes," I said. "Now I know. Let's put up a sign: Lemonade and Cake, 50 cents—we'd do a serious business."

The next morning, after organizing my cookbooks, laptop, and recipe-testing forms, I put on my blue "lucky" apron, stuck my notepad between neighbor Doris Early's blue KitchenAid mixer and Linda's mixing bowls, and went to work. My first test cake was a 1-2-3-4 layer cake. It didn't take long to get it into the oven and set the timer.

As in any new location, my first test results here were erratic because I had not yet learned the personality of the oven, let alone the quirks of the altitude. Invariably, the ovens were fussy, out of calibration, and not holding a true temperature. I put a second auxiliary oven thermometer in each chamber and began to regulate temperature only by watching the inner readings. That helped. It took a few tries to bake muffins with both good shape and texture, and four versions of the 1-2-3-4-cake before I had that one right. I discovered that everything was better with 25 degrees more heat, that most recipes needed less sugar, and that some needed a little more flour. Cakes stuck in the greased pans until I also dusted them with flour or lined them with parchment. As always, each recipe became a multi-testing adventure.

The mound of plastic-wrapped "wannabes" grew on the table. "Any idea who we could give them to?" I asked. "How about the hospital?" Dan suggested. Their daughter Linda was an emergency room nurse at McCall Memorial Hospital. We called her. "Sure, that's a great idea," she said. "Bring everything to the staff lounge for the nurses and doctors." Dan took me over to introduce me, and we began to make hospital runs every few days.

"Incoming goodies!" the admitting desk attendant would roar as I carried a tray of cakes past her desk and down the hall to the lounge conference table. I taped a comment sheet beneath each plate. Linda came by the house one day to tell me her colleagues thought writing comments was just as much fun as sampling my wares and often stood around arguing and comparing notes. I couldn't wait to read my reviews each time. Orange sponge cake: "delicious, better than the orange chiffon beside it"; "good texture and taste!" Mocha chiffon: "light and chocolatey"; "Yuck, too dry." Pumpkin Bundt was the winner, with seventeen "good," two "moist and flavorful," and one "pretty darn yummy!"

The hospital connection gave me much more than a cake outlet. I made new friends among the staff, including nurses Maureen Perseo, who picked me a bushel of special baking apples for a chopped apple cake, and Donna Harjung. After their shifts together, they often dropped by the house. And when Donna and Maureen decided I needed to get out of the kitchen, they took me out to dinner, or to the Bistro 45 Wine Bar, "dedicated to exploring the passions of living well." Ann and Dan also showed me their favorite spots, including Lardo's, a colorful cross between a family hamburger joint and a crazed Wild West saloon that captured perfectly the spirit and character of the town.

When I mentioned that I'd like to talk to some local bakers, everyone agreed that I needed to go to Flight of Fancy in nearby Donnelly. "They have good cake and a great story." With one of my previous cookbooks and a notepad under my arm, I found owner Susan Dorris behind the cake-filled glass counter. When I introduced myself and my project, she stepped out to meet me with a beaming smile, a buttery apron around her middle and her hair in a tight ponytail. "What an idea! I wish we had that

book to use. We could sell it to people who complain about the altitude, except if they knew how to bake at home, maybe they'd stop buying my cakes!" She called her husband, George, to join us for coffee at a tiny round table in the front. I autographed my cookbook for them, and asked them to tell me their story. "I'd always loved to bake," Susan said, cutting samples of cheesecake for us. "About seven years ago, I finally got up the courage to quit my day job and expand my hobby into a business. It seemed only natural to locate my new kitchen in our small airport hangar." George jumped right in. "That hanger housed my 1981 Britten Norman Islander, a nine-passenger plane." He had flown for the air force for twenty years before "molting" into an air-cowboy. "Now I'm a backcountry pilot," he said with pride. "I'll fly anywhere, for anything. I arrange charter flights for elk hunters and haul freight into the wilderness. My customers are always hungry on the flights, and they loved Susan's desserts, so we started bringing them on board to sell." Soon the bakery outgrew its allotted corner in the hangar and Susan moved into her present shop. "I still bake for George's clients, but here I can do everything from breads to pies and wedding cakes. I cater parties too, but my real specialty is cheesecake," she said, pointing proudly to a gaily crayoned wall sign: "Cheesecakes—plain, turtle, raspberry, swirled Grand Marnier, and amaretto."

"Did you ever have problems baking at this 5,000-foot altitude?" I asked, taking out my pad. "Oh, sure. Some things I just won't do here anymore, like meringues cookies or meringue pie. It's not only the altitude, we also get wild humidity swings and changes in barometric pressure around here. Be sure to write that down! My meringues fell all the time. Cheesecakes are a lot more reliable here, because they don't have to rise." "Any secrets?" "After years of trial and error," she said, "I've learned to underbeat egg whites when I'm leavening cakes with egg foam, cut back leavening in certain breads, and add a little solid shortening to the butter in my chocolate chip cookies. I also chill that dough before baking." Two customers came in, and it seemed like a good time to polish off my cheesecake with a gulp of coffee, buy a slice of lemon–poppy seed cake, and say goodbye.

One sunny Saturday morning when I couldn't resist being outside, I took my watercolors to sketch McCall's boat-filled harbor on Payette Lake. A few small sailboats drifted in the distance, burgundy shrubs dotted the sandy beach, and the water was the same deep ultramarine blue as the cloudless sky. After painting for a couple of hours, I joined Ann for tea at the Mountain Monkey Café. I found one of my cookbooks there for sale and bought it for Ann. I was writing an inscription when the woman at the next table leaned over. "Sorry to interrupt, but I couldn't help overhearing you. Did you really write that cookbook? Listen, sweetheart," she said sincerely, "What you've got to do is write a book about baking at this altitude. I haven't been able to make my favorite cakes since I moved here from Minnesota."

Another suggestion led me to Corey McDonald at the Evening Rise Bread Company, where the tall, rangy, twenty-six-year old baker met us in front of his shop. I told him about my new book. "Great idea. Really needed, especially out here." Eager to tell me his own story, he continued, "I've only been open about two years, but folks really like my bread. I sell forty different kinds, from nine-grain to baguettes, ciabatta to basil pesto to German rye. We bake about two hundred loaves in a typical day. Summer, fall, and winter business is good; spring's mud season, when locals and smart folks go on vacation.

"Do I have any problems baking bread at this altitude? Absolutely. But I'm used to it," he said. "I was born in Albuquerque [5,000 feet]. I've studied this altitude thing very carefully. It's important. Let's look out back." He led us into a cavernous open space filled with huge mixers, massive ovens, long worktables, and racks of rising bread. We were surprised not to see any other workers. "I do most of the baking myself," Corey explained. "My brother, Bill, who's a brewer, is my partner. When we set up, I chose the best equipment I could find." He pointed with pride to the huge Pavailler dough mixer effortlessly curling a 220-pound batch of dough around its spiraled stainless steel hook. "Those are steam-injected French ovens in the back. Taste this," he said, tearing off crusty chunks of just-baked baguette. "Take some home." He piled loaves into my arms. "Do you have any tips for other bread bakers up here?" "Sure do. I'll write some notes and send them to you."

His handwritten letter came a few days later: "Susan: Watch out for sudden changes in barometric pressure, use extra-strength high-gluten flour that gives a strong elastic dough. . . . Judge rising by bread's bulk, not by the time it takes. Make small adjustments to recipes until you see what works. Hope this helps. Love, Corey."

As my departure date approached, my hosts wanted to make sure I didn't miss any local attractions. Dan and his best friend, George, planned an elaborate day-long sightseeing adventure. They even rented a guided tour audiotape from the chamber of commerce.

We started out early in the morning. I packed up a basket of test scones and cake; the men brought coffee and potato chips. The road, easy at first, gradually changed from lakeside blacktop to forest floor gravel, as we climbed into the Payette National Forest. Dan leaned over, pressed the on button, and a deep voice announced that we were at the 0.1 mile marker, beginning the Warren Auto Tour. Keeping a carefully modulated speed to match our tape, we soon came to mile marker 4.9: "Payette

Lake, carved by alpine glaciers 75,000 years ago . . ." Then Marker 18.4: The fires of 1994 and 2000 "burned over wildfire areas, . . . started by lightning and fueled by hot dry weather. . . . Your ears may be popping, you have reached the elevation of 6,434 feet above sea level, ascending about 63 feet per mile . . . snow depths here reach more than 14 feet. . . ." Fascinating, and also gorgeous. The blue-green pine-covered mountains were punctuated by exclamation points of bright gold tamarack trees.

I was glad pilot Dan was driving his sturdy SUV, as we were often looking down on clouds, high enough up to be in a cockpit. White-knuckled beside him, I held my breath as we inched up and down narrow dirt washboard roads barely chiseled into the sides of terrifying cliffs. At last, we reached Warren, our first destination of the day. An 1860s gold rush boom-town with a peak population of 660, it is now a near–ghost town, with a few weather-beaten wood houses strung along Main Street and a year-round population of nine. We were the only souls in sight. The place looked like the back lot at Universal Studios. We drove past a boarded-up dance hall and stopped in front of a rickety structure that could have been a saloon stage set. The covered porch sagged under the weight of too many years and racks of moose and elk antlers, but its sign, "Warren Winter Inn," had an optimistically fresh coat of paint.

"Ready for lunch?" the men asked. We were the only people in the smoky, pine-paneled room. Greasy dollar bills were thumbtacked all over the ceiling. We sat at stools by the bar along the back wall and watched while a slight woman with a tousled shock of gray hair pushed herself through the swinging doors. She tied a red plaid apron around her waist and rubbed her eyes. Obviously we had woken her up. "Not been too busy round here today. You want to eat?" she said with a yawn, passing out menus as if she were used to waiting on real cus-

tomers. "Today's selection [emphatically singular] is chili 'n' buns," she muttered, and almost immediately began serving up bowls of steaming hot chili and a plastic basket of warm golden biscuits. I quickly picked one up. "Who made these?" I asked, taking a bite. The crumb was delicate, tender, and just faintly sweet. "Me, of course. Name is Shannon. I do everything here, cooking, the works, been here eight years . . . keep the only restaurant in town." We quickly polished off the biscuits and asked for more. Shannon began to warm up. "We're nearly 6,000 feet up. How do you make these so light?" I asked. "I have my tricks," she winked conspiratorially. "I can cook 'em anywhere. I like 'em high and fluffy, and always use the same old recipe. But up here I keep the baking powder the same, use all-purpose flour instead of cake flour, and add more liquid than you're s'posed to. Works perfect!" It was hard to believe she hadn't been given a script and sent out by central casting just for my visit.

Our route along the Wagon Road took us next to Burgdorf, the area's oldest hot mineral springs. Not long ago, it was an outdoor public bath where loggers and miners soaked off their grime, but the rustic 1890s cabins had been hosed down, modestly restored, and reopened to the public. Glad to be out of the car, we took a long relaxing soak into the steaming green open-air pool, which smelled slightly of rotten eggs. I floated on my back and could have stayed for hours, but the men lured me out of the water with the promise of a coffee-and-cake picnic.

As we began our dizzying descent, we stopped a couple of times for photo ops, to catch our breath, and to look across amazing alpine valleys. We crossed over Hershey's Point (8,322 feet), wound down and around a craggy ridge following forty-three miles of S-curving summer-only dirt "track," and dropped 4,000 feet over a couple of scenic, and scary hours. Eventually we reached French Creek, a fisherman's paradise leading into the broad, wild Salmon River. The golden rays of the late-afternoon sun sparkled across the river's choppy surface as if, in a miner's dream, it was strewn with real gold dust. Following the river on a relatively flat course, we soon came to the bustling camper-packed town of Riggins, then climbed out of the river valley, crossed the Time Zone Bridge (going from Mountain to Pacific Time), and, just as the sun began to set, returned to McCall. After such a dazzling finale, there was nothing left to do but to pack my pots and pans and move on.

There was just one problem: after three weeks in Idaho, I still had not completed my testing at 5,000 feet. I needed to find another kitchen at that altitude for a week or two

longer. I had been in touch with some Colorado friends, and just as my time was running out, I found a lucky opportunity. Denver (5,000 feet) friends Tracy and Randy Spalding e-mailed that they were going away for two weeks and offered me the use of their home. Tracy, who grew up next door to me in Connecticut, loves to bake and wanted to help with this book. I shipped her my boxes of equipment, flew in the day after they left, and settled into another immaculate kitchen. This time, I packed my extra test cakes into the freezer for the Spalding children to share with friends. I concentrated on baking, allowing myself few distractions. The day before Tracy and Randy's return, I finished my cake chapter, vacuumed up my crumbs, and flew home.

## Santa Fe, New Mexico

To tell the truth, my ulterior motive in writing this book was to have an excuse to return to Santa Fe. I had visited and baked there often in the past, loved the town, and always wished I could stay longer. When I was ready to start testing these recipes, I knew Santa Fe would be my first choice for a 7,000-foot location.

Calendar in hand, I picked up the phone to call Marilyn Abraham and her husband, Sandy MacGregor, longtime friends and enthusiastic foodies. They were just in the process of planning a trip to Europe and needed someone to "house- and cat-sit" while they were away. "Stay at least six weeks, including August, season of Indian Market and the opera," they said, adding even more enticement. And if that weren't gift enough, they added two spectacular bonuses—their kitchen would be totally renovated by the time I arrived and Marilyn's new lipstick-red Dodge pickup truck was at my disposal. Who could resist?

My friendship with Marilyn and Sandy goes

Santa Fe, NM

back more than twenty years, to the days when they were both in the New York publishing business. Marilyn, as executive editor of Ballantine Books, acquired the paperback rights to my first cookbook, *As Easy as Pie*. After they quit their jobs, this remarkable couple turned their executive skills toward new horizons, touring the country in their recreational vehicle several months of each year and writing books about it: *First We Quit Our Jobs* and *The Happy Camper's Cookbook*. When they decided to move to Santa Fe, they bought a contemporary adobe-style home with typical Southwestern details— Ponderosa pine beamed ceilings, terra-cotta tile floors, and sunny rooms centered around a spacious kitchen. A world-class cookbook library and pantry filled with state-of-the-art baking equipment made this the house—and test kitchen—of my dreams.

When I arrived in Santa Fe, I was traveling light (for me)—just a bag of clothes, a laptop computer, and a carry-on filled with recipes— not even a rolling pin or pie plate to weigh me down. This was the one test location where I didn't have to haul in, or ship out, my own pots and pans.

The new kitchen was efficient and designed for two people who like to cook together. The original skylights were still there, but Marilyn and Sandy had replaced hard-surface tiles with maple flooring. They also added white Corian countertops, a generous center island, and double work stations with two sinks, two dishwashers, and double ovens. Cherry cabinets and Mexican tile trim in primary colors gave a playful touch to the serious work space.

I couldn't wait to start baking. Pete and Norman, my feline charges, were glad to see me again, knowing they could count on cake crumbs in their chow. I woke up every morning glad to be there. Even when my cakes refused to rise, the kitchen, and the views from it, lifted my spirits. Washing dishes at the corner sink, I faced the towering Sangre de Cristo Mountains. The back windows overlooked a private garden, rolling hills of juniper and sage, and the distant Jemez Range to the west. It was way too easy to daydream, watching the mountains and the shifting patterns of the endless sky. I hate to admit it, but it occasionally took the smell of

nearly burned cookies to bring me back to work.

Even though I had previously developed some "Santa Fe cakes for 7,000 feet" to use in a baking class (see page xiv), I had more than ninety sea level recipes left to adapt for this book. My earlier tests had taught me a few tricks, but I still found baking at this altitude hard going. Thin air and reduced air pressure gave a boost to rising batters, but water boiled at just about 198°F and everything took much longer to cook. Sea-level batters wanted to rise but couldn't get hot inside fast enough to hold up; when they did rise, their protein structures were so weak they collapsed. Muffins stayed dense and soggy, fruit pie fillings took so long to bake through that their crusts burned. I did know that most batters required more flour for strength, and some needed more liquid because the air was so dry and evaporation so fast, but I quickly learned that there was no such thing as a rule of thumb. Each recipe was unique. Most recipes improved with less leavening; some improved with higher oven heat but others overbaked on top and stayed wet below; and some preferred longer baking times and reduced temperatures. Every cake needed airtight wrapping as soon as it cooled, or it staled while you watched because of the ultra-rapid evaporation. Even my steaming cups of tea cooled off before I could finish them.

My pattern was to rise early and bake while the morning was cool, shopping for groceries in the heat of midday. When I ran out of ingredients, I usually went to the closest market, where I quickly made friends with Maria, the grandmotherly checkout lady. After a couple of weeks of observing my frequent stops for six pounds of butter, three quarts of buttermilk, and at least four dozen eggs, she couldn't contain her curiosity. "What ever are you cooking, girl?" When I explained that I was working on a cookbook, she burst out laughing. "I'll tell you a secret," she whispered, not wanting her manager to overhear. "I am, too! Tomorrow I'll bring it in . . . maybe you can give me some tips." I returned to "my" kitchen in the afternoons and baked late into the nights. While sifting and stirring, I took copious notes. I photographed everything so I could sketch it later, then wrapped up each carefully labeled piece (dating and numbering each version of each recipe) for Stacy, my baking assistant, before freezing or giving away the leftovers.

I was lucky to have Stacy Pearl helping me on her days off from catering. We had met a couple of years before, when she assisted me at a class at Cookworks Cooking School in Santa Fe. A transplanted New Yorker, Stacy was quick, smart, and very funny. She had an impressive background as an artist, newspaper columnist (advice to the lovelorn), chef, and caterer, and no matter what happened, she could fix it and make me roar with laughter.

She arrived early in the morning once or twice each week. We would start with mugs of tea at the dining room table while we tasted and critiqued our way through a pile of plastic-wrapped goodies, the "stinkers (or sinkers) of the week." Then we went into the kitchen to try out revised versions of problem recipes. Troubleshooting together, we stirred and folded our way through oceans of finely tuned batters, scraped bits of fallen cakes from the bottoms of the pristine ovens, and generally tried to keep our buttered notes and floury fingers from sticking together in the 101°F August heat. Between the double ovens and the hot desert summer, the portable fan we set on the kitchen floor gave us little relief.

Some days we were exhausted by the weather, fresh out of ideas and frustrated, while other days we were elated by breakthrough results (see Lemon–Poppy Seed Loaf, page 69). We took time out in our garden to pick lavender

to put in the biscotti (page 248) and herbs to top the fig tart (page 304). My journal entry from August 25: "Until the timer tells me the poppy seed cake is baked, I get to stretch out in the hammock and inhale the warm breeze perfumed by rosemary and lemon thyme. Spikes of blue-violet Russian sage share a border with pink echinacea, pale gold California poppies, and fat white daisies. Tall wispy grasses edge the coyote fence beneath an apricot tree. I feel dwarfed by the immense sky overhead, too overwhelming to contemplate. Considering the scale of life from this perspective, adjusting quarter teaspoon measurements of leavening seems utterly inconsequential if not absolutely foolish."

When we weren't in the kitchen baking, Stacy and I snacked our way through local bakeries, including Sage and the renowned Cloud Cliff, on the lookout for baking-at-altitude problems and solutions. I always tried to chat with professional bakers. Some bluffed and said they had no trouble baking at all. Some admitted to frustration and told tales of crashed cakes and wounded egos. Several chefs refused to share altitude tips with home bakers because they knew how hard it was to do and they didn't want to lose their captive audience. My favorite was the baker who told me that by the time she had successfully developed one butter cake that didn't fall on its face, she was so undone by the process she stopped right there. She now bases her entire cake business on variations of a single recipe, although her eight-page brochure offers cakes in several dozen flavors and frostings from almond to vanilla.

In the name of my hard work (tasting as many local baked goods as possible and working through entire dessert menus), I dined out in Santa Fe whenever I could find time. Pat West-Barker, food editor of the *Santa Fe New Mexican*, offered me helpful advice, as did local food writer, teacher, and culinary expert John

Vollertsen. Marilyn and Sandy had introduced me to the great breakfast muffins and scones at Harry's Roadhouse, and my friend Lorraine Schechter refined my tastes with serious restaurant travels. We lunched at Mark Miller's Coyote Café and the Inn at Chimayó (see page 300), and dined at Geronimo's, Gabriel's, and Casa Sena, to name a few favorites with exceptional desserts. My cousin Bessy took me to the Tesuque Reservation, where we watched the antler-costumed deer hunter dance and joined a Native American family for lunch (venison stew, posole, chili and beans, Jell-o molds, and apple pie). We also cruised the popular Chocolate Maven bakery (rich brownies, no recipe sharing). I spoke at length with Santa Fe's two reigning freelance pastry experts, Donna Brand and Maggie Faralla. Both make a wide variety of baked goods and developed their recipes after "agonizing trial and error." Donna prefers to bake sponge cakes because "the altitude really helps the [rising] action of the whipped eggs." Maggie works with sponge as well as butter cake, but specializes in wildly creative, highly styled designs and decorations.

After gathering so much information, I worked on perfecting my own techniques. It didn't take long before I was faced with my recurring problem—what to do with my growing pile of baked goods. I could always count on giving away treats to Mark Hopkins, the young craftsman finishing up the new kitchen, when he stopped by for an early morning coffee break. One day I wrapped up a batch of cookies for his children, but he had other ideas. "I guess I can spare a few cow and star shapes for my kids, but the rest of the good stuff goes with me this weekend to Wyoming . . . these cookies will be happiest at a fisherman's campsite." And whatever cakes would fit went into my hosts' freezer. But when space ran out, I began to spread the wealth, expanding my fan club from the resident cats to new neighborhood friends.

When I knocked on Virginia Grey's door, she welcomed me as if I was expected, saying Sandy had told her a "baking lady" was coming to town. (I'm pretty sure Virginia, a psychic, already knew I was there and was waiting for me.) Although she said she didn't usually eat sweets, she agreed to taste a small bite of the carrot cake in my basket. Surprised that it was not too sweet, she decided to serve it for lunch, "because she could taste the love with which it was baked." Another neighbor, Olivia Ogorek, gave me much-needed massages and, with her partner, Katherine, tried out my lemon meringue pie and a satchel of scones ("perfect").

When I branched out beyond my neighborhood, I found both new and old friends who were eager to help. In one marathon dessert-tasting evening, David Jenness and Ken Collins proved their friendship by critiqueing their way through a Blitz Torte, Chocolate Truffle Cake, Gingerbread, and Aspen Apple Cake. When I began testing popovers, I discovered to my surprise that they were the specialty of transplanted Connecticut artist Carol Anthony. In a typically generous gesture, she not only loaned me her favorite popover pan and shared baking secrets, but also hosted a popover party so we could taste the results with friends.

The Santa Fe Opera is a major summer happening, a unique experience because you can watch the sunset during the performance. I was thrilled to be able to go one evening with my friend Jane Reid. Wearing chic black dresses and high heels, we made a grand entrance pulling into the parking lot in the shiny red Dodge 4×4. We parked neatly between a Mercedes and a BMW, spread our blue and red patchwork quilt in the truck's flatbed, and proceeded to join the other opera tailgaters. Around us in the gravel lot there was everything from a tiny damask-topped card table set up with chairs, lighted candles, and crystal to a

Jeep with an opened trunk proffering silver platters of sturgeon and caviar. Women in high heels and gauzy cocktail dresses clustered about their men in Santa Fe formals (cowboy boots, jeans, and tuxedo jackets). Not to be outdone, we set up our canvas chairs and drank Champagne from crystal flutes as we picnicked on tabbouleh and Thai shrimp. For dessert we polished off test slices of fig tart, then quickly took our seats in the theater to watch the sun set along with the opening measures of *La Traviata*.

If I had any problem (beside the altitude) in Santa Fe, it was that there were so many diversions to distract me from my hot oven. Santa Fe appealed to all my senses, not only as an artist and food writer, but also as a sun worshipper. The blue sky and endless sunny days seduced my New England soul. I relished the food, espe-cially the sharp flavors of chile (infinite varieties, in myriad colors, served fresh, roasted, smoked, stuffed, and dried) added to everything from ubiquitous blends of beans-rice-corn to cheesecake. I loved the colorful palette of the landscape, seeing brilliantly hued paintings wherever I looked—terra-cotta adobe earth against turquoise doors, cadmium-yellow sunflowers, sage-green grasses, violet shadows on ochre mountains. I carried a camera, watercolors, and a sketch pad, trying to capture it all. To me, Santa Fe's unique personality is an exciting, eclectic mix of creative artists and musicians; Wild West, Native American, Mexican, and Hispanic culture; and a heavy dash of Hollywood kitsch—all tossed together in a vibrant community. Beneath the town's veneer of glamour and glitz, I felt its warmth and spirit, and its energy kept me going when my own flagged.

I knew high altitude cooking was different, but didn't realize how different until I was preparing toasted almonds to add to a dish I was demonstrating at the Food and Wine Classic in Aspen (7,800 feet). I put the nuts in a pan on the stove expecting them to take about ten minutes, as they do at home in San Francisco. I kept shaking the pan, in between all my other prepping tasks, trying to hurry them along. I thought the stove was dead. I am an impatient cook, and I knew something was wrong. Control is a big issue for me, and this made me feel totally out of control; it threw off my sense of ease and sense of timing in the kitchen. Finally, after twenty-five to thirty minutes, the nuts began to brown.

—Joyce Goldstein, chef/cookbook author,
*Solo Suppers* and *Italian Slow and Savory*

My Santa Fe stories could go on forever, and I hope that they will. The tales you will find throughout the recipes in this book reflect my delight in the people and places that make up that extraordinary community. When I re-turned to my Connecticut kitchen and un-packed, I found my dessert recipes scented with chile powder and cilantro from the many packets of spices I brought home to keep my memories, and taste buds, alive.

## Breckenridge, Colorado

Talk about friends in high places. . . . I knew there was an angel with a sweet tooth nibbling pie in the sky when my friend Mari Frohne told me about Porterfield Peak, an alpine ski chalet facing the Ten Mile Mountain Range in Breck-enridge, Colorado (10,000 feet), owned by friends of her sister, Kit. They called the own-ers, Sandy and Skip Porterfield, to tell them about my project and this generous couple didn't hesitate to offer me their vacation home. "You're welcome to stay and bake," they wrote in a warm and enthusiastic note. "We'd love to be part of your story."

After a flurry of e-mails, I finalized plans, shipped out five crates of baking equipment, and flew into Denver. My first stop was a quick visit with my friend Tracy Spalding, who guided me through a whirlwind Whole Foods/Costco stocking-up spree.

The next afternoon, I drove my bulging rental car up the 5,000-foot rise in elevation to the mountains of Breckenridge. To my surprise, when I pulled into the chalet's driveway in the early evening, I found a string of white fairy lights twinkling across the front deck and a wel-coming dinner party, arranged in my honor by my energetic hosts, who were flying back east the next morning, so I could meet them and their friends and not feel like a stranger in town. As we gathered around the fireplace, they filled me with good food and friendly advice. "Taste the scones at Clint's Bakery." "Take extra cakes to a shelter called the House with the Red

Breckenridge, CO

Door." The DeCarli, Hunt, and Scollard families eagerly volunteered to be taste-testers, and they took their jobs seriously, stopping by for sam-ples and offering thoughtful critiques through-out my stay. Pat, Karen, and Judy invited me to lunch, movies, and hikes, giving me an instant community.

On my first morning, I awoke early to ab-solute silence in a totally new world. The party over, my hosts long gone, I was alone on yet an-other mountaintop . . . a realization that never ceased to thrill me. Still sleepy, I stepped out onto the bedroom balcony, totally unprepared for the view. Brilliant pink and magenta light splashed across the craggy mountains as the sun rose, focusing its theatrical spotlight on the panorama facing my window. A straggly V of geese flapped across the sky high above my head. I inhaled the serenity and stillness of the early chill (and quite breathlessly thin) air and realized that watching the scenery could easily become a full-time job. When I lowered my gaze, however, my packed car stared back at me, bringing me quickly to the business at hand.

Unpacking and sorting ingredients, carving out work areas in someone else's kitchen. . . . By now the tasks were familiar, my categorizing skills well honed. The pine dining room table quickly looked like the supermarket baking aisle. The narrow but efficient L-shaped kitchen opened onto the dining/living room with views that more than made up for the lack of space. Over my sea of supplies, I looked across hunter green log couches and a stone fireplace, through broad windows, onto the front deck. In one corner lodged an oversized bird feeder that, at my hosts' request, I kept filled (with more cake than birdseed to the apparent joy of the crested blue Steller's jays, who favored chocolate). Beyond that, I saw nothing but pine forest and mountaintops. Inside, I added work space by setting up a couple of folding tables to hold my indispensable KitchenAid mixer and Cuisinart food processor (both shipped out to Denver), and I was ready to begin work.

I began by testing muffin recipes, thinking they would be easy and feeling confident that baking in three other high altitude locations had taught me something. Not a chance. Instead of easy incremental add-ins, I soon found that at a stratospheric 10,000 feet, all bets were off. Bran muffins were my worst nightmare. They sank like wet mudpies, resisting even my

most creative lifesaving techniques. After five or six trial batches, a few phone consultations with Utah pastry chef Letty Flatt, and about a ton of soggy bran, I had yet to see a domed top or a perfect crumb. My tattered notes now seem both instructive and hilarious, but at the time, I was in tears. I added, then cut back on eggs; added, then reduced, and finally reproportioned flour and leavening; and tinkered with the measurements of sugar and oil. No matter what, the muffin tops stayed depressingly flat. I raised the oven heat to give a quicker set and instead caused a quick peak and a fast fall. Flat tops turned crusty, the batter remained pasty. I was ready to give up when, on my eighth attempt, I left the ingredients alone and tried lowering the oven temperature and increasing the baking time. When I saw the results, I was nearly too tired to jump for joy: rounded tops and fully baked crumbs—miraculous! The only remaining problem was what to do with the pile of edible but imperfect test muffins that had narrowly escaped the garbage can and the bird feeder.

Fortunately, I remembered Pat DeCarli's suggestion the night of my arrival, and phoned the Red Door shelter run by St. John's Episcopal Church. I headed out, my muffins in a basket, my head in a muddle. How could I cope with 100 recipes as difficult as this? I started to believe that all the baked goods I saw in shops were trucked up from Denver.

The red door at the shelter was opened by the personable young manager, Nathan Griffin, who was thrilled to receive homemade treats—fair or failed—to give to the young people who dropped in seeking help, healing, or just a bowl of ever-ready hot soup. The boys who were there quickly snapped up the muffins and urged me to bring more. There's nothing like positive reinforcement. Cheered by my reception, I returned home to face my second-greatest 10,000 foot–challenge, lemon meringue pie. It was a recipe I had originally expected to be easy (see page 296). How hard could it be? After all, high altitude piecrust was do-able, the filling was prepared on the stovetop, and meringue topping should be light and lofty in this land of minimal air pressure. Wrong again! Words can't describe my frustration when, after repeated adjustments to sugar (superfine, regular, powdered) and cream of tartar, cornstarch, and/or arrowroot, my luscious whipped meringue topping . . . toppled. Repeatedly, I made what I thought were perfect pies and they crashed. Each time, just as I started to pull the pie from the oven, the gossamer mountain sagged like a popped balloon, turning into slushy white glue.

Frantic to solve the meringue mystery, I started phoning local bakers. "Give it up," they said, "are you crazy? No one makes meringue-topped pies at 10,000 feet!" My first break-through clue was from David Fair, owner of Mollie MacDuff's Bakery in Fairplay. "Try whipping the whites in a double boiler." A second, more detailed tip came from Victor, the baker at the Butterhorn Bakery in Frisco. He chuckled at my frustration and let me in on the secret: 7-minute boiled icing! "Whip your whites and sugar over boiling water for however long it takes to reach 160°F. That's it!" He made it sound so simple, but he was right. Once I made an old-fashioned boiled icing, the whipped whites were so stable I could do anything with them . . . piling them on top of a pie was child's play.

Excited to have achieved a "10K" lemon meringue pie, I packed it up to share with my Red Door fan club. Nathan's eyes lit up when he saw the pie, and he suggested I might want to talk about high altitude pies with his mother. I phoned as soon as I got home. "I'd love to meet you," she said, "where do you live?" Vague about town geography, I told her my address. "That can't be right," she laughed, "are you quite sure?" I repeated the street and the number. "Go to the front window of your house and look through the pine trees. Do you glimpse a house through the woods?" Charlotte and her husband, Father Ron Griffin, founder/director of the Red Door and minister of the church, were my next-door neighbors! Needless to say, many afternoon tastings followed, as well as a delightful dinner at their home. Charlotte came to my rescue when I tested pecan pie (see page 270), helped me lighten up my Buttermilk Biscuits, and arranged my most ambitious tasting party—the cake buffet for a reception following her piano students' Clementi Festival.

In between my tests and testers, I commuted to the supermarket across town, using the eggs-and-buttermilk run as an excuse to get out and explore the colorful village. Winding through a valley beneath ski run–striped mountains, the main street of Breckenridge is lined with narrow wooden shops painted cheerfully muted yellows, rust tones, sage, and blue. The few central streets are a jumble of cafés, restaurants, yoga studios, bike shops, and outfitters of mountaineering gear. I quickly found my favorite haunt, a little white pushcart selling made-to-order Brittany-style crêpes (formed on a flat round burner straight from Paris, the young baker proudly explained).

By the time I worked through all my sponge and Bundt cakes, they were stacked on every available surface in the house. The freezer was packed for the Porterfields' return. So I made another Red Door delivery, then phoned Pat DeCarli and Karen Hunt, staunch testers, who stopped by for a friendly cup of tea and "whatever I had to offer this time."

After another week of baking, I knew I needed professional taste buds to review my results. I looked up one young baker who advertised herself as a wedding cake specialist. When I asked about her recipes, she confessed that she in fact had only one: cheesecake (made with a variety of decorations), since it didn't have to rise. "You can't count on any other type of cake at this altitude," she assured me. I had a more productive meeting with Laura Komeshian, the owner of Clint's Bakery/Café, on Main Street. An attractive thirty-one-year-old ex-New Yorker, she had graduated from a baker's degree program in Portland and worked her way to Breckenridge. With the help of Michelle Gapp, who makes the vegan products, Laura bakes an impressive number of muffins, scones, pies, cakes, and cookies, plus an occasional "traditional" wedding cake.

We settled into a corner of the shop to sample my latest efforts in what became a weekly ritual. Laura offered comments and advice. "I'm used to this," she laughed. "My customers ask me for help when their home baking fails, or they just give up and buy it. There really are tricks to baking up here. You need to strengthen batter by adding flour and cutting sugar as you would at say, 7,000 feet, but that's not all. Our scones and cakes don't get brown enough on top, and everything dries out too fast."

Her main tips for baking at 10,000 feet (summarized in my shorthand notebook) were: "Add more liquid. Try to work in corn syrup or honey, for moisture as well as color. Some cakes need longer baking times at lower temperatures. Add extra eggs or egg whites for strength. Add buttermilk or sour cream wherever you can. For cookies, cut back fat and sugar, add a yolk and/or flour for strength." Once I returned to Connecticut, I was able to repay Laura's kindness in a small way when she called to ask for the recipe for my 10K popovers, an item she didn't make at the shop.

I was eager to introduce Laura to my friend Kristin, a professional baker who came from Boston for a long weekend visit. I had many projects lined up, several problem recipes for her to tackle, and a long list of sights to see. After perfecting a recipe for trail bars so she had a worthy hiking snack, we took time off. Driving into the mountains north of town, we explored the scenery around Fairplay and South Park (of television fame), small sleepy villages with the endearing, slightly dilapidated look of the old mining towns they once were.

While we were in the area, we stopped to see friends from my arrival party, Judy Scollard (a local sheriff) and her husband, Tom, a creative log-furniture maker/sculptor. They showed us around fantastic piles of his raw material—sun-silvered, gnarled and twisted logs and tree branches—to the studio where he fashions beds, tables, and chairs out of native woods.

By that time, we had worked up an appetite. Fortunately, we were near David Fair's bakery, Mollie MacDuff's, in Fairplay (elevation 9,970 feet). A native of Montana, David looks far younger than his forty-one years, much of it spent in the worlds of business finance and hotel management. It took him a while, he said, to give in to his true calling as a baker. We tasted our way through his whole wheat–honey, cinnamon, and fruit breads, but our favorite was a crunchy Dakota seed loaf, made with pumpkin, sunflower, sesame, and poppy seeds. With partners Gretchen and Hope, he turns out about forty loaves of bread each day, plus rolls and bagels ranging in flavor from plain and poppyseed to jalapeño-Cheddar. David and Kristin talked about kneading techniques and I asked questions about altitude adjustments to yeast and liquid proportions in his bread doughs. After the shop talk, Kristin and I bought a selection of David's bagels and set off to picnic at Cottonwood Hot Springs, near Buena Vista. In a totally rustic non-resort setting we soaked our ache-and-bake troubles away in a series of steamy little rock-edged pools set into the ice-cold tree-lined river. Just before sunset, we finally scraped ourselves off the rocks and drove home to meet hiking friends who wanted to sample Kristin's trail bars.

Before leaving Colorado, the Porterfields had prepared a list of people for me to call, putting a star beside the name of Suzanne Pedersen, a local theatrical producer and actress. When I phoned, she was working on a production at the Dillon Theater, and she invited me to an upcoming performance followed by a gathering at her home. Always looking for an audience of my own, I volunteered to bring cookies for the backstage cast party, and a cran-apple crostata with a trio of cakes for her dessert table. The evening was great fun. Suzanne's guests, all living very high lives at 9,000 to 10,000 feet, vied to tell tales of calamitous cakes and overrisen breads. An enthusiastic cook and bread baker herself, Suzanne contributed to my research by lending me her favorite high altitude cookbook, a butter-spattered, string-bound compilation of tried and true recipes by friends of the Summit County Library in Frisco.

I was testing brownies from that book when friends Marianne O'Carroll and Timm Fautsko invited me for a weekend visit to their home in Glenwood Springs. I packed up a basket of samples and headed west on Route 70, passing dense pine forests, snow-frosted mountains, narrow valleys filled with yellow-gold aspens, and scary "runaway truck" lanes approaching the dramatic tunnels and crags of Glenwood Canyon. By the time I arrived, I was dizzy from the head-spinning scenery and glad to stop moving.

The next, action-packed, day, Marianne showed me around their spectacular area. We took a breathtaking (swinging-in-the-air) tram ride up Iron Mountain to the mouth of the Fairy Caves, then made a dizzying descent, tunnelling along wooden footpaths deep into an awesome world of dark red-brown caverns. We inched our way past stalactites and stalagmites, the path lit by flickering candles stuck in wrinkles of rock. When we finally emerged, we were ready for a soothing finale, a sunset soak in the famed Hot Springs Pool next to Teddy Roosevelt's Hotel Colorado.

My last excursion from Breckenridge was a nearby drive to Nancy Hassett's elegant Savory Inn and Cooking School in Vail (8,380 feet). I was in for a serendipitous surprise when I met the delightful young executive chef/baker, Deanna Scimio, who turned out to be a fan of my books. She had prepared an afternoon tea for me so I could taste her biscotti (see page 245), and was full of high altitude baking stories. By the time I was ready to go, Deanna had volunteered not only to help test bread recipes, but also, a couple of weeks later, to spend her day off helping me pack and driving me to the Denver airport for my return to Connecticut. Talk about angels!

# Twelve High Altitude Myths
# Brought Down to Earth

When I researched the subject of high altitude baking, I found ubiquitous tips and lists of rules—do's and don't's for success. Some were printed on little bookmarks given away or sold for a dollar in bookstores of ski resort towns, others were notes in sea-level cookbooks. Other sources were university extension service pamphlets and high altitude websites. The admonitions seemed to come from the combined wisdom of anecdotal experience, computer calculations extrapolating tests from one altitude (usually 5,000 feet) to another, and, in the case of the university labs, scientific calculations tested in pressurized laboratories that (more or less) mimic changes in elevation and atmospheric pressure. With few exceptions, the rules had rarely been systematically tested in mountaintop home kitchens. But when I set out to do just that, these guidelines were all I had to go by. I was in for a big surprise when I discovered that many of the "rules" were wrong.

**1. "Always substitute extra-large eggs for large or medium eggs in sea-level recipes."** Sometimes. When this works, it is because

many high altitude recipes need extra liquid and more protein and, presumably, an extra-large egg is bigger than a large or medium egg. Unfortunately, this is not always true, because egg grading and size vary. The recipes in this book were developed for U.S. Grade A large eggs (24 ounces per dozen). The baker also needs to consider the properties of the egg itself: the yolk is all fat (and an emulsifier), the white is protein (which has drying properties and adds strength), and the total egg equals 3 tablespoons of liquid. I believe the "all-purpose" high altitude egg solution was first recorded by covered-wagon cooks traveling to uncharted western mountain territories. The extra-large egg substitution is still a popular recommendation.

If you have a recipe to try, you can start the adjustment process by substituting one extra-large egg for a medium or large egg or adding one more large egg, but this may not solve all the problems—you may need to adjust other ingredients as well. Refer to the High Altitude Notes for similar recipes in this book and also see the Adjustment Guide on page 323.

2. **"At higher altitudes, add extra flour to all baked goods."** Right and wrong. Often it helps to add flour to a cake batter to give it more strength, enabling it to resist collapsing when it rises at high altitude with less air pressure. However, this is not an all-purpose fix. Sometimes recipes need a little extra liquid and no more flour, and sometimes the reduction of a little sugar adds sufficient strength without adding flour. Excess flour can make cookies and other baked goods tough, so indiscriminate additions aren't wise.

3. **"Always cut the leavening as altitude increases."** Wrong some of the time. Up through 5,000 feet, the leavening in cakes often (but not always) should stay the same. Leavening adjustments are critical: you need carefully balanced proportions of baking powder and baking soda to effect a good rise.

Most high altitude guides tell bread bakers to cut the amount of leavening (yeast). It is true that dough rises more quickly as the elevation increases, but cutting back on the yeast is not always the best solution, and in any case, it is not necessary until you get over 5,000 feet. It is often better just to monitor the dough temperature, keeping it cooler so it takes longer to rise and punching it down to allow an extra rise or two.

4. **"Cut out the baking soda at high altitudes."** Wrong. Less is more, but none is too little! The more acidic a batter or dough, the more quickly it will set in the heat of the oven, but you cannot remove all the soda just to get more acidity unless you replace it with baking powder or another leavening. See Baking Soda, page 41. And when you reduce the baking powder in a recipe, you should often—but not always—reduce the soda—the two must be in balance for high altitude products to rise well.

5. **"Reduce the fat in rich cakes and cookies at high elevations."** Rarely necessary. I did this occasionally around 10,000 feet. The reasoning is that while fat, which coats the protein/gluten in flour and weakens it, makes cakes tender (a

good thing), at high elevations, when liquids evaporate quickly, the residual higher concentration of fat and sugar may weaken the cell walls too much (a bad thing), causing the cake to collapse. Most of the time, instead of cutting fat, you can strengthen the batter by adding flour (and sometimes an egg), and reducing the sugar. To prevent moisture loss from evaporation, you can start by adding extra liquid, so there is enough to dissolve the sugar and blend it with the other ingredients in correct proportion.

6. **"Always raise the oven temperature by 25 degrees at high altitudes."** Wrong. This doesn't always work, and in fact it is often better to leave the temperature the same or even reduce it, baking at a more moderate heat for a longer time. It depends upon what you are baking. Raising the heat by 25 degrees to bake cookies and cakes works very well at 5,000 feet, but at 7,000 and 10,000 feet, the oven may be too hot, crusting over the top of a cake before the inside bakes through. Instead of changing the temperature, it is often better to change the position of the rack in the oven, so your cake is closer to (or farther away from) intense heat (see the section on ovens, page 34).

7. **"When using a glass baking dish, always reduce the oven temperature by 25 degrees."** Wrong. I always bake pies in glass (Pyrex) pie plates and never reduce temperature. In fact, the higher you go in altitude, the more heat you want to reach whatever you are baking.

8. **"Batter will overflow in cake pans at high altitude."** Right and wrong. At high altitudes, reduced air pressure contributes to rapid expansion of gases, so sea-level leavening can be too expansive. In addition, liquids evaporate more quickly at high altitudes; such evaporation leaves excess concentrations of sugar in a batter or pie filling, which can then boil up and easily overflow (see Red Door Pecan Pie, page 270). Carefully developed recipes prevent such situations. Use pan sizes called for.

And, as a corollary, I found this statement on one bookmark of high altitude tips: **"At higher altitudes, use smaller pans."** Wrong. If anything, you would need a larger pan. Overflow occurs if you put too much batter in a too-small pan or overfill the pan; remember to leave rising room. If you are worried, put a sheet of foil on the oven floor to catch spills. In all my high altitude testing, I very rarely had a cake batter overflow, but I did see a pecan pie disaster. Do not use pans larger than those called for, because the batter will then be too thin and over-bake, with a dry or tough result.

**9. "Cookie recipes don't need adjustment at high altitude."** Wrong. Many sea-level cookies will work without any changes, but most are improved with slight adjustments. At high altitudes, cookies tend to overspread as they bake. The more they spread, the thinner and crisper (or tougher) they get. Also, because liquids evaporate faster at high altitudes, the dough loses moisture as it bakes, leaving behind a high concentration of sugar and fat that can alter the texture. To remedy these conditions and reduce spreading, strengthen the batter by reducing the sugar, leavening, and very occasionally, fat; sometimes you can also add a little flour (but too much flour makes cookies tough). To help cookies hold their shape, add a little solid shortening (which has a higher melting point than butter) along with the butter. To counter loss of moisture by evaporation in dry mountain air, add liquid. Sometimes you can also add a little corn syrup or honey, to improve browning and add moisture. Raising the baking temperatures by about 25 degrees often enables cookies to set faster before they spread and/or dry out, but you have to be sure the higher temperature doesn't simply cause over-browning instead.

**10. "Pie crusts don't need adjustment because they are not affected by high altitudes."** Wrong. Pie crusts are affected (see page 264), but not as much as cakes. At 5,000 feet and above, especially in dry mountain air, pastry dough often requires a little more liquid to become pliable enough to shape and to bake without cracking. However, moisture is one of the factors that activates gluten, and too much liquid can lead to a tough crust.

**11. "Pie fillings don't need adjustment because they are not affected by high altitude."** Wrong (see page 263). For fruit tarts and crumb-topped pies, baking times and techniques are about the same as at sea level, as long as the fruit is not too hard and the altitude is below 7,000 feet. It does take longer for a juicy pie to thicken because it takes more time for the juices to come to a boil and gelatinize the starch (flour, cornstarch, or tapioca), and these pies often take longer to bake.

At 7,000 feet and above, it takes much longer to bake a pie filled with firm, crisp fruit. For example, if you sandwich a high mound of Granny Smith apple slices between two crusts, the top crust will often burn before the apples are baked. There are two solutions: Use a softer variety of apple, or precook the fruit in a pot on the stove; but again be aware that it will take longer at high altitude than at sea level to boil the juices and soften the fruit. As an added consideration, I have found that at 7,000 feet and above, food tastes blander than at sea level; you'll need to increase spices or seasonings in your pies to brighten their flavors.

**12. "When using boxed mixes, you can count on their high altitude directions to work every time."** Wrong (see About Cake Mixes, page 317). Boxed mixes are developed to work to about 6,500 feet in altitude, not higher.

# About the Recipes

The recipes in this book have been individually developed for use at five elevations: sea level, 3,000 feet, 5,000 feet, 7,000 feet, and 10,000 feet, and all altitudes in between. There's no need to guess on the measurements, just follow them as written, though you may find the chart format unconventional at first glance.

If you are baking between sea level and just below 2,000 feet, select the measurements in the first (sea-level) column, then follow the directions for mixing and baking that come after the chart. If you are at between 2,000 and 3,500 feet, use the column for 3,000 feet; from 3,500 to about 6,500 feet, use the column for 5,000 feet; from 6,500 to 8,500 feet, use the column for 7,000 feet; and from 8,500 to about 11,500 feet, use the column for 10,000 feet.

When you use the ingredients charts, keep your eyes on the correct column; if you need to, cover the others with a strip (or strips) of paper. The introduction to each recipe gives "General High Altitude Notes" that cover the theoretical background of the adjustments and also tell the story of my trial-and-error journey with that recipe. You will also find specific "High Notes" to the baker, with pointers for each altitude that needs particular attention. The procedure steps are almost always the same for all altitudes; if changes are made, they are noted. If you want generalized adjustment advice that you can apply to your own recipes, see the Recipe Adjustment Guide on page 323.

If you study the ingredients charts, you will see that in many recipes, the adjustments in measurement, temperature, or time are not in direct linear progression across the board. This reflects the reality of my testing experience. Often theoretically logical adjustments did not produce the best result, and my goal was to bake the best item, not write a recipe that made sense mathematically but not practically.

# Tips for Success at All Altitudes

- Before starting any recipe, read the high altitude information at the beginning of each chapter to understand some of the theory behind the altitude adjustments. This information will also be useful if you want to adjust your own recipes. Also read the Equipment and Ingredients chapter, page 28, to understand the peculiarities of certain items at altitude; many things are surprisingly different at high altitudes.

- Heat source and intensity are critical in high altitude baking. For success, always position the oven rack(s) as indicated in the recipe (see the section on ovens on page 34). Put an auxiliary oven thermometer inside your oven to monitor temperature; adjust the external control indicator as needed to keep the correct internal temperature.

- Since baked goods tend to stick to the pans more at higher altitudes, pay particular attention to the pan preparation instructions.

- When a range is given for doneness, always check the oven at the first time, then watch closely until the second, and observe the visual signs of doneness given in the recipe. Oven temperatures tend to vary widely.

- Standard volume measurements are used for all ingredients in this book except for items (like fruit, nuts, and raisins) that are usually purchased by weight (ounces). If you prefer to use a scale to measure, see the table on page 324.

- All dry measurements are level: fill a dry measuring cup or measuring spoon until slightly heaping, then level it off with a straightedge or the back of a knife.

- Use the type of flour specified in the recipe, as different flours have different properties, absorb different amounts of water, and react very differently at high altitudes. See page 36 for sifting and measuring information and techniques.

   *Note:* 1 cup all-purpose flour, *unsifted*, weighs 5 ounces; 1 cup *sifted* all-purpose weighs 4¼ ounces. A level cup of unsifted flour contains about 2 tablespoons more than a cup of sifted. In this book, flour is not sifted unless specifically called for. However, *unsifted* flour always means that the flour is first whisked in the canister to lighten it, then spooned into a measuring cup and leveled with a straightedge.

- The recipes in this book are designed for U.S. Grade A large eggs (2 ounces); just because you are at a higher altitude, do not be tempted to substitute an extra-large egg or add more eggs; prepare the recipes as written.

- Butter is unsalted unless otherwise noted. Butter gives baked goods the best flavor. Don't substitute soft margarine—its water content varies and will affect the results (use only hard stick margarine if necessary for dietary reasons).

- Lemon zest refers only to the brightly colored part of the lemon peel; avoid the bitter white pith.

- When a recipe calls for "½ cup chopped nuts," the nuts are chopped before measuring; if it specifies "½ cup nuts, chopped," they are chopped after measuring.

- Room temperature is about 68° to 72°F. Usually ingredients should be at room temperature (except the chilled ingredients for pastry dough) so they will blend properly. If cold ingredients are needed for high altitude purposes, that is indicated in the recipe.

# Equipment and Ingredients

## Equipment

You don't need different equipment for baking at high altitudes, but you do need to be aware of a few potential problems. Some tips and special techniques will make your baking high life much easier.

During my testing, I had good results at every altitude using my own equipment, shipped from my home, which, to be honest with you, is well worn and slightly beaten up, but of good quality. I heard stories, however, from high altitude home bakers that provide cautionary tales.

### Cake, Muffin, and Loaf Pans

For cakes, muffins, and loaves, use shiny or matte-finish pans of fairly heavy quality rather than ones that are thin, warped, or with scratched nonstick surfaces. Avoid heavy black steel pans; they hold heat and give cakes a dark crust.

As Charlotte Griffin, at 10,000 feet in Colorado, told me, "Up here, the condition of your baking pans counts. When I moved here from sea level, I learned how to adjust recipes for the altitude but still got poor tex-

ture and less rise with my thin, warped pans. So I did a test, baking the same (altitude-adjusted) brownie recipe at the same time, on the same oven shelf—one batch in my oldest pan and one in a newer, shiny aluminum pan. No contest. In the old thin pan, the brownies were dense and rubbery; in the heavier new pan, they had a perfect texture." And Jeannie Daubar, at 3,600 feet in North Carolina, said, "When I moved here from Florida, my cakes rose better in shiny new pans than they did in my old thinner pans or those that were Teflon-scratched."

### Tube Pans

At 7,000 feet and above (and especially at 10,000 feet), heavy, dense cake batters rise much better in tube pans than in any other shape because the heat reaches the center of the batter to help it set before the top crusts over. If you don't have a tube pan, create one by setting a (well-greased and floured) ovenproof custard cup or metal measuring cup upside down in the center of your pan (see sketch; sure, the handle

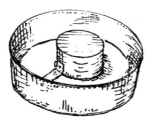

*Pan with measuring cup*

*Pan with cake tube*

will leave a mark in the cake top, but you can cover it with frosting or fruit). Or you can buy a "cake tube" at a bakeware shop. This is a metal cone used specifically for turning regular pans into tube pans; grease and flour its outside surface before using.

### Bread Pans and Lames (Razors)

For baking French bread, I prefer the long curved double- or triple-loaf baguette pans of solid, rather than perforated, metal.

To cut a decorative pattern or make slash lines in the top of a bread, use a single-edged razor blade, sold in packets in hardware stores, or the French *lame,* a razor blade with a handle designed specially for this purpose, available in bakeware shops or by mail order.

### Cookie Sheets

Use only regular cookie sheets at any altitude above sea level. Double-layer insulated or cush-

ioned cookie sheets prevent adequate heat from reaching the bottoms of the cookies, so they either don't brown fast enough or don't brown at all. For good results and crisply browned cookies, you need plenty of heat.

### Double Boilers

At high altitudes, water boils at a lower temperature than at sea level (at 7,500 feet, water boils at 198.9°F). Therefore, melting butter and chocolate in a double boiler, for example, will take longer than at sea level. When melting chocolate, you can ignore the admonishment about keeping the top pan from touching the boiling water below—nothing bad will happen if the top pan touches the hot water, which can be simmering or even gently boiling. Just be sure to watch the chocolate carefully, to stir often, and to remove it from the heat as soon as it melts. The higher the elevation, the more quickly the water in the bottom of the double boiler will evaporate. Keep a kettle of water boiling on the stove to replenish it so the level remains constant.

When making puddings or sauces that require boiling a liquid to gelatinize a starch, I found that above 3,000 feet a double boiler does not allow the pan of ingredients to get hot enough. It is better to cook over direct heat, keeping the temperature moderate and stirring constantly. Watch closely to avoid scorching or burning.

### Water Baths

Some delicate cakes (Flourless Espresso Truffle Cake, page 215) and soufflés are baked in a larger pan of water to ensure gentle heat. At high altitudes, be aware, again, that water boils at a lower temperature the higher you go and that it also evaporates more quickly. So be sure the water is hot enough to start. I found it was easiest to preheat the water bath in the oven, then add the cake with more vigorously boiling water. If the water bath isn't hot enough at the start, the cake may start to sink or even collapse before the water gets hot enough to transmit enough heat. Keep a kettle of water boiling on the stove, and replace water that evaporates so the water bath level remains fairly constant.

## Silpat or Nonstick Baking Mats, Baking Parchment, and Wax Paper

At high altitudes, baked goods have a tendency to stick to the pans more than they do at sea level. Nonstick precautions should be taken seriously, and a few products will make life easier.

Silpats, silicone baking mats imported from France, come in various sizes to fit most baking sheets (they cannot be cut with scissors). These silicone-coated flexible baking pads are far sturdier than parchment or wax paper. They don't need greasing, nothing sticks to them, and breads set on them brown well. They last for years. The pads are easy to lift from the baking pan to a wire rack for cooling, and after use, you simply rinse them off. But cookies baked at above 5,000 feet on silicone baking mats don't brown on the bottom quite as well as they do on baking parchment, because the mat is thicker and insulates the cookies slightly. There are various other similar products, such as Teflon-coated mats from Germany and thinner nonstick sheets that can be cut with scissors to fit your pans. All of these are sold in bakeware shops or by mail order (see Sources, page 329).

To line baking pans, baking parchment and wax paper can be used interchangeably, but parchment is preferable because it is sturdier and less likely to scorch. It is sold in most supermarkets and in specialty baking and food stores, in rolls or precut sheets. It is designed for baking without pregreasing, but at high altitudes, I always grease both parchment and wax paper.

To line most baking pans with parchment or wax paper, you can simply set the pan on top of the paper and draw around it, then cut it to fit. To line loaf pans, cut two strips, one large enough to cover the bottom and long sides, the other large enough to cover the bottom and ends, and stack the strips (they will be double on the bottom—sketch a). Or, draw around pan as shown (b, c), then cut out liner and fit it in pan (d). To line a tube pan, set the pan upside down on a sheet of parchment, draw a circle around the rim, and cut it out. Fold the circle in half, then fold it in half several more times, making a fairly thin multilayered wedge. Turn the pan right side up, hold the paper wedge with the point at the pan center, and with a pencil mark the points where the edges touch, as shown (page 31, sketch a). Cut at these points, open the paper ring, and trim to fit if necessary.

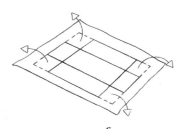

*a*                    *b*                    *c*                    *d*
**Overlap lining strips**

*a*    *Mark paper wedge to cut ring*

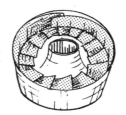

*b*    *Fringe strip in pan*

If the edges of the paper ring don't lie flat in the pan, cut them into a fringe all the way around the paper ring, then overlap the fringe sections when you set it back in the pan (sketch b). For Bundt pans, you can also cut a ring from aluminum foil, which can more easily be molded into the shape of the pan; see page 34.

## Measuring Cups and Spoons, and High Altitude Measurement Math

At high altitudes, tiny adjustments in measurement are critical, spelling success or failure in cake baking, so it is important to use the right equipment.

Liquid and dry measuring cups are different. Liquid measuring cups have a handle and a lip. They must be set flat and level on a counter be-fore filling to the desired mark; bring your eyes down to the cup level to see that it is properly filled. Don't fill a liquid cup to the brim, or you will have too much; the extra space at the top is there so you can carry and pour liquids without spilling.

Dry measuring cups are commonly available in nested sets, in sizes graduated from ⅛ (2 tablespoons) to 2 cups. To measure dry ingredients, spoon them into the cup, then level the top by scraping the back of a knife blade or other straightedge across it. Invest in a set of sturdy metal measuring cups with flat bottoms. Measuring spoons are equally important, and their accuracy is critical in high altitude baking. Avoid decorative plastic spoons and instead select a set made of sturdy metal, preferably with ⅛- and ¾-teaspoon measures.

*Level sugar with knife*

*Liquid cup*

*Dry cups*

At high altitude, measurements of many ingredients may be different from at sea level. Small, incremental changes are common. For example, at sea level, you might use a neat ½ cup sugar, but at 5,000 feet, the recipe will call for "½ cup minus 1 tablespoon." To do this, fill a sturdy metal ½-cup measuring cup with sugar and level it off by running the flat edge of a knife across the top. Set it on the counter and, with a 1-tablespoon measure, scoop out the unneeded sugar and return it to the canister.

- To measure ¾ teaspoon, use ½ teaspoon plus ¼ teaspoon.
- To measure ⅛ teaspoon, use two generous pinches or half of ¼ teaspoon.
- To measure 6 tablespoons, use ¼ cup plus 2 tablespoons.

## Sifter/Strainer

Many recipes call for a sifter, either to sift confectioners' sugar or flour or to set over a bowl and stir/sift a combination of dry ingredients into the bowl. The word *sieve* usually refers to a single-screen mesh used for draining fruits,

straining sauces, and other tasks, but I use my all-purpose "sifter/strainer" for almost everything, making sure it is completely dry and clean between uses. I use a 6- to 8-inch-diameter bowl-shaped strainer with a medium-fine mesh and a comfortable handle. To sift cocoa, or small amounts of flour or sugar, I use a 3-inch-diameter strainer with a 3- to 4-inch-

long handle. For sifting flour or cocoa into a greased pan, you can use this small strainer or a shaker with a wire-mesh sifter top; these are especially helpful for getting flour or cocoa onto the center pillar of a tube pan. I don't use double- or triple-sifters.

To sift flour, see page 36.

## Cardboard Cake Disks

For baking cakes, you will quickly find it hard to live without these disks of corrugated cardboard sold in dimensions that correspond to cake pan sizes—6, 8, 9, 10, 12 inches. Some manufacturers refer to them as "cardboard cake circles." They come covered with glazed white or plain brown paper or gold or silver foil and with plain or fluted edges. They are available in restaurant supply houses, party and paper goods shops, and more and more frequently in bakeware shops. If you have trouble finding them, ask at a local pizzeria; these are the same boards put under baked pizzas. If you cannot find these boards, simply cut your own out of any corrugated box and cover them with foil. They are indispensable for handling cakes, especially when spreading on icing or pressing crumbs or chopped nuts onto the iced cake sides.

## Graters

A stainless-steel box grater or flat mandoline-style grater with a variety of hole sizes is good for most purposes. My favorite grater for citrus zest (peel) and chocolate is the Microplane®, a rasp-type grater available in various sizes and shapes; it is sharp, efficient, and easier to clean than a box grater. It is available in cookware shops and by mail order (see Sources, page 329). For grating nuts into a very fine, dry powder (as for Wilton Walnut Torte, page 179), it is

best to use a rotary nut mill (see sketch), but you can also whirl the nut in a food processor with some sugar or flour.

## Bench Scrapers

One of my favorite tools, the bench scraper (dough scraper, dough knife, or *coupe-pâte*), is simply a metal rectangle about 4½ × 5½ inches, with a wooden or plastic bar-shaped handle along one edge. I like to use it for cutting, lifting, and scraping bread dough, releasing the edges of rolled pie crust from a board, or scraping dough off countertops. Substitutes: a broad pancake turner or a wide putty knife purchased in a hardware store. Similar tools,

made in both stiff and flexible plastic with curved edges, are great for scraping dough out of bowls. Another gadget I couldn't live without, which is related to the bench scraper but larger and more flexible, is the giant spatula, or cake or pastry lifter, about 10 × 12 inches, with a plastic handle on one end (see Sources, page 329). It is ideal for lifting and moving rolled-out pie dough, loaves of bread, or cake layers.

## Cake Testers

At high altitudes, cakes may appear baked on top but still be unbaked and wet inside, so it is especially important to test the doneness by inserting a wooden skewer or cake tester into the center. My favorite testers are long thin bamboo saté sticks sold in packages in Asian markets, and some supermarkets and bakeware shops. Metal cake testers also work, but the metal gets hot quickly and tends to pick up crumbs more easily than the wood, so it may give a false reading. You can use toothpicks, but these are too short for many cakes.

## Aluminum Foil

At high altitudes, dense cake batters tend to overbrown on top before the interior bakes through. To slow the process, near the end of the baking time, you can cut a piece of aluminum foil a little larger than your pan and set it lightly over the cake (or bread) in the oven. Be sure to set it shiny side down, because the shiny side will deflect the heat away from your cake.

It is especially important at high altitudes to protect pastry-topped pies from overbrowning before the fruit filling is cooked through. Cut a 10- or 12-inch rectangle of foil, fold it into quarters, and tear out the center, leaving about a

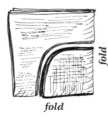

**fold**

**unfolded frame**

*a*                    *b*

2-inch frame (see sketches a and b) all around. Unfold the foil, flatten it out, and gently curl under the edges. Place the foil frame over your pie or tart as directed in the recipe. To cover the center if necessary during baking, unfold and flatten out the torn piece of foil (or shape it into a shallow bowl) and set it over the crust center. As your recipe directs, you may need to remove the foil during the final few minutes of baking to be sure the top crust is evenly golden brown.

Foil can also be cut into a ring and molded onto the bottom of a greased Bundt pan to prevent a cake from sticking. Foil's flexibility makes it better than baking parchment or wax paper when the pan has a pattern in the bottom. To cut a ring, place the pan upside down on a piece of foil, and draw around the outer edge; then reach through the tube (I use a chopstick, which is longer than a pencil) and draw or press a mark around the tube. Cut out the ring, cutting slightly inside the marks, because the top of the pan is larger than the bottom. Press the foil ring in place to test, and trim if needed.

### Ovens, Oven Racks, and Oven Thermometers

Ovens are notoriously inaccurate, but most bakers get used to their cranky appliances and learn how to adapt to their foibles. Even brand-new ovens rarely hold accurate calibration for long, and most have hot spots that cause uneven baking. Oven temperatures are especially critical in high altitude baking: a variation of 15 to 25 degrees can make the difference between a cake that rises and one that falls. To ensure accuracy, invest in one or two oven thermometers and keep them sitting on the oven racks, one in front on top and one in back on the bottom.

The most widely available oven thermometers have a spring-type mechanism and a dial.

Mercury thermometers with a glass tube mounted on a metal stand are not safe if the tube should break, and are not recommended. I use the spring type thermometer when I travel. Oven thermometers are sold in hardware and cookware shops and some supermarkets and are fairly inexpensive. Once you have your auxiliary thermometer in the oven, use it, not the exterior heat indicator, to determine the actual heat.

For accurate high altitude baking, always preheat the oven for at least 15 to 20 minutes. If your oven has hot spots, you will need to rotate the baking pans from shelf to shelf or front to back about halfway through the baking period.

The recipes in this book always specify the position of the oven rack, because heat circulation varies within the chamber. Many ovens have a heat source on the bottom only, but some have one at both top and bottom. Because heat rises, the lowest shelf will usually put the baked goods close to the heat in most ovens, but in those with a top heat source as well, the top shelf may do the same. For more moderate heat, use the middle rack. My oven is 16½ inches high. The center rack is at about 7½ inches; when the oven is divided into thirds, the "lower-third" rack is about 5½ inches above the floor of the oven and the "upper-third" rack is about 9½ inches above the oven floor.

Allow at least 1 to 2 inches between pans so heat can circulate. If baking several layers at a time, stagger the pans on two shelves, so they are not directly lined up.

Convection ovens have an interior fan to blow the heat around. This constant circulation causes quicker baking, and recipes need to be adjusted accordingly. I avoided using convection ovens if possible, or turned off the fans if given the choice, in order to have standard conditions for all my high altitude recipes in all locations. If you are using a convection oven for the recipes in this book, turn off the fan if possible. If not, try reducing the baking temperature by about 25 degrees—but bear in mind that at high altitudes you may not get optimal results the first time. If a recipe doesn't work, take notes and try again.

## Microwave Ovens

In my high altitude tests, I did not bake in the microwave. I did use the microwave to soften and/or melt butter (both good ideas) and melt chocolate (okay, but not my favorite method). Foods, like butter, that contain liquid can splatter very easily in the microwave unless lightly covered. Since microwave units vary widely in size and power, my recommendation, whatever your altitude, is to go slowly, using moderate settings (*defrost* instead of *cook*, for example) and brief few-second pulses of time until you get the desired results.

Be sure to put either butter or chocolate in a microwaveable bowl, and cover lightly with wax paper or plastic wrap (but do not seal) before turning on the oven.

**To soften or melt 1 stick (8 tablespoons) butter:** If your butter is cold or frozen and you need to thaw or soften it quickly, use the *defrost* setting (rather than *cook*) for 45 to 60 seconds. If the butter is still too hard, continue on *defrost* for 10 to 15 seconds at a time as necessary (the total time depends on the power of your microwave and how soft you want the butter to be). To melt the butter, you can continue on *defrost* for a few seconds longer. Or, to melt cold butter, use the *cook* setting for 1 minute, check

the result, and continue in 10- to 15-second pulses until melted.

**To melt chocolate:** Always chop the chocolate first. To melt 1 ounce of chocolate, *cook* on full power about 30 seconds. Check, stir, and continue with 10- to 20-second pulses, checking and stirring after each one, until melted. Larger amounts of chocolate will take slightly longer, but the procedure is the same. *Note:* Melting chocolate in blocks or squares in the microwave is unsatisfactory because solid chocolate does not lose its shape as it melts, so you cannot judge its state by simply looking at it; you must stir it. Chopped chocolate is easier to judge, but you still need to stir (not just look) until melted. I find it easier to melt chopped chocolate in a double boiler, though this will take longer at 10,000 feet than at sea level.

## Instant-Read Thermometers

At high altitudes, water boils at a lower temperature than it does at sea level, so it takes longer for the interior of a batter or dough to get hot enough to set properly. Knowing the internal temperature can often make the difference between success and failure. Instant-read thermometers have a stainless-steel stem and a large round dial mounted on top. These are meant to be inserted in food just to check the temperature, not to remain in the food during cooking in the oven. Instant-read thermometers are available with dial or digital read-outs.

# Ingredients

Whether you are at sea level or a high altitude, you obviously will use the same ingredients. However, the way they work can be affected by differences in elevation. At high altitudes,

some ingredients are more effective than others and some need special handling. The ingredients discussed below are those with properties that affect baking at high altitudes.

## Flour

Different types of flour have different characteristics depending upon many factors, including geographic and climatic conditions and the type of wheat from which they are milled. In high altitude baking, batter strength is critical: whether a cake rises or falls can depend upon just a small difference in the amount of flour. It is also especially important to use the type of flour specified in the recipe. Do not use self-rising flour, because you are unable to control the amount of leavening and baked goods can easily overexpand.

For bakers at all altitudes, the amount of gluten-producing protein in flour is important. Gluten is the stretchy elastic substance that develops when two of the many proteins present in wheat (gluten and gliadin) blend with liquid. Bread flour is milled from hard wheat and has about 12 to 16 percent gluten. For example, King Arthur unbleached bread flour contains about 12.7 percent protein, or 16 grams per cup (this was my favorite at all altitudes); King Arthur Sir Lancelot high-gluten flour (good for extra-chewy breads) has 14.2 percent protein. Gold Medal bread flour has 16 percent protein. High Altitude Hungarian Flour (sold primarily in Colorado, New Mexico, and some other Southwestern markets), milled from hard wheat grown in the West, contains 12 percent protein and is bleached and very finely milled (it feels like cake flour); it also gives a good rise. All-purpose flour is milled from a blend of hard and soft wheats and contains roughly 10 to 13 percent gluten. King Arthur unbleached all-purpose flour (11.7 percent protein) worked well in the layer cakes in this book and other recipes specifying all-purpose flour. By contrast, bleached cake flour contains about 8 percent protein and is more acidic. It would seem to be a good flour for high altitude use, and it does work well in delicate sponge cakes. However, cake flour's low protein content also means it lacks strength, and many high altitude cakes and pastries require the strength of all-purpose flour.

To make your own cake flour from all-purpose, add 2 tablespoons cornstarch to a 1 cup measure, then fill it with all-purpose flour. One cup all-purpose flour equals one cup plus 2 tablespoons cake flour.

Since very dry high altitude climates cause rapid evaporation of moisture from baked goods, bakers, especially bread bakers, must be aware of the absorption qualities of their flour. The flour with the highest protein content (high-gluten bread flour) will absorb the most water (so you won't need to add much extra flour) while the flour with the lowest protein content (cake flour) absorbs much less (you may need to add more flour).

**To sift flour:** The label "presifted" on flour packages should be ignored, because flour compacts as it settles, whether or not it has been sifted, and it must be aerated or stirred before use. High altitude bakers frequently must add extra flour to sea-level formulas in order to add strength to the batter or dough. Be aware, however, that excess flour can toughen baked goods, so be sure to use the precise measurements given in the recipes. Note whether flour is sifted before measuring or not.

In this book, if a recipe calls for "1 cup flour," you don't have to sift it before measuring, but you do need to start by whisking or stirring the flour in its canister or a bowl to lighten it. Then spoon the flour into a dry measuring cup until it is slightly heaped, and level it off with a straightedge. Do not tap the cup, or the flour will compact. You may then be asked to sift this flour together with other dry ingredients, but that is just to blend them together well.

If the recipe calls for "1 cup sifted flour," you must sift it before measuring. To do this, put some flour into a sifter and shake it out onto a piece of wax paper. Spoon the sifted flour lightly into a dry measuring cup until it is slightly heaped, then level it off with a straight-edge. Do not tap the cup, or the flour will compact. Gather up the edges of the wax paper and pour the excess flour back into the canister.

## Potato Starch and Potato Flour

Potato starch and potato flour are different products that are not interchangeable, although both are gluten-free. Marketing is often misleading and the two items are often given the same name, making it easy to mistake one for the other. *Potato starch*, commonly used for Jewish holiday baking, is a superfine white powder resembling talc. It is extracted from water after soaking grated raw or ground cooked and dried potatoes. Use it instead of wheat flour for the delicate Passover sponge cakes in this book, or as a thickener (like cornstarch) for sauces. *Potato flour* is made from cooked, dried, and ground potatoes. It is coarse and crumbly, good in some bread doughs and for thickening sauces; it has a slight potato flavor, but the texture is definitely not fine enough for it to be used for delicate cakes. If you can't tell what you have from the label, touch it and you will know right away.

I ran into the labeling problem while testing the Passover Mocha Sponge Cake (page 187) in New Mexico. I had run out of the Manischewitz potato starch I'd brought out in my suitcase, and so I went to a local market where I found a box labeled "potato starch." It had quite coarse granules and I worried that I was making a mistake but went ahead anyway to see what would happen. The result was a lumpy, wet, sodden mess (hardly a cake) that would not rise at all—as if I had added mashed potatoes, which in effect, I did. (In Great Britain, "potato starch flour" is available, and its texture should be examined before use, as it may be either one of the above.)

## Cornmeal, Corn Flour, and Cornstarch

These three items are neither the same nor interchangeable. *Cornmeal* is made from dried corn kernels that have been ground to a texture that may be fine, medium, or coarse. In baking, medium or coarse-ground is preferable for corn bread and muffins, and it imparts a nutty flavor and slight crunch. Finely ground cornmeal is the texture of flour and mainly used to make cornmeal puddings. Masa de harina is cornmeal that has been ground from kernels treated with limewater before grinding, and it is used primarily for making tortillas and tamales.

*Corn flour* is finely ground cornmeal; it looks like flour. In baking, it can be used along with other types of flour, for example in multigrain bread.

Both cornmeal and corn flour can be made from yellow, white, or blue corn; yellow and white are most widely available. Stone-ground cornmeal, preferably organic, is available in natural food stores and specialty markets. Hispanic markets sell both yellow and white cornmeal and corn flour.

*Cornstarch* (called cornflour in Britain), is a soft, fine powder made from the endosperm of the corn kernel. It is used as a thickener in sauces and as a coating agent in cooking. In baking, it adds starch without gluten and is sometimes blended with all-purpose flour.

## Sugar

Sugar has many functions in baking. It provides sweetness and aids in creaming, because the crystals open tiny pockets of air in fat as it is whipped. It contributes to grain and texture; it also helps cakes stay fresh longer, aids in yeast fermentation in bread baking, and caramelizes when cooked or baked, adding color to cake and bread crusts.

Sugar interferes with the coagulation of egg proteins, so they (and the batters containing them) need more heat in order to set. Thus, the less sugar in a batter, the less heat needed and the more quickly the batter will set in the oven—a great virtue at high altitudes. Sugar also interferes with the ability of gluten strands to join together; the more sugar present, the weaker the gluten strands and the more tender the product. Some sugar, then, is necessary for tender baked goods. However, at high altitudes, liquids evaporate more quickly, leaving behind a high concentration of sugar, which will weaken the structure of a batter—so much so that a cake or sweet bread can fall flat. To avoid such overconcentration of sugar, most cake and quick bread recipes baked above 3,000 feet reduce the sugar by 1 to 3 tablespoons. Cookies also need less sugar, about 1 to 2 tablespoons per cup of sugar, to prevent overspreading.

Regular *granulated sugar* is used for most baking, but *superfine sugar* (also called bar or ultrafine sugar, sold in 1-pound boxes in the baking aisles of supermarkets) is best for making meringues because its smaller crystals dissolve very quickly in liquid or eggs. You can make your own superfine sugar by whirling granulated sugar in a food processor. British "castor sugar" is similar to superfine sugar (British "icing sugar" refers to confectioners' sugar).

*Brown sugar* is added to baked goods for color, flavor, and moisture (a boon at high altitudes). It is essentially white sugar that contains some molasses; the darker brown the sugar, the more intense the flavor and the more molasses it contains. Both dark and light brown sugar have the same sweetening power as an equal weight of white sugar and can be used interchangeably. However, white sugar is more dense; therefore, to achieve an equivalent degree of sweetness, brown sugar must always be firmly packed before measuring by volume.

Brown sugar always has a tendency to lump, but that is a special problem at high altitudes where everything dries out quickly. To prevent lumping, store brown sugar in a tightly covered glass jar or sealed heavy-duty plastic bag in the refrigerator. If it does lump, add a slice of apple or a piece of bread to the container, and it will soften. To make your own brown sugar, combine 1 cup granulated sugar with 3 to 4 tablespoons unsulfured molasses.

*Confectioners' sugar* is finely powdered sugar. It tends to lump and should always be sifted before measuring. Lightly spoon the sifted sugar into a dry measuring cup, then level it off with a straightedge.

## Salt

Table salt (sodium chloride) is used in the recipes in this book. It has a finer grain than either kosher or sea salt, and it dissolves quickly. Salt has the ability to enhance flavors and it actually makes sweets taste sweeter. In high altitude baking, it is an essential ingredient because higher altitudes tend to rob food of flavor; therefore, the higher you go, the more salt is needed to bring out flavors. In bread baking, salt slows down the development of yeast, an important consideration at high altitudes, because reduced air pressure causes yeast to expand too quickly. Even if you are on a low-salt diet, don't omit salt from high altitude baked goods, or they will taste flat and flavorless.

## Eggs

The recipes in this book use U.S. Grade A large eggs. Eggs add leavening as well as richness, vitamins, and minerals to baked goods. They also contribute to the structure, texture, and color, and help to bind batter ingredients together. As a cake rises during baking, the proteins in the egg combine with the proteins in the flour to support the structure. Eggs also contribute liquid (3 tablespoons per each large egg). In high altitude baking, whole eggs and/or yolks are often added as an "all-purpose" remedy, to provide more strength, richness, and liquid.

The yolk, which contains all the fat and most of the protein of the egg, not only adds richness and color, but also contains lecithin, an emulsifier that helps yolks whip into a stabilized foam. In addition, the presence of lecithin enables a batter to hold more sugar than would otherwise be possible—this can be important in high altitude baking because, in some cakes, the sugar is concentrated by rapid evaporation of liquid. In other cake recipes, you might need to reduce the sugar in order to strengthen batter—but by cutting down the sugar, you would also cut taste. Adding an extra yolk may let you keep more sugar, thereby saving a cake's taste as well as its texture.

Egg whites (albumen) contain some protein, traces of minerals and fats, and water. Whites add strength to a batter, a virtue at high altitudes. But it's important to know that too many whites can be drying to a cake batter, because at high altitudes, faster evaporation already causes excessive dryness in baked goods.

When eggs or egg whites are whipped full of air, the bubbles created expand in the oven to leaven the product. If air is the primary leavening in cakes at high altitudes, the eggs must be handled with care to achieve—and retain—maximum volume.

Eggs separate most easily when cold, but whites beat to their fullest volume when at room temperature. At high altitudes, egg temperature is particularly important for two reasons. First, you need good volume in whipped whites, and second, you want all the ingredients in a batter to be at room temperature so they will blend together smoothly and get hot quickly enough to rise in the oven (cold batter takes longer to heat through). To warm cold

eggs that will be used whole, set them (in their shells) in a bowl of very warm water for about 10 minutes. Or, separate the eggs while still cold, and put the yolks in one bowl and the whites in another, which can be set into a container of warm water for a few minutes to reduce the chill.

Whites will not whip properly if there is even a trace of fat in the bowl or on the beaters. To be sure your equipment is absolutely clean, wipe down the bowl and beater with white vinegar.

To whip whites properly, add cream of tartar and/or salt if called for and whip with an electric mixer on medium-high speed just until foamy. The lower the speed you start with, the smaller the air bubbles and the more stable the foam, important for a reliable rise at high altitudes. Gradually whip in the sugar, increasing the mixer speed to high.

Watch the whites closely as they whip. As soon as you see beater tracks on top, stop the machine, lift the beater, and check the stiffness of the foam. The stiffness of the whipped whites depends upon the recipe. In general, for whites that will leaven a batter *at sea level*, you want them to stand up in stiff peaks, *but at 2,500 feet and above*, you only want soft, droopy peaks. If the whites look too soft, continue beating for just a few more seconds, then check again; do not overbeat. At this stage there is still room in the air cells for them to expand when baked. At high altitudes, if whites are beaten to stiff peaks, the air cells, and the cake, will collapse when the cake cools.

Egg safety is important for good health. When buying eggs, inspect the carton and avoid any with cracked eggs. At home, eggs should be kept refrigerated. Wash your hands, utensils, and counters after handling raw eggs. To the baker, there is no difference between brown and white eggs.

## Butter and Margarine

Butter gives better flavor than margarine, and it should be used at any altitude unless margarine is a dietary necessity. If you must use margarine, select only the hard stick type; soft margarine and butter substitutes contain water and other additives that can cause unpredictable changes and/or baking failures. Above 8,500 feet in altitude, recipes for rich cakes and some cookies may produce better results if you reduce the fat in the sea-level recipe by 1 to 2 tablespoons per cup (half-pound).

## Buttermilk

Traditionally buttermilk was the liquid by-product of churned milk or cream; today it is commercially made by "enhancing" milk. After the solids are removed, the remaining buttermilk is naturally either low fat or nonfat. Cultured buttermilk is low-fat or nonfat milk mixed with a lactic-acid bacteria culture. You can use any type of buttermilk in the recipes in this book. Powdered cultured buttermilk (sold with the baking ingredients in many supermarkets) should be added to a batter along with the other dry ingredients, then the water needed to reconstitute it is added along with the other liquids. Although powdered buttermilk works in high altitude baking, I much prefer to use liquid buttermilk.

Buttermilk is used in baking to contribute acidity as well as richness, moisture, flavor, and tenderness. Its lactic acid weakens the elasticity and/or strength of gluten in wheat flour, thereby keeping baked products tender.

As a substitute for buttermilk, make your own sour milk by adding 1 tablespoon white vinegar or lemon juice to each 1 cup whole or 2% milk; let it sit for about 3 minutes before using it. Or blend about 3 tablespoons plain yogurt into 1 cup milk.

## Cream

There are many different types of cream on the market, and unfortunately, most producers do not indicate the butterfat content on the label, although that is what determines its use. I always use *heavy cream* or *heavy whipping cream*, which has a butterfat content of between 36 and 40 percent. When well chilled and whipped to stiff peaks, this type can hold a piped design without "wilting." Avoid *whipping cream,* which has only about 30 percent butterfat; it will whip, but it will not hold a shape for long. *Light cream* has only 18 to 20 percent butterfat and *half-and-half* has about 10½ to 12 percent; neither will whip or hold a shape.

## Leavening Agents

Air, steam, and carbon dioxide gas produced by baking powder and baking soda are the principal leaveners for most baked goods (yeast leavens bread; see following page). As the altitude increases, air pressure lessens. When there is less air pushing down on the surface of a batter, it can rise much more easily. The higher the elevation, the less air resistance and the more easily the leavening (of any type) works. The amount of leavening in most recipes developed for sea level must be reduced at higher altitudes, or the baked goods will rise too much and then collapse. If both baking powder and baking soda are used in the same recipe, they are usually but not always reduced by the same amount, as indicated in the recipe (or see the table of adjustments on page 323). The amount of air whipped into batters or egg foams must also be carefully controlled, or reduced, or you risk overexpansion when heated (see Eggs, page 38).

**Baking powder:** Baking powder is a combination of acid-reacting ingredients and an alkali (bicarbonate of soda). Most brands also have a starch filler, such as cornstarch, as a stabilizer. There are several types of baking powder, but for successful high altitude baking, double-acting baking powder is the only one I can recommend. Available in any supermarket, it is composed of cream of tartar, tartaric acid, sodium aluminum sulfate, and monocalcium phosphates, and it produces two separate reactions. The first occurs when the baking powder is mixed with liquid in a batter, causing a reaction between the acid and the alkali, which starts to produce carbon dioxide gas. The second occurs in the hot oven, when the heat results in a second burst of carbon dioxide.

Baking powder absorbs moisture from the air and can lose its strength if it gets too old; the average shelf life is about 1 year. If you suspect yours is not fresh, test it by stirring 1 teaspoon of it into about ½ cup of hot water. If it bubbles up quickly, it is fine: if not, toss it out and replace it with a new container (on which you write the purchase date).

**Baking soda:** Also called bicarbonate of soda, baking soda is an alkaline product that is used when there is acid in a batter (such as buttermilk, sour milk, yogurt, lemon juice, vinegar, molasses, honey, chocolate, or cocoa), in order to neutralize some of the acidity. It also provides leavening when it reacts with the acid, releasing carbon dioxide gas. This effect is similar to that of baking powder, but the leavening action only happens once, as soon as the batter is mixed. Batters with baking soda as the only leavening must be put into a preheated oven as soon as they are prepared, before the rising action dissipates.

Many recipes call for both baking soda and baking powder. In that case, the powder is the primary leavening agent and the soda is present to neutralize some of the acidity, as well as to contribute some leavening. In high altitude baking, batters with a high acidity are desirable because they set more quickly in the oven.

Baking soda has four times the strength of baking powder. In some high-altitude recipes, you can cut back the quantity of baking soda so not all the acidity in the batter is neutralized. Too much baking soda can produce off odors and a soapy aftertaste. If your baking soda is lumpy when you measure it, pour it into the palm of your hand and smooth it out or press it through a strainer before adding to the batter.

In recipes that contain chocolate or cocoa, baking soda has another function: as an alkali, it darkens and reddens the color of the chocolate or cocoa (see Cocoa, below).

**Cream of tartar:** A mildly acidic salt, cream of tartar is a by-product of winemaking. Sold in supermarkets with other baking products, it is used to add stability to egg white foam and acidity to batters. In high altitude recipes, the quantity of cream of tartar is often increased to add extra acidity.

**Yeast:** Yeast is available to the home baker in several forms: granulated dry, compressed, and instant active dry. The breads in this book use granulated (active) dry, sold in all supermarkets and specialty food stores. *Instant* active dry is designed to eliminate the need for proofing and to hasten rising. It is fine for sea-level baking with recipes for quick-rise products (sweet breads, especially), but quantities must be greatly cut for high altitude breads, because the reduced air pressure itself encourages rapid yeast expansion; the combination of instant yeast and low air pressure can make bread rise too fast.

Yeast is a living organism sensitive to temperature changes. To activate dry yeast, you must mix it with warm liquid (105° to 110°F); very cold liquid will prevent the yeast from growing and very hot liquid will kill it.

As a substitute for active dry yeast, you can use compressed yeast, which must be very fresh, pale tan in color, and have a clean aroma. One 0.6-ounce cake compressed yeast equals one envelope dry yeast (1 scant tablespoon, ¼ ounce, 7 grams). Crumble it before using in the recipe.

## Flavorings and Extracts

At high altitudes, flavors tend to be less perceptible, or less pungent, than at sea level. For this reason, at 3,000 feet and above, measurements for extracts are usually increased slightly. It is also important to use the best-quality pure extracts available (see Sources, page 329). Quantities of citrus zest (the brightest part of the peel) are also increased at high altitudes to give more flavor. Select fruit with bright color. (See Graters, page 32.)

## Cocoa

Cocoa is produced when chocolate liquor (an essence, not an alcohol) is pressed to remove more than half of its cocoa butter. The resulting dry cake is then pulverized and sifted to make fine unsweetened cocoa powder. Natural cocoa, like solid chocolate, is acidic and has the fruity flavor of the cocoa bean from which it origi-nated. To neutralize some of the acidity and to darken and redden the color, cocoa may be Dutch processed, or factory-treated with alkali (a process invented by a Dutchman, Conrad van Houten). Some widely available Dutch-process brands include Droste, Fedora, Van Houten, and Hershey's European. Widely known American brands of natural unsweetened cocoa (with higher acidity) are regular Hershey's, Baker's, Nestlé, and Ghirardelli. In my high altitude tests, I found that Hershey's natural gave better flavor and color than most other natural cocoas.

When baking soda is added to recipes containing cocoa, the soda balances and/or reduces the acidity and also reddens the cocoa's color (see Daredevil's Food Cake, page 121).

A recipe using Dutch-process cocoa needs less baking soda than one with natural cocoa, because the processed cocoa contains less acid. Take care when using baking soda, because an excess amount gives baked goods an unpleasant soapy taste.

When preparing pans for chocolate cakes, I like to dust the greased pans with sifted cocoa instead of flour. The cocoa gives a richer brown color to the crust.

# Muffins

## Baking Muffins at High Altitudes

A great muffin should look as good as it tastes, with a rounded or domed top, golden brown color, and a crunchy sugar or streusel topping that makes your mouth water. The crumb should be tender and moist, with a fairly open texture, less fine than a layer cake.

Theoretically, baking muffins at high altitudes would seem to be an easy task. In fact, compared to cakes, muffin recipes change relatively little as the altitude increases. This is mainly because when baking a muffin, you have a small quantity of batter surrounded by a hot metal cup that conducts heat quickly throughout the batter. Because it heats fast, there are not the same concerns about evaporation as with a cake. If any extra liquid is added to the recipe, it is to counter the dryness of flour at high altitudes. That said, however, heavy batters like that for Raisin Bran Muffins (page 54) are another story. The challenge here is to get a good rise with the weighty, dense batter. The solution—arrived at after mixing my way through several boxes of bran and countless bags of raisins—

involved many changes in the sea-level formula. I replaced the whole milk with buttermilk to increase the batter's acidity, omitted the baking soda (again to maintain acidity, rather than neutralize it), substituted white sugar for the weightier dark brown, and altered the proportions of the bran and flour.

To get a moister crumb with heavier muffins at higher elevations, I discovered that oil (which is 100 percent fat and coats the gluten strands in flour, keeping products tender) was better than melted butter (about 81 percent fat), although the latter contributes more flavor.

Getting the proper rise is not always as easy as it sounds. Like other members of the quick bread family, muffins are leavened with baking powder and/or baking soda. Although a heavy raisin bran batter will never rise as high as a blueberry muffin batter, even muffins made from a dense batter should have a slightly rounded top. Muffins made with a less dense batter rise more easily into a rounded top. I didn't have to reduce leavening for them until I was at

10,000 feet and, in fact, I was glad for the rising help provided naturally by the reduced atmospheric pressure. But at 10,000 feet, I found that I had too much chemical leavening combined with the reduced air pressure, so my muffins rose and then sank! Balance is the key, and I had to reduce the leavening.

For the best rise, fill muffin cups to the rim (rather than the usual two-thirds full) with batter. If you use 2½-inch-diameter muffin cups, the yield will be 12 muffins. Larger cups will hold more batter and yield fewer muffins. If your pan has any empty cups, add a little water to them before baking.

Above 3,000 feet, it's sometimes necessary to increase baking temperature and time slightly to give a richer golden color. But don't overbake muffins, or they will dry out and have a crumbly texture (the higher, the drier).

Some experts warn that shiny muffins pans result in muffins with pale bottoms, but this is not true when baking temperature and time are correct. I prefer shiny pans to black pans, especially heavy steel, which can result in too dry a crust because they retain so much heat.

To freeze muffins at high altitudes (for up to 2 months), seal them individually in plastic wrap, then store in a heavy-duty plastic bag. To warm thawed muffins, wrap them tightly in foil. Heat for about 5 minutes at 400°F. Or to warm muffins in a microwave, wrap them loosely in paper towels and use full power for 45 seconds for two to four muffins (30 seconds for just one muffin).

# Mom's Blueberry Muffins

**B**LUEBERRY MUFFINS were one of my mother's specialities, and I dedicate this recipe to her memory. These are the muffins I dream about, and wake up hoping someone has whipped them up for my breakfast the way she used to. Their presence makes any morning special. I often double the recipe to put some in the freezer. There is no limit to the variations you can create with this recipe: try combining different types of berries, or use blueberries and peach or nectarine slices, or sliced plums and raspberries.

**General High Altitude Notes:** Oven temperatures vary, and baking times and liquid increase with altitude. This recipe was totally stable at higher altitudes, needing only more liquid, until I reached 10,000 feet—then it gave me a very hard time. It took at least six batches before I found a formula that gave good rise and texture. I tried varying amounts of leavening and replacing the whole milk with buttermilk, but I ultimately rejected that because it resulted in too much leavening action—it made the muffin tops rise, then fall as they cooled. To get the desired results, I added a little salt for more flavor, cut out one egg, and reduced the leavening as well as the sugar to strengthen the structure.

**Special Equipment:** 2½-inch muffin cups; sifter; wooden skewer or cake tester

**Pan Preparation:** Coat the muffin cups with nonstick vegetable spray (then wipe the top of the pan with a paper towel) or coat with solid shortening, or use paper muffin cup liners. At 10,000 feet, coat with nonstick spray, then dust with flour and tap out the excess flour.

**Makes** 12 muffins

**High Notes**
> *At 3,000 feet and above,* increase the milk as the elevation climbs.
> *At 10,000 feet,* omit 1 egg, reduce the sugar and leavening, and increase the salt.

**1.** Position the rack and preheat the oven as indicated for your altitude in the chart on the next page. Prepare the pan as directed.

If using fresh berries, pick them over and remove the stems, rinse, and gently blot dry on paper towels. If using frozen berries, remove any ice particles. Set aside.

| Ingredients | Sea Level | 3,000 feet | 5,000 feet | 7,000 feet | 10,000 feet |
|---|---|---|---|---|---|
| **Oven rack position, temperature, and baking time** | Rack in center; bake at 400°F for 20 to 22 minutes | Rack in center; bake at 400°F for 22 to 25 minutes | Rack in center; bake at 425°F for 22 to 25 minutes | Rack in center; bake at 400°F for 23 to 25 minutes | Rack in lower third of oven; bake at 425°F for 23 to 25 minutes |
| **Blueberries, fresh or frozen** | 1½ cups | 1½ cups | 1½ cups | 1½ cups | 1½ cups |
| **Large egg(s), at room temperature** | 2 | 2 | 2 | 2 | 1 |
| **Milk** | ½ cup plus 2 tablespoons | ½ cup plus 2 tablespoons | ¾ cup | ¾ cup | 1 cup |
| **Unsalted butter, melted and cooled, or canola oil** | 4 tablespoons (¼ cup) | 4 tablespoons (¼ cup) | 4 tablespoons (¼ cup) | 4 tablespoons (¼ cup) | 4 tablespoons (¼ cup) |
| **All-purpose flour** | 2 cups | 2 cups | 2 cups | 2 cups | 2 cups |
| **Baking powder** | 1 tablespoon | 1 tablespoon | 1 tablespoon | 1 tablespoon | 2 teaspoons |
| **Salt** | ½ teaspoon | ½ teaspoon | ½ teaspoon | ½ teaspoon | ¾ teaspoon |
| **Granulated sugar** | ⅔ cup | ⅔ cup | ⅔ cup | ⅔ cup | ½ cup minus 1 tablespoon |
| **TOPPING** | | | | | |
| **Granulated sugar** | 3 tablespoons | 3 tablespoons | 3 tablespoons | 3 tablespoons | 3 tablespoons |

**2.** In a large bowl, whisk together the egg(s), milk, and melted butter or oil. Place a sifter over the bowl and measure the flour, baking powder, salt, and sugar into it. Stir/sift the dry ingredients onto the wet, add the berries, and stir everything together just to blend; don't overbeat.

**3.** Divide the batter evenly among the muffin cups, filling them nearly full. (Half-fill any empty cups with water.) Generously sprinkle sugar on top of each muffin. Bake for the time indicated for your altitude in the chart above, or until the muffins are golden brown and well risen and a cake tester inserted in the center comes out clean. (Muffins made with frozen berries will take a few more minutes to bake through.) Cool slightly on a wire rack, and serve warm.

# Cranberry Pecan Streusel Muffins

How can you resist? Cinnamon-nut streusel tops an orange-scented muffin packed with cranberries and pecans—at every altitude, this is an unbeatable combination. In Breckenridge, Colorado, as I was dropping off a batch of muffins at the Red Door shelter one morning I saw a carton of extra-high-topped muffins on the table. I was struggling so hard to make my own muffins rise in that rarified atmosphere, I took a second, closer look at them. "These muffins are really glamorous, do you know who baked them?" I asked Nathan, the young manager. "No one real, and not up here, for sure," he replied. "Starbucks bakes them down in Denver (5,000 feet) and trucks them up."

I knew all the good muffins in town weren't imported, though, because I had tasted some beauties at Laura Komeshian's bakery/café, Clint's, on Main Street in Breckenridge (see page 21). As she raced between the kitchen and the cash register, Laura would stop at my table, taste my latest efforts, share her recipes, and commiserate. Although Laura mixes her muffin batters in thirty-gallon buckets and bakes them in four-dozen batches, she took the time to break down her recipes so we could compare them with mine. And she offered many tips: "Add an egg or a yolk," she advised. "Cut back on the sugar and add flour. Try yogurt or buttermilk for the liquid."

To get the best rise in this recipe, use 1 cup cranberries and ½ cup nuts. Any more fruit weighs down the batter and reduces the rise, but the taste is still great—if you don't care about looks, you can add up to ½ cup more cranberries, or combine fresh cranberries with Craisins. I use wheat germ for its nutritional value and texture, but you can substitute oat or wheat bran. Oil gives a slightly moister crumb than melted butter.

**General High Altitude Notes:** Yogurt adds moisture and flavor as well as acidity, which helps the batter set fast at high altitudes.

At 10,000 feet, the acidity of the yogurt plus the baking powder created too much leavening and caused "flat-tops," so I replaced yogurt with milk. Because the batter is weighted down by the fruit and nuts, it needs extra strength to hold its rise at high altitudes. For a stronger structure and quicker set (except at 10,000 feet; see below), I added more flour and another egg. To enhance the batter's acidity, I omitted the baking soda, which normally neutralizes some of yogurt's acidity.

**Special Equipment:** 2½-inch muffin cups; sifter; wooden skewer or cake tester

**Pan Preparation:** Coat the muffin cups with nonstick vegetable spray (then wipe the top of the pan with a paper towel) or coat with solid shortening. At 10,000 feet, coat the pan, then dust with flour and tap out the excess flour; or use paper muffin cup liners.

**Makes** 12 muffins

**High Notes**

*At 10,000 feet,* replace the yogurt with whole milk and add strength by cutting down the sugar. Muffins tend to stick in the pan at this altitude; bake them in paper cups or flour the greased muffin tins.

I learned to cook in my twenties, when I lived in Albuquerque, New Mexico (5,000 feet). A passionate foodie, I was trying very hard and really cared about the results. I found that general cooking was easy for me, though it took a little longer than at sea level, but I had disasters every time I tried to bake! I couldn't find reliable adjustments, did each cake three or more times with different changes, but never had a success. I got so fearful that my hands shook whenever I baked. I'm sure that early trauma is the reason I am now what I call a reluctant baker. I'm still afraid to bake and hardly ever try, even though I have moved to sea level in Long Beach, California.

—Russ Parsons, food columnist for the *Los Angeles Times*; author, *How to Read a French Fry*

| Ingredients | Sea Level | 3,000 feet | 5,000 feet | 7,000 feet | 10,000 feet |
|---|---|---|---|---|---|
| Oven rack position, temperature, and baking time | Rack in center; bake at 400°F for 20 to 22 minutes | Rack in center; bake at 400°F for 20 to 22 minutes | Rack in lower third of oven; bake at 400°F for 22 to 25 minutes | Rack in lower third of oven; bake at 400°F for 22 to 25 minutes | Rack in lower third of oven; bake at 425°F for 25 to 27 minutes |

**TOPPING**

| Ingredients | Sea Level | 3,000 feet | 5,000 feet | 7,000 feet | 10,000 feet |
|---|---|---|---|---|---|
| All-purpose flour | 2 tablespoons | 2 tablespoons | 2 tablespoons | 2 tablespoons | 2 tablespoons |
| Granulated sugar | 2 tablespoons | 2 tablespoons | 2 tablespoons | 2 tablespoons | 2 tablespoons |
| Salt | Pinch | Pinch | Pinch | Pinch | Pinch |
| Ground cinnamon | ¼ teaspoon | ¼ teaspoon | ¼ teaspoon | ¼ teaspoon | ¼ teaspoon |
| Unsalted butter, cut up | 1 tablespoon | 1 tablespoon | 1 tablespoon | 1 tablespoon | 1 tablespoon |
| Pecans or walnuts, finely chopped | ¼ cup (1 ounce) | ¼ cup (1 ounce) | ¼ cup (1 ounce) | ¼ cup (1 ounce) | ¼ cup (1 ounce) |

**MUFFINS**

| Ingredients | Sea Level | 3,000 feet | 5,000 feet | 7,000 feet | 10,000 feet |
|---|---|---|---|---|---|
| Granulated sugar | ½ cup | ½ cup | ½ cup plus 2 tablespoons | ⅔ cup | ¼ cup plus 2 tablespoons |
| Cranberries, coarsely chopped | 1 cup | 1 cup | 1 cup | 1 cup | 1 cup |
| Pecans or walnuts, chopped | ½ cup (2 ounces) | ½ cup (2 ounces) | ½ cup (2 ounces) | ½ cup (2 ounces) | ½ cup (2 ounces) |
| Grated orange zest | 1 teaspoon | 1 teaspoon | 1 teaspoon | 1 teaspoon | 1 teaspoon |
| Orange extract | 1 teaspoon | 1 teaspoon | 1 teaspoon | 1 teaspoon | 1 teaspoon |
| Large egg(s), at room temperature | 1 | 2 | 2 | 2 | 1 |

(continued)

| Ingredients | Sea Level | 3,000 feet | 5,000 feet | 7,000 feet | 10,000 feet |
|---|---|---|---|---|---|
| **Plain or orange yogurt, top liquid poured off** | 1 cup | 1 cup minus 2 tablespoons | 1 cup minus 2 tablespoons | ³⁄₄ cup, plus 2 tablespoons water | None |
| **Whole milk** | None | None | None | None | 1 cup |
| **Unsalted butter, melted, or canola oil** | 4 tablespoons (¹⁄₄ cup) | 4 tablespoons (¹⁄₄ cup) | ¹⁄₃ cup oil | ¹⁄₃ cup oil | ¹⁄₄ cup oil |
| **Wheat germ** | 2 tablespoons | 2 tablespoons | 2 tablespoons | 3 tablespoons | 2 tablespoons |
| **Unsifted All-purpose flour** | 1¹⁄₂ cups | 1³⁄₄ cups | 1³⁄₄ cups | 1³⁄₄ cups | 2 cups minus 2 tablespoons |
| **Baking powder** | 2 teaspoons | 1 tablespoon | 1 tablespoon | 1 tablespoon | 2 teaspoons |
| **Baking soda** | ¹⁄₂ teaspoon | None | None | None | None |
| **Salt** | ¹⁄₂ teaspoon | ¹⁄₂ teaspoon | ¹⁄₂ teaspoon | ¹⁄₂ teaspoon | ³⁄₄ teaspoon |
| **Ground cinnamon** | ¹⁄₂ teaspoon | ¹⁄₂ teaspoon | ¹⁄₂ teaspoon | ¹⁄₂ teaspoon | ¹⁄₂ teaspoon |

**1.** Position the rack and preheat the oven as indicated for your altitude in the chart above. Prepare the pan as directed.

In a medium bowl, toss together all the streusel topping ingredients and pinch everything together with your fingertips to make crumbs. Set aside.

**2.** Measure the sugar. In another bowl, toss together the cranberries and nuts with the grated orange zest, extract, and 1 tablespoon of the sugar. Set aside.

**3.** In a large bowl, whisk together the egg(s), yogurt or milk, melted butter or oil, the remaining sugar, and the wheat germ. Place a sifter over the bowl and measure the flour, baking powder, baking soda (if using), salt, and cinnamon into it. Stir/sift the dry ingredients onto the wet, add the cranberry-nut mixture, and stir everything together just to blend; don't overbeat.

**3.** Divide the batter evenly among the muffin cups, filling them nearly full. Sprinkle generously with the streusel crumbs. (Half-fill any empty cups with water.) Bake for the time indicated for your altitude in the chart above, or until the muffins are golden brown and well risen and a cake tester inserted in the center comes out clean. Cool slightly on a wire rack, and serve warm.

# Whole-Wheat Apple-Oat Muffins

THESE NUTRITIOUS muffins are perfect for fall picnics and lunch boxes. While they are baking, your house will be filled with the perfume of apples and cinnamon. The crumb is tender, the flavor not too sweet, and the textural contrast between the soft, sweet apples and the crunchy streusel topping is very satisfying. To make Maple-Nut Apple-Oat Muffins, add ¼ cup chopped walnuts and ½ teaspoon maple extract to the batter.

**General High Altitude Notes:** At 3,000 feet and above, the rise is improved by changing the flour proportions: less whole-wheat, more white. At 5,000 feet and above, oil gives a moister crumb than melted butter, yogurt or sour cream provides the extra acidity needed for a quick set and good rise, and a tiny bit of baking soda adds leavening and neutralizes just the right amount of the yogurt's acidity.

**Special Equipment:** 2½-inch muffin cups; sifter; wooden skewer or cake tester

**Pan Preparation:** Coat the muffin cups with nonstick vegetable spray (then wipe the top of the pan with a paper towel) or coat with solid shortening. At 10,000 feet, coat the pans with nonstick spray, then dust with flour and tap out the excess flour; or use paper muffin cup liners.

**Makes** 12 muffins

**High Notes**

*At 10,000 feet,* the baking temperature and time are increased and the oven rack position is different; the tops will be rounded but the rise will be a little less than at other elevations. Muffins tend to stick in the pan at this altitude; bake them in paper cups or flour the greased muffin tins.

| Ingredients | Sea Level | 3,000 feet | 5,000 feet | 7,000 feet | 10,000 feet |
|---|---|---|---|---|---|
| **Oven rack position, temperature, and baking time** | Rack in center; bake at 400°F for 20 to 22 minutes | Rack in center; bake at 400°F for 22 to 25 minutes | Rack in center; bake at 400°F for 22 to 25 minutes | Rack in center; bake at 400°F for 22 to 25 minutes | Rack in lower third of oven; bake at 425°F for 35 to 37 minutes |

*(continued)*

| Ingredients | Sea Level | 3,000 feet | 5,000 feet | 7,000 feet | 10,000 feet |
|---|---|---|---|---|---|
| **TOPPING** | | | | | |
| **All-purpose flour** | 3 tablespoons | 3 tablespoons | 3 tablespoons | 3 tablespoons | 3 tablespoons |
| **Light brown sugar, packed** | 3 tablespoons | 3 tablespoons | 3 tablespoons | 3 tablespoons | 3 tablespoons |
| **Old-fashioned rolled oats** | 2 tablespoons | 2 tablespoons | 2 tablespoons | 2 tablespoons | 2 tablespoons |
| **Ground cinnamon** | ½ teaspoon | ½ teaspoon | ½ teaspoon | ½ teaspoon | ½ teaspoon |
| **Unsalted butter, cut up** | Generous 1 tablespoon | Generous 1 tablespoon | Generous 1 tablespoon | Generous 1 tablespoon | Generous 1 tablespoon |
| **Salt** | Pinch | Pinch | Pinch | Pinch | Pinch |
| **MUFFINS** | | | | | |
| **Apple, Golden Delicious or other soft eating type** | 1 | 1 | 1 | 1 | 1 |
| **Raisins** | ½ cup (3 ounces) | ½ cup (3 ounces) | ½ cup (3 ounces) | ½ cup (3 ounces) | ½ cup (3 ounces) |
| **Vanilla extract** | 1 teaspoon | 1 teaspoon | 1 teaspoon | 1 teaspoon | 1 teaspoon |
| **Old-fashioned rolled oats** | ⅓ cup | ⅓ cup | ¼ cup | ⅓ cup | ¼ cup |
| **All-purpose flour** | 1 cup | 1 cup plus 2 tablespoons | 1 cup plus 2 tablespoons | 1 cup plus 2 tablespoons | 1 cup |
| **Whole-wheat flour** | 1 cup | ¾ cup | ¾ cup | ¾ cup | ¾ cup |
| **Baking powder** | 2 teaspoons | 2 teaspoons | 2 teaspoons | 2 teaspoons | 1 teaspoon |
| **Baking soda** | None | None | ⅛ teaspoon | ⅛ teaspoon | ½ teaspoon |
| **Salt** | ½ teaspoon | ½ teaspoon | ¾ teaspoon | ¾ teaspoon | ¾ teaspoon |
| **Ground cinnamon** | 1 teaspoon | 1 teaspoon | 1 teaspoon | 1 teaspoon | 1¼ teaspoons |

(*continued*)

| Ingredients | Sea Level | 3,000 feet | 5,000 feet | 7,000 feet | 10,000 feet |
|---|---|---|---|---|---|
| **Light brown sugar, packed, or granulated sugar** | 1/3 cup | 1/3 cup | 1/2 cup | 1/2 cup | 1/4 cup plus 2 tablespoons |
| **Large eggs, at room temperature** | 2 | 2 | 2 | 2 | 2 |
| **Unsalted butter, melted, or canola oil** | 4 tablespons (1/4 cup) butter | 4 tablespons (1/4 cup) butter | 1/4 cup oil | 1/4 cup oil | 1/4 cup oil |
| **Plain yogurt or sour cream** | None | None | 1/4 cup | 1/4 cup | 1/4 cup |
| **Apple cider or apple juice** | 1/2 cup plus 2 tablespoons | 1/2 cup plus 2 tablespoons | 2/3 cup | 3/4 cup | 3/4 cup |

**1.** Position the rack and preheat the oven as indicated in the chart above. Prepare the pan as directed.

In a medium bowl, toss together all the topping ingredients, and pinch everything together with your fingertips to make crumbs. Set aside.

**2.** Peel and core the apple. Chop it into small (about 1/4-inch) bits and put it in a small bowl with the raisins. Add the vanilla, toss, and set aside.

**3.** In a large bowl, whisk together the oats, white and whole-wheat flours, baking powder, baking soda (if using), salt, and cinnamon. Crumble in the sugar, breaking up any lumps of brown sugar with your fingers.

**4.** Make a well in the middle of the dry mixture and add the eggs, melted butter or oil, yogurt or sour cream (if using), and apple cider or juice. With a whisk or fork, first blend the wet ingredients together, then work in the dry ingredients. Stir in the apples and raisins; do not overmix.

**5.** Divide the batter evenly among the muffin cups, filling them nearly full. Sprinkle generously with the streusel crumbs. (Half-fill any empty cups with water.) Bake for the time indicated for your altitude in the chart above, or until the muffins are golden brown and well risen and a cake tester inserted in the center comes out clean. Cool slightly on a wire rack, and serve warm.

# Smoky Mountain Raisin Bran Muffins

THESE FLAVORFUL sugar-topped muffins have a surprisingly light, moist crumb even though they are full of bran. The taste is not too sweet, with just a hint of molasses, and because the batter is heavy, the tops are gently rounded rather than peaked. Bran muffins are heavenly for breakfast served warm with cream cheese, or split in half, toasted lightly, and topped with butter; they also travel well, and make a nutritious lunch-box snack.

Of all the muffins in this book, this was the most difficult to perfect at each high altitude location because the original (sea-level) balance of ingredients was so heavy in weight and not sufficiently acidic for higher altitude. Each time, it took me about eight tests before I got it right. However, except for being flat-topped, the wannabes were not bad, and they made me quite a few friends.

I was up to my elbows in bran and feeling on edge from frustration early one morning in Breckenridge when, suddenly, I was surrounded by a terrifying roar of chain saws. I rushed out to the deck, muffin in hand, to confront the assault team headed my way: one black Labrador puppy and four young men in T-shirts from A Cut Above Forestry. I waved the muffin (my secret weapon) and they stopped sawing. They were quick to explain that they were part of a forest fire prevention program (requested by my host), removing any lodgepole pines that grew too close to houses. I don't know whether it was the muffin in my hand or the sweet baking perfume wafting out my kitchen door, but almost as soon as I returned to the kitchen, there was a tentative

knock at the door. It was a blond young man named Ben, with the jumping puppy, asking if he could, "please, ma'am," fill his Thermos with cold water. At my suggestion, Ben and company were delighted to take a muffin break, while reassuring me that they were way too expert to drop a tree on my roof or even hang it up in the tangle of surrounding woods. "It's hard to cut straight in a crooked forest," Ben mumbled with a mouth full of muffin, "but that's our specialty. We're glad muffins are yours."

**General High Altitude Notes:** In order to get a rise out of this heavy batter above sea level, several changes were necessary. First I lightened the batter by replacing some of the heavy bran with lighter-weight flour. Then, although butter has a great taste, I found that oil gave a moister crumb at 3,000 feet and above. I also switched from brown to granulated sugar. To make the batter set more quickly at 5,000 feet and above, I increased acidity by omitting the baking soda and substituting buttermilk for milk.

For better rise and quicker set, I altered the oven temperature, baking time, and rack position with rises in elevation. When the oven temperature was over 425°F, the tops of the muffins crusted over before the interior baked through. Baking on the lowest rack gave best rise at 5,000 feet and above.

**Special Equipment:** 2½-inch muffin cups; wooden skewer or cake tester

**Pan Preparation:** Coat the muffin cups with nonstick vegetable spray (then wipe the top of the pan with a paper towel) or coat with solid shortening. At 10,000 feet, coat the pans with nonstick spray, then dust with flour and tap out the excess flour; or use paper muffin cup liners.

**Makes** 12 muffins (13 at 10,000 feet)

**High Notes**

*At 3,000 feet and above,* switch from brown sugar to white; at 5,000 feet, switch from whole milk to buttermilk.

*At 7,000 feet,* reduce baking temperature to 400°F.

*At 10,000 feet,* return the baking temperature to 425°F; the muffin tops will be slightly rounded but the rise will be a little less high than at other elevations. To get the best rise, add an egg to increase the amount of liquid and add volume; the yield will be thirteen (2½-inch) muffins.

| Ingredients | Sea Level | 3,000 feet | 5,000 feet | 7,000 feet | 10,000 feet |
|---|---|---|---|---|---|
| **Oven rack position, temperature, and baking time** | Rack in center; bake at 400°F for 15 to 17 minutes | Rack in center; bake at 425°F for 15 to 17 minutes | Rack in lower third of oven; bake at 425°F for 17 to 20 minutes | Rack in lower third of oven; bake at 400°F for 22 to 25 minutes | Rack in lower third of oven; bake at 425°F for 22 to 25 minutes |

(*continued*)

| Ingredients | Sea Level | 3,000 feet | 5,000 feet | 7,000 feet | 10,000 feet |
|---|---|---|---|---|---|
| **100% All-Bran cereal (not flakes)** | 1⅓ cups | 1 cup | 1 cup | 1 cup | 1 cup |
| **Milk** | 1¼ cups | 1⅓ cups | None | None | None |
| **Buttermilk** | None | None | 1⅓ cups | 1½ cups | 1½ cups plus 2 tablespoons |
| **Unsulfured Molasses** | 2 tablespoons | 2 tablespoons | 2 tablespoons | 2 tablespoons | 2 tablespoons |
| **Light or dark brown sugar, packed** | ½ cup | None | None | None | None |
| **Granulated sugar** | None | ½ cup minus 1 tablespoon | ¼ cup plus 2 tablespoons | ¼ cup plus 2 tablespoons | ⅓ cup plus 1 tablespoon |
| **Vanilla extract** | 1 teaspoon | 1 teaspoon | 1 teaspoon | 1 teaspoon | 1 teaspoon |
| **Raisins** | 1 cup (6 ounces) | 1 cup (6 ounces) | 1 cup (6 ounces) | 1 cup (6 ounces) | 1 cup (6 ounces) |
| **All-purpose flour** | 1 cup | 1⅓ cups | 1⅓ cups | 1⅓ cups | 1½ cups plus 3 tablespoons |
| **Baking powder** | 2 teaspoons | 1½ teaspoons | 1¼ teaspoons | 1¾ teaspoons | 2 teaspoons |
| **Baking soda** | ½ teaspoon | None | None | ½ teaspoon | ¼ teaspoon |
| **Salt** | ½ teaspoon | ½ teaspoon | ½ teaspoon | ½ teaspoon | ½ teaspoon |
| **Ground cinnamon** | 1 teaspoon | 1 teaspoon | 1 teaspoon | 1 teaspoon | 1 teaspoon |
| **Large egg, at room temperature, lightly beaten** | 1 | 1 | 1 | 1 | 2 |
| **Unsalted butter, melted, or canola oil** | 4 tablespoons (¼ cup) butter | ¼ cup oil | ¼ cup oil | ¼ cup oil | 3 tablespoons oil |
| **TOPPING** | | | | | |
| **Granulated sugar** | 1½ tablespoons | 1½ tablespoons | 1½ tablespoons | 1½ tablespoons | 1½ tablespoons |

**1.** Position the rack and preheat the oven as indicated in the chart above. Prepare the pan as directed.

**2.** In a large bowl, stir together the bran, milk or buttermilk, molasses, brown or granulated sugar, vanilla, and raisins. Set aside to soak for about 10 minutes, or until the bran is very soft.

**3.** In a medium bowl, whisk together the flour, baking powder, baking soda (if using), salt, and cinnamon. When the bran mixture is soft, stir the egg and melted butter or oil into it. Add the flour mixture all at once and stir just until well blended; do not overmix.

**4.** Divide the batter evenly among the muffin cups, filling them to just below the brim. Note that at 10,000 feet, there will be a little more batter (see High Notes). Sprinkle the topping sugar on top of the muffins. (Half-fill any empty cups with water.)

**5.** Bake for the time indicated for your altitude in the chart above, or until the muffins are slightly rounded on top and deep golden brown and a cake tester inserted in the center comes out clean. Cool the muffins in the pan on a wire rack for about 5 minutes, then lift them out of the pan and let cool slightly on the rack. Serve warm.

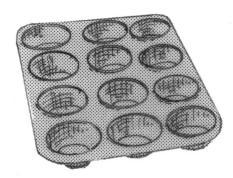

# Quick Breads, Scones, Biscuits, and Popovers

## Baking Quick Breads, Scones, Biscuits, and Popovers at High Altitudes

The quick bread family includes scones, biscuits, popovers, corn bread, and Irish soda bread, as well as quick breads. They are related because they share several characteristics: they all use chemical leaveners—baking powder and/or baking soda (except popovers, which use hot air)—and they all have a more tender crumb when their batters are beaten as little as possible.

At high altitude, members of the quick bread family all share the same adjustments. When altitude increases, the baking powder and/or baking soda must be reduced slightly. Baking soda (an alkali; see page 41) has two important functions. First, it neutralizes some of the acidity in ingredients like buttermilk or yogurt (½ teaspoon baking soda will neutralize 1 cup buttermilk), and second, it reacts with the acidic ingredient, such as buttermilk, to produce carbon dioxide gas, a leavener.

At high altitudes, the more acidic the bat-ter, the more quickly it will set up in a hot oven. Since the boiling point of water is lower at high altitudes, the higher the elevation, the longer it will take to heat up the inside of a batter and the longer it will take to set; an acidic batter speeds the process. To increase acidity (leaving more of the batter's acidity intact), you can reduce the baking soda, but don't try to omit it entirely (unless you replace it with baking powder for leavening).

Because liquids evaporate faster at high altitudes, the high concentrations of sugar that remain can weaken the batter's structure, interfering with the strength-giving proteins (gluten) in the flour, and leading to its eventual collapse. To strengthen a batter, reduce the sugar and increase flour as the elevation increases. To compensate for the dryness of high altitude air, add extra liquid; it is especially helpful if the liquid is buttermilk or yogurt, because both contribute acidity while also adding flavor, tenderness, and moisture.

Quick breads all require careful attention to technique at high altitude. Scones and biscuits need very light handling during the blending of very cold butter with flour (the same procedure used for making piecrust). This is easily accomplished using a food processor because the steel blade quickly dices hard or frozen butter. If you don't have a processor, grate frozen butter by rubbing it across the large holes of a box grater.

Many quick breads (also called tea breads) are baked in loaf pans. These present a particular challenge for the high altitude baker because the narrow rectangular pan exposes a relatively small amount of batter to direct heat, and this top surface can easily crust over before the wet interior batter is baked through. To prevent this, look at the color of your loaf about halfway through the baking time, and if it seems to be browning too quickly, lightly cover it with a piece of aluminum foil (shiny side down).

To give all quick breads a good rise, the oven temperature can be increased by 15 to 25 degrees at elevations between 4,000 and 6,000 feet. If using a loaf pan above that elevation, however, it is better to keep the temperature at a moderate heat (350°F) so the top of the loaf will not set so quickly and the inside has a little longer to bake through.

# Ann's Irish Soda Bread

THIS RECIPE is named for Ann Endresen, my Dublin-born friend who, with her husband, Dan, invited me to test recipes in their Idaho kitchen. This round golden-brown, raisin-studded bread makes a dramatic presentation at any time, but especially on St. Patrick's Day, when it has a cross cut into the top. The dough is quick and easy to mix together, and the less you handle it, the more tender the bread will be.

The recipe traditionally uses buttermilk, a bonus for high altitude bakers, because it is one of our favorite acidic ingredients. It helps batter set quickly at high elevations and contributes tenderness, moisture, and leavening when mixed with baking soda and baking powder. For variations, you can add 1 tablespoon caraway seeds, or make wheaten bread, or brown soda bread (as it is called in Northern Ireland), by replacing half the white flour with stone-ground organic whole-wheat flour and adding a couple of tablespoons of wheat bran or wheat germ.

Traditional recipes such as the one below use about 8 tablespoons butter. You can easily reduce the fat without compromising taste or texture by cutting the butter to only 2 tablespoons and using nonfat buttermilk.

For easy preparation, I like to use a food processor to cut the butter into the flour. Alternatively, you can whisk together all the dry ingredients, then work in room-temperature butter with a fork or wire pastry cutter.

**General High Altitude Notes:** The large ball of dough is quite thick and dense, so at all altitudes be sure to leave the bread in the oven long enough to bake the inside completely (test it like a cake, with a skewer). You can increase the baking time if necessary, but don't raise the oven temperature, or you will risk overbrowning the crust before the inside is set. If you see the top overbrowning, cover it loosely with a piece of aluminum foil (shiny side down). At 10,000 feet, I got a better rise when I cut the butter slightly, strengthening the gluten in the flour.

**Special Equipment:** A cookie sheet; Silpat or other nonstick baking mat or baking parchment; pastry brush; single-edged razor blade or sharp knife; wooden skewer or cake tester; aluminum foil

**Pan Preparation:** Line the cookie sheet with a nonstick mat or baking parchment or spray with nonstick vegetable spray.

**Makes** 1 large round loaf; about 16 slices

**High Notes**

*At 3,000 feet and above,* decrease the baking soda and increase the liquid.

*At 10,000 feet,* decrease the baking soda, baking powder, and butter.

| Ingredients | Sea Level | 3,000 feet | 5,000 feet | 7,000 feet | 10,000 feet |
|---|---|---|---|---|---|
| **Oven rack position, temperature, and baking time** | Rack in center; bake at 375°F for 40 to 45 minutes | Rack in center; bake at 375°F for 50 to 55 minutes | Rack in center; bake at 375°F for 50 to 55 minutes | Rack in center; bake at 375°F for 50 to 55 minutes | Rack in center; bake at 375°F for 45 to 50 minutes |
| **All-purpose flour** | 4 cups | 4 cups | 4 cups | 4 cups | 4 cups |
| **Granulated sugar** | 2½ tablespoons | 3 tablespoons | 3 tablespoons | 3 tablespoons | 3 tablespoons |
| **Baking powder** | 1 tablespoon | 1 tablespoon | 1 tablespoon | 1 tablespoon | 1¾ teaspoons |
| **Baking soda** | 1 teaspoon | 1 teaspoon minus ⅛ teaspoon | ¾ teaspoon | ¾ teaspoon | ½ teaspoon |
| **Salt** | 1 teaspoon | 1 teaspoon | 1 teaspoon | 1 teaspoon | 1 teaspoon |
| **Unsalted butter, cold** | 8 tablespoons (1 stick) | 8 tablespoons (1 stick) | 8 tablespoons (1 stick) | 8 tablespoons (1 stick) | 7 tablespoons |
| **Raisins or currants** | 1½ cups (9 ounces) | 1½ cups (9 ounces) | 1½ cups (9 ounces) | 1½ cups (9 ounces) | 1½ cups (9 ounces) |
| **Buttermilk** | 1½ cups plus 2 tablespoons | 1½ cups plus 3 tablespoons | 1½ cups plus 3 tablespoons | 1¾ cups | 1¾ cups |
| **Large egg, at room temperature** | 1 | 1 | 1 | 1 | 1 |
| **GLAZE** | | | | | |
| **Large egg** | 1 | 1 | 1 | 1 | 1 |
| **Buttermilk** | 1 teaspoon | 1 teaspoon | 1 teaspoon | 1 teaspoon | 1 teaspoon |

1. Position the oven rack as indicated in the chart above. Prepare the baking sheet as directed.

2. Measure the flour, sugar, baking powder, baking soda, and salt into the bowl of a food processor. Pulse a couple of times to blend, then add the cold butter and pulse until finely chopped and blended. Add the raisins and pulse quickly 1 or 2 times, just to coat them with flour.

3. In a large bowl, whisk together the butter-milk and egg. Dump in the flour-butter mixture and stir with a sturdy wooden spoon until well combined; don't overmix. The dough will feel quite sticky.

4. Sprinkle 2 to 3 tablespoons flour onto the counter and turn out the dough. With lightly floured hands, knead the dough 5 or 6 times, adding a little more flour if necessary. It should feel neither wet nor totally dry to the touch, and the surface should look a little shaggy.

Form the dough into a ball about 8 inches in diameter and place it on the prepared baking sheet.

5. Use a single-edged razor blade or *very* sharp knife to cut the cross on top, making cuts about ½ inch deep. Beat an egg with buttermilk and brush this glaze over the top of the dough ball.

6. Bake the bread for the time indicated for your altitude in the chart above, or until it is well risen and a rich golden brown on top; a long skewer inserted in the center should come out dry. If the top seems to be browning too quickly, loosely cover it with a piece of aluminum foil, shiny side down. Cool the bread on a wire rack.

7. To serve, cut the bread into wedges with a serrated knife. Store covered with a cloth if it will be served within an hour or two. Or, once it is completely cool, store in an airtight tin or sealed plastic bag to retain its moisture.

# Carsons' Corn Bread

THIS CLASSIC corn bread has a nutty texture and a moist crumb, and it is not too sweet. It is named for my cousins Stacey and Jim Carson, who make it often in their North Carolina mountaintop home. The flavor and color vary slightly depending upon the type of cornmeal used (see page 37); I prefer stone-ground organic yellow cornmeal, found in natural foods stores and specialty markets, but any yellow or white medium-ground cornmeal will give good results. To enhance the recipe, you can add a little more sugar, or ½ cup raisins, or about 3 tablespoons crumbled crisply cooked bacon. For a variation, Spicy Santa Fe Corn Bread (see page 65) is a popular treat, especially when served with chili, salad, and cold beer.

**General High Altitude Notes:** This recipe contains a high proportion of baking powder and the dough will start to rise slightly as soon as the liquid is added; get it into a hot oven as soon as the batter is mixed. As altitude increases, the sugar and baking powder are cut slightly and more liquid is added. From sea level to 5,000 feet, I used both metal and Pyrex pans with success. At 5,000 feet and above, I preferred the Pyrex pan because I wanted to be able to see the color on the bottom as the bread baked. Be sure to use a square pan rather than a loaf pan, which would expose only a relatively small amount of batter to the heat; at high altitudes, the heat would crust over the top of a loaf before the batter below baked through.

**Special Equipment:** An 8-inch-square metal pan or Pyrex baking dish; wooden skewer or cake tester

**Pan Preparation:** Grease the pan with butter, nonstick vegetable spray, or oil, then dust lightly with flour and tap out the excess flour.

**Makes** 9 to 12 servings

**High Notes**

*At 10,000 feet,* increase the flour to strengthen the batter.

| Ingredients | Sea Level | 3,000 feet | 5,000 feet | 7,000 feet | 10,000 feet |
|---|---|---|---|---|---|
| **Oven rack position, temperature, and baking time** | Rack in center; bake at 425°F for 20 to 22 minutes | Rack in center; bake at 425°F for 20 to 22 minutes | Rack in center; bake at 425°F for 22 to 25 minutes | Rack in center; bake at 425°F for 22 to 25 minutes | Rack in center; bake at 425°F for 22 to 25 minutes |
| **Unsalted butter, melted and cooled, or canola oil** | 4 tablespoons (¼ cup) | 4 tablespoons (¼ cup) | 4 tablespoons (¼ cup) | 4 tablespoons (¼ cup) | 4 tablespoons (¼ cup) |
| **Large egg, at room temperature** | 1 | 1 | 1 | 1 | 1 |
| **Milk** | 1 cup | 1 cup | 1 cup plus 1 tablespoon | 1 cup plus 2 tablespoons | 1 cup plus 2 tablespoons |
| **Plain yogurt (top liquid poured off) or sour cream** | ¼ cup | ¼ cup | ¼ cup | ¼ cup | ¼ cup |
| **Granulated sugar** | ¼ cup | 3½ tablespoons | 3 tablespoons | 3 tablespoons | 3 tablespoons |
| **Cornmeal** | 1 cup | 1 cup | 1 cup | 1 cup | 1 cup |
| **All-purpose flour** | 1 cup | 1 cup | 1 cup | 1 cup | 1 cup plus 3 tablespoons |
| **Baking powder** | 1 tablespoon | 1 tablespoon | 2¾ teaspoons | 2¾ teaspoons | 2½ teaspoons |
| **Baking soda** | ⅛ teaspoon | ⅛ teaspoon | ⅛ teaspoon | ⅛ teaspoon | Pinch |
| **Salt** | ½ teaspoon | ½ teaspoon | ½ teaspoon | ½ teaspoon | ½ teaspoon |

**1.** Position the oven rack as indicated in the chart above. Prepare the baking pan as directed.

**2.** In a large bowl, whisk together the melted butter or oil, egg, milk, yogurt or sour cream, and sugar. Add the cornmeal, flour, baking powder, baking soda, and salt and stir or whisk together just until well blended; do not overmix.

**3.** Turn the batter out into the prepared pan.

Bake for the time indicated for your altitude in the chart above, or until the top is beginning to look golden brown and a cake tester inserted in the center comes out clean; the top may crack slightly. Don't overbake, or the texture will be dry. Cool in the pan on a wire rack.

**4.** Cut into squares to serve. Wrap airtight to store.

## Spicy Santa Fe Corn Bread

Prepare the recipe as above, following the instructions for your altitude, with the following changes: Reduce the sugar to 1½ tablespoons. At the end, stir in ¾ cup grated sharp Cheddar (2½ ounces), ¼ cup chopped mild or hot green chiles, 2 tablespoons minced red bell pepper, 3 tablespoons chopped pitted black olives (about 6 large), 3 tablespoons chunky medium or hot salsa, 2 tablespoons packed chopped fresh cilantro (or 1 teaspoon dried), and a dash of cayenne pepper, or to taste.

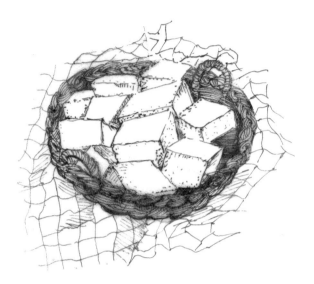

# Apricot-Almond Gift Bread

THIS FLAVORFUL sweet bread is packed with dried fruit and nuts and has a very moist crumb. The recipe makes one large loaf or three small loaves that you can give for holiday gifts: leave them in their baking pans, wrap in a colorful napkin, and tie on a card with the recipe printed on it. I often play with the flavor combinations in this festive recipe, using pecans or walnuts with dried sweet cherries and/or cranberries, plus orange juice, orange extract, and 1 tablespoon grated orange zest instead of the almond extract and apricot nectar.

A food processor makes quick work of chopping the dried fruit and nuts, but you can also snip the apricots with kitchen shears wiped with a little oil, or chop all the fruit and nuts with a sharp knife on a cutting board.

**General High Altitude Notes:** *Above 3,000 feet,* this heavy batter needs to be strengthened so it won't collapse as it cools. Add a little more flour and another egg and use a little less sugar. As the altitude rises, reduce the leavening slightly. Buttermilk contributes extra acidity, which helps the batter set at higher elevations; it is preferred over apricot nectar at 7,000 feet and above. For proper rise at 3,000 feet and above, adjust the oven temperature, time, and rack as noted.

Loaf pans allow only a relatively small amount of batter to be exposed directly to the oven's heat, and that top surface can quickly crust over before the heavy, fruit-laden batter is baked through. To prevent problems, monitor the oven temperature carefully; if the cake looks as if it is overbrowning, cover it loosely with a piece of aluminum foil (shiny side down).

**Special Equipment:** 9 × 5 × 3-inch loaf pan or three 5¾ × 3¼ × 2-inch baby loaf pans; baking parchment or wax paper (at 7,000 feet and above); food processor and kitchen shears or cutting board and knife; wooden skewer or cake tester

**Pan Preparation:** Butter the pan(s) or spray with butter-flavor nonstick vegetable spray and dust with flour. Tap out the excess flour. At 7,000 feet and above, line with baking parchment or wax paper (see page 30), grease the paper, and dust with flour; tap out the excess flour.

**Makes** 1 large loaf or 3 baby loaves

**High Notes**

*At 3,000 feet and above,* add flour and 1 egg and reduce the sugar.

*At 3,000 feet to 5,000 feet,* increase the oven temperature by 25 degrees.

*At 7,000 feet and above,* reduce the oven temperature to 350°F and increase the baking time.

| Ingredients | Sea Level | 3,000 feet | 5,000 feet | 7,000 feet | 10,000 feet |
|---|---|---|---|---|---|
| Oven rack position, temperature, and baking time | Rack in center; bake large loaf at 350°F for 60 to 65 minutes, baby loaves for 40 to 45 minutes | Rack in center; bake large loaf at 375°F for 50 to 55 minutes, baby loaves for 30 to 35 minutes | Rack in lower third of oven; bake large loaf at 375°F for 48 to 50 minutes, baby loaves for 35 to 40 minutes | Rack in lower third of oven; bake large loaf at 350°F for 60 to 62 minutes, baby loaves for 30 to 35 minutes | Rack in lower third of oven; bake large loaf at 350°F for 60 to 65 minutes, baby loaves for 32 to 37 minutes |
| All-purpose flour | 2 cups | 2 cups plus 1 tablespoon | 2 cups plus 1 tablespoon | 2 cups plus 2 tablespoons | 2 ¼ cups |
| Baking powder | 1½ teaspoons | 1½ teaspoons | 1¼ teaspoon + ⅛ teaspoon | 1¼ teaspoons | 1¼ teaspoons |
| Baking soda | ½ teaspoon | ¼ teaspoon | ¼ teaspoon | ¼ teaspoon | ⅛ teaspoon |
| Salt | ½ teaspoon | ½ teaspoon | ½ teaspoon | ½ teaspoon | ½ teaspoon + ⅛ teaspoon |
| Granulated sugar | 1 cup | 1 cup minus 1 tablespoon | 1 cup minus 2 tablespoons | ¾ cup | ¾ cup minus 1 tablespoon |
| Wheat germ | 3 tablespoons | 3 tablespoons | 3 tablespoons | 3 tablespoons | 3 tablespoons |
| Dried apricots (moist-style) | 1 cup | 1 cup | 1 cup | 1 cup | 1 cup |
| Almonds, blanched | ½ cup (2½ ounces) | ½ cup (2½ ounces) | ½ cup (2½ ounces) | ½ cup (2½ ounces) | ½ cup (2½ ounces) |
| Canola or light olive oil | ⅓ cup | ⅓ cup | ⅓ cup | ⅓ cup | ⅓ cup |
| Large egg(s), at room temperature | 1 | 2 | 2 | 2 | 2 |
| Apricot nectar or buttermilk | ¾ cup | ¾ cup | ¾ cup plus 2 tablespoons | 1 cup buttermilk | 1 cup buttermilk |
| Almond extract | 1 teaspoon | 1 teaspoon | 1 teaspoon | 1 teaspoon | 1 teaspoon |
| Vanilla extract | 1 teaspoon | 1 teaspoon | 1 teaspoon | 1 teaspoon | 1 teaspoon |

*(continued)*

| Ingredients | Sea Level | 3,000 feet | 5,000 feet | 7,000 feet | 10,000 feet |
|---|---|---|---|---|---|
| **ICING (OPTIONAL)** | | | | | |
| **Sifted confectioners' sugar** | ⅔ cup | ⅔ cup | ⅔ cup | ⅔ cup | ⅔ cup |
| **Milk, water, or fruit juice** | 2 to 3 tablespoons, or as needed | 2 to 3 tablespoons, or as needed | 2 to 3 tablespoons, or as needed | 2 to 3 tablespoons, or as needed | 2 to 3 tablespoons, or as needed |

**1.** Position the oven rack as indicated in the chart above. Prepare the pan(s) as directed.

**2.** In a large bowl, whisk together the flour, baking powder, baking soda, salt, sugar, and wheat germ. If using a food processor, add the apricots and a generous tablespoon of the flour mixture to the bowl and pulse until the fruit is cut into small (¼-inch) bits. Or, cut up the apricots with oiled kitchen shears or an oiled knife. Scrape the apricot bits into the bowl with the flour. Chop the nuts and add them to the dry ingredients.

**3.** In a medium bowl, whisk together the oil, egg(s), nectar or buttermilk, and extracts. Make a well in the middle of the dry ingredients and pour in the oil-egg mixture. Whisk or stir just to blend well; don't overmix.

**4.** Scrape the batter into the prepared pan(s), filling them about two-thirds full. Bake for the time indicated for your altitude in the chart above, or until the bread is golden brown and a cake tester inserted in the center comes out clean. Cool in the pan(s) on a wire rack.

**5.** To make the optional icing, whisk together the sugar and liquid in a small bowl until thick and smooth. When the bread is completely cooled, drizzle the icing over the top; it will harden as it dries.

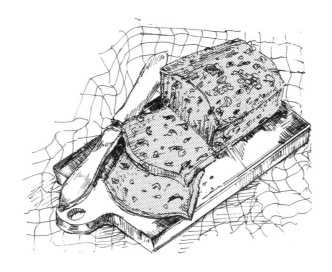

# Vail Lemon–Poppy Seed Loaf

Perfect for afternoon tea or a midnight snack, a slice of this not-too-sweet fine-grained tea bread is always a special treat. The tangy citrus flavor is enhanced by the buttermilk, which also adds acidity, tenderness, and moisture.

You need a total of 1 tablespoon packed grated lemon zest for the full recipe. With a box grater, that can take two to three medium lemons, but with a Microplane grater (see page 32), you should need only one large lemon. Normally this loaf is a pale, creamy color; if you prefer a deeper yellow color, use organic eggs, which generally have more natural color in their yolks. (Commercially made lemon loaves usually contain a little yellow food coloring.)

**General High Altitude Notes:** Since acidity helps batter set faster, I expected this recipe to work perfectly at high altitude. It did not. At 5,000 feet and above, the cake had a dense texture and heavy crumb. At 7,000 feet, it took more than a dozen tests before I balanced the ingredients properly. The problem was that I could not cut out too much sugar without losing the desired sweet-sour taste, and the high proportion of acidity from the lemon threw off the reaction of the leavening agents and weakened the starch structure too much. At sea level, yogurt provides acidity, moisture, and tenderness, but at 3,000 feet and above, I prefer to use buttermilk because it has all yogurt's virtues plus it adds more liquid, which is needed at higher, drier elevations. Note that the oven temperature and baking times vary; at each elevation I tried to find the best combination to completely bake the interior batter before the top crusted over.

**Special Equipment:** A 9 × 5 × 3-inch loaf pan; baking parchment or wax paper (at 7,000 feet and above); grater; sifter; wooden skewer or cake tester

**Pan Preparation:** Coat the loaf pan with solid shortening or butter-flavor nonstick vegetable spray, dust with flour, and tap out the excess flour. At 7,000 feet and above, also line the pan with baking parchment or wax paper (see page 30), then grease or spray the paper, dust with flour, and tap out the excess flour.

**Makes** 1 loaf; 14 to 16 slices

**High Notes**

*At 3,000 feet and above,* strengthen the batter with a little more flour and less sugar. Adjust the baking soda as noted. At 3,000 and 5,000 feet, raise the oven temperature by 25 degrees.

*At 7,000 feet and above,* bake at the sea-level oven temperature.

| Ingredients | Sea Level | 3,000 feet | 5,000 feet | 7,000 feet | 10,000 feet |
|---|---|---|---|---|---|
| **Oven rack position, temperature, and baking time** | Rack in center; bake at 350°F for 55 to 60 minutes | Rack in lower third of oven; bake at 375°F for 45 to 47 minutes | Rack in lower third of oven; bake at 375°F for 50 to 55 minutes | Rack in lower third of oven; bake at 350°F for 55 to 60 minutes | Rack in center of oven; bake at 350°F for 55 to 60 minutes |
| **Unsalted butter, melted and cooled** | 8 tablespoons (1 stick) | 8 tablespoons (1 stick) | 8 tablespoons (1 stick) | 8 tablespoons (1 stick) | 8 tablespoons (1 stick) |
| **Granulated sugar** | 1 cup | 1 cup minus 1 tablespoon | 1 cup minus 2 tablespoons | 1 cup minus 2 tablespoons | 1 cup minus 2 tablespoons |
| **Large eggs, at room temperature** | 2 | 2 | 2 | 2 | 2 |
| **Grated lemon zest, packed** | 1 tablespoon | 1 tablespoon | 1 tablespoon | 1 tablespoon | 1 tablespoon |
| **Fresh lemon juice** | 3 tablespoons | 3 tablespoons | 3 tablespoons | 3 tablespoons | 3 tablespoons |
| **Lemon extract** | 1 teaspoon | 1¼ teaspoons | 1½ teaspoons | 1½ teaspoons | 2 teaspoons |
| **Lemon yogurt (top liquid poured off)** | 1 cup | None | None | None | None |
| **Buttermilk** | None | 1 cup | 1 cup plus 3 tablespoons | 1¼ cups | 1⅓ cups |
| **All-purpose flour** | 2¼ cups | 2⅓ cups | 2⅓ cups plus 1 tablespoon | 2½ cups | 2½ cups plus 2 tablespoons |
| **Baking powder** | 2 teaspoons | 2 teaspoons | ¾ teaspoon | ¾ teaspoon | ¾ teaspoon |
| **Baking soda** | ½ teaspoon | ¼ teaspoon | ½ teaspoon | ½ teaspoon | ¼ teaspoon |
| **Salt** | ½ teaspoon | ½ teaspoon | ½ teaspoon | ½ teaspoon | ½ teaspoon |
| **Ground nutmeg** | ¼ teaspoon | ¼ teaspoon | ¼ teaspoon | ⅛ teaspoon | ⅛ teaspoon |
| **Poppy seeds** | ¼ cup | ¼ cup | ¼ cup | ¼ cup | ¼ cup |

**1.** Position the oven rack as indicated in the chart above. Prepare the baking pan as directed.

**2.** In a large bowl, whisk together the melted butter, sugar, eggs, lemon zest, juice, extract, and yogurt or buttermilk. Place a sifter over the bowl and measure the flour, baking powder, baking soda, salt, and nutmeg into it. Stir/sift the dry ingredients onto the wet mixture below, then stir or beat them together to blend; don't overmix. Stir in the poppy seeds. Scrape down the bowl and beat a little longer, until the batter is thick and creamy.

**3.** Scoop the batter into the prepared baking pan. Bake for the time indicated for your altitude in the chart above, or until the loaf is golden on top and slightly cracked and a cake tester inserted in the center comes out clean.

Cool in the pan on a wire rack for 10 to 15 minutes.

**4.** Run a knife between the loaf and the pan sides, tip out the loaf, and peel off the paper if you used it. Turn right side up on the rack and cool completely. Slice with a serrated knife.

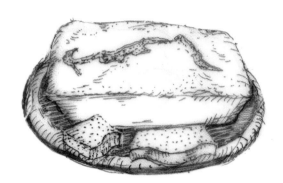

# Highland Currant Scones

T HESE ARE classic wedge-shaped currant scones with a buttery flavor and a tender crumb. They are similar to the Blueberry Scones that follow, but without the egg and with a little more buttermilk.

Techniques for mixing scones vary; any way you can blend the ingredients together without overworking them is the right way for you. You can cut the butter into the flour in a bowl using a fork or wire pastry cutter, or you can pulse the butter and dry ingredients together in a food processor (the method I prefer), then dump the mixture into a bowl before working in the liquid and berries. For light, tender scones, handle the dough as little as possible.

**General High Altitude Notes:** Looking for the best rise and texture, I tested this recipe with many different variations: with and without egg, with more or less butter, and with different proportions of leavening and liquid. You will see that the measurements vary slightly between elevations—don't try to find a pattern, just trust that I found the best combination after multiple tests.

**Special Equipment:** Cookie sheet; Silpat or other nonstick baking mat, baking parchment, or wax paper (optional); pastry brush; wooden skewer or cake tester

**Pan Preparation:** Line the cookie sheet with a nonstick mat, baking parchment, or wax paper, or spray it with butter-flavor nonstick vegetable spray.

**Makes** 8 scones

**High Notes**

*At 3,000 feet and above,* adjust leavening as noted and add buttermilk.

*At 5,000 feet and above,* texture and rise are improved by omitting the egg and adjusting flour and butter.

*At 10,000 feet,* the oven is preheated to 25 degrees higher than the actual baking temperature, then the heat is reduced when the scones are put into the oven. The baking soda is omitted, and the sugar and butter are reduced.

| Ingredients | Sea Level | 3,000 feet | 5,000 feet | 7,000 feet | 10,000 feet |
|---|---|---|---|---|---|
| **Oven rack position, temperature, and baking time** | Rack in center; bake at 425°F for 10 to 12 minutes | Rack in center; bake at 425°F for 15 to 18 minutes | Rack in center; bake at 425°F for 16 to 20 minutes | Rack in center; bake at 425°F for 20 to 24 minutes | Rack in center; *preheat* oven to 400°F, *bake* at 375°F for 25 to 30 minutes |
| **All-purpose flour** | 2 cups | 2 cups | 2 cups plus 2 tablespoons | 2 cups plus 2 tablespoons | 2 cups |
| **Wheat germ** | 2 tablespoons | 2 tablespoons | 2 tablespoons | 2 tablespoons | 2 tablespoons |
| **Baking powder** | 2½ teaspoons | 1 tablespoon | 1 tablespoon | 1 tablespoon | 1½ teaspoons |
| **Baking soda** | ¼ teaspoon | ⅛ teaspoon | ⅛ teaspoon | ⅛ teaspoon | None |
| **Salt** | 1 teaspoon | ¾ teaspoon | ¾ teaspoon | 1 teaspoon | ½ teaspoon |
| **Granulated sugar** | ⅓ cup | ⅓ cup | ⅓ cup | ⅓ cup | 3½ tablespoons |
| **Unsalted butter, cold, cut up** | 6 tablespoons (¾ stick) | 6 tablespoons (¾ stick) | 7 tablespoons | 8 tablespoons (1 stick) | 6 tablespoons (¾ stick) |
| **Large egg, at room temperature** | 1 | 1 | None | None | None |
| **Buttermilk** | ½ cup | ½ cup plus 1 tablespoon | ¾ cup plus 2 tablespoons | ¾ cup | 1 cup |
| **Dried currants or raisins, lightly packed** | ¾ cup | ¾ cup | ¾ cup | ¾ cup | ¾ cup |
| **GLAZE** | | | | | |
| **Buttermilk** | 2 tablespoons | 2 tablespoons | 2 tablespoons | 2 tablespoons | 2 tablespoons |
| **Granulated Sugar** | 2 tablespoons | 2 tablespoons | 2 tablespoons | 2 tablespoons | 2 tablespoons |

**1.** Position the rack and preheat the oven as indicated for your altitude in the chart above. Prepare the cookie sheet as directed.

**2.** Measure the flour, wheat germ, baking powder, baking soda (if using), salt, and sugar into a large bowl or the bowl of a food processor. Add the butter and blend it in with a fork or wire pastry blender or pulse until it is the size of small peas. If using the processor, dump the dry mixture into a large bowl.

**3.** If using the egg, whisk it together with the buttermilk in a small bowl. Make a well in the dry mixture. Pour in the buttermilk (mixture), add the currants, and stir everything together gently with a fork just until the dough comes together into a sticky ball.

**4.** Turn out the dough onto the prepared cookie sheet. With floured fingers, gently pat it into a 7- or 8-inch disk about 1 inch thick. With a floured knife, divide the dough into quarters, then eighths. Cut gently if using a baking mat so you don't mar its surface. If you leave the wedges touching each other, they will rise a little higher while baking but will have soft sides.

For crisp sides, slide a floured spatula under each wedge and pull it about ½ inch away from its neighbors.

**5.** To glaze the scones, brush the tops with the buttermilk and sprinkle with the sugar. Bake for the time indicated for your altitude in the chart above, or until the tops are golden brown and a cake tester inserted in the center comes out clean. Cool on a wire rack.

# Blueberry Scones or Shortcakes

These golden scones are studded with blueberries and have a tender buttery texture. Serve them warm with coffee for breakfast, or split them in half, fill them with strawberries, and top them with whipped cream for a festive Fourth of July dessert. Shortcake purists can, of course, omit the blueberries. You could also easily add an extra ½ cup of blueberries, or, for Cranberry-Nut Scones, replace the blueberries with coarsely chopped fresh or frozen cranberries, a teaspoon of grated orange zest, and about ⅓ cup chopped walnuts.

Techniques for mixing scones vary; any way you can blend the ingredients together without overworking the dough is the right way for you. You can cut the butter into the flour in a bowl using a fork or wire pastry cutter or pulse the butter and dry ingredients together in a food processor (the method I prefer), then dump the mixture into a bowl before working in the liquid and berries. For light, tender scones, handle the dough as little as possible.

---

**General High Altitude Notes:** Above 3,000 feet, the measurements vary slightly between elevations—don't try to find a pattern, just trust that I found the best combination for that location after multiple tests. If there is any discernible pattern, it is that liquid and fat are increased as the elevation increases, and buttermilk gives a better result except at 7,000 feet, where I prefer whole milk, though the difference is not great.

I tried this recipe with and without the egg at every altitude, and found that at up to 10,000 feet it was an improvement, adding more moisture and richness (from the fat in the yolk). At 10,000 feet, the results are best without the egg.

**Special Equipment:** Cookie sheet; Silpat or other nonstick baking mat, baking parchment, or wax paper (optional); pastry brush; wooden skewer or cake tester

**Pan Preparation:** Line the cookie sheet with a nonstick mat, baking parchment, or wax paper or spray with butter-flavor nonstick vegetable spray.

**Makes** 8 scones

## High Notes

*At 10,000 feet,* the oven is preheated to 25 degrees higher than the actual baking temperature, then the heat is reduced when the scones are put into the oven. The texture is improved by omitting the egg and adding a little more butter and flour; the sugar is slightly reduced.

| Ingredients | Sea Level | 3,000 feet | 5,000 feet | 7,000 feet | 10,000 feet |
|---|---|---|---|---|---|
| **Oven rack position, temperature, and baking time** | Rack in center; bake at 425°F for 13 to 15 minutes | Rack in center; bake at 425°F for 12 to 15 minutes | Rack in center; bake at 425°F for 18 to 20 minutes | Rack in center; bake at 425°F for 20 to 22 minutes | Rack in center; *preheat* oven to 425°F, *bake* at 400°F for 22 to 24 minutes |
| **Blueberries, fresh or frozen** | 1 cup | 1 cup | 1 cup | 1 cup | 1 cup |
| **All-purpose flour** | 2 cups | 2 cups | 2 cups plus 3 tablespoons | 2 cups | 2 cups plus 3 tablespoons |
| **Baking powder** | 2½ teaspoons | 2½ teaspoons | 1 tablespoon | 2½ teaspoons | 2½ teaspoons |
| **Baking soda** | None | None | ⅛ teaspoon | None | ⅛ teaspoon |
| **Granulated sugar** | ⅓ cup | ⅓ cup | ⅓ cup | ⅓ cup | ¼ cup plus 2 teaspoons |
| **Salt** | 1 teaspoon | 1 teaspoon | 1 teaspoon | 1 teaspoon | ¾ teaspoon |
| **Ground nutmeg** | ½ teaspoon | ½ teaspoon | ½ teaspoon | ½ teaspoon | ½ teaspoon |
| **Cold butter, cut up** | 6 tablespoons (¾ stick) | 6 tablespoons (¾ stick) | 7 tablespoons | 7 tablespoons | 8 tablespoons (1 stick) |
| **Large egg, at room temperature** | 1 | 1 | 1 | 1 | None |
| **Buttermilk** | ½ cup | ½ cup plus 2 tablespoons | ½ cup plus 2 tablespoons | None | ¾ cup |
| **Whole milk** | None | None | None | ¾ cup | None |
| **GLAZE** | | | | | |
| **Milk** | 2 tablespoons | 2 tablespoons | 2 tablespoons | 2 tablespoons | 2 tablespoons |
| **Granulated sugar** | 2 tablespoons | 2 tablespoons | 2 tablespoons | 2 tablespoons | 2 tablespoons |

1. Position the rack and preheat the oven as indicated for your altitude in the chart (opposite). Prepare the cookie sheet as directed.

If using fresh berries, pick over and remove the stems, rinse, and gently blot dry on paper towels. If using frozen berries, remove any ice particles. Set aside.

2. Measure the flour, baking powder, baking soda (if using), sugar, salt, and nutmeg into a large bowl or the bowl of a food processor. Add the butter and blend it in with a fork or wire pastry blender or pulse until it is the size of small peas. If using the processor, dump the dry mixture into a large bowl.

3. If using the egg, whisk it together with the buttermilk or milk in a small bowl. Make a well in the dry mixture. Pour in the milk mixture, add the berries, and stir everything together gently with a fork just until the dough comes together in a sticky ball.

4. With floured fingers or a large spoon, scoop out 8 lumps of dough, each roughly 2 by 2½ inches, and set them about 2 inches apart on the prepared baking sheet. Leave the dough rounded, or pat it into wedges. To glaze the scones, brush the tops with the milk and sprinkle generously with the sugar.

5. Bake the scones for the time indicated for your altitude in the chart above, or until the tops are golden brown and a cake tester inserted in the center comes out dry. Cool on a wire rack.

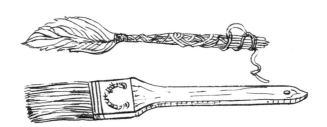

# Breckenridge Biscuits

THESE GOLDEN, tender biscuits have a good rise, buttery taste, and delicate crumb that will win raves at any table, especially when heaped in a basket and served warm. For the lightest texture, handle the dough as little as possible.

Techniques for mixing biscuits vary. You can cut the butter into the flour in a bowl using a fork or wire pastry cutter or you can pulse the butter and dry ingredients together in a food processor (the method I prefer), then dump the mixture into a bowl before adding the liquid. Whichever method you use, add just enough liquid to make a sticky dough.

---

**General High Altitude Notes:** These were just called Buttermilk Biscuits until I took them to Breckenridge, Colorado (10,000 feet), where they became the center of my universe for quite a while. My first trials rose and fell in amazingly short order. It took me about a dozen attempts and even more conversations with local bakers before Janet Crispell, former owner/baker of Bull Moose Restaurant in Breckenridge, set me straight. The usual leavening combination of baking powder plus buttermilk with baking soda (along with extra help from the reduced air pressure at high altitude) made way too much leavening, so they "overreacted," went into a swoon, and fainted dead away. When I substituted regular milk and cut out the baking soda, they rose high and stayed put.

**Special Equipment:** Cookie sheet; Silpat or other nonstick baking mat, baking parchment, or wax paper; fork, wire pastry blender, or food processor; bench scraper (optional); pastry brush

**Pan Preparation:** Line the cookie sheet with a nonstick mat, baking parchment, or wax paper.

**Makes** 12 biscuits

**High Notes**
> *At 5,000 feet and above,* adjust the baking powder and baking soda as noted.
> *At 7,000 feet and above,* omit the baking soda.
> *At 10,000 feet,* add an extra tablespoon of milk if the dough feels too dry.

| Ingredients | Sea Level | 3,000 feet | 5,000 feet | 7,000 feet | 10,000 feet |
|---|---|---|---|---|---|
| **Oven rack position, temperature, and baking time** | Rack in center; bake at 425°F for 15 to 17 minutes | Rack in center; bake at 450°F for 15 to 18 minutes | Rack in center; bake at 450°F for 15 to 17 minutes | Rack in center; bake at 450°F for 15 to 17 minutes | Rack in center; bake at 450°F for 15 to 17 minutes |
| **All-purpose flour** | 2 cups | 2 cups | 2 cups | 2 cups | 2 cups |
| **Baking powder** | 1 tablespoon | 1 tablespoon | 1½ teaspoons | 1 tablespoon | 1 tablespoon plus 1 teaspoon |
| **Baking soda** | ½ teaspoon | ½ teaspoon | ¼ teaspoon | None | None |
| **Salt** | ¾ teaspoon | ¾ teaspoon | ¾ teaspoon | ¾ teaspoon | ¾ teaspoon |
| **Unsalted butter, cold, cut up** | 6 tablespoons (¾ stick) | 6 tablespoons (¾ stick) | 6 tablespoons (¾ stick) | 6 tablespoons (¾ stick) | 6 tablespoons (¾ stick) |
| **Buttermilk** | 1 cup | 1 cup | 1 cup | 1 cup | None |
| **Whole milk** | None | None | None | None | ¾ cup plus 2 to 3 tablespoons |
| **GLAZE** | | | | | |
| **Buttermilk or whole milk** | 3 tablespoons | 3 tablespoons | 3 tablespoons | 3 tablespoons | 3 tablespoons |

1. Position the rack and preheat the oven as indicated for your altitude in the chart above. Prepare the cookie sheet as directed.

2. Measure the flour, baking powder, baking soda (if using), and salt into a large bowl or the bowl of a food processor. Add the butter and blend it in with a fork or wire pastry blender or pulse until it is the size of small peas. If using the processor, dump the pulsed mixture into a large bowl.

3. Add the buttermilk or milk and stir it in with a fork until the dough just clings together. At 10,000 feet, the dough may feel too dry and may need an extra tablespoon of liquid. It is better to have the dough too moist than too dry; don't overmix.

4. Lightly flour the counter, turn out the dough, and knead it 2 or 3 times just to bring it together; it should still feel quite sticky. Pat the dough into a rough 6 × 8-inch rectangle about 3/4 inch thick. With a floured bench scraper or knife, cut it into 12 squares.

5. With a floured spatula or your fingers, lift each biscuit and set it on the prepared baking sheet. To get the highest rise, the biscuits should touch one another; for crisper edges but slightly less rise, set them apart. With a pastry brush, lightly glaze the biscuit tops with the buttermilk or milk.

6. Bake for the time indicated for your altitude in the chart above, or until the biscuits are well risen and golden brown. Cool slightly on a wire rack.

7. Serve the biscuits warm with butter. (They can be reheated in a 300°F oven for about 5 minutes.)

I was planning to demonstrate the making of profiteroles in Boulder, Colorado (5,300 feet), at the Cooking School of the Rockies, but I was worried about the effect of altitude on my sea-level recipe for pâte à choux. The school suggested three changes: substituting unbleached all-purpose flour for bleached (for a slight increase in gluten), raising the oven temperature about ten degrees (for a stronger steam burst and to set the dough faster), and using an extra half-egg, for a crisper shell structure. To see for myself while there, I did side-by-side tests: one using my original recipe, one with the adjustments. The results were dramatic. My originals needed about ten minutes extra baking time and even then were too soft and did not puff enough; the batch using their suggestions was perfect.

—Rick Rodgers, cooking teacher and cookbook author, *Kaffeehaus*

# Durango Popovers

Popovers are fun to eat and even more fun to make. Crusty, golden brown hollow shells with tall quirky shapes that resemble chefs' toques, they have an eggy, slightly moist interior like nothing else, except maybe their cousin, Yorkshire pudding. Making popovers is all about action—whipping up a batter, placing it quickly in a very hot oven, making steam for the POP that gives the rise. It is showy, a trick of temperature, and it always works, no matter what your altitude, if you have enough moisture in the batter and enough heat in the oven. After the big puff, the oven heat is reduced in order to bake the shell all the way through and dry it out.

I tested this recipe with different types of pans, from pottery custard cups and aluminum muffin tins to designer popover pans with narrow tapered cups made of cast iron or steel. All containers worked, but I got the highest rise and best texture with cast iron or steel. Some bakers preheat their baking pans before adding the batter, but I tried both cold and preheated pans and found no difference in the result, as long as the oven was very hot when the popovers went in. The quicker the heat turns the liquid in the batter to steam, the faster and higher the puff.

Popovers should be served warm and crisp. They can be reheated, uncovered, in a 325°F oven for about 10 minutes.

**General High Altitude Notes:** This is a great high altitude recipe because the reduced air pressure helps the rise, as long as the oven is hot enough to make good steam and a crisp crust. Aside from the variations in oven temperatures and baking times, the changes from sea level, adding an egg and cutting out a little butter, give the batter more strength. Before baking, be sure to remove or raise the upper oven rack so the popovers don't bump into it when they rise; the height from the bottom of the pan to the top of the risen popovers can easily be 4½ inches! Whatever the altitude, before baking, be sure to preheat the oven for at least 15 minutes so it is good and hot.

**Special Equipment:** Six large (¾-cup-capacity) black-steel or cast-iron popover cups or twelve small (⅓-cup-capacity) cups or twelve 2½-inch muffin cups

**Pan Preparation:** Spray the cups with butter-flavor nonstick vegetable spray or coat with butter.

**Makes** 5 or 6 large or 12 small popovers

**High Note:**
> At **10,000 feet,** the oven is preheated to 25 degrees higher than the actual baking temperature, then the heat is reduced when the popovers are put into the oven.

| Ingredients | Sea Level | 3,000 feet | 5,000 feet | 7,000 feet | 10,000 feet |
|---|---|---|---|---|---|
| **Oven rack position, temperature, and baking time** | Rack in lower third of oven; bake at 450°F for 15 minutes, then at 350°F for 15 to 20 minutes if using large cups, 10 to 12 minutes if using small cups | Rack in lower third of oven; bake at 450°F for 15 minutes, then at 350°F for 10 to 15 minutes if using large cups, 10 to 12 minutes if using small cups | Rack in lower third of oven; bake at 450°F for 15 minutes, then at 350°F for 17 to 20 minutes if using large cups, 10 minutes if using small cups | Rack in lower third of oven; bake at 450°F for 15 to 17 minutes, then at 350°F for 20 minutes if using large cups, 10 to 12 minutes if using small cups | Rack in lower third of oven; *preheat* oven to 475°F; *bake* at 450°F for 20 minutes, then at 350°F for 15 minutes if using large cups, 10 to 12 minutes if using small cups |
| **Sifted all-purpose flour** | 1 cup | 1 cup | 1 cup | 1 cup | 1 cup |
| **Salt** | ½ teaspoon | ½ teaspoon | ½ teaspoon | ½ teaspoon | ½ teaspoon |
| **Granulated sugar** | 1 teaspoon | 1 teaspoon | 1 teaspoon | 1 teaspoon | 1 teaspoon |
| **Large eggs, at room temperature** | 2 | 3 | 3 | 3 | 3 |
| **Milk** | 1 cup | 1 cup | 1 cup | 1 cup | 1 cup |
| **Unsalted butter, melted and cooled, or vegetable oil** | 2 tablespoons | 1 tablespoon | 1 tablespoon | 1 tablespoon | 1 tablespoon |

**1.** Position the rack and preheat the oven as indicated in the chart above. Be sure to remove the rack above the one you will use for baking. Prepare the pan(s) as directed.

**2.** In a large bowl, whisk together the flour, salt, and sugar. Make a well in the center of the dry ingredients and add (without mixing) the eggs, milk, and melted butter or oil. With a whisk, blend together the wet ingredients, then gradually work in the dry mixture, pulling it to the center as you whisk, until everything is combined. Don't worry if there are a few lumps.

**3.** Pour or spoon the batter into the prepared pan(s), filling the cups just half-full. At sea level, with just 2 eggs, the batter will make only 5 large popovers instead of 6; half-fill any empty cups with water.

**4.** Bake at 450°F for the time indicated for your altitude in the chart above, then reduce the heat to 350°F and bake for the time indicated, or until the popovers are well risen and rich golden brown and feel crisp on the outside. Set the pan of popovers on a wire rack: At this point, the dough inside the popovers will still be a little moist. If you want to dry it out more, cut a small slit in the side of each popover with a paring knife, set it back in its baking cup, and return the pan to the still-hot oven, with the heat off, for 5 to 10 minutes. Or serve right away.

# Yeast Breads

## Baking Bread at High Altitudes

Changes in altitude primarily affect the rising times of yeast bread doughs. Yeast dough rises because of fermentation, a process in which carbon dioxide gas and alcohol are produced as live yeast cells react to sugar, warm liquid, and flour. As the gas expands into air bubbles in the dough, it is trapped and held by gluten (stretchy proteins in wheat flour). The longer and slower the rise, the better the texture and more developed the flavor.

At sea level, there is enough air pressure pushing down to resist the dough's rise, and this balance (depending, of course, on ambient temperature) allows for a relatively slow, leisurely rising time. For many doughs at sea level, two rises are sufficient to create the proper texture. However, as the altitude increases, there is less air pressure pushing down to resist the rising of the dough. Above 3,000 feet, yeast at warm temperatures can get overly enthusiastic and the dough may rise too fast for its own good, losing out on both texture and flavor development. The remedy is to punch down the dough more often, giving it at least three

rises. Since warmth encourages rising and cold discourages it, you can also enhance the results by refrigerating the dough overnight; it will still rise in the cold environment, but much more slowly. The next day, bring the dough to room temperature and complete the process. Above 3,500 feet, you must also prevent overrising (overproofing), by not allowing the dough to double in bulk each time it is set to rise; it is much better to underproof, letting it rise until not quite double in bulk the first and second rises, and much less, only about one-third larger, on the final rise just before baking.

At elevations above 7,000 feet, some types of dough, especially in hot weather, can rise surprisingly fast, exhaust themselves, and collapse. Don't be tempted to use instant yeast at high altitude—it only exacerbates this problem. As a general rule, to prevent overrising, use a little less yeast in a white bread than you would at sea level. For example, I reduced the yeast slightly in Boulder's Best White Bread for altitudes of 7,000 feet and above. However, I don't reduce the yeast in heavier whole-wheat and multigrain doughs. Weightier doughs need all the help they can get to lift and aerate them: the natural lift of the reduced air pressure plus the oomph of yeast.

A bread's first quick rise in a hot oven is called oven spring, and it is essential for good volume. By restricting the dough's final rise to only one-third larger than its original bulk instead of double, the oven spring will be higher; oven spring can increase the size of a loaf by almost one third. This effect is enhanced at 7,000 feet and above if you preheat the oven slightly above the actual baking temperature, then reduce the heat as soon as the bread goes into the oven.

Wheat flour contains gluten, stretchy elastic strands that develop when the wheat's proteins combine with liquid and are worked together. The greater the amount of protein, the more water the flour will absorb. Bread flour contains more protein, which gives greater elasticity, but it absorbs more liquid than all-purpose flour; it can cause breads to be too dry unless liquid is carefully monitored.

High, dry mountain air also dries out flour, whereas humid climates and rainy weather may add a little moisture, but the primary factor influencing the amount of liquid the flour will absorb is the flour type. All-purpose flour is preferred by some bread bakers at 7,000 feet and above because it absorbs less liquid and requires less tinkering with the liquid proportions. David Fair, owner/baker at Mollie McDuff's in Fairplay, Colorado (9,970 feet), splits the difference, using an unbleached all-purpose flour with a moderate amount of gluten rather than an extra-high-gluten bread flour. David adds more liquid to his doughs but relies on his experience to sense how the dough should feel in his hands. In McCall, Idaho (5,023 feet), I talked to bread baker Corey Mc-Donald at Evening Rise Bread Company, who prefers high-gluten flour but also bakes "by

feel," adding liquid as needed. Corey considers the mineral content of his water as well, noting that its hardness, especially iron content, influences results. To retard rise, he always adds a little extra salt and starts with cool water to allow for slow fermentation and buildup of flavor.

My best advice to the high altitude baker is to watch the dough, not the recipe. I did many side-by-side trials at each test altitude using different types of flour. I agree with David and Corey that you have to judge by the feel of the dough, but in my tests, I preferred bread flour (sometimes called high-gluten bread flour) to regular all-purpose flour at all altitudes, and I saw no significant improvement with High Altitude Hungarian flour (see page 36), which has about the same amount of gluten as all-purpose: loaves made with it rose well and had a finer, slightly more dense crumb than those made with bread flour. The recipes in this book will give good results if you use the type of flour called for.

Yeast is available to the bread baker in several forms. I tested all the breads in this book with granulated active dry yeast, which is reliable and sold in supermarkets in sealed foil packets containing 7 grams (¼ ounce) or in jars. Fleischmann's and Red Star are two widely available brands. Although this yeast is labeled "dry," it contains 8% moisture, and must be refrigerated if the packet is opened. Store sealed active dry yeast at room temperature, or refrigerate or freeze it. Do not confuse active dry with instant dry yeast (Fleischmann's RapidRise), which is a different strain altogether, engineered to avoid proofing and make bread rise faster—not a desirable trait at high altitudes, where breads rise too quickly anyway.

Sugar, which caramelizes to help give bread its golden brown color, is essential for the growth of yeast, but it also tenderizes and weakens the gluten, or elasticity, of the dough.

For this reason, too much sugar, honey, or other sweeteners, especially at high altitudes, can contribute to the collapse of a loaf. Therefore, sweeteners are reduced as elevation increases.

Salt (I use table salt) is absolutely essential for bread baking at high altitudes. It not only contributes flavor and enhances the strength of the gluten, but, most important, it also slows down the growth of yeast, which can go too fast at high altitudes. In addition, at high altitudes, the taste of salt is less pronounced, or less perceived by the palate. For good flavor, add salt as elevation increases.

Fats, in small amounts, are good additions to bread dough. Liquefied fat is usually added to a liquid mixture, then worked into the flour. Fat contributes to the flavor and texture of the dough and also increases its ability to contain the carbon dioxide gas.

Milk, yogurt, sour cream, and sweet cream improve bread's nutritional value, help yeast growth, and add flavor, color, and tenderness to the crumb. Water is the liquid of choice in the majority of bread recipes, but fruit juices can also be used (they vary in acidity, which can affect texture and flavor slightly). The temperature of the water used to dissolve the yeast is important because it is critical to the life, and growth, of the yeast. Very cold water slows down and can actually prevent yeast growth. After the yeast is dissolved, though, you can add ice water to retard the growth at high altitudes in hot weather. Warm water (about 110° to 115°F, comfortable to the touch) encourages yeast to grow, and very hot water (140°F to 145°F) kills it. *Note*: When a recipe says to use hot water (120°F), you may not be able to get tap water hot enough at 7,000 feet or above. If necessary, heat the water in a pan or in the microwave and test the temperature with an instant-read thermometer before adding it to the yeast.

Eggs contribute nutritional value, richness, color, leavening, and structural strength to bread dough. Egg yolks both bind ingredients and contain lecithin, an emulsifier that helps breads retain moisture and stay fresh.

At high altitudes, steam is one of the bread baker's most dramatic helpers. As soon as a loaf is placed in a hot oven, it is at risk of crusting over on top before the moist, sticky dough below gets hot enough to set. Low air pressure encourages rapid evaporation, so the surface of the loaf gives up its moisture very quickly. When you put a pan of water on the oven floor, or spray water into the chamber during baking, the added moisture turns to steam. These water molecules moisten the oven air. Once it can't absorb any more moisture, the evaporation on the surface of the dough stops, allowing the interior dough cells to rise and expand without restriction.

In addition, steam transfers liquid to the starch molecules on the bread's surface, allowing them to swell and creating a crisper crust. Near the end of the baking time, once the rise is complete, you can remove the pan of water so you have a hot dry oven to finish the bake and make the crust more crunchy. If you notice your bread browning too quickly, cover it loosely with a piece of aluminum foil.

To test the doneness of bread, watch for the visual signs, rather than just the times, in the recipes ("when the crust is golden brown and makes a hollow sound when rapped with your knuckle"). A loaf is completely baked inside when an instant-read thermometer inserted into the center reads between 190° and 200°F.

When storing bread at high altitudes, remember that dry air causes rapid evaporation, quickly making uncovered baked goods stale. To keep bread fresh, as soon as it is completely cooled, wrap it in plastic wrap. At 3,000 feet and above, I use plastic wrap plus a heavy-duty plastic bag or foil. Leftovers can be double-wrapped and frozen.

# Bread Machines

The white and multigrain breads in this chapter were tested at approximately 5,000 feet using a Zojirushi Bread Machine, Model BBCCQ20, which holds 4 cups of flour. It has several settings, including a basic cycle that can mix dough, give two rises, and bake and a dough cycle that mixes and gives two rises. The single loaf of white bread was made with great success using the full basic cycle to mix, rise, and bake. I also tested the dough cycle for both the white and multigrain breads: the machine mixed the dough and gave it two rises. Then I took it out, and by hand shaped, proofed, and baked it. Results were excellent, comparable to completely handmade loaves.

Up to about 6,500 feet, I can vouch for the fact that these two recipes work as described above in a bread machine. But because machines vary, you need to follow the manufacturer's directions to mix your dough. Allow it to rise in the machine, or follow the recipe for rising. You will have best results with the multigrain bread if shaping and the final rise are done outside the machine. At higher elevations, you may need to add more liquid to your recipes to make a softer dough. Bakers at around 10,000 feet told me bread machines did not perform properly at that altitude, but I did not test this myself.

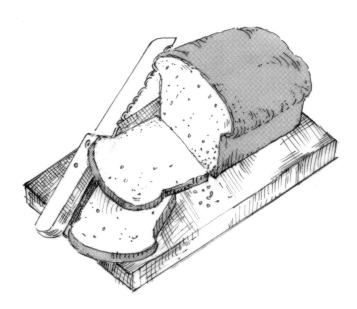

# Boulder's Best White Bread

THIS BASIC recipe has always been a part of my life, as necessary as the proverbial basic black dress: it is all-purpose and reliable, and it can be dressed up or down. While it is baking, its sweet yeasty perfume will fill your home. Note that the recipe can easily be doubled. For variations, see Honey Whole-Wheat and Cinnamon-Raisin Bread following the master recipe. (See "Baking Bread at High Altitudes," page 84).

Start making this bread early in the morning if you want to serve it that day. It is always best when fresh, but if wrapped airtight, it keeps well for several days. You can also prepare, raise, and shape the dough in advance then double-wrap and freeze it for up to 1 month before baking. Thaw the dough at room temperature for 4 to 5 hours before glazing and baking. Baked loaves can be wrapped airtight and frozen for up to 2 months.

---

**General High Altitude Notes:** At 5,000 feet and above, the oven spring and bake benefit from starting the loaf in a hot oven, then finishing it at a lower heat. As altitude increases, you need to boost the flavor with a little more salt and reduce the yeast slightly to take advantage of the help provided by the lower atmospheric pressure.

**Special Equipment:** A 9 × 5 × 3-inch loaf pan; electric mixer with paddle and dough hook or large mixing bowl and sturdy wooden spoon; bench scraper or wide spatula; 1- to 2-gallon self-sealing plastic bag or plastic wrap and a tea towel; pastry brush; roasting pan; mister or spray bottle of water (optional); instant-read thermometer (optional); serrated knife

**Pan Preparation:** Grease the loaf pan with vegetable oil or coat it with nonstick vegetable spray.

**Makes** 1 loaf

**High Notes**

*At 5,000 feet,* bake at 400°F for the first 15 minutes, then reduce the heat by 25 degrees to complete the baking.

*At 7,000 feet and above,* add salt for more flavor and reduce the yeast. Bake at 425°F for the first 15 minutes, then reduce the heat to 350°F to complete the baking.

| Ingredients | Sea Level | 3,000 feet | 5,000 feet | 7,000 feet | 10,000 feet |
|---|---|---|---|---|---|
| Oven rack position, temperature, and baking time | Rack in center; bake at 375°F for 30 minutes | Rack in center; bake at 375°F for 30 to 38 minutes | Rack in center; bake at 400°F for 15 minutes, then at 375°F for 30 minutes | Rack in center; bake at 425°F for 15 minutes, then at 350°F for 18 to 20 minutes | Rack in center; bake at 425°F for 15 minutes, then at 350°F for 20 to 25 minutes |
| Active dry yeast | 2¼ teaspoons | 2¼ teaspoons | 2¼ teaspoons | 2⅛ teaspoons | 1¾ teaspoons |
| Warm water | ¼ cup | ¼ cup | ¼ cup | ¼ cup | ¼ cup |
| Granulated sugar | 1 tablespoon | 1 tablespoon | 1 tablespoon | 1 tablespoon | 1 tablespoon |
| Whole milk | ½ cup | ½ cup | ½ cup | ½ cup | ½ cup |
| Water | ½ cup | ½ cup | ½ cup | ½ cup | ½ cup |
| Unsalted butter, melted, or vegetable oil | 1 tablespoon | 1 tablespoon | 1 tablespoon | 1 tablespoon | 1 tablespoon |
| Salt | 1 teaspoon | 1 teaspoon | 1 teaspoon | 1 teaspoon plus a pinch | 1¼ teaspoons |
| Unbleached bread flour | 2¼ to 2½ cups, or as needed | 2¼ to 2½ cups, or as needed | 2¼ to 2¾ cups, or as needed | 2¼ to 2½ cups, or as needed | 2¼ to 2¾ cups, or as needed |
| GLAZE (CHOOSE ONE: MILK OR EGG BEATEN WITH WATER) | | | | | |
| Milk | 2 tablespoons | 2 tablespoons | 2 tablespoons | 2 tablespoons | 2 tablespoons |
| Large egg | 1 | 1 | 1 | 1 | 1 |
| Water | 1 teaspoon | 1 teaspoon | 1 teaspoon | 1 teaspoon | 1 teaspoon |

1. In a cup, combine the yeast, warm water, and sugar. Stir, and set aside for 3 or 4 minutes, until the mixture bubbles up.

2. Meanwhile, in a small saucepan, combine the milk, the ½ cup water, butter or oil, and salt and set over low heat until it feels quite warm (about 120°F) and bubbles just begin to show around the edges.

3. Pour the warm liquid into a large bowl or the bowl of a stand mixer and let it cool until you can touch it comfortably (about 110°F). When you are sure it is not too hot, stir in about 2 cups of the flour and then the yeast mixture. Beat hard for several minutes using a sturdy spoon or the paddle attachment. You will have a thick, soupy mass with a few lumps. With a spoon or with the paddle on low speed, gradually stir in another ¼ cup of flour. Continue to mix, adding 1 to 2 tablespoons more flour as needed, until the dough begins to come together and looks stretchy.

4. You can knead the dough with the dough hook attachment or with your hands. *To knead with the mixer*, switch to the dough hook. With

the mixer on the lowest speed, add another 2 or 3 tablespoons flour and work the dough for about 5 minutes. As the flour is incorporated, continue to add more, a tablespoon at a time as needed, until the dough is no longer sticky, has pulled away from the sides of the bowl, and looks fairly smooth. Scrape the dough onto a lightly floured counter and knead it for 3 to 4 minutes by hand, working in a little more flour only if it is still sticky. The total flour used will range from 2¼ to 2¾ cups or more, depending upon your altitude and the humidity in the air. Form the dough into a ball.

*To knead by hand,* sprinkle 2 or 3 tablespoons of flour onto the counter and turn out the dough. Flour your hands, fold the dough in half toward you, and push it away with the heels of your hands, then give it a quarter turn and repeat. Reflour the surface if necessary to prevent sticking, and continue kneading for 5 to 8 minutes, or until the dough looks smooth and satiny and no longer feels sticky to the touch. As you work, use a bench scraper or broad spatula to scrape any dough off the counter and back into the dough mass. Form the dough into a ball.

**5.** At this point, if you wish, you can refrigerate the dough overnight in a lightly oiled bowl with a plate and heavy weight on top (this counts as the first rise). The next day, remove the dough from the bowl, set it on a sheet of oiled plastic wrap or foil, and bring it to room temperature (3 to 4 hours) before giving it the second rise as described below.

Alternatively, you can give the dough its first rise right away: Put about a tablespoon of oil in a 1- or 2-gallon self-sealing plastic bag or large clean bowl, add the dough, and turn it once to coat with oil. Seal the bag or cover the bowl with oiled plastic wrap and a tea towel. The best location for rising is a warm (not hot) spot free from drafts, about 75° to 85°F. I use my microwave oven (turned off) or my regular oven (heat off) with the dough on the center rack (on a cookie sheet if in plastic bag) and a roasting pan of very hot water beneath it on the lowest oven shelf. **See chart below for rising times.**

**6.** Let the dough rise until nearly double in bulk; you will be able to poke two fingers into the top and have the marks remain.

**7.** Once the dough has risen, punch it down to remove large air bubbles, turn it out onto a lightly floured counter, and knead once or twice. Return it to the oiled container for the second rise. While the dough rises, prepare the pan as directed.

### Approximate Rising Times at 80° to 85°F for Varying Elevations

| Elevation | Sea Level | 3,000 feet | 5,000 feet | 7,000 feet | 10,000 feet |
|---|---|---|---|---|---|
| 1st Rise | 60 to 90 minutes | 60 to 70 minutes | 55 minutes | 45 to 50 minutes | 45 to 50 minutes |
| 2nd Rise | 60 minutes | 45 to 50 minutes | 40 to 45 minutes | 40 to 45 minutes | 40 to 45 minutes |
| 3rd Rise | 45 minutes | 20 minutes | 20 minutes | 20 minutes | 15 minutes |

**8.** Once the dough has risen again, shape the loaf. Turn the dough out onto the counter and knead a few times, then pat and press it into a flattened rectangle about 8 by 11 inches. Working from one short end, roll the dough up into a log about 3½ by 8 inches, and pinch the seam and ends to seal. Set the dough seam side down in the prepared loaf pan, cover lightly with oiled plastic wrap, and set to rise in a warm location (not the oven, which will now be preheating). From sea level to 3,000 feet, the dough should rise this time until slightly *less than double in bulk*; above 3,000 feet, the dough should rise even less, *only until it is about one-third larger* (it will rise more in the oven if not overproofed now).

**9.** While the dough rises, position the oven rack as indicated in the chart above, set a roasting pan of very hot water on the lowest oven shelf, and preheat the oven to the temperature indicated for your altitude. (Instead of, or in addition to, the pan of water, you can add steam by spraying water into the oven chamber or throwing ice cubes onto the oven floor 3 or 4 times during the baking.)

**10.** Use a pastry brush to coat the top of the loaf either with milk or egg glaze (beat egg with water), then set the pan in the oven to bake for the time indicated for your altitude in the chart, or until the top is a rich golden brown and an instant-read thermometer inserted in the center of the bread reads 190° to 195°F. Tip the loaf out of the pan and rap your knuckle on the bottom; it should sound hollow. If it needs more time, return the loaf to the oven and bake for about 5 minutes longer before retesting.

**11.** Tip the bread out of its pan and cool on a wire rack. When cool, slice with a serrated knife.

## Honey Whole-Wheat Bread

This is a deliciously aromatic, slightly sweet wheat bread with a tender crumb and a brown crust. It makes great toast.

Prepare the white bread as above, with the following changes: For all altitudes, begin mixing the dough with 1¼ cups white bread flour *plus* 1 cup whole-wheat flour; use only whole-wheat flour for any additional flour needed. (Total flour used will be approximately 1¼ cups white, 1¼ cups whole-wheat). The amount of sweetener (honey and sugar) is reduced as the altitude increases:

> **From sea level up** through 5,000 feet, use only 1 teaspoon sugar. Add ⅓ cup honey to the milk mixture before heating it, and stir until dissolved.
> **Above 5,000 feet,** use 2 teaspoons sugar. Add ¼ cup honey to the milk mixture before heating it, and stir until dissolved.
> **At 10,000 feet,** use 2 teaspoons yeast. Add an additional 6 to 7 tablespoons whole wheat flour during the kneading process to achieve a smooth, elastic dough.

## Cinnamon-Raisin Bread

Prepare the white bread as above, with the following changes, mixing the cinnamon-raisin filling while the bread rises. To make the filling, melt 2 tablespoons salted butter in a small saucepan or in the microwave. In a small bowl, mix together ⅓ cup granulated sugar and 2 teaspoons ground cinnamon. In Step 8, before shaping the bread, press the dough into a flat rectangle about 6 by 16 inches. Brush on the melted butter and sprinkle evenly with the cinnamon sugar. Top with about ¾ cup raisins. Working from one short end, roll the dough up into a tight roll, pinch the seam to seal, and pinch the ends closed, tucking them underneath. Place the loaf seam side down in the prepared pan and give it the last rise, then bake as directed.

# Celestial Challah

CHALLAH IS an egg-rich, slightly sweet yeast bread traditionally served on the Jewish Sabbath and other holidays. Throughout the year, challah is braided, but on Rosh Hashanah, the New Year, it is shaped into either a spiral or a ball, symbolizing a round, full year.

This recipe has been in my family as long as I can remember, though we have tinkered with it, sacrilegiously, for just as long. Another yolk, a touch more or less sugar—but we never veered too far from my grandmother's original formula. When my sister Nancy's sons, David and Scott, showed an interest in shaping dough as toddlers, I passed on the recipe, and they started a tradition of making holiday challah. Although they are now in college, they remain the family's challah makers, and they helped me perfect this recipe at sea level.

My challah originally had 3 whole eggs, but we added 3 additional yolks for extra richness and color; organic eggs will usually give an even deeper yellow color. David and Scott prefer a not-too-sweet bread and cut the sugar from the original ¾ cup to ½ cup; it also works with just ⅓ cup sugar, the amount preferred for altitudes above 7,000 feet.

Challah makes fabulous French toast and the best breakfast toast in the world spread with unsalted butter and apricot jam. And leftovers raise bread pudding to new heights. (See "Baking Bread at High Altitudes," page 84.)

Start making the bread early in the morning if you want to serve it that day. It is always best when fresh, but if wrapped airtight, it keeps well for several days. You can also prepare, raise, and shape the dough in advance, then double-wrap and freeze it for up to 1 month before baking. Baked loaves can be wrapped airtight and frozen for up to 2 months.

**General High Altitude Notes:** All-purpose flour may be substituted, but bread flour contains more gluten and, in my experience, gives a slightly higher rise. In my high altitude tests, regular bread flour produced essentially the same results as High Altitude Hungarian flour, although the latter produced a finer, denser crumb (not my favorite). From sea level through 3,500 feet, this recipe needs only two rises: the first comes right after kneading, the second after it has been punched down and braided. Above 3,500 feet, the flavor and texture benefit from three rises: two before and one after braiding.

**Special Equipment:** Two cookie sheets; baking parchment or 2 Silpats or other nonstick baking mats (optional); electric mixer with whip, paddle, and dough hook, or large mixing bowl and sturdy wooden spoon; bench scraper or wide spatula; 2-gallon self-sealing plastic bag (or two 1-gallon bags), or plastic wrap and a tea towel; pastry brush; roasting pan; instant-read thermometer

**Pan Preparation:** Line the cookie sheets with baking parchment or a nonstick mat or coat with nonstick vegetable spray.

**Makes** 2 large braided loaves (about 6 inches wide by 17 inches long)

**High Notes**

*At 7,000 feet and above,* for a better rise, reduce the sugar to ⅓ cup, reduce the yeast to 4¼ teaspoons, and add more salt.

*At 10,000 feet,* increase the baking temperature to 425°F for the first 15 minutes, decrease yeast.

| Ingredients | Sea Level | 3,000 feet | 5,000 feet | 7,000 feet | 10,000 feet |
|---|---|---|---|---|---|
| **Oven rack position, temperature, and baking time** | Rack in center; bake at 350°F for 40 to 50 minutes | Rack in center; bake at 350°F for 35 to 40 minutes | Rack in center; bake at 350°F for 38 to 40 minutes | Rack in center; bake at 350°F for 25 to 35 minutes | Rack in center; bake at 425°F for 15 minutes, then at 350°F for 20 minutes |
| **Active dry yeast** | 4½ teaspoons | 4½ teaspoons | 4½ teaspoons | 4¼ teaspoons | 3½ teaspoons |
| **Warm water** | ¼ cup | ¼ cup | ¼ cup | ¼ cup | ¼ cup |
| **Granulated sugar, divided** | 1 tablespoon for yeast, ½ cup for dough | 1 teaspoon for yeast, ½ cup minus 1 tablespoon for dough | 1 teaspoon for yeast, ½ cup minus 1 tablespoon for dough | 1 teaspoon for yeast, ⅓ cup for dough | 1 teaspoon for yeast, ⅓ cup for dough |
| **Large whole eggs** | 3 | 3 | 3 | 3 | 3 |
| **Large egg yolks** | 3 | 3 | 3 | 3 | 3 |
| **Canola or other vegetable oil** | ½ cup | ½ cup | ½ cup | ½ cup | ½ cup |

*(continued)*

| Ingredients | Sea Level | 3,000 feet | 5,000 feet | 7,000 feet | 10,000 feet |
|---|---|---|---|---|---|
| **Salt** | 1 tablespoon | 1 tablespoon | 1 tablespoon | 1 tablespoon plus ⅛ teaspoon | 1 tablespoon plus ¼ teaspoon |
| **Hot water (120°F)** | 1 ¾ cups | 1 ¾ cups | 1 ¾ cups | 1 ¾ cups | 1 ¾ cups |
| **Unbleached bread flour** | 6 ¼ to 7¾ cups, or as needed | 6½ to 7¾ cups, or as needed | 6½ to 7¾ cups, or as needed | 6¼ to 7¾ cups, or as needed | 7¾ cups, or as needed |
| **GLAZE** | | | | | |
| **Large whole egg** | 1 | 1 | 1 | 1 | 1 |
| **Egg whites** | 2 | 2 | 2 | 2 | 2 |
| **Water** | 1 teaspoon | 1 teaspoon | 1 teaspoon | 1 teaspoon | 1 teaspoon |
| **TOPPING** | | | | | |
| **Poppy seeds or sesame seeds** | ¼ cup | ¼ cup | ¼ cup | ¼ cup | ¼ cup |

**1.** In a cup, combine the yeast, water warm, and the 1 tablespoon or 1 teaspoon sugar, depending on your altitude. Stir and set aside for 3 to 4 minutes, until the mixture bubbles up.

**2.** In the bowl of a stand mixer or other large bowl, whisk together the eggs and yolks (save 2 of the whites for the glaze), then beat in the oil, salt, the remaining sugar, and the hot water. Touch the mixture—when it feels warm but not hot to the touch, scrape in the yeast, along with about 2 cups of the flour. Whisk until smooth or use the mixer's whip attachment for this stage.

**3.** Switch to the paddle attachment, or use a sturdy spoon, and mix or stir in an additional 1 to 2 cups flour. Mix hard until the dough comes together in a sticky mass and begins to look stretchy, 3 to 5 minutes with the mixer's paddle, longer if stirring vigorously with the spoon.

**4.** You can now knead the dough with the dough hook attachment or with your hands. *To knead with the mixer*, switch to the dough hook. With the mixer on the lowest speed, continue adding flour ¼ cup at a time until you've added about 1¾ more cups. This can take 10 to 15 minutes, and you should scrape the dough off the hook several times during this period. The total flour used will be about 6¼ to 7¾ cups, but it will vary depending upon the humidity and altitude; above 8,000 feet, you may even need to add more flour, until the dough looks smooth and no longer feels sticky to the touch. Scrape the dough out onto a lightly floured counter and knead it for 3 to 4 minutes by hand, working in a little more flour if necessary. Form the dough into a large ball, with a smooth, satiny surface.

*To knead by hand,* sprinkle about ¼ cup flour onto the counter and turn out the dough. Flour your hands, fold the dough in half toward you, and push it away with the heels of your hands, then give it a quarter turn and repeat. Reflour the surface as necessary to prevent sticking, and continue kneading for 10 to 12 minutes, or until the dough looks smooth and no longer feels sticky to the touch. As you work, use a bench scraper or broad spatula to scrape any dough off the counter and back into the dough mass. Form the dough into a ball.

**5.** At this point, if you wish, you can refrigerate the dough overnight in a lightly oiled bowl with a plate and heavy weight on top (this counts as the first rise). The next day, remove the dough from the bowl, set it on a sheet of oiled plastic wrap or foil, and bring it to room temperature (3 to 4 hours) before giving it the second rise as described below.

Alternatively, you can give the dough its first rise right away: Put about a tablespoon of oil in a 2-gallon self-sealing plastic bag or large clean bowl, add the dough, and turn it once to coat with oil. (Or, if you do not have a 2-gallon bag, divide the dough in half and let each portion rise in an oiled 1-gallon bag.) Seal the bag(s) or cover the bowl with oiled plastic wrap and a tea towel. The best location for rising is a warm (not hot) spot free from drafts, about 75°F to 85°F. I use my microwave oven (turned off) or my regular oven (heat off) with the dough on the center rack (on a cookie sheet if in a plastic bag), and a roasting pan of very hot water beneath it on the lowest oven rack.

**6.** Let the dough rise until nearly double in bulk; you will be able to poke two fingers into the top and have the marks remain. *See chart below for rising times.*

**7.** Once the dough has risen, punch it down to remove large air bubbles, turn it out onto a lightly floured counter, and knead once or twice. Return it to the oiled container for the second rise. While the dough rises, prepare the pan as directed.

## Approximate Rising Times at 80° to 85°F for Varying Elevations

| Elevation | Sea Level | 3,000 feet | 5,000 feet | 7,000 feet | 10,000 feet |
|---|---|---|---|---|---|
| 1st Rise | 60 minutes | 45 minutes | 45 minutes | 45 to 50 minutes | 45 minutes |
| 2nd Rise | 45 minutes | 30 minutes | 25 minutes | 25 to 30 minutes | 25 to 30 minutes |
| 3rd Rise | 40 minutes | 20 minutes | 20 minutes | 20 minutes | 12 to 15 minutes |

**8.** Once the dough has risen again, punch it down and divide it in half. To shape the braids, work with one portion at a time. Divide it into thirds, using the bench cutter or a knife. With the palms of your hands, roll each piece into a rope about 1 inch thick and 20 inches long. Place the ropes side by side, (see page 96, a). Cross the ropes over each other at their midpoints (b), then start braiding from the center out to one end. To make a symmetrical braid, try to twist over and gently pull on each rope while braiding. Pinch the ends of the 3 ropes together and tuck them under; repeat with the other end (c). The finished braid will measure approximately 3 inches wide by 15 to 17 inches long. Set the braid in the center of a prepared baking sheet. Divide and braid the second portion of dough.

**9.** Cover the braided loaves with lightly oiled plastic wrap or wax paper and set them to rise in a warm, draft-free location (not the oven, which will now be preheating). Allow the loaves to increase by about one-third in bulk (not double).

**10.** Meanwhile, position the racks as indicated in the chart above, put a roasting pan of very hot water on the lowest oven rack, and preheat the oven to the temperature indicated for your altitude.

**11.** Beat 1 whole egg with 2 egg whites and water, then brush this glaze on top of the braids. Sprinkle on the poppy or sesame seeds. Bake for the time indicated for your altitude in the chart above, or until the loaves are a rich golden brown, the crust sounds hollow when rapped with your knuckle, and an instant-read thermometer inserted in the center reads about 190 to 195°F. At 10,000 feet, bake at 425°F for 15 minutes, then reduce the heat to 350°F and bake for 20 minutes, or until the braids are done. For a crisper crust, you can remove the pan of water from the oven for the final 10 minutes of baking time. For a darker brown crust, turn off the oven and leave the loaves in the oven an additional 4 or 5 minutes, watching their color carefully.

**12.** Slide the baked braids off their pans and cool them on a wire rack.

*a*
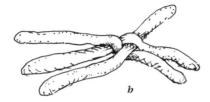
*b*
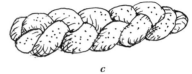
*c*

# Buckhorn Baguettes

CRUNCHY OUTSIDE, chewy-tender inside, these classic French loaves have the irresistible appeal of the mouthwatering (pre-industrial) baguettes I loved to slather with sweet butter and Camembert when I was a student in Paris. They also remind me of the long golden loaves my friend Joan Moore used to bake when she was my Connecticut neighbor, before moving to the Eastern Shore of the Chesapeake. In Joan's artistic hands, the humble baguette was elevated to an art form, filled with extra flavors and decorated on top. My favorites were made with either a half-cup of finely minced onion or a few tablespoons of chopped fresh dill added to the dough and topped appropriately with either several overlapping thinly sliced onion rings or fresh sprigs of flowering dill "glued" to the crust with egg glaze just before baking. I have altered Joan's basic recipe somewhat for the purposes of this book, but if you want to experiment with add-ins, I recommend her creative touches. (See "Baking Bread at High Altitudes," page 84.)

**General High Altitude Note:** At each altitude, I baked dozens of baguettes using different types of flour. I worked with various brands and combinations of unbleached all-purpose flour, high-gluten bread flour, and High Altitude Hungarian flour (see page 36). From sea level to about 3,500 feet, I had good results with a combination of all-purpose and high-gluten unbleached bread flour, though looking back at my side-by-side photos, my best results came from using bread flour by itself. Above 3,500 feet, I consistently got the best rise, texture, and shape with unbleached bread flour because its high gluten content makes it more elastic and best able to support the protein structure during the quick-paced rise at high elevations. However, several bread bakers I spoke with in the Denver-Boulder area (5,000 feet) were successfully using unbleached all-purpose flour or High Altitude Hungarian flour. At 7,000 feet and above, bakers were using both all-purpose and regular bread flour, but at 10,000 feet, bread flour was the favorite, the only one with enough strength to support a good rise.

The total flour used will vary depending upon humidity and altitude. The longer you knead this dough, the more elastic and chewy it will be; by keeping the dough slightly moist, you get more steam, more holes, and a less dense crumb. When climbing in altitude, it isn't necessary to reduce the yeast, though I did cut back a little at 10,000 feet. The main thing is to watch the air temperature and rising times: the higher you go and the warmer the air, the quicker the rise. At sea level, if you are pressed for time, it is good to know that this recipe works with only two rises (one in the bowl and one on the pan just before baking), though I like it best with three rises.

Flavor and texture are enhanced by long, slow rising, which can be achieved at high altitudes by multiple rises and/or a first overnight rise in the refrigerator. Also, at higher (drier) altitudes, the flour will be drier, so you may need to add a little more water to the dough—this recipe benefits from being slightly more moist than regular white bread. Preheating the oven to a temperature higher than required for the bake helps oven spring, giving the dough extra oomph in the first few minutes so steam and expanding gases can create larger air pockets in the dough. Take care not to overbake this bread, or it will be dry.

Different baking pans produce quite-different-looking loaves. French curved metal pans make nicely shaped rounded loaves. I found that solid metal pans made crisper loaves than perforated pans (though you would expect the reverse), but both tended to bake loaves that remained a little pale in color even after they were completely baked. To brown the crust more, I simply removed them from the pans and baked them on the oven racks for a few minutes at the end. Without the support of metal sides, baguettes baked on flat cookie sheets may have a slightly less rounded shape.

If you are using a bread machine, program it for "manual" and let the dough work through its final cycle, then remove the dough and follow the directions below for raising, shaping, and baking.

**Special Equipment:** 2 double-loaf curved metal French bread pans (solid metal rather than perforated) or 1 or 2 cookie sheets; baking parchment (for cookie sheets only); electric mixer with paddle attachment and dough hook or large mixing bowl and sturdy wooden spoon; bench scraper or wide spatula; instant-read thermometer (optional); 2-gallon self-sealing plastic bag (or two 1-gallon bags), or plastic wrap and a tea towel; roasting pan; mister or spray bottle of water; single-edged razor blade, *lame*, or very sharp knife; pastry brush

**Pan Preparation:** Coat curved French pans with nonstick vegetable spray; line cookie sheets with baking parchment or coat with nonstick vegetable spray.

**Makes** 3 baguettes (each about 17 inches by 2¾ inches)

**High Notes**

*At 5,000 feet and above in very hot weather,* rising times will be much shorter than noted in the recipe; watch the dough, not the clock.

*At 7,000 feet and above in dry mountain climates,* add a little more liquid; in humid areas, add a little more flour if necessary.

*At 10,000 feet and above,* use a higher preheating and baking temperature.

| Ingredients | Sea Level | 3,000 feet | 5,000 feet | 7,000 feet | 10,000 feet |
|---|---|---|---|---|---|
| Oven rack position, temperature, and baking time | Rack in center; *preheat* to 425°F; *bake* at 400°F for 15 minutes, then at 350°F for 15 to 20 minutes | Rack in center; *preheat* to 425°F; *bake* at 400°F for 15 minutes, then at 350°F for 15 to 20 minutes | Rack in center; *preheat* to 425°F; *bake* at 400°F for 20 minutes, then at 350°F for 15 minutes | Rack in center; *preheat* to 425°F; *bake* at 400°F for 20 to 22 minutes, then at 350°F for 20 minutes | Rack in center; *preheat* to 475°F; *bake* at 425°F for 15 minutes, then at 350°F for 20 minutes |
| Water | 1½ cups | 1½ cups | 1½ cups | 1½ cups | 1½ cups |
| Olive or canola oil | 1½ tablespoons | 1½ tablespoons | 1½ tablespoons | 1½ tablespoons | 1½ tablespoons |
| Salt | 2 teaspoons | 2 teaspoons | 2 teaspoons | 2 teaspoons | 2¼ teaspoons |
| Active dry yeast | 2¼ teaspoons | 2¼ teaspoons | 2¼ teaspoons | 2⅛ teaspoons | 2 teaspoons |
| Warm water | ¼ cup | ¼ cup | ¼ cup | ¼ cup | ¼ cup |
| Granulated sugar | 1 tablespoon | 1 tablespoon | 1 tablespoon | 1 tablespoon | 1 tablespoon |
| Unbleached all-purpose flour | 1 cup | 1 cup | None | None | None |
| Unbleached bread flour | 3 to 3½ cups | 3 to 3½ cups | 4½ to 4¾ cups | 4 to 4½ cups | 4 to 4½ cups |
| GLAZE (OPTIONAL) | | | | | |
| Large egg white | 1 | 1 | 1 | 1 | 1 |
| Water | 1 teaspoon | 1 teaspoon | 1 teaspoon | 1 teaspoon | 1 teaspoon |
| TOPPING (OPTIONAL) | | | | | |
| Flour or sesame seeds | ¼ cup | ¼ cup | ¼ cup | ¼ cup | ¼ cup |

1. Combine the 1½ cups water, oil, and salt in a small saucepan, set on low heat, and warm until just barely hot to the touch (about 115°F). Remove from the heat.

2. In a small bowl, combine the yeast, warm water, and sugar. Stir and set aside for 3 to 4 minutes, until the mixture bubbles up.

3. Measure about 2½ cups of the flour (from sea level to 3,500 feet, use 1 cup all-purpose flour plus 1½ cups bread flour) into the large bowl of an electric mixer or another large bowl, and scoop out a well in the center of the flour. Test the liquid mixture in the saucepan; when it is just warm (about 110°F), pour it into the flour well and add the yeast mixture. Mix hard for 3 to 4 minutes using the mixer's paddle attach-

ment or a wooden spoon; this will begin to develop the gluten and enhance the elasticity of the dough. Then continue beating or stirring slowly as you work in another 1½ to 2 more cups flour, using just enough to make a soft, slightly gooey, stretchy dough that begins to come together in a ball. It is better to use less flour here than too much.

**4.** You can knead the dough with the dough hook or your hands. *To knead with the mixer,* switch to the dough hook. With the mixer on the lowest speed, knead the dough for 10 to 12 minutes, or until it looks smooth and stretchy on the surface but still feels soft and a little sticky on the inside. Work in a little more flour if required, but don't make a dry dough.

*To knead by hand,* sprinkle 2 to 3 tablespoons of flour onto the counter and turn out the dough, scraping out all the sticky bits from the bowl bottom. Flour your hands, fold the dough in half toward you, and push it away with the heels of your hands, then give it a quarter turn and repeat. Add a little more flour to the counter as you work to prevent sticking, and continue kneading for 8 to 10 minutes, or until the dough looks smooth and stretchy outside but still feels a little sticky inside; it should not feel too dry. As you work, use a bench scraper or broad spatula to scrape bits of dough off the counter and back into the dough mass. Form the dough into a ball.

**5.** At this point, if you wish, you can refriger-ate the dough overnight in a lightly oiled bowl with a plate and heavy weight on top (this counts as the first rise). The next day, remove the dough from the bowl, set it on a sheet of oiled plastic wrap or foil, and bring it to room temperature (3 to 4 hours) before giving it the second rise as described below.

Alternatively, you can give the dough its first rise right away. Put about a tablespoon of oil into a 2-gallon self-sealing plastic bag or a large clean bowl, add the dough, and turn it once to coat with oil. (Or, if you do not have a 2-gallon bag, divide the dough in half and let each por-tion rise in an oiled 1-gallon bag.) Seal the bag(s) or cover the bowl with oiled plastic wrap and a tea towel. The best location for rising is a warm (not hot) spot free from drafts, about 80° to 85°F. I use my microwave oven (turned off) or my regular oven (heat off) with the dough sitting on the center rack (on a cookie sheet if in a plastic bag) and a roasting pan of very hot water beneath it on the lowest oven rack.

**6.** Let the dough rise until almost double in bulk; you will be able to poke two fingers into the top and have the marks remain. **See chart on page 101 for rising times.**

**7.** Once the dough has risen, punch it down to remove large air bubbles, turn it out onto a lightly floured counter, and knead once or twice. Return it to the oiled container for the second rise. While the dough is rising, prepare the pans as directed.

## Approximate Rising Times at 80° to 85°F for Varying Elevations

| Elevation | Sea Level | 3,000 feet | 5,000 feet | 7,000 feet | 10,000 feet |
|---|---|---|---|---|---|
| 1st Rise | 60 to 80 minutes | 45 minutes | 55 to 60 minutes | 50 to 55 minutes | 50 to 60 minutes |
| 2nd Rise | 50 minutes | 30 to 35 minutes | 38 to 40 minutes | 35 to 40 minutes | 30 to 35 minutes |
| 3rd Rise | 30 minutes | 20 to 25 minutes | 22 to 25 minutes | 20 minutes | 12 to 15 minutes |

**8.** Once the dough has risen again, punch it down to flatten it, knead it a couple of times, and form it into a ball. Divide the ball into thirds with a knife or bench scraper. To shape the baguettes, flatten each ball with your fingertips and pat it into a rough rectangular shape about ¼ inch thick, 4 to 5 inches wide, and about 10 inches long. Working from a short end, roll it up into a log, like a fat jelly roll. To lengthen the rolls into the classic baguette shape, place both your palms side by side on top of each roll and rock it gently back and forth while working your palms toward the ends. The shaped baguettes should be about 15 to 16 inches long and 1½ to 2 inches in diameter.

**9.** Place the shaped loaves in the prepared pans and cover lightly with oiled plastic wrap. (If you only have one double-loaf French pan, bake the third loaf at the same time on a cookie sheet instead of waiting for the first 2 loaves to bake.) Place in a warm rising location (not the oven, which will now be preheating) for the third and final rise. From sea level to 3,000 feet, the dough should rise until slightly *less than double* in bulk; above 3,000 feet, the dough should rise even less, *only until about one-third larger* (it will rise more in the oven if not over-proofed now).

**10.** While the dough rises, position the oven rack as indicated in the chart above, set a roasting pan of boiling or very hot water on the bottom shelf (steam does *not* make the crust crisp) and preheat the oven to the temperature indicated for your altitude. (Instead of, or in addition to, the pan of water, you can spray water into the oven chamber or throw ice cubes onto the oven floor 3 or 4 times during the baking.)

**11.** Using a single-edged razor blade, French *lame*, or very sharp knife, make 3 or 4 slashes (see below) about ⅛ inch deep in the top of each loaf. For the floury finish often used in

*Baguette with razor cuts along top*

professional bakeries, toss a little flour on top of the baguettes. Or if you want a shiny surface, beat the egg white with water, then use a pastry brush to coat the baguettes with this glaze; try not to drip glaze inside the slashes in the dough. If you wish, sprinkle the glazed loaves with sesame seeds.

**11.** Reduce the heat as directed in the chart above just before you put the loaves in the oven, and bake the baguettes for the time indicated for your altitude. Watch the loaves more than the clock, baking the baguettes until their tops are golden brown and make a hollow thump when rapped with your knuckle. About 10 minutes before the end of the baking time, remove the pan of water. When fully baked, the interior of the loaves should register 185° to 190°F on an instant-read thermometer. If you want an extra-crisp crust, turn off the oven, place the baked loaves directly on the oven shelf, prop the door open slightly with a wooden spoon, and bake for an additional 5 minutes.

**12.** Remove the loaves from the pans and cool on the wire rack.

**Note:** Baguettes baked on cookie sheets brown more quickly than those in curved metal pans. If your loaves seem crisp outside but look too pale, remove them from the pan(s) and set them directly on your oven shelf to bake for 3 to 5 minutes longer (watch carefully).

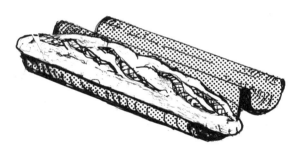

*Double-curved French pan with baked baguette*

# Grassy Creek Multigrain Bread

THIS SATISFYING round rustic loaf is all about texture and flavor: it contains three types of flour, three kinds of seeds, wheat germ, and honey. The crumb is lighter than you might expect, the taste is heavenly, and the nutritional value high—all that's needed is some sweet butter to spread on top! You'll love it warm from the oven, but it's also great for breakfast toast, sandwiches, or served with a selection of cheeses and beer.

Feel free to substitute different grains and seeds; the recipe works as long as you start with 2 cups of white flour and keep the other basic proportions the same. Special flours, grains, and seeds are available at natural food stores or in the baking sections of many supermarkets. (See "Baking Bread at High Altitudes," page 84.)

**General High Altitude Notes:** The basic procedure is to give this dough three rises, two in a bowl or plastic bag, and the third after shaping on the baking pan. The use of the multigrains makes a fairly weighty dough, but the amount of yeast plus the gluten in the bread flour is sufficient for a nice rise and keeps the crumb from being too dense. You will see from the recipe chart that the ingredients change very little from one elevation level to the next (more salt in higher elevations; the yeast is not reduced, because it helps lighten the heavy dough); the basic difference when baking this heavy dough at different altitudes is rising time, and that depends primarily upon room temperature and humidity. Complex multigrain breads develop greater flavor with a long, slow rise. I found that this bread was especially good when it had its first rise overnight in the refrigerator; the next morning, I brought it to room temperature and allowed it to rise twice more before baking. But if you don't have time for the refrigerated rise, the bread will still be a success. In very hot weather, you will find the rising times shorter than noted in the table, so watch the dough, not the clock; if your dough was chilled overnight, rising times will take longer.

**Special Equipment:** Cookie sheet; baking parchment, Silpat, or other nonstick baking mat (optional); instant-read thermometer (optional); electric mixer with paddle attachment and dough hook or large bowl and sturdy wooden spoon; bench scraper or wide spatula; 2-gallon self-sealing plastic bag (or two 1-gallon bags), or plastic wrap and a tea towel; roasting pan; mister or spray bottle of water (optional); pastry brush; single-edged razor blade, *lame*, or very sharp knife

**Pan Preparation:** Line the cookie sheet with baking parchment or a nonstick mat or coat with nonstick vegetable spray.

**Makes** 1 large *boule* (rounded loaf about 9¼ inches in diameter and 3½ to 4½ inches high; 2½ pounds)

**High Notes**

*At 5,000 feet and above,* add salt to boost flavor, and extra white flour.

*At 7,000 feet and above,* preheat the oven to 425°F, then reduce the heat to 400°F when the bread is put into the oven to bake for 15 minutes; finally reduce the heat to 375°F to complete the baking.

| Ingredients | Sea Level | 3,000 feet | 5,000 feet | 7,000 feet | 10,000 feet |
|---|---|---|---|---|---|
| **Oven rack position, temperature, and baking time** | Rack in center; bake at 400°F for 15 minutes, then at 375°F for 20 minutes | Rack in center; bake at 400°F for 15 minutes, then at 375°F for 20 to 30 minutes | Rack in center; bake at 400°F for 15 minutes, then at 375°F for 25 to 35 minutes | Rack in center; *preheat* to 425°F; *bake* at 400°F for 15 minutes, then at 375°F for 20 to 27 minutes | Rack in center; *preheat* to 425°F; *bake* at 400°F for 15 minutes, then at 375°F for 25 to 30 minutes |
| **Active dry yeast** | 2¼ teaspoons | 2¼ teaspoons | 2¼ teaspoons | 2¼ teaspoons | 2¼ teaspoons |
| **Warm water** | ¼ cup | ¼ cup | ¼ cup | ¼ cup | ¼ cup |
| **Granulated sugar** | 1 tablespoon | 1 tablespoon | 1 tablespoon | 1 tablespoon | 1 tablespoon |
| **Water** | ½ cup plus 2 tablespoons | ½ cup plus 2 tablespoons | ½ cup plus 2 tablespoons | ½ cup plus 2 tablespoons | ½ cup plus 2 tablespoons |
| **Plain yogurt, low-fat or regular** | ½ cup | ½ cup | ½ cup | ½ cup | ½ cup |
| **Salt** | 1 teaspoon | 1 teaspoon | 1¼ teaspoons | 1¼ teaspoons | 1¼ teaspoons |
| **Olive or canola oil** | 2 tablespoons | 2 tablespoons | 2 tablespoons | 2 tablespoons | 2 tablespoons |
| **Honey** | 3 tablespoons | 3 tablespoons | 3 tablespoons | 3 tablespoons | 3 tablespoons |
| **Unbleached white bread flour** | 2 cups, or as needed | 2 cups, or as needed | 2⅓ cups, or as needed | 2½ cups, or as needed | 2½ cups, or as needed |
| **Whole wheat flour** | ½ to ¾ cup | ½ to ¾ cup | ½ to ¾ cup | ½ to ¾ cup | ½ to ¾ cup |
| **Spelt flour** | ½ cup | ½ cup | ½ cup | ½ cup | ½ cup |

*(continued)*

| Ingredients | Sea Level | 3,000 feet | 5,000 feet | 7,000 feet | 10,000 feet |
|---|---|---|---|---|---|
| **Wheat germ, toasted or plain** | ¼ cup, plus some for sprinkling on top | ¼ cup, plus some for sprinkling on top | ¼ cup, plus some for sprinkling on top | ¼ cup, plus some for sprinkling on top | ¼ cup, plus some for sprinkling on top |
| **Flaxseed meal (or ground seeds)** | 3 tablespoons | 3 tablespoons | 3 tablespoons | 3 tablespoons | 3 tablespoons |
| **Flaxseeds or sesame seeds** | 3 tablespoons | 3 tablespoons | 3 tablespoons | 3 tablespoons | 3 tablespoons |
| **Sunflower seeds or chopped walnuts** | ¼ cup | ¼ cup | ¼ cup | ¼ cup | ¼ cup |
| **Poppy seeds, optional** | 1 tablespoon | 1 tablespoon | 1 tablespoon | 1 tablespoon | 1 tablespoon |
| **GLAZE** | | | | | |
| **Large egg** | 1 | 1 | 1 | 1 | 1 |
| **Water** | 1 teaspoon | 1 teaspoon | 1 teaspoon | 1 teaspoon | 1 teaspoon |

**1.** In a small bowl, combine the yeast, warm water, and sugar. Stir, and set aside for 3 to 4 minutes, until the mixture begins to bubble up.

**2.** In a medium saucepan, combine the ½ cup plus 2 tablespoons water, yogurt, salt, oil, and honey and heat just until hot to the touch, 115° to 120°F on an instant-read thermometer. Remove from the heat.

**3.** In the large bowl of an electric mixer or another large bowl, toss together all the flour (use just ½ cup whole-wheat flour), wheat germ, meal, and seeds or nuts. Stir in the bubbling yeast mixture. Test the temperature of the liquid in the saucepan; it should feel comfortably warm (not hot) to the touch; cool it if necessary, then stir it into the flour and yeast.

**4.** With the paddle attachment or a wooden spoon, beat the dough slowly until it is well blended and the gluten begins to develop (about 5 to 7 minutes). The dough will look quite rough; if it feels very sticky, sprinkle on another 2 to 3 tablespoons bread flour and beat for a few more minutes.

**5.** You can knead the dough with the dough hook attachment or with your hands. *To knead with the mixer,* switch to the dough hook. With the mixer on the lowest speed, knead the dough until it forms a cohesive ball and is no longer sticky to the touch, about 6 to 7 minutes, adding another 2 or 3 tablespoons bread or whole-wheat flour if necessary. Form the dough into a ball.

*To knead by hand,* sprinkle 2 to 3 tablespoons bread flour onto the counter and turn out the dough. Flour your hands, fold the dough in half toward you, and push it away with the heels of your hands, then give it a quarter turn and repeat. Reflour the surface with 1 or 2 tablespoons more bread or whole-wheat flour if necessary to prevent sticking, and continue kneading for 7 to 10 minutes, until the dough no longer feels sticky. As you work, use a bench scraper or wide spatula to scrape any dough off the counter and back into the dough mass. Form the dough into a ball.

**6.** At this point, if you wish, you can refrigerate the dough overnight in a lightly oiled bowl with a plate and heavy weight on top (this counts as the first rise). The next day, remove the dough from the bowl, place it on a sheet of oiled plastic wrap or foil, and let come to room temperature (about 2 hours) before giving it the second rise as described below.

Alternatively, you can give the dough the first rise right away. Put about a tablespoon of oil into a 2-gallon self-sealing plastic bag or a large clean bowl (or, if you do not have a 2-gallon bag, divide the dough in half and let each portion rise in an oiled 1-gallon bag), add the dough, and turn it once to coat with oil. Seal the bag, or cover the bowl with oiled plastic wrap and a tea towel. The best location for rising is a warm (not hot) spot free from drafts, about 75° to 80°F. I use my microwave oven (turned off) or my regular oven (heat off) with the dough on the center rack (on a cookie sheet if in a plastic bag) and a roasting pan of very hot water beneath it on the lowest oven rack.

**7.** Let the dough rise until just about double in bulk; you will be able to poke two fingers into the top and have the marks remain. ***See chart below for rising times***.

**8.** Once the dough has risen, punch it down to remove large air bubbles, turn it out onto a lightly floured counter, and knead it once or twice. Return it to the oiled container for the second rise. While the dough is rising, prepare the cookie sheet as directed.

### Approximate Rising Times at 80° to 85°F for Varying Elevations

| Elevation | Sea Level | 3,000 feet | 5,000 feet | 7,000 feet | 10,000 feet |
|---|---|---|---|---|---|
| 1st Rise | 60 to 75 minutes | 60 to 75 minutes | 45 to 55 minutes | 35 to 40 minutes | 50 to 55 minutes |
| 2nd Rise | 40 to 45 minutes | 40 to 45 minutes | 35 to 40 minutes | 35 minutes | 45 minutes |
| 3rd Rise | 30 to 40 minutes | 30 to 40 minutes | 15 to 20 minutes | 20 minutes | 15 minutes |

**9.** Once the dough has risen again, punch it down, knead once or twice, and then form it into a round smooth ball, pinching the edges under the bottom. Set the ball on the prepared baking sheet and cover loosely with oiled plastic wrap. Let the dough rise (not in the oven, which will now be preheating) only until it is about one-third larger (not double); it will spring back if you give it a very light poke.

**10.** Meanwhile, position the oven rack as indicated above, place a roasting pan of very hot water on the lowest oven rack, and preheat the oven to the temperature for your altitude. (In addition to or instead of using the water pan, you can toss some ice cubes onto the oven floor during the first 15 minutes or spray the oven several times with a mister.)

**11.** Beat egg with water, then brush this glaze on top of the dough. With a single-edged razor blade, *lame*, or very sharp knife, slash a cross-hatch design in the top, making 4 or 5 sets of cuts perpendicular to each other, about 1/4 inch deep and 1/2 inch apart as shown. Toss a little wheat germ on top.

**12.** Place the dough in the oven and bake for 15 minutes. Reduce the oven temperature to 375°F and bake for 20 to 35 minutes longer, according to the chart; watch the bread, not the clock. Remove the pan of water after the first 10 minutes at 375°F, and bake until the bread is a rich brown color and sounds hollow when rapped with your knuckle. When fully baked, the interior of the loaf should register about 190°F on an instant-read thermometer.

Slide the bread off the pan and cool it on a wire rack. (Both flavor and ease of slicing are best on the second day.)

# Cakes

## Baking Cakes at High Altitudes

Cake baking is the most dramatic and challenging part of the high altitude story. More than any other baked goods, cakes begin to react strongly to changes in atmospheric pressure at elevations as low as 2,000 feet above sea level, and reactions grow more intense as elevation increases. A cake may rise and then collapse, or not rise at all; it may be cracked, convex or concave, or crusted over on top but sodden inside; or it may have a coarse, heavy crumb. It may overflow the pan or stick to it. And that's just the beginning.

Three major altitude factors affect cake baking. First, the higher in elevation you go, the less air pressure there is and the lower the boiling point of water; second, the higher the altitude (with its reduced air pressure), the more quickly leavening gases expand; and third, the higher the altitude, the faster liquids (and moisture) evaporate. Each of these poses a threat to the relatively delicate, leavened structure of cakes developed for sea level use and must be met with specific adjustments and corrections.

As elevation increases, and water boils at a lower temperature, it gets harder to deliver sufficient heat to the inside of a heavy, wet batter (see pages 109–10). At the same time, liquids evaporate quickly, leaving behind a higher than usual concentration of sugar and fat. Extra sugar makes the texture of a cake coarse and an excess of sugar and fat weakens the strength of the gluten in the flour. A weakened structure can cause a cake to fall.

In my testing, I discovered that there are no all-purpose remedies: each recipe is unique and requires special adjustments, so you must follow the recipes carefully; also see the table of adjustments on page 323). But there are some general guidelines. The first thing to do is strengthen the batter, by reducing the sugar or other sweetener. This also helps the proteins in the batter set up more quickly in the oven. You can also add one or more whole eggs or an extra yolk, or more flour or other starch. (For more detail, read about eggs and flour in the ingredients section, page 35.) Be sure to use the type of flour called for. All-purpose is often better than cake flour for high altitude cakes because its slightly higher protein content contributes to batter strength. But angel cake and sponge cake benefit from softer cake flour, which contributes just enough protein and adds a little more acidity. With rich formulas like pound cakes, you may need to reduce the fat, especially at altitudes around 10,000 feet. And to compensate for faster evaporation at high altitudes and the dryness of high mountain air, you often need to add liquid.

The acidity of a cake batter is important at high altitudes because the more acidic the batter, the more quickly it will set up in the heat of the oven. My favorite high altitude liquid is buttermilk, but soft yogurt or soured milk works (add a tablespoon of vinegar or lemon juice to each cup of milk). Thick yogurt and sour cream also add acidity, but they lack the liquefying property of buttermilk. Greater acidity also contributes to the tenderness of a cake, because acid breaks down the strength and elasticity of gluten in wheat flour.

The leavening measurements for sea-level cakes must be cut back at high altitudes, because the lower air pressure allows leavening gases to expand with such exuberance that they can push up the batter before cell walls have time to set in the heat. The result is a free fall when the cake starts to cool. My high altitude leavening rule of thumb is *less is more:* reduce the baking powder and baking soda as well as the amount of air whipped into egg foams or beaten egg whites (see "About Sponge Cakes and Egg Whites," below). This may seem counterintuitive since, theoretically, you want a cake to rise as high as possible. You might assume, in fact, that the combination of lowered air pressure, chemical leavening, and/or whipped egg whites would produce a sensational high-rise cake. My tests with Mocha Chiffon Cake are a good example of the reality. At sea level, leavened by 1 tablespoon of baking powder plus stiffly beaten egg whites, it baked to lofty perfection. However, at an altitude of 10,000 feet, the same formula caused a crash. After many trials, I re-created the stable rise when I cut out about one-third of the baking powder, reduced the sugar and oil, and added acidity. This solution is fairly typical. With some cakes, you will get a perfect rise simply by cutting back on the leavening; with others, you must also strengthen and reformulate the batter. The key is to find the correct balance of ingredients.

Flavors and aromas are less sharp at higher altitudes, especially over 7,000 feet. The higher you go, the more you need to increase the salt (which makes sweets taste sweeter) and increase the extracts and other flavoring agents.

The amount of air whipped into the batter affects the texture of the cake. A properly prepared butter cake has a moist, fine-grained crumb with evenly distributed airholes. When you are creaming the butter and sugar together, be sure to achieve a smooth, light mixture; the sugar crystals open tiny air pockets in the fat, which expand and multiply as beating continues. Underbeating can cause a heavy, coarse crumb, while overbeating can develop the gluten in the flour and toughen the cake or add excess air that causes the batter to rise too much.

Baking pan size and preparation are also important to success. Use the size pan called for in the recipe. If the pan is too small, the batter may overflow; if the pan is too large, the cake will be thin, dry, and tough. As elevation increases, cakes tend to stick to pans; be sure to grease and flour the pans as directed. Above 5,000 feet, many recipes also require greased pans to be lined with baking parchment or wax paper.

Proper temperature control and oven heat are essential for high altitude cakes. It helps to have all ingredients at room temperature before you start mixing so they blend smoothly. Once the cake is in the oven, the trick is to get enough heat inside the cake to enable it to set up before the top forms a hard (or burned) crust. Sometimes this can be accomplished simply by switching the type of pan: instead of a round, square, or loaf pan, use a tube pan that can deliver heat directly to the center of the batter. In many cases, you can improve a cake's rise simply by shifting the position of the baking rack, placing the cake in the lower third of the chamber so it is closer to the heat source. With some cake recipes (but not all), you can increase the oven temperature by 15 to 25 degrees. In every case, it is essential to use an auxiliary thermometer inside your oven so you know the exact temperature; most home ovens are at least slightly (if not hugely) inaccurate, and a few degrees can make all the difference at high altitudes. At around 10,000 feet, you often get the best results with a two-step approach: preheat the oven to 25 degrees above the baking temperature, then lower the heat as soon as the cake goes into the oven. The extra heat boost helps the batter warm up quickly and also compensates for heat lost when the oven door is opened.

Cool cakes on wire racks for the time indicated in your recipe in order to allow the batter to settle and the steam to escape. The heavier and more dense the cake, the more time it needs to cool. If a cake is unmolded too soon, part of it may remain stuck to the pan. (If this happens, you can try to stick it back together, using jam for glue. Or scoop it all out, sprinkle the pieces with liqueur, cut them into cubes, and make a trifle, layering the cake with fruit or berries, jam, and vanilla pudding topped with whipped cream and toasted nuts.)

Proper cake storage is also an issue. Most mountain locations have extra-dry air that literally sucks moisture from the surface of baked goods. Uncovered cakes will dry out before you know it, and cake slices will stale quickly.

Whole cakes should be frosted or glazed as soon as possible, to seal the surface and prevent moisture loss. They should be stored in airtight containers or covered with plastic wrap, then stored in heavy-duty plastic bags. For longer storage, double-wrap cakes in plastic, then foil or a heavy-duty plastic bags. The higher the fat content of a cake, the longer it can be frozen without loss of flavor or texture; double-wrap and bag cakes before freezing.

### About Sponge Cakes and Egg Whites

Sponge cakes, also called foam cakes, are leavened primarily with whipped eggs or egg whites rather than baking powder and/or baking soda. This family includes sponge cakes, jelly rolls, angel food cakes, chiffon cakes, and tortes. For successful sponge cakes, eggs must be handled with care. To whip whites, bring them to room temperature in a grease-free bowl, add the salt and/or cream of tartar, and beat until foamy. Then begin to add the sugar gradually, starting with the mixer on medium speed and gradually increasing it. The lower the whipping speed at the beginning, the smaller the air bubbles and the more stable the foam. Between sea level and 2,500 feet, egg whites used for leavening a cake can be beaten to stiff peaks, but at altitudes of 2,500 feet and above they should be beaten only to soft, droopy peaks so there is enough room left in the air cells to expand during baking. At high altitudes, overwhipped whites collapse, taking the cake down with them.

With the exception of angel food cake, sponge cakes contain yolks whipped with sugar. At sea level, the yolk mixture is "ribboned," or whipped until it nearly triples in volume and forms a ribbon falling back on itself when the beater is lifted. At about 8,500 feet and above, it is better to whip the yolk-sugar foam slightly less. It should still form a ribbon, but it should contain a little less air than usual, leaving room for rising in the oven.

At high altitudes, it is essential to get foam cake batters into the hot oven as soon as they are mixed. The quick surface evaporation caused by high, dry air makes foam batters dry out and deflate if allowed to stand.

Although some sponge cakes are baked in greased and floured pans, angel food cake and chiffon cake pans are never greased, so that the batter can cling to the slides as it rises in the oven. These cakes are cooled by turning the pan upside down, usually over the neck of a tall bottle, so gravity can help stretch the fragile cell structure until it is cooled and set; if left to cool right side up, angel food and chiffon cakes can collapse.

## About Cheesecakes

Cheesecakes are the easiest cakes to bake at high altitudes. In fact, I met a professional wedding cake baker at 10,000 feet in Colorado whose only recipe was for cheesecake (varying in size and decoration). That's a cop-out in my opinion, but cheesecakes are much less temperamental than leavened cakes: all you have to do is apply steady low-to-moderate heat until their proteins coagulate and set. The main thing to remember is that since water boils at a lower temperature at high altitudes, it will take longer for the inside of your heavy cheesecake batter to heat up and bake. To prevent overbrowning the cake top before the inside sets, you can reduce oven heat sightly and increase the baking time. Judge doneness of cheesecakes more by the visual guidelines given in the recipes than by exact timing, as times can vary at high altitudes.

To understand the changes in cake baking caused by high altitudes, read "Into Thin Air: The Science Behind High Altitude Baking" (page 319), and the ingredients section on page 35. If you use cake mixes, see page 317. When following one of the cake recipes in this chapter, pay special attention to the General High Altitude Notes and the individual High Notes—they will not only help you with that recipe, but will also give you information you can apply to similar recipes that need altitude adjustments.

# Classic 1-2-3-4 Cake

THIS NINETEENTH-century cake originated—at sea level—as an easy and reliable formula. To make it even easier for my students, I translated 1-2-3-4 into the acronym "Be SaFE": 1 cup Butter, 2 cups Sugar, 3 cups Flour, 4 Eggs.

This was the first recipe I tried when I began this book. Its initial test at 7,000 feet was made in Santa Fe by my friend Sandy MacGregor, an enthusiastic home baker who, with his wife, Marilyn, later hosted my stay there. Though it was some years ago, I still treasure Sandy's note: "I think you will be delighted with the result of these modifications. . . . The cake was really delicious." My penciled-in postcript, "It worked! I have my story," was the official start of this manuscript.

This recipe lends itself to nearly infinite variations. For example, along with vanilla extract, you can add 1 teaspoon of almond, lemon, orange, or hazelnut extract. You can make two round layers or split them into four by slicing each one in half with a serrated knife, or you can bake the cake in a sheet pan. Fill a layer cake with your favorite fruit preserves and dust the top with sifted confectioners' sugar, or use one of the icing recipes that follow. For a vanilla cake I like to use Bittersweet Chocolate Icing (page 119) or Mocha Buttercream Icing (page 123); for a lemon-almond-vanilla cake, use the Honey Cream Icing below. Two variations on the cake recipe follow: Spice Cake, which pairs well with the rich and mellow Honey Cream Icing, and Coconut Cake with Coconut Icing.

~~~~~

**General High Altitude Notes:** This is a foundation recipe for endless variations at sea level, but when I took the recipe to higher altitudes, the proportions changed quite radically. I used this recipe for my first test at every altitude on my testing route because the results and required adjustments usually indicated a pattern of adjustments I could follow with other butter cakes. In general, at 5,000 feet and above, to hold a good rise I found it necessary to strengthen the batter by reducing the leavening and sugar while adding a little flour and one egg. To enhance flavor, I doubled the vanilla; to increase the acidity of the batter and add moisture to the crumb in dry atmospheres, I switched from whole milk to buttermilk and increased the amount of liquid.

**Special Equipment:** Two 9 × 1½-inch round cake pans or one 9 × 13-inch baking pan (for sheet cake); baking parchment or wax paper; wooden skewer or cake tester; 2 foil-covered 9-inch cardboard cake disks or flat plates

**Pan Preparation:** Coat the pans with butter-flavor nonstick vegetable spray or solid shortening. Line round cake pans (not the baking pan) with baking parchment or wax paper, then spray or grease it. At 7,000 feet and above, also dust all pans with flour and tap out the excess flour.

**Makes** one 2-layer 9-inch cake; serves 8; or one 9 × 13-inch sheet cake; serves 12

**High Notes**

*At 5,000 feet and above,* strengthen the batter with extra flour and another egg, but reduce the leavening and the sugar. Use buttermilk instead of whole milk to make the batter more acidic. Add more salt and extract.

*At 7,000 feet and above,* enhance the flavor by adding 1 teaspoon almond and/or lemon extract along with the vanilla.

*From 7,000 to 10,000 feet,* bake the cake in the center of the oven at more moderate heat (350° instead of 375°F) for a better rise and moister crumb.

| Ingredients | Sea Level | 3,000 feet | 5,000 feet | 7,000 feet | 10,000 feet |
|---|---|---|---|---|---|
| **Oven rack position, temperature, and baking time** | Rack in center; bake at 350°F: layers for 30 to 35 minutes, sheet cake for 32 to 38 minutes | Rack in center; bake at 375°F: layers for 30 to 35 minutes, sheet cake for 38 minutes | Rack in center; bake at 375°F: layers for 22 to 28 minutes, sheet cake for 30 to 33 minutes | Rack in lower third of oven; bake at 350°F: layers for 22 to 27 minutes, sheet cake for 30 to 32 minutes | Rack in center; *preheat* oven to 375°F; *bake* at 350°F: layers for 28 to 30 minutes, sheet cake for 30 to 35 minutes |
| **Sifted all-purpose flour** | 3 cups | 3 cups | 3 cups plus 1 tablespoon | 3 cups plus 3 tablespoons | 3 cups plus 3 tablespoons |
| **Baking powder** | 1 tablespoon | 2½ teaspoons | 2 teaspoons | 2 teaspoons | 1½ teaspoons |
| **Salt** | ½ teaspoon | ½ teaspoon | ¾ teaspoon | ¾ teaspoon | ¾ teaspoon |
| **Unsalted butter, at room temperature** | ½ pound (2 sticks) | ½ pound (2 sticks) | ½ pound (2 sticks) | ½ pound (2 sticks) | ½ pound (2 sticks) |
| **Granulated sugar** | 2 cups | 2 cups minus 1 tablespoon | 2 cups minus 1 tablespoon | 2 cups minus 2 tablespoons | 2 cups minus 2 tablespoons |
| **Large eggs, at room temperature** | 4 | 4 | 5 | 5 | 5 |

*(continued)*

| Ingredients | Sea Level | 3,000 feet | 5,000 feet | 7,000 feet | 10,000 feet |
|---|---|---|---|---|---|
| **Vanilla extract** | 1 teaspoon | 1 teaspoon | 2 teaspoons | 2 teaspoons | 2 teaspoons |
| **Whole milk** | 1 cup | None | None | None | None |
| **Buttermilk** | None | 1 cup | 1 cup plus 2 tablespoons | 1¼ cups | 1⅓ cups |

**1.** Position the rack and preheat the oven as indicated for your altitude in the chart above. Prepare the pan(s) as directed.

**2.** In a medium bowl, whisk together the sifted flour, baking powder, and salt.

**3.** In the large bowl of an electric mixer, cream together the butter and sugar until well blended. Scrape down the bowl and beater. Beat in the eggs 2 or 3 at a time, along with the vanilla (and the other extract; see recipe headnote above), beating well to blend, then scrape down bowl and beater again. Don't worry if the batter looks curdled—the flour will bring it together.

**4.** With the mixer on the lowest speed, slowly add the dry ingredients, alternating with the milk or buttermilk. Once the batter is blended together, increase the speed and beat for about a minute, until smooth and creamy.

**5.** Divide the batter evenly between the two pans or spread it in the sheet pan; smooth the top. Bake for the time indicated for your altitude in the chart above, or until golden, nicely risen, and springy to the touch; a cake tester inserted in the center should come out dry. Cool in the pan(s) on a wire rack for about 10 minutes.

**6.** Run a knife between the cake layers and pan sides to release the cakes, then top each with a foil-covered cardboard cake disk or flat plate and invert. Remove the pan and peel off the parchment. The sheet cake can be removed or left in the pan. Cool completely, then fill and frost as desired (see recipe headnote for suggestions).

## Santa Fe Spice Cake

Prepare the cake as above, but in Step 2, whisk the following into the dry ingredients:

| Ingredients | Sea Level | 3,000 feet | 5,000 feet | 7,000 feet | 10,000 feet |
|---|---|---|---|---|---|
| **Ground cinnamon** | 1½ teaspoons | 1½ teaspoons | 1½ teaspoons | 1½ teaspoons | 1¾ teaspoons |
| **Ground nutmeg** | ½ teaspoon | ½ teaspoon | ¾ teaspoon | ¾ teaspoon | ¾ teaspoon |
| **Ground ginger** | ½ teaspoon | ½ teaspoon | ½ teaspoon | ½ teaspoon | 1 teaspoon |
| **Ground cloves** | ¼ teaspoon | ¼ teaspoon | ¼ teaspoon | Generous ¼ teaspoon | Generous ¼ teaspoon |
| **Cayenne pepper, optional** | Pinch | Pinch | Pinch | Scant ⅛ teaspoon | Scant ⅛ teaspoon |
| **Unsweetened cocoa** | 1 tablespoon | 1 tablespoon | 1 tablespoon | 1 tablespoon | 1 tablespoon |

# Honey Cream Icing
*(recipe is the same at all altitudes)*

**Makes** 2⅔ cups, enough to fill and frost 2 layers or to frost 1 sheet cake

1 pound Philadelphia regular cream cheese
(not low-fat), at room temperature
4 tablespoons (½ stick) unsalted butter, at
room temperature
⅓ cup honey, or more as needed
¾ cup sifted confectioners' sugar, or more as
needed
Pinch of salt
½ teaspoon vanilla extract
½ teaspoon lemon extract or juice

In a food processor or the bowl of an electric mixer, preferably with a paddle attachment, cream together the cream cheese and butter until completely smooth. Add the honey, confectioners' sugar, salt, and extracts and process or beat until smooth and spreadable. Adjust the texture with more sugar or honey if needed. (The icing can be made a day in advance and refrigerated, covered; bring to room temperature and beat until smooth before using.)

# Coconut Cake

This recipe gets its rich coconut flavor from both coconut extract and shredded sweetened coconut (sold in any supermarket). The coconut tends to clump together in the packet and must be pulled apart and crumbled into the dry ingredients. Since coconut is a drying agent and also adds weight to the batter, at higher elevations you need to reduce the flour and add a little more liquid; at 2,000 to 6,500 feet, you also use less sugar. Resist the temptation to substitute unsweetened coconut milk (not enough taste) or canned coconut cream (too much sugar, which destroys the cake's texture) for the

buttermilk, which adds the required acidity (trust me, I tried it). For a layer cake, fill with about 1 cup apricot preserves and frost with Coconut Icing (below).

Prepare the cake as above, with the following changes: At all altitudes, use only 3 cups sifted flour and 1 teaspoon vanilla extract, plus ¾ teaspoon coconut extract. The other altitude variables (for sugar, coconut, and liquid) are listed below. Crumble the shredded coconut into the flour mixture in Step 2.

**Sea Level:** 1 cup (3 ounces) lightly packed
shredded sweetened coconut
**3,000 feet:** 2 cups minus 2 tablespoons granulated sugar; 1 cup (3 ounces) shredded
sweetened coconut
**5,000 feet:** 2 cups minus 2 tablespoons granulated sugar; 1 cup (3 ounces) shredded
sweetened coconut; 1½ cups plus 1 tablespoon buttermilk
**7,000 feet:** 1 cup (3 ounces) shredded sweetened coconut; 1½ cups buttermilk
**10,000 feet:** ¾ cup (about 2 ounces) shredded
sweetened coconut; 1⅓ cups plus 1 tablespoon buttermilk

# Coconut Icing
*(recipe is the same at all altitudes)*

The food processor makes quick work of smoothing the cream cheese and blending the ingredients.

**Makes** 2⅓ cups, enough to frost the top and sides of a two-layer 8- or 9-inch cake or the top of a 9 × 13-inch sheet cake

**Garnish**
1 cup (3 ounces) shredded sweetened coconut

8 tablespoons (1 stick) unsalted butter, at
room temperature

One 3-ounce package Philadelphia regular
   cream cheese (not low-fat)
1 teaspoon vanilla extract
1½ teaspoons coconut extract
One 1-pound box confectioners' sugar, sifted
   (about 5¼ cups)
3 tablespoons milk, or as needed

Preheat the oven to 375°F. Spread the
coconut on a cookie sheet and bake for 6 to 10
minutes, tossing occasionally, until evenly
golden brown. Let cool.

In a food processor or the large bowl of an
electric mixer, preferably with the paddle
attachment, cream together the butter and
cream cheese until completely smooth. Add
the extracts and about 2 cups of the sifted
sugar and process or beat until smooth.
Add the remaining sugar and 3 tablespoons
milk and process or beat to spreading consistency, adding just a few drops more milk if
needed.

Frost the cake, then sprinkle on the toasted
coconut.

# Chocolate Buttermilk Cake with Bittersweet Chocolate Icing

THIS OLD-FASHIONED, moist chocolate cake has a fine grain and a tender crumb. It is my personal favorite at every altitude; sensational at sea level and (almost) made-to-order for high elevations because it contains buttermilk, a favored high-altitude ingredient that contributes moisture and tenderness as well as extra acidity, which helps the batter set quickly.

This is the ideal cake for every occasion, plain to fancy. For a picnic, bake it in a sheet pan. For birthdays, bake round or heart-shaped layers. And for sophisticated galas, bake two round layers, split them horizontally with a serrated knife to make a four-layer cake, and fill with raspberry preserves and fresh berries. Frost the cake with the delectable Bittersweet Chocolate Icing, following, or use Mocha Buttercream Icing (page 123).

For a Double Chocolate Cake, add 1 cup semisweet mini–chocolate chips to the batter at the end of Step 5, right after mixing in the melted chocolate.

**General High Altitude Notes:** At home (540 feet), I always found this recipe easy and totally reliable. Because the recipe contains buttermilk, I theorized that it might work without adjustment at higher altitudes. I was taken by surprise, though, when I baked it at 5,000 feet in Idaho. My first test, as usual, was without changing the sea-level recipe, just to see if something would happen—and it did. A typical high altitude failure, it rose fast, then sank, and it had a dense, wet texture; but it was not easy to fix. To strengthen the batter, I added varying amounts of flour, reduced the sugar, and played with different proportions of baking powder and baking soda. My worst idea was substituting baking powder for the baking soda; the color turned gray

and the taste was dull and flat! When I finally I got it right, I was surprised once again when that version failed at 10,000 feet. At that high elevation, I ran into new problems (see High Notes) that required even greater adjustments.

**Special Equipment:** Two 9 × 1½-inch shiny metal round pans; or a 9 × 13-inch baking pan (for sheet cake); baking parchment or wax paper; double boiler (optional); wooden skewer or cake tester; foil-covered 9-inch cardboard cake disks or flat plates.

**Pan Preparation:** Coat pans with butter-flavor nonstick vegetable spray or solid shortening. At 5,000 feet and above, line with baking parchment or wax paper, grease again, and dust with sifted cocoa; tap out the excess cocoa.

**Makes** one 2- or 4-layer 9-inch cake; serves 8 to 10; or one 9 × 13-inch sheet cake; serves 12

### High Notes

*At 3,000 feet and above,* add a little flour and reduce the sugar. Decrease the leavening as the elevation increases, and add a little more buttermilk and salt. From 3,000 to 5,000 feet, increase the oven temperature but position the rack in the center of the oven, rather than the lower third, for more moderate heat.

*At 10,000 feet,* the flour is unsifted (just whisked, spooned into the cup, and leveled off), so the cup will hold a little more. Normally you would cut back the sugar to further strengthen the batter; however, at this elevation, reducing the sugar leaves the taste too flat. After endless adjustments and several phone calls, food scientist Shirley Corriher suggested adding an extra egg plus a yolk. The yolk adds emulsification that helps the batter hold more sugar without weakening the structure. Because the eggs also add liquid, you do not need to add as much buttermilk as at 7,000 feet.

| Ingredients | Sea Level | 3,000 feet | 5,000 feet | 7,000 feet | 10,000 feet |
|---|---|---|---|---|---|
| **Oven rack position, temperature, and baking time** | Rack in lower third of oven; bake at 325°F: layers for 35 to 45 minutes, sheet cake for 40 to 45 minutes | Rack in center; bake at 375°F: layers for 25 to 27 minutes, sheet cake for 25 to 27 minutes | Rack in center; bake at 375°F: layers for 25 to 30 minutes, sheet cake for 30 to 32 minutes | Rack in lower third of oven; bake at 350°F: layers for 30 to 32 minutes, sheet cake for 35 minutes | Rack in lower third of oven; bake at 350°F: layers for 32 to 35 minutes, sheet cake for 35 minutes |
| **Unsweetened chocolate, chopped** | 4 ounces | 4 ounces | 4 ounces | 4 ounces | 4 ounces |
| **Sifted all-purpose flour** | 2 cups | 2 cups plus 2 tablespoons | 2 cups plus 3 tablespoons | 2 cups plus 3 tablespoons | 2 cups plus 2 tablespoons unsifted flour |
| **Baking soda** | 1½ teaspoons | 1¼ teaspoons plus ⅛ teaspoon | 1¼ teaspoons | 1 teaspoon | ½ teaspoon |
| **Salt** | ¼ teaspoon | ½ teaspoon | ½ teaspoon | ½ teaspoon | ½ teaspoon |
| **Ground nutmeg** | ¼ teaspoon | ¼ teaspoon | ¼ teaspoon | ¼ teaspoon | ¼ teaspoon |
| **Unsalted butter, at room temperature** | ½ pound (2 sticks) | ½ pound (2 sticks) | ½ pound (2 sticks) | ½ pound (2 sticks) | 12 tablespoons (1¼ sticks) |

*(continued)*

| Ingredients | Sea Level | 3,000 feet | 5,000 feet | 7,000 feet | 10,000 feet |
|---|---|---|---|---|---|
| Granulated sugar | 1¾ cups | 1½ cups plus 3 tablespoons | 1½ cups plus 3 tablespoons | 1½ cups plus 2 tablespoons | 1½ cups plus 3 tablespoons |
| Vanilla extract | 1 teaspoon | 1 teaspoon | 1 teaspoon | 1 teaspoon | 1½ teaspoons |
| Large eggs, at room temperature | 4 | 4 | 4 | 4 | 5, plus 1 yolk |
| Buttermilk | 1⅓ cups | 1½ cups | 1½ cups | 1½ cups plus 2 tablespoons | 1½ cups |

BITTERSWEET CHOCOLATE ICING (RECIPE FOLLOWS), OPTIONAL

**1.** Position the rack and preheat the oven as indicated for your altitude in the chart above. Prepare the pan(s) as directed.

**2.** Put the chocolate in the top of a double boiler set over simmering (at sea level to 3,000 feet) or boiling (at 5,000 feet and above) water and heat, stirring occasionally, until smooth; or melt the chocolate in the microwave (see page 35). Remove from the heat and set aside to cool.

**3.** In a medium bowl, whisk together the flour, baking soda, salt, and nutmeg. Set aside.

**4.** In the large bowl of an electric mixer, cream together the butter and sugar until well blended. Scrape down the bowl and beater. Beat in the vanilla and then the eggs, adding them 2 at a time. Beat well to blend, then scrape down the bowl and beater.

**5.** With the mixer on the lowest speed, alternately add the flour mixture and the buttermilk. Stir the melted chocolate to make sure it is smooth, then scrape it into the batter and beat until an even color and no longer streaked.

**6.** Divide the batter evenly between the two pans or spread it all into the sheet pan; smooth the top. Bake for the time indicated for your altitude in the chart above, or until the cake is springy to the touch and a cake tester inserted in the center comes out clean.

**7.** Let the sheet cake cool completely in its pan on a wire rack, then frost. Cool the layers in their pans on a wire rack for 10 to 15 minutes, then run a knife between the layers and the sides to release them. Top each layer with a foil-covered cardboard cake disk or a plate, invert, and remove the pan. Peel off the parchment, if you used it, and cool layers completely. Fill and frost as desired.

## Bittersweet Chocolate Icing
*(recipe is the same at all altitudes)*

This is a classic ganache (blend of chocolate and heavy cream); the flavor is best when made with fine-quality bittersweet or semisweet chocolate (such as Callebaut, Lindt Excellence, Tobler Tradition, or Baker's bittersweet). The flavor can be varied: for Mocha Icing, add 2 teaspoons instant coffee powder dissolved in 1 tablespoon hot water, or 3 tablespoons coffee liqueur; for Raspberry Icing, add 3 tablespoons

Chambord liqueur; for Hazelnut Icing, add 3 tablespoons Frangelico (hazelnut) liqueur plus ½ teaspoon hazelnut or almond extract, or to taste.

**Special Equipment:** Double boiler (optional); hand-held electric mixer; medium metal bowl (if using a glass double boiler); large metal bowl; icing spatula

**Makes** 2½ to 3½ cups (depending on whipping time), enough to fill a 3-layer 9-inch cake or fill and frost a 2-layer 8- or 9-inch cake or 1 chocolate sponge roll (see page 170); or use about 2 cups to frost the top of a 9 × 13-inch sheet cake (freeze any leftover icing)

> 8 ounces semisweet or bittersweet chocolate, finely chopped
> 1 cup heavy cream, or more as needed
> 2 to 3 tablespoons liqueur (see above), brandy, or rum, or 1 teaspoon vanilla extract

Combine the chocolate and cream in the top of a double boiler, set over simmering (at sea level to 3,000 feet) or boiling (at 5,000 feet and above) water, and heat, stirring occasionally, until smooth. Remove from the heat and set aside to cool. Or melt the chocolate in the microwave (see page 35). At 7,000 feet and above, it will take longer for the water to boil; watch closely, and add more water if it evaporates.

Whisk the flavoring into the chocolate cream. If using a glass double boiler, transfer the mixture to a metal bowl.

Prepare an ice water bath (place some ice cubes and cold water in a large metal bowl) and set the bowl of chocolate in it. Beat the chocolate with a hand-held electric mixer for a few minutes, or until it is cool, lighter in color, and nearly doubled in volume. It should be thick, creamy, and of spreading consistency; if necessary, add a little more cream to soften it, or refrigerate (or freeze, wrapped in plastic wrap) to firm. *Note:* If you are not pressed for time, you can chill the cream in the refrigerator for about 1 hour before beating it instead of using the ice water bath. *Note:* Total quantity will vary somewhat depending upon the length of time the mixture is beaten.

Spread the icing on the cake with an icing spatula. At first you will see lots of bubbles in the icing, but as you work the spatula over the surface, the texture will smooth out.

# Daredevil's Food Cake with Mocha Buttercream Icing

AN AMERICAN classic, devil's food cake has a moist, tender crumb and satisfying chocolate flavor. The characteristically red (devil) brown color of the cake comes from the baking soda, an alkali that reddens chocolate as it neutralizes some of its acidity and leavens the cake. This recipe is specifically developed for use with natural, not Dutch-process, cocoa (see page 42). Because cocoa packs and clumps in its container, you will get the most accurate measurement if you first sift it onto wax paper, then spoon it into the measuring cup and level it off.

You can bake this cake as two layers, fill it with your favorite fruit preserves (try black cherry or raspberry), and frost it with the Mocha Buttercream Icing, following. Or bake it in a tube pan and top it with any icing (see index) or just a light sifting of cocoa or confectioners' sugar (like snow on mountaintops!).

**General High Altitude Notes:** As altitude increases, both the leavening and sugar are reduced. In search of the best version of this cake at high altitudes, I tried different proportions of baking soda with and without baking powder. I also tried using baking powder alone (a huge mistake, which resulted in a dull gray color and bland flavor). Baking soda alone produced the best rise and color at all elevations. Note that the oven heat and baking rack position vary. At sea level, the cake is baked at 350°F in the center of the oven; at 3,000 to 5,000 feet, the oven temperature is 375°F. At 7,000 feet and above, the heat is 350°F but the cake is baked in the lower third of the oven for greater exposure to the heat.

**Special Equipment:** Two 8 × 1½-inch round cake pans or 9- to 9½-inch (6½ to 8-cup) tube or Bundt pan; baking parchment, wax paper, or foil; 1 or 2 foil-covered 8- or 9- or 10-inch cardboard cake disks or flat plates; wooden skewer or cake tester

**Pan Preparation:** Generously coat the pan(s) with solid shortening, line with baking parchment or wax paper (for a tube or Bundt pan, cut a paper or foil ring; see page 31 or page 34), grease the liner, and dust with sifted cocoa; tap out the excess cocoa.

**Makes** one 2-layer 8-inch cake; serves 8; or one 9-inch tube cake; serves 8 to 10

**High Notes**

*At 3,000 feet and above,* strengthen the batter by adding flour. From 3,000 to 5,000 feet, increase the heat to 375°F.

*At 5,000 feet and above,* reduce the sugar and increase the buttermilk.

*At 10,000 feet,* add one egg.

| Ingredients | Sea Level | 3,000 feet | 5,000 feet | 7,000 feet | 10,000 feet |
|---|---|---|---|---|---|
| **Oven rack position, temperature, and baking time** | Rack in center; bake at 350°F: layers for 30 to 35 minutes, tube cake for 38 to 40 minutes | Rack in center; bake at 375°F: layers for 30 to 35 minutes, tube cake for 30 to 32 minutes | Rack in center; bake at 375°F: layers for 30 to 35 minutes, tube cake for 35 to 40 minutes | Rack in lower third of oven; bake at 350°F: layers for 30 to 35 minutes, tube cake for 35 to 40 minutes | Rack in lower third of oven; bake at 350°F: layers for 30 to 33 minutes, tube cake for 40 to 43 minutes |
| **Sifted all-purpose flour** | 2¼ cups | 2¼ cups plus 1 tablespoon | 2⅓ cups | 2⅓ cups | 2½ cups minus 1 tablespoon |
| **Baking soda** | 1¼ teaspoons | 1⅛ teaspoons | 1 teaspoon | 1 teaspoon | ¾ teaspoon |
| **Salt** | ¼ teaspoon | ½ teaspoon | ½ teaspoon | ½ teaspoon | ½ teaspoon |
| **Sifted natural cocoa, such as Hershey's regular** | ½ cup | ½ cup | ½ cup | ½ cup | ½ cup |
| **Unsalted butter, at room temperature** | 8 tablespoons (1 stick) | 8 tablespoons (1 stick) | 8 tablespoons (1 stick) | 8 tablespoons (1 stick) | 8 tablespoons (1 stick) |
| **Granulated sugar** | 1½ cups | 1½ cups | 1½ cups minus 1 tablespoon | 1½ cups minus 2 tablespoons | 1½ cups minus 2 tablespoons |
| **Vanilla extract** | 1 teaspoon | 1 teaspoon | 1 teaspoon | 1 teaspoon | 1 teaspoon |

*(continued)*

| Ingredients | Sea Level | 3,000 feet | 5,000 feet | 7,000 feet | 10,000 feet |
|---|---|---|---|---|---|
| Large eggs, at room temperature | 2 | 2 | 2 | 2 | 3 |
| Buttermilk | 1½ cups | 1½ cups | 1½ cups plus 3 tablespoons | 1¾ cups | 1½ cups plus 3 tablespoons |

COCOA OR CONFECTIONERS' SUGAR, FOR TUBE CAKE

MOCHA BUTTERCREAM ICING (RECIPE FOLLOWS), FOR LAYERS

**1.** Position the rack and preheat the oven as indicated for your altitude in the chart above. Prepare the pan(s) as directed.

**2.** In a medium bowl, whisk together the flour, baking soda, salt, and cocoa. Set aside.

**3.** In the large bowl of an electric mixer, cream together the butter and sugar for 3 to 4 minutes, until very well blended. Scrape down the bowl and beater. Beat in the vanilla and eggs and scrape down the bowl and beater again.

**4.** With the mixer on the lowest speed, alternately add the flour mixture and the buttermilk. Once the ingredients are blended together, increase the speed and whip for about 30 seconds (no longer, because at high altitudes you don't want to incorporate excess air).

**5.** Divide the batter between the two pans or scrape it all into the tube pan. Bake for the time indicated for your altitude in the chart above, or until the cake top feels springy to the touch and a cake tester inserted in the center comes out clean. Cool in the pan(s) on a wire rack for 10 to 15 minutes.

**6.** Run a knife between the layers and the pan sides to release them, or run the tip of a knife around the pan sides and the top of the tube to loosen the cake. Top each layer, or the tube pan, with a foil-covered cardboard cake disk or flat plate, invert, and give a sharp downward shake to release the cake. Remove the pan and peel off the parchment. Cool completely.

**7.** Fill the layers and frost with the buttercream, or dust the tube cake lightly with cocoa or confectioners' sugar (or frost as desired).

## Mocha Buttercream Icing
*(recipe is the same at all altitudes)*

**Makes** 3 cups, enough to fill and frost one 2-layer 8-inch cake or 1 chocolate sponge roll (see page 170); volume varies slightly with mixing method

8 tablespoons (1 stick) unsalted butter, at room temperature

6 cups sifted confectioners' sugar, or more as needed

⅓ cup sifted unsweetened natural cocoa, such as Hershey's regular

5 to 6 tablespoons extra-strength coffee or espresso (or 1 tablespoon instant coffee powder dissolved in ½ cup hot water)

1 teaspoon vanilla extract

In a food processor or the large bowl of an electric mixer, preferably with the paddle attachment, process or beat the butter until soft. Add 2 cups of the sifted sugar and beat until smooth. Scrape down the bowl and blade or beaters. Add the remaining sugar plus cocoa, 5 tablespoons coffee, and vanilla and process or beat until completely smooth and creamy. Add more sugar or coffee if necessary to bring the icing to spreading consistency. (The icing can be made a day in advance and refrigerated, covered; bring to room temperature and beat until smooth before using.)

# Anna's Butter Cake

THIS TRADITIONAL Swedish butter cake is my family's favorite. The grain is fine and tender, the taste rich and buttery. Purists like it best with a hint of almond flavoring and just a light sifting of confectioners' sugar on top. For special occasions, I substitute pure orange extract for the almond and add the grated zest of one orange.

**General High Altitude Notes:** This is one of my favorite, most reliable recipes at sea level, and I expected it to be easy to make at high altitudes. Instead, it began to behave badly even at 3,000 feet. The cake would collapse or sink in the center or have a coarse, dense texture. The problem was the high proportion of fat and sugar, as in a pound cake. It took four to five attempts at each altitude to achieve the proper rise and balance between richness, density, and tenderness of crumb. Baking temperature and time also vary with altitude. Contrary to the procedure for most butter cakes, I had to add a little baking powder and reduce the flour. For strength and liquid, I added both an egg and more milk. At 5,000 feet and above, the flavor needed a boost with more extract. I also replaced the whole milk with buttermilk because its acidity helps the batter set quickly and it also adds moisture to the crumb.

**Special Equipment:** A 9- to 9½-inch (6½- to 8-cup) tube pan; baking parchment or wax paper; foil-covered 9-inch cardboard cake disk or a flat plate; wooden skewer or cake tester

**Pan Preparation:** Coat the pan with butter-flavor nonstick vegetable spray or solid shortening, line with baking parchment or wax paper (see page 30), regrease, then dust with flour; tap out the excess flour. (At sea level, omit the paper liner.)

**Makes** one 9-inch tube cake; serves 8 to 10

### High Notes
*At 3,000 feet,* increase the leavening slightly, add an egg, and reduce the sugar. Increase the baking temperature but shorten the time.

*At 5,000 feet and above,* add extra flavoring extract. Replace the milk with buttermilk.

*At 7,000 feet and above,* return the baking temperature to 350°F and increase the time slightly to improve the rise.

*At 10,000 feet,* decrease the leavening.

| Ingredients | Sea Level | 3,000 feet | 5,000 feet | 7,000 feet | 10,000 feet |
|---|---|---|---|---|---|
| **Oven rack position, temperature, and baking time** | Rack in center; bake at 350°F for 40 to 43 minutes | Rack in center; bake at 375°F for 32 to 35 minutes | Rack in center; bake at 375°F for 35 to 37 minutes | Rack in lower third of oven; bake at 350°F for 40 to 43 minutes | Rack in lower third of oven; bake at 350°F for 35 to 45 minutes |
| **Sifted all-purpose flour** | 2 cups plus 2 tablespoons | 2 cups plus 2 tablespoons | 2 cups | 2 cups | 2 cups plus 1 tablespoon |
| **Baking powder** | 1 teaspoon | 1¼ teaspoons | 1½ teaspoons | 1½ teaspoons | ¾ teaspoon |
| **Salt** | ½ teaspoon | ½ teaspoon | ½ teaspoon | ½ teaspoon | ½ teaspoon |
| **Unsalted butter, at room temperature** | ½ pound (2 sticks) | ½ pound (2 sticks) | 14 tablespoons (1¾ sticks) | 12 tablespoons (1½ sticks) | 12 tablespoons (1½ sticks) |
| **Granulated sugar** | 1½ cups | 1⅓ cups | 1⅓ cups | 1⅓ cups | 1⅓ cups plus 1 tablespoon |
| **Large eggs, at room temperature** | 2 | 3 | 3 | 3 | 3 |
| **Vanilla extract** | 1 teaspoon | 1 teaspoon | 1 teaspoon | 1 teaspoon | 1 teaspoon |
| **Almond extract** | 1 teaspoon | 1 teaspoon | 1½ teaspoons | 1½ teaspoons | 1½ teaspoons |
| **Whole milk** | ¾ cup | 1 cup | None | None | None |
| **Buttermilk** | None | None | 1 cup | 1 cup plus 2 tablespoons | 1 cup plus 2 tablespoons |
| **TOPPING** | | | | | |
| **Confectioners' sugar** | ¼ cup | ¼ cup | ¼ cup | ¼ cup | ¼ cup |

1. Position the rack and preheat the oven as indicated for your altitude in the chart above. Prepare the pan as directed.

2. In a medium bowl, whisk together the sifted flour, baking powder, and salt. Set aside.

3. In the large bowl of an electric mixer, cream together the butter and sugar until well blended. Scrape down the bowl and beater. Add the eggs and extracts, beating well to blend. Don't worry if the batter looks curdled—the flour will bring it together.

4. With the mixer on the lowest speed, alternately add the flour mixture and the milk or buttermilk. Scrape down the bowl and beaters, then beat until the batter is creamy, smooth, and thick.

5. Scoop the batter into the prepared baking pan and smooth the top. Bake for the time indicated for your altitude in the chart above, or until the cake is risen, springy to the touch, and golden brown; a cake tester inserted in the center should come out clean. Don't overbake, or the cake will be dry.

6. Cool the cake in the pan on a wire rack for at least 15 minutes. Run a knife between the cake and pan sides and the top of the tube to release the cake. Top with a foil-covered cardboard cake disk or plate, invert, and remove the pan. Peel off the paper, if you used it, and cool the cake completely.

7. Before serving, sift the confectioners' sugar over the top of the cake.

# Aspen Apple Cake

THIS BIG cake filled with apples, raisins, and walnuts is one of my family's favorites. The cinnamon-spiced crumb is moist and rich, not too sweet. Because it is made with oil, the cake stays fresh a long time, even at high altitudes, making it a perfect choice for picnics, bake sales, and brunch. It is equally appropriate for dessert at any fall or winter celebration, from Halloween or Thanksgiving to Christmas.

———❦———

**General High Altitude Notes:** This is a big, heavy batter, but it adapted to high altitudes with minimal adjustments. I replaced the whole milk with buttermilk to increase the acidity of the batter, helping it set up quickly in the oven. To strengthen the batter, I added an egg. I played with baking times and temperatures at various elevations, looking for the best rise. The biggest challenge came at 10,000 feet, when the cake tended to sink slightly and crust over before baking through. To improve the rise, I reduced the baking soda and oil and added a little liquid. I cut just ¼ cup of sugar—I would have reduced it even more to strengthen the batter structure, but the sugar is critical to the flavor and texture. The solution was to add an extra egg yolk to provide more emulsification, enabling the batter to contain the sugar without weakening its structure.

**Special Equipment:** A 9- or 10-inch angel food cake pan or plain springform or tube pan (12- to 16-cup capacity); food processor or nut chopper; 2 foil-covered 10-inch cardboard cake disks or flat plates; wooden skewer or cake tester

**Pan Preparation:** Coat the pan with butter-flavor nonstick vegetable spray or solid shortening, dust generously with flour, and tap out the excess flour.

**Makes** one 9- or 10-inch tube cake; serves 10 to 12

### High Notes

*At 3,000 feet and above,* replace the whole milk with buttermilk.

*At 5,000 feet,* raise the oven temperature, reduce the baking time, and add an egg.

*At 7,000 feet,* return the oven to 350°F but bake for a longer time. Add extra buttermilk.

*At 10,000 feet,* add more flour, cut back on the sugar and oil, and reduce the baking soda. Add an extra yolk, plus a little liquid to offset evaporation. The oven is preheated to 25 degrees above the actual baking temperature and the heat is reduced when the cake goes into the oven.

| Ingredients | Sea Level | 3,000 feet | 5,000 feet | 7,000 feet | 10,000 feet |
|---|---|---|---|---|---|
| **Oven rack position, temperature, and baking time** | Rack in center; bake at 350°F for 75 to 85 minutes | Rack in center; bake at 350°F for 70 to 75 minutes | Rack in center; bake at 375°F for 55 to 60 minutes | Rack in center; bake at 350°F for 65 to 70 minutes | Rack in center; *preheat* oven to 375°F; *bake* at 350°F for 65 to 70 minutes |
| **Sifted all-purpose flour** | 3 cups | 3 cups | 3 cups | 3 cups | 3 cups plus 3 tablespoons |
| **Baking powder** | ½ teaspoon | ½ teaspoon | ½ teaspoon | ½ teaspoon | ½ teaspoon |
| **Baking soda** | ½ teaspoon | ½ teaspoon | ½ teaspoon | ½ teaspoon | ¼ teaspoon |
| **Salt** | ¼ teaspoon | ½ teaspoon | ½ teaspoon | ½ teaspoon | ½ teaspoon |
| **Ground cinnamon** | ½ teaspoon | ½ teaspoon | ½ teaspoon | ½ teaspoon | ½ teaspoon |
| **Ground nutmeg** | ½ teaspoon | ½ teaspoon | ½ teaspoon | ½ teaspoon | ½ teaspoon |
| **Apples (about 3 large, 6½ ounces each), peeled, cored, and chopped into ¼- to ½-inch bits** | 3 cups chopped | 3 cups chopped | 3 cups chopped | 3 cups chopped | 3 cups chopped |
| **Raisins, lightly packed** | 1 cup (6 ounces) | 1 cup (6 ounces) | 1 cup (6 ounces) | 1 cup (6 ounces) | 1 cup (6 ounces) |
| **Walnuts, coarsely chopped** | 1 cup (4 ounces) | 1 cup (4 ounces) | 1 cup (4 ounces) | 1 cup (4 ounces) | 1 cup (4 ounces) |
| **Canola or light olive oil** | 1½ cups | 1½ cups | 1½ cups | 1½ cups | 1⅓ cups |

*(continued)*

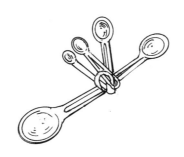

| Ingredients | Sea Level | 3,000 feet | 5,000 feet | 7,000 feet | 10,000 feet |
|---|---|---|---|---|---|
| **Granulated sugar** | 2 cups | 2 cups | 2 cups | 2 cups | 1¾ cups |
| **Large eggs, at room temperature** | 3 | 3 | 4 | 4 | 4, *plus* 1 yolk |
| **Vanilla extract** | 2 teaspoons | 2 teaspoons | 2 teaspoons | 2 teaspoons | 2 teaspoons |
| **Whole milk** | 3 tablespoons | None | None | None | None |
| **Buttermilk** | None | ¼ cup | 3 tablespoons | ¼ cup | ⅓ cup plus 1 tablespoon |
| TOPPING (OPTIONAL) | | | | | |
| **Sifted confectioners' sugar** | 2 tablespoons | 2 tablespoons | 2 tablespoons | 2 tablespoons | 2 tablespoons |

**1.** Position the rack and preheat the oven as indicated for your altitude in the chart above. Prepare the pan as directed.

**2.** In a medium bowl, whisk together the sifted flour, baking powder, baking soda, salt, and spices. Put the apples, raisins, and chopped nuts in a bowl and toss together with about 2 tablespoons of the flour mixture, coating all the pieces. Set both bowls aside.

**3.** In the large bowl of an electric mixer, beat together the oil, sugar, eggs, vanilla, and milk or buttermilk. With the mixer on the lowest speed, gradually beat in the flour mixture. Scrape down the bowl and beaters. Stir in the apple mixture, blending well. The batter will feel quite stiff.

**4.** Scoop the batter into the prepared pan and smooth the top. Bake for the time indicated for your altitude in the chart above, or until the cake has risen and is springy to the touch, and a cake tester inserted in the center comes out clean. Cool the cake in its pan on a wire rack for no less than 20 minutes.

**5.** Run a knife between the cake and pan sides and the top of the tube to release the cake. Top with a foil-covered cardboard cake disk or plate, invert, and remove the pan. Top with another covered cardboard cake disk or plate and invert again. Cool completely.

**6.** Before serving, sift a little confectioners' sugar over the top of the cake if you wish.

# El Rancho Gingerbread with Warm Rum-Lemon Sauce

GRATED FRESH ginger gives a sophisticated kick to the taste of this old-fashioned favorite. You can still serve squares from the pan for picnics and snacks, but the serious flavor boost elevates it from homey to high art, and you'll receive raves when you serve it to dinner party guests on your best dishes napped with the rum-lemon sauce and a sprinkle of slivered candied ginger. In Santa Fe, I brought this cake, along with five others, to a dessert tasting at the home of David Jenness and Ken Collins, who pronounced it "the best ever of all gingerbreads." High praise, indeed, from tough cake and art critics.

If you are a ginger fanatic, you can double the grated fresh ginger.

---

**General High Altitude Notes:** At 10,000 feet, this "old reliable" recipe suddenly became problematic, requiring four trials before I was able to balance the leavening, acidity, and texture of its very wet batter. My first attempts were dense, coarse, and soupy, with little or no rise. The problem was that both molasses and sour cream are acids that lend moisture and flavor to the cake but also interact with the baking soda. At very high elevations, they "overreacted" to make excess leavening, causing the cake to rise fast, then fall. Cutting out the baking powder and reducing the soda helped, and cutting out a little of the butter increased the batter's strength. However, it wasn't until I baked it in a tube pan, which delivered more direct heat to the inner batter, that the rise and texture were perfect.

**Special Equipment:** From sea level to about 10,000 feet, a 9 × 2-inch square baking pan; at or near 10,000 feet, a 9-inch (6½-cup) tube pan

**Pan Preparation:** Coat the square pan with solid shortening or butter-flavor nonstick vegetable spray, dust generously with flour, and tap out the excess flour. Or, coat the tube pan with solid shortening or vegetable spray, line with a ring of baking parchment or wax paper (see pages 30–31), and grease and flour the paper; tap out the excess flour.

**Makes** one 9-inch square cake; serves 9; or one 9-inch tube cake; serves 8 to 10

**High Notes**
- *At 3,000 feet and above,* add an egg and reduce the leavening as the altitude increases.
- *At 5,000 feet to 7,000 feet,* add flavor by increasing the salt.
- *At 7,000 feet,* reduce the oven temperature to 350°F so the cake top doesn't crust over before the batter bakes through.
- *At 10,000 feet,* bake the cake in a tube pan instead of a square pan. Omit the baking powder, and reduce the butter and sugar.

| Ingredients | Sea Level | 3,000 feet | 5,000 feet | 7,000 feet | 10,000 feet |
|---|---|---|---|---|---|
| **Oven rack position, temperature, and baking time** | Rack in center; bake at 350°F for 35 minutes | Rack in center; bake at 375°F for 35 minutes | Rack in center; bake at 375°F for 40 minutes | Rack in center; bake at 350°F for 45 to 47 minutes | Rack in center; bake at 375°F for 42 to 44 minutes |
| **All-purpose flour** | 2½ cups | 2½ cups | 2½ cups | 2½ cups | 2½ cups |
| **Baking powder** | ½ teaspoon | ½ teaspoon | ½ teaspoon | ½ teaspoon | None |
| **Baking soda** | 1 teaspoon | ¾ teaspoon | ½ teaspoon plus ⅛ teaspoon | ¾ teaspoon | ½ teaspoon |
| **Salt** | ½ teaspoon | ½ teaspoon | ¾ teaspoon | ¾ teaspoon | ½ teaspoon |
| **Ground ginger** | 2½ teaspoons | 2½ teaspoons | 2½ teaspoons | 2½ teaspoons | 2½ teaspoons |
| **Ground cinnamon** | 1 teaspoon | 1 teaspoon | 1 teaspoon | 1 teaspoon | 1 teaspoon |
| **Unsalted butter, at room temperature** | 8 tablespoons (1 stick) | 8 tablespoons (1 stick) | 8 tablespoons (1 stick) | 8 tablespoons (1 stick) | 6 tablespoons (¾ stick) |
| **Granulated sugar** | ½ cup plus 2 tablespoons | ½ cup plus 2 tablespoons | ½ cup plus 2 tablespoons | ½ cup plus 2 tablespoons | ½ cup |
| **Large egg(s), at room temperature** | 1 | 2 | 2 | 2 | 2 |
| **Sour cream** | ½ cup | ½ cup | ⅔ cup | ⅔ cup | ⅔ cup |
| **Fresh ginger, grated (about a 1 × 2-inch piece)** | 2 teaspoons | 1 tablespoon | 1 tablespoon | 1 tablespoon | 1 tablespoon |
| **Unsulfured molasses** | ½ cup | ½ cup | ½ cup | ½ cup | ½ cup |
| **Very hot water** | 1 cup | 1 cup | 1 cup | 1 cup plus 2 tablespoons | 1 cup |

WARM LEMON-RUM SAUCE (RECIPE FOLLOWS), OPTIONAL

1. Position the rack and preheat the oven as indicated for your altitude in the chart above. Prepare the pan as directed.

2. In a medium bowl, whisk together the flour, baking powder (if using), baking soda, salt, and spices.

3. In the large bowl of an electric mixer, cream together the butter and sugar until well blended. Scrape down the bowl and beater. Beat in the egg(s), then beat in the sour cream and grated ginger. Scrape down the bowl again.

4. Combine the molasses with the hot water in a 2-cup measure and stir until dissolved. With the mixer on the lowest speed, alternately add the flour mixture and the molasses liquid. Once the batter is blended together, scrape down the bowl again and beat a few seconds longer. The batter will be quite runny.

5. Scrape the batter into the prepared pan. Bake for the time indicated for your altitude in the chart above, or until the top is springy to the touch and a cake tester inserted in the center comes out clean; there may be a few cracks on the cake top. Cool the cake in the pan on a wire rack for 20 to 30 minutes.

6. Cut the cake into squares and serve from the pan with a broad spatula. If using a tube pan, run a knife around the pan sides and the top of the tube to release the cake, then top with a foil-covered cardboard cake disk or flat plate and invert. Lift off the pan. (The cake is easier to remove from the pan after it has cooled slightly; when hot, it is fragile and tends to stick.) Serve with the warm sauce, if desired.

# Warm Lemon-Rum Sauce
*(recipe is the same at all altitudes)*

**Special Equipment:** Strainer

**Makes** about 1½ cups

1 large egg, lightly beaten
¼ cup water
1 cup granulated sugar
⅛ teaspoon salt
1 teaspoon grated lemon zest
3 tablespoons fresh lemon juice
8 tablespoons (1 stick) unsalted butter, cut into small pieces
3 tablespoons dark rum, or to taste

Whisk together the egg and water in a small pan, then add the sugar, salt, lemon zest, lemon juice, and butter. Place over medium heat and stir to melt the butter and dissolve the sugar, then increase the heat slightly, bring to a boil, whisking, and boil for 1 full minute, whisking. (Altogether, this takes under 5 minutes at sea level to 5,000 feet, slightly longer at higher altitudes.) Strain the sauce, then stir in the rum and serve. The sauce can be made a day in advance, covered, and refrigerated; rewarm before serving.

# Applesauce Cake with Icing Glaze

THIS IS a marvelous holiday cake, with a rich moist crumb and good balance between sweet and spicy. As one of my Colorado friends said, "It tastes just like Christmas smells." When it is baking, your home will be filled with the irresistibly aromatic perfume of cinnamon, nutmeg, cloves, and apples.

For easy entertaining, or for a do-ahead holiday gift, you can freeze the cake for up to two months, double-wrapped and then placed in a heavy-duty plastic bag. Wheat or oat bran can be substituted for the wheat germ, and other chopped dried fruits can be substituted for the cranberries. For decoration, set halved nuts or candied fruits on the glazed cake top.

---

**General High Altitude Notes:** To strengthen the batter at high altitudes, I added one egg and reduced the sugar as the elevation increased. To improve the texture, I increased the liquid by just over one tablespoon. You can use either light brown or white sugar, but avoid dark brown sugar because it makes the batter, and cake crumb, too heavy. To strengthen the batter, I reduced the sugar as altitude increased. I test-baked this recipe in square, loaf, and tube pans. In loaf and square pans at 5,000 feet and above, the dense, wet batter crusted over on top before the center baked through. When I switched to a tube pan, which delivers heat to the center of the batter, it baked through easily, rose well, and had an excellent texture.

**Special Equipment:** A 9-inch (6½-cup) tube pan or Bundt pan; baking parchment, wax paper, or aluminum foil; nut chopper or food processor; foil-covered 10-inch cardboard cake disk or flat plate; wooden skewer or cake tester

**Pan Preparation:** Coat the pan with solid shortening or butter-flavor nonstick vegetable spray. Line with a ring of wax paper, baking parchment, or foil (see pages 30–31 or 34), grease the liner, and dust with flour; tap out the excess flour.

**Makes** one 9-inch tube cake; serves 8 to 10

**High Notes**

*At 3,000 feet and above,* reduce the wheat germ and sugar but add a little more honey or maple syrup, which contributes both flavor and liquid.

*At 10,000 feet,* add flour and reduce the maple syrup slightly.

| Ingredients | Sea Level | 3,000 feet | 5,000 feet | 7,000 feet | 10,000 feet |
|---|---|---|---|---|---|
| Oven rack position, temperature, and baking time | Rack in center; bake at 350°F for 45 to 50 minutes | Rack in center; bake at 375°F for 35 to 40 minutes | Rack in center; bake at 375°F for 30 to 35 minutes | Rack in center; bake at 350°F for 40 to 45 minutes | Rack in center; bake at 375°F for 35 to 40 minutes |
| All-purpose flour | 1½ cups | 1½ cups | 1½ cups | 1½ cups | 1½ cups plus 2 tablespoons |
| Baking soda | 1 teaspoon | 1 teaspoon | 1 teaspoon | 1 teaspoon | 1 teaspoon |
| Salt | ½ teaspoon | ½ teaspoon | ½ teaspoon | ½ teaspoon | ½ teaspoon |
| Ground cinnamon | ½ teaspoon | ½ teaspoon | ½ teaspoon | ½ teaspoon | ½ teaspoon |
| Ground nutmeg | ½ teaspoon | ½ teaspoon | ½ teaspoon | ½ teaspoon | ½ teaspoon |
| Ground allspice or cardamom | ½ teaspoon | ½ teaspoon | ½ teaspoon | ½ teaspoon | ½ teaspoon |
| Ground cloves | ¼ teaspoon | ¼ teaspoon | ¼ teaspoon | ¼ teaspoon | ¼ teaspoon |
| Wheat germ, preferably toasted | ¼ cup | 3 tablespoons | 3 tablespoons | 3 tablespoons | 2 tablespoons |
| Golden raisins, packed | ½ cup (3 ounces) | ½ cup (3 ounces) | ½ cup (3 ounces) | ½ cup (3 ounces) | ½ cup (3 ounces) |
| Fresh cranberries, coarsely chopped, or dried cranberries or dark raisins | ½ cup | ½ cup | ½ cup | ½ cup | ½ cup |
| Finely chopped walnuts | 1 cup (4 ounces) | 1 cup (4 ounces) | 1 cup (4 ounces) | 1 cup (4 ounces) | 1 cup (4 ounces) |
| Unsalted butter, at room temperature | 8 tablespoons (1 stick) | 8 tablespoons (1 stick) | 8 tablespoons (1 stick) | 8 tablespoon (1 stick) | 8 tablespoons (1 stick) |
| Light brown sugar, packed, or granulated sugar | 1 cup | 1 cup minus 2 tablespoons | 1 cup minus 2 tablespoons | ¾ cup | ¾ cup |

(continued)

| Ingredients | Sea Level | 3,000 feet | 5,000 feet | 7,000 feet | 10,000 feet |
|---|---|---|---|---|---|
| **Honey or pure maple syrup** | 2 tablespoons | 3 tablespoons | 3 tablespoons | 3 tablespoons | 2 tablespoons |
| **Large egg(s), at room temperature** | 1 | 2 | 2 | 2 | 2 |
| **Apple juice or sweet cider** | ¼ cup | ¼ cup plus 1 tablespoon | ⅓ cup | ⅓ cup | ⅓ cup |
| **Thick applesauce, preferably unsweetened** | 1 cup | 1 cup | 1 cup | 1 cup | 1 cup |
| **GLAZE** | | | | | |
| **Sifted confectioners' sugar** | 1⅓ cups, or as needed | 1⅓ cups, or as needed | 1⅓ cups, or as needed | 1⅓ cups, or as needed | 1⅓ cups, or as needed |
| **Milk or water** | 2 to 3 tablespoons | 2 to 3 tablespoons | 2 to 3 tablespoons | 2 to 3 tablespoons | 2 to 3 tablespoons |
| **Vanilla extract** | ¼ teaspoon | ¼ teaspoon | ¼ teaspoon | ¼ teaspoon | ¼ teaspoon |

**GARNISH (OPTIONAL): NUT HALVES, DRIED CRANBERRIES, OR CANDIED FRUITS**

**1.** Position the rack and preheat the oven as indicated for your altitude in the chart above. Prepare the pan as directed.

**2.** In a medium bowl, whisk together the flour, baking soda, salt, spices, and wheat germ. In a second medium bowl, toss together the raisins, cranberries, and nuts with about 2 tablespoons of the flour mixture. Set both bowls aside.

**3.** In the large bowl of an electric mixer, cream together the butter and sugar until well blended and pasty. Scrape down the bowl and beater. Beat in the honey or maple syrup, egg(s), apple juice, and applesauce. Scrape down the bowl and beater again. The batter will look curdled, but that's okay. Little by little, beat in the flour mixture

until combined. Stir in the raisin mixture.

**4.** Scoop the batter into the prepared pan. Bake for the time indicated for your altitude in the chart above, or until the top feels springy to the touch and shows some cracks, and a cake tester inserted in the center comes out moist but clean. Cool the cake in its pan on a wire rack for 10 to 15 minutes.

**5.** Top the cake with a foil-covered cardboard cake disk or flat plate and invert. Lift off the pan and peel off the paper, if you used it. Leave the cake upside down or invert it once more, and cool completely before glazing.

**6.** To make the glaze, beat together all the ingredients (start with 2 tablespoons milk or water) in a small bowl until the glaze slowly drips from a spoon (it should be very slightly runny, neither thick nor liquid); adjust the consistency if necessary by adding a little more sifted sugar or liquid. Drizzle the glaze over the top of the cake (it should be thick enough to be visible). Press a few nut halves, dried cranberries, or candied fruits into the glaze, if desired. The glaze will harden as it dries; wrap the cake for storing after the glaze hardens.

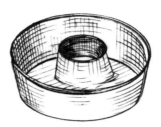

# Hot Springs Honey Cake

RADITIONALLY BAKED in celebration of Rosh Hashanah, the Jewish New Year, honey cake symbolizes the wish for a sweet year. And every year, a few irreverent voices declare that it makes a better symbol than a dessert. In fact, the whispered secret about honey cake is that it is baked but not beloved. Why? In my experience it is because most are dry, dense, rubbery, and overly sweet. When no one is looking, the heavy, dark loaves are quietly consigned to that special limbo reserved for holiday fruitcakes. This recipe, however, will change your mind. It is a honey of a cake, with a lighter, moister crumb than my Grandma used to make, and its flavor is not too sweet because the honey is balanced by coffee and spices. Don't be surprised if you want a second slice. The cake freezes well, so you can make it in advance, and it keeps for up to a week at room temperature if wrapped airtight and stored in an airtight (nosh-proof) container.

The technique for this recipe was streamlined by my Santa Fe assistant, Stacy Pearl, who was determined to make this one of the easiest, best, and quickest cakes in the book because it was so often requested by her catering customers. Although I didn't know it at the time, I was probably sitting next to one of those customers a few years ago when attending the morning Rosh Hashanah service of Santa Fe's Congregation Beit Tikva. In the few minutes before the service began, my elegantly garbed neighbor

leaned over to introduce herself. Remarking that I was obviously new and not a member, she asked my name, my astrological sign, and my occupation (in one breath—a fairly typical quick study in that town). When she learned she was sitting next to a Taurus writing a high altitude cookbook, her face brightened, then fell. "Great idea . . . but it won't be for us, right?" she said. "Us?" I replied. "I've lived here at 7,000 feet for twenty-five years and never found a single high altitude recipe for Jewish baking," she answered. "Watch for *Pie in the Sky*, coming soon to your neighborhood sisterhood. . . ." This recipe is one of many included in this book as my answer to her.

—✦—

**General High Altitude Notes:** When you look at the ingredients chart, you will see that from sea level to about 9,000 feet there are very few altitude adjustments other than the expected reduction in leavening as altitude increases. But once I hit the range of 9,000 feet, dramatic changes occurred, getting even worse at 10,000 feet. During my tests at that elevation, the wet, dense batter would not set in the loaf pan before the top crusted over no matter what temperature I used, even if I tented it with foil to protect the top from heat. For my first five attempts, I tried various combinations and reductions of baking powder and baking soda, strengthened the structure by adding flour and cutting back on the sweeteners (sugar as well as honey), and added another egg, then two. I could get the cake to rise in the oven, but every time, it sank as it cooled, leaving a neat-but-strange sarcophagus-like shape (uncooked batter, it turned out) sinking down in the middle. At last, I realized that I was just not getting enough heat to the center of the batter. For the sixth test, I used a tube pan to bring the heat into the middle, and the rise and texture were perfect.

**Special Equipment:** At sea level to 7,000 feet, use a 9 × 5 × 3-inch loaf pan; at 9,000 feet and above, a 9-inch (6½-cup) plain tube pan; baking parchment or wax paper; wooden skewer or cake tester; aluminum foil if needed.

**Pan Preparation:** Coat the pan with butter-flavor nonstick vegetable spray or solid shortening, line the loaf or tube pan with baking parchment or wax paper (see page 30 or 33), grease the paper, and dust with flour; tap out the excess flour.

**Makes** 1 loaf cake; serves 8; or one 9-inch tube cake; serves 8 to 10

**High Notes**

At **3,000 feet and above,** check the cake after the first 20 minutes of baking time; if the top has begun to brown too much, loosely cover with a piece of aluminum foil, shiny side down.

At **10,000 feet,** the ingredients need major adjustments and most important, the cake must be baked in a tube pan, which delivers direct heat to the center of the batter and therefore takes less time to bake. To strengthen the batter, add 2 eggs and a little flour, but reduce the sugar, honey, and leavening.

| Ingredients | Sea Level | 3,000 feet | 5,000 feet | 7,000 feet | 10,000 feet |
|---|---|---|---|---|---|
| **Oven rack position, temperature, and baking time** | Rack in center; bake at 350°F for 60 to 64 minutes | Rack in center; bake at 350°F for 53 to 60 minutes | Rack in center; bake at 350°F for 55 to 60 minutes | Rack in lower third of oven; bake at 350°F for 50 to 53 minutes | Rack in center; bake at 350°F for 35 to 40 minutes |
| **Instant espresso powder or regular instant coffee powder** | 1 tablespoon instant espresso or 1 tablespoon plus 1 teaspoon regular instant coffee powder | 1 tablespoon instant espresso or 1 tablespoon plus 1 teaspoon regular instant coffee powder | 1 tablespoon instant espresso or 1 tablespoon plus 1 teaspoon regular instant coffee powder | 1 tablespoon instant espresso or 1 tablespoon plus 1 teaspoon regular instant coffee powder | 1 tablespoon instant espresso or 1 tablespoon plus 1 teaspoon regular instant coffee powder |
| **Very hot water** | ¾ cup | ¾ cup | ¾ cup | ¾ cup | ¾ cup |
| **Honey** | 1 cup | 1 cup | 1 cup | 1 cup | ¾ cup |
| **Granulated sugar** | 1 cup | 1 cup | 1 cup | 1 cup | 1 cup minus 2 tablespoons |
| **Large eggs, at room temperature** | 3 | 3 | 3 | 3 | 5 |
| **Canola or light olive oil** | ¾ cup | ¾ cup | ¾ cup | ¾ cup | ½ cup plus 2 tablespoons |
| **All-purpose flour** | 2½ cups | 2½ cups | 2½ cups | 2½ cups | 2½ cups plus 3 tablespoons |
| **Baking powder** | 2 teaspoons | 2 teaspoons | 1¾ teaspoons | 1½ teaspoons | ½ teaspoon |
| **Baking soda** | ¼ teaspoon | ⅛ teaspoon | ⅛ teaspoon | ¼ teaspoon | ⅛ teaspoon |
| **Salt** | ½ teaspoon | ½ teaspoon | ½ teaspoon | ½ teaspoon | ½ teaspoon |
| **Ground cinnamon** | 2 teaspoons | 2 teaspoons | 2 teaspoons | 2 teaspoons | 2 teaspoons |
| **Ground nutmeg** | ½ teaspoon | ½ teaspoon | ½ teaspoon | ½ teaspoon | ½ teaspoon |
| **Ground ginger** | ¼ teaspoon | ¼ teaspoon | ¼ teaspoon | ¼ teaspoon | ¼ teaspoon |
| **Ground cloves** | ¼ teaspoon | ¼ teaspoon | ¼ teaspoon | ¼ teaspoon | ¼ teaspoon |

1. Position the rack and preheat the oven as indicated for your altitude in the chart above. Prepare the pan as directed.

2. In a medium bowl, dissolve the espresso or coffee powder in the hot water. Whisk in the honey until dissolved. Whisk in the sugar and eggs, then the oil.

3. In a large bowl, whisk together the flour, baking powder, baking soda, salt, and spices. Make a well in the center of the dry ingredients and pour in the honey mixture. Beat the batter to blend well until smooth and slightly runny.

4. Scrape the batter into the prepared pan. Bake for the time indicated for your altitude in the chart above, or until the top is springy to the touch and nicely risen, perhaps with a crack in the center, and a cake tester inserted in the middle comes out clean. Check cake color during bake; if it seems to be getting too brown, cover it loosely with a piece of aluminum foil for the last 10 minutes or so. Cool the cake in the pan on a wire rack for at least 30 minutes.

5. Slide a knife around the pan sides, and the top of the tube, if using, to release the cake. Tip out the cake onto a rack, peel off the parchment, and turn the cake right side up on the rack to cool completely.

# Apricot Upside-Down Cake with Cardamom-Honey Sauce

THIS BEAUTIFUL old-fashioned dessert makes a dramatic presentation, and it tastes even better than it looks. It is impossible to resist the appeal of the sweet-tart apricots, honey-spiced cake, crunchy nuts, and buttery caramel sauce. Add a dollop of whipped cream or vanilla ice cream, and you have a celestial treat. This cake is not only great to eat, but fun for bakers of any age, who always gets a kick out of the upside-down magic.

There are three easy steps to making an upside-down cake: First the caramel sauce–fruit-nut topping is prepared on top of the stove, then the batter is added, and it is all baked together. When the cake is inverted onto a platter, the caramel sauce becomes the cake topping.

Cardamom is an aromatic spice available as small dry seed pods or ground into powder, sold in gourmet shops and most supermarkets. If you have pods (which give a more pungent flavor), grind them in a spice or (clean) coffee mill. If you can't get cardamom, use a little more nutmeg, cinnamon, and ginger, to give the cake a strong flavor. If you want a strong caramel flavor, use light (not dark) brown sugar in the topping sauce; white sugar gives a weaker flavor. If you don't want to use nuts, substitute raspberries or blueberries (fresh or frozen) or cranberries.

**Note:** To measure honey easily, oil the cup first.

**General High Altitude Notes:** Because this cake has liquefied syrup and fruit beneath the cake batter, it presents special problems when baking at 3,000 feet and above: the top risks crusting over before the wet batter is baked through. The solution is to lower the oven temperature, increase the baking time, and cover the cake loosely with a piece of foil for the last 10 minutes of baking to avoid overbrowning.

**Special Equipment:** A 9 × 1½- or 2-inch round cake pan or nonreactive 9- to 10-inch ovenproof skillet; aluminum foil; 12-inch flat serving platter with a lip; wooden skewer or cake tester

**Makes** one 9-inch cake; serves 8 to 10

**High Notes**

*At 3,000 feet and above,* omit the baking soda to keep the batter more acidic, but (at 3,000 feet) add a pinch more baking powder. Replace the milk with buttermilk. To prevent overbrowning, loosely cover the cake with a piece of foil (shiny side down) for the last 10 minutes of baking.

*At 5,000 feet and above,* reduce oven temperature and bake longer.

*At 10,000 feet and above,* add a little flour and reduce the baking powder and sugar.

| Ingredients | Sea Level | 3,000 feet | 5,000 feet | 7,000 feet | 10,000 feet |
|---|---|---|---|---|---|
| **Oven rack position, temperature, and baking time** | Rack in center; bake at 375°F for 30 to 35 minutes | Rack in center; bake at 375°F for 32 to 35 minutes | Rack in center; bake at 350°F for 38 to 40 minutes | Rack in center; bake at 325°F for 38 to 42 minutes | Rack in center; bake at 325°F for 32 to 37 minutes |
| **TOPPING** | | | | | |
| **Unsalted butter** | ⅓ cup (5⅓ tablespoons) | ⅓ cup (5⅓ tablespoons) | ⅓ cup (5⅓ tablespoons) | ⅓ cup (5⅓ tablespoons) | ⅓ cup (5⅓ tablespoons) |
| **Light brown sugar, packed, or granulated white sugar** | ⅔ cup | ⅔ cup | ⅔ cup | ⅔ cup | ⅔ cup |
| **Fruit juice (orange, apple, or reserved canned apricot syrup)** | 2 tablespoons | 2 tablespoons | 2 tablespoons | 2 tablespoons | 2 tablespoons |
| **Honey** | ¼ cup | ¼ cup | ¼ cup | ¼ cup | ¼ cup |
| **Ground cardamom** | ¼ teaspoon | ¼ teaspoon | ¼ teaspoon | ¼ teaspoon | ¼ teaspoon |
| **Salt** | Pinch | Pinch | Pinch | Pinch | Pinch |

*(continued)*

| Ingredients | Sea Level | 3,000 feet | 5,000 feet | 7,000 feet | 10,000 feet |
|---|---|---|---|---|---|
| **7 or 8 ripe apricots (about 18 ounces), halved and pitted, or two (15¼-ounce) cans unpeeled apricots in syrup** | 14 to 16 apricot halves | 14 to 16 apricot halves | 14 to 16 apricot halves | 14 to 16 apricot halves | 14 to 16 apricot halves |
| **Pecan or walnut halves** | ½ cup (2 ounces) | ½ cup (2 ounces) | ½ cup (2 ounces) | ½ cup (2 ounces) | ½ cup (2 ounces) |
| CAKE | | | | | |
| **Unsalted butter, melted and cooled** | ⅓ cup (5⅓ tablespoons) | ⅓ cup (5⅓ tablespoons) | ⅓ cup (5⅓ tablespoons) | ⅓ cup (5⅓ tablespoons) | ⅓ cup (5⅓ tablespoons) |
| **Granulated sugar** | ½ cup | ½ cup | ½ cup | ½ cup | ⅓ cup |
| **Honey** | ¼ cup | ¼ cup | ¼ cup | ¼ cup | ¼ cup |
| **Large eggs, at room temperature** | 2 | 2 | 2 | 2 | 2 |
| **Vanilla extract** | 1 teaspoon | 1 teaspoon | 1 teaspoon | 1 teaspoon | 1 teaspoon |
| **Whole milk** | ⅓ cup | None | None | None | None |
| **Buttermilk** | None | ⅓ cup | ⅓ cup | ⅓ cup | ⅓ cup |
| **All-purpose flour** | 1½ cups | 1½ cups | 1½ cups | 1½ cups | 1½ cups plus 2 tablespoons |
| **Baking powder** | 1½ teaspoons | 1½ teaspoons plus a pinch | 1½ teaspoons | 1½ teaspoons | 1 teaspoon |
| **Baking soda** | ¼ teaspoon | None | None | None | None |
| **Salt** | ¼ teaspoon | ½ teaspoon | ¼ teaspoon | ¼ teaspoon | ½ teaspoon |
| **Ground cardamom** | 1 teaspoon | 1 teaspoon | 1 teaspoon | 1 teaspoon | 1 teaspoon |
| **Ground ginger** | 1 teaspoon | 1 teaspoon | 1½ teaspoons | 1½ teaspoons | 1½ teaspoons |

*(continued)*

| Ingredients | Sea Level | 3,000 feet | 5,000 feet | 7,000 feet | 10,000 feet |
| --- | --- | --- | --- | --- | --- |
| Ground cinnamon | ½ teaspoon | ½ teaspoon | ½ teaspoon | ½ teaspoon | ½ teaspoon |
| Ground nutmeg | ½ teaspoon | ½ teaspoon | ½ teaspoon | ½ teaspoon | ½ teaspoon |

**1.** Position the rack and preheat the oven as indicated for your altitude in the chart above.

**2.** If using canned apricots, drain them, reserving the juice. Set the apricot halves on paper towels to drain.

**3.** Prepare the topping: Combine the butter and sugar in the cake pan. Set the pan on the stovetop over medium heat and stir until the butter is melted. Slowly stir in the fruit juice, honey, cardamom, and salt and cook, stirring, for another minute or two, until the honey is dissolved and the ingredients are well blended. (This process takes just a few minutes at altitudes up to 5,000 feet, slightly longer at higher elevations.) Remove the pan from the heat, and set it on a heatproof surface.

**4.** Place the halved apricots cut side up in the pan of caramel sauce, arranging them in a random pattern or in neat rings. If using fresh fruit, return the pan to medium heat for a couple of minutes to precook and soften the fruit slightly; remove from the heat. Arrange the pecans or walnuts curved side down in between the apricots.

**5.** Prepare the cake batter: In a large bowl, whisk together the melted butter, sugar, honey, eggs, vanilla, and milk or buttermilk. Set a sifter over the bowl and measure the flour, bak-

ing powder, baking soda (if using), salt, and spices into it. Stir/sift the dry ingredients onto the wet mixture below, then stir well to blend. The batter will be quite thick.

**6.** Spoon the batter over the apricots. The batter will look a little sparse in a 10-inch pan but it will spread out as it bakes; a 9-inch pan will look full but shouldn't overflow. As insurance, place a piece of aluminum foil, shiny side up, on the oven shelf under the pan.

**7.** Bake the cake for about 25 minutes, then loosely cover the top with a piece of foil, shiny side down, and continue baking for the remaining time indicated for your altitude in the chart above, or until the cake top is springy to the touch and a cake tester inserted in the center comes out clean. Cool the cake in its pan on a wire rack for 3 to 4 minutes, until the juices stop bubbling.

**8.** Cover the cake with a serving plate that has a lip to catch the sauce. Slide pot holders under the hot pan, grip the pot holders on the bottom and the plate on top, and invert, with a sharp downward shake. Lift off the pan. Use a fork to reposition any fruit or nut pieces left in the pan. Cool the cake for 4 to 5 minutes, and serve warm.

# Payette Pound Cake with Raspberry Sauce

THIS IS not a true pound cake by weight of ingredients, but it has the right spirit, and a less dense texture. Homey and appealing, it is a big tube cake with a fine-grained, tender crumb and a not-too-sweet taste. Serve it with the sweet-tart raspberry sauce, or, for an unusual presentation, serve lightly toasted wedges topped by a scoop of vanilla ice cream or raspberry sherbet and the sauce.

This recipe was shared with me by Helga Carpenter, a friend of my cousins Stacey and Jim Carson, in Grassy Creek, North Carolina. When I told Helga I was having difficulty finding a reliable high altitude pound cake, she gave me her favorite recipe to try. As she said, "It's a big cake that takes a bit of doing," but it is well worth the trouble because it serves a crowd and is always a success. Helga flavors her cake with lemon and brandy and serves it with homegrown raspberries and the raspberry sauce. Once I'd tested her recipe at different altitudes, I decided it was definitely a keeper.

An enthusiastic home baker and public school teacher, Helga, and her husband, Jack, are well known in the Greensboro, North Carolina, area because they are the second generation of his family to cultivate the divinely flavorful purple Carpenter Heirloom Raspberries. Jack's organic raspberry operation is located on a half-acre of intensely planted land carved out of four hundred acres under continuous cultivation by his family since the Civil War. At the height of the one-month-long high season, Jack has just two helpers plus Helga and their immediate family. Their relatively small but highly prized harvest is eagerly sought by some twenty-five of the finest restaurants—such as Fabian's and Marisol—in the Winston-Salem and Greensboro area.

Celestial Challah

(page 92)

Chocolate Buttermilk
Cake with Bittersweet
Chocolate Icing

(page 117)

Porterfield
Pumpkin Bundt
with Snow White
Glaze (page 154)

Alpine Angel Cake

(page 166)

Taos Lemon
Sponge Roll with
Light Lemon Curd
Filling (page 194)

Old-Fashioned Sugar Cookies (page 221), Black-and-White Chocolate Chip Cookies (page 236), Mexican Wedding Cookies (page 239), Double Chocolate–Pecan Biscotti (page 245), Lavender-Honey-Rosemary Biscotti (page 248), Independence Pass Brownies (page 250), Cinnamon-Nut Rugelach (page 253)

Pike's Peak Apple
Pie with Flaky
Pastry (page 265)

Mile-High Lemon
Meringue Pie

(page 296)

**General High Altitude Notes:** From sea level to 5,000 feet, my favorite pound cake recipe was completely reliable, but at altitudes of 7,000 feet and above, I ran into many problems. Pound cakes have a high proportion of butter and sugar compared to other types of cake, and the rich formula caused trouble. I tried different recipes and many adjustments, reducing the sugar and/or fat, changing flour quantities and leavening proportions, but the cakes continued to collapse, sink in the center, or have a coarse or heavy crumb; not one worked perfectly at each elevation. Cakes baked in loaf pans crusted over on top while the inner batter remained gooey and wet no matter how long it was baked, and tube pans did not solve all problems.

In frustration, I had decided to omit pound cake from this book until I tried Helga's recipe. It is leavened with both baking powder and whipped egg whites and includes sour cream for moisture, acidity, and tenderness. I took the cake to every elevation and it passed all trials with flying colors, though I have tinkered slightly with the original formula, making changes for various altitudes. The trick to success is to be careful when whipping the whites—from sea level to about 2,500 feet, you can whip them just to stiff peaks, but above that, you should stop whipping as soon as the whites form soft peaks. The recipe is large and you will need a 5-quart or larger mixing bowl to blend it all together. Bake this pound cake in a tube pan, not a loaf, and to be sure the cake bakes through before the top overbrowns, loosely cover the cake top with a piece of foil after the first 30 minutes of baking.

**Special Equipment:** A 10-inch (12- to 16-cup) plain tube pan or angel food pan (not a fancy Bundt); baking parchment or wax paper (at 7,000 feet or above); sifter; 5-quart or larger bowl; 2 foil-covered 10-inch cardboard cake disks or flat plates; long-handled flexible spatula (optional); aluminum foil

**Pan Preparation:** Coat the pan with butter-flavor nonstick vegetable spray or solid shortening. At 7,000 feet and above, line the greased pan with a ring of baking parchment or wax paper (see pages 30–31), grease the paper, and dust with flour; tap out the excess flour.

**Makes** one 10-inch tube cake; serves 14 to 16

### High Notes

*At 5,000 feet and above,* add one egg. As the elevation increases, add more flour, and reduce the sugar.

*At 7,000 feet and above,* line the baking pan with parchment to prevent sticking. Preheat the oven to 25 degrees above the baking temperature, then reduce it as soon as the cake is put in the oven. Increase the cream of tartar.

| Ingredients | Sea Level | 3,000 feet | 5,000 feet | 7,000 feet | 10,000 feet |
|---|---|---|---|---|---|
| **Oven rack position, temperature, and baking time** | Rack in center; bake at 375°F for 50 to 52 minutes | Rack in lower third of oven; bake at 375°F for 55 to 60 minutes | Rack in lower third of oven; bake at 375°F for 45 to 50 minutes | Rack in lower third of oven; *preheat* oven to 375°F; *bake* at 350°F for 45 to 55 minutes | Rack in lower third of oven; *preheat* oven to 375°F; *bake* at 350°F for 55 to 60 minutes |
| **Sifted all-purpose flour** | 3 cups | 3 cups | 3 cups plus 1 tablespoon | 3 cups plus 2 tablespoons | 3¼ cups |
| **Baking powder** | 1½ teaspoons | 1½ teaspoons | 1½ teaspoons | 1¼ teaspoons | 1 teaspoon |
| **Large eggs, separated, at room temperature** | 8 | 8 | 9 | 9 | 9, *plus* 2 yolks |
| **Cream of tartar** | ½ teaspoon | ½ teaspoon | ½ teaspoon | ¾ teaspoon | 1 teaspoon |
| **Salt** | ¾ teaspoon | ¾ teaspoon | ¾ teaspoon | ¾ teaspoon | ¾ teaspoon |
| **Granulated sugar, divided** | ¾ cup plus 2 cups | ¾ cup plus 2 cups | ¾ cup plus 1¾ cups | ¾ cup plus 1½ cups | 1 cup plus 1¼ cups |
| **Unsalted butter, at room temperature** | ¾ pound (3 sticks) | ¾ pound (3 sticks) | ¾ pound (3 sticks) | ¾ pound (3 sticks) | ¾ pound (3 sticks) |
| **Sour cream** | 1 cup | 1 cup | 1 cup | 1 cup | 1 cup |
| **Vanilla extract** | 1 tablespoon | 1 tablespoon | 1 tablespoon | 1 tablespoon | 1 tablespoon |
| **Lemon or almond extract (or 1 teaspoon of each)** | 2 teaspoons | 2 teaspoons | 2 teaspoons | 2 teaspoons | 2 teaspoons |
| **Brandy or rum** | 3 tablespoons | 3 tablespoons | 3 tablespoons | 3 tablespoons | 3 tablespoons |

RASPBERRY SAUCE (RECIPE FOLLOWS)

**1.** Position the rack and preheat the oven as indicated for your altitude in the chart above. Prepare the pan as directed.

**2.** In a medium bowl, whisk together the sifted flour and baking powder. Set aside.

**3.** Place the egg whites in the large bowl of an electric mixer and check the whites to make sure they no longer feel cold. Add the cream of tartar and salt, and whip until foamy. Gradually whip in ¾ cup of the sugar (1 cup at 10,000 feet), increasing the mixer speed to high, but watch closely. As soon as you see beater tracks on top of the whites, stop the machine, lift the beater, and check the stiffness of the foam. At sea level, you want whites that just begin to stand up in stiff peaks, but at 2,500 feet and above, you want soft, droopy peaks (see page 150). If the whites look too soft, continue beating for just a few more seconds and check again; do not overbeat. The whites should be glossy and smooth.

Remove the bowl of whites from the mixer stand and set aside. Or, if you don't have another mixer bowl, scrape the whites out into another bowl so you can reuse the mixer bowl (without washing it).

**4.** Combine the butter and the remaining sugar in the mixer bowl and cream together until well blended. Scrape down the bowl and beater. Beat in the sour cream, vanilla, lemon and/or almond extract, and brandy or rum. Beat in the yolks two at a time. Scrape down the bowl and beaters and whip a few seconds longer. Don't worry if the batter looks curdled—the flour will smooth it out.

You'll need a 5-quart or larger bowl for the next step for ease in folding together the large quantity of batter. If the batter is in a smaller bowl, scoop it out into a larger one.

**5.** Fold or whisk about 2 cups of the whipped whites into the batter to lighten and soften it. Then, in 5 or 6 additions, alternately fold in the flour mixture and the remaining whites; it helps to use a long-handled spatula for this job. Fold until you no longer see streaks of flour; the mixture will quickly smooth out into a thick, creamy batter.

**6.** Scoop the batter into the prepared tube pan. Without touching the pan sides, draw the spatula or a knife once through the batter to break up any large air pockets, then smooth the top. Bake for the time indicated for your altitude in the chart above, but, after the first 30 minutes (set a timer) cover the cake loosely with a piece of aluminum foil, shiny side down, so the top doesn't overbrown. Then continue

baking until the top is golden brown, slightly cracked, and springy to the touch, and a cake tester inserted in the center comes out clean or with just a couple of crumbs.

**7.** Cool the cake in its pan on a wire rack for 45 to 60 minutes, or until the pan bottom feels comfortable to the touch.

**8.** Slide a knife between the cake and the sides of the pan to release it. Top the cake with the foil-covered cardboard cake disk or a flat plate, invert, and remove the pan. Peel off the paper, top with another plate or disk, and invert again. Cool completely. Pound cake will cut most easily and taste even better after the flavors mellow, the day after it is baked (if you can wait).

**9.** Serve with the raspberry sauce.

# Raspberry (or Blueberry-Raspberry) Sauce
*(recipe is the same at all altitudes)*

This tangy, ruby-hued sauce is just the right flavor to complement a slice of pound cake. You can use half blueberries, or a blend of other berries, or, out of season, use frozen berries. The sauce can be made a day or two in advance, covered, and refrigerated.

**Special Equipment:** Strainer

**Makes** 1 cup plus 2 tablespoons strained; 1½ cups with some seeds left in

3 cups fresh raspberries, picked over, and rinsed, or one 12-ounce bag frozen unsweetened berries
3 tablespoons granulated sugar, or to taste
3 tablespoons water or orange juice
1 tablespoon cornstarch
3 tablespoons raspberry liqueur (Chambord), eau-de-vie (framboise), or other fruit liqueur, optional

In a nonreactive saucepan, combine the berries, sugar, and 2 tablespoons of the water or juice. Place over medium heat and cook, stirring and mashing the berries with the back of a large spoon, until the berries release their juice and the sugar dissolves. If you want to remove the seeds, strain the mixture through a sieve into a bowl, pressing hard on the berries to be sure you get all the liquid. Return the puree to the saucepan, and discard some or all the seeds.

In a small cup, dissolve the cornstarch in the remaining 1 tablespoon water or juice. Stir it into the berry puree and bring to a boil over medium-high heat, stirring constantly. Boil for 45 to 60 seconds at sea level, 2 to 3 minutes, or longer, at higher altitudes, until the sauce is thickened and no longer looks cloudy. Remove from the heat, add the liqueur, if desired, and adjust the sugar to taste. Cool completely.

*Whipped Egg Whites*

*droopy peaks*

*stiff peaks*

# Gold Rush Triple Ginger Bundt Cake with Ginger-Honey Icing Glaze

Make no mistake, this is *not* gingerbread. A big cake with a buttery, tender crumb, it packs surprising flavors that bite the tongue and excite the palate. The tongue tingling comes from a triple play of grated fresh ginger, chopped candied ginger, and powdered ginger (¼ cup, one whole little jar), plus other aromatic spices and a touch of cayenne pepper. Top it with the Ginger-Honey Icing Glaze, and serve it with lemon sorbet or vanilla ice cream.

---

**General High Altitude Notes:** As altitude increases, you need to strengthen the batter structure with another egg, more flour, and less sugar. Add liquid to compensate for evaporation and dry atmosphere. Since flavors seem blander as elevation increases, add spices to keep up the sharp taste.

**Special Equipment:** A 9½- to 10-inch (10- to 12-cup) Bundt or plain tube pan; baking parchment, wax paper, or aluminum foil; sifter; foil-covered 10-inch cardboard cake disk (optional) or flat plate; wooden skewer or cake tester

**Pan Preparation:** Generously coat the pan with butter-flavor nonstick vegetable spray or solid shortening, dust with flour, and tap out the excess flour. At 5,000 feet and above, line the greased pan with a ring of baking parchment or wax paper (see pages 30–31), grease the paper and dust with flour; tap out the excess flour.

**Makes** one 10-inch Bundt or tube cake; serves 12 to 14

**High Notes**

*At 3,000 feet and above,* bake in the lower third of the oven. Add 1 egg; replace the whole milk with buttermilk up to 10,000 feet.

*At 5,000 feet and above,* the cake tends to stick to the pan, so baking pan needs a paper or foil liner.

*At 10,000 feet,* cut back the butter. Use whole milk rather than buttermilk.

| Ingredients | Sea Level | 3,000 feet | 5,000 feet | 7,000 feet | 10,000 feet |
|---|---|---|---|---|---|
| **Oven rack position, temperature, and baking time** | Rack in center; bake at 375°F for 45 to 52 minutes | Rack in lower third of oven; bake at 375°F for 50 to 55 minutes | Rack in lower third of oven; bake at 375°F for 45 to 50 minutes | Rack in lower third of oven; bake at 375°F for 50 to 52 minutes | Rack in lower third of oven; bake at 375°F for 42 to 45 minutes |

*(continued)*

| Ingredients | Sea Level | 3,000 feet | 5,000 feet | 7,000 feet | 10,000 feet |
|---|---|---|---|---|---|
| **Fresh ginger, peeled** | Piece about 1 × 3 inches | Piece about 1 × 3 inches | Piece about 1 × 3 inches | Piece about 1 × 3 inches | Piece about 1 × 3 inches |
| **Candied (crystallized) ginger, finely chopped** | 3½ ounces (⅔ cup chopped) | 3½ ounces (⅔ cup chopped) | 3½ ounces (⅔ cup chopped) | 3½ ounces (⅔ cup chopped) | 3½ ounces (⅔ cup chopped) |
| **Grated lemon zest (1 to 2 lemons)** | 2 tablespoons | 2 tablespoons | 2 tablespoons | 2 tablespoons | 2 tablespoons |
| **Sifted all-purpose flour** | 3 cups | 3 cups plus 1 tablespoon | 3 cups plus 2 tablespoons | 3 cups plus 3 tablespoons | 3 cups plus 3 tablespoons |
| **Baking powder** | 1 tablespoon | 2¾ teaspoons | 2¼ teaspoons | 2 teaspoons | 1½ teaspoons |
| **Salt** | ½ teaspoon | ½ teaspoon | ¾ teaspoon | ¾ teaspoon | ¾ teaspoon |
| **Ground cinnamon** | 1 teaspoon | 1 teaspoon | 1 teaspoon | 1 teaspoon | 2 teaspoons |
| **Ground nutmeg** | ½ teaspoon | ½ teaspoon | ½ teaspoon | ½ teaspoon | 1 teaspoon |
| **Ground ginger** | ¼ cup | ¼ cup | ¼ cup | ¼ cup | ¼ cup |
| **Ground cloves** | ⅛ teaspoon | ⅛ teaspoon | ⅛ teaspoon | ⅛ teaspoon | ⅛ teaspoon |
| **Cayenne pepper** | ⅛ teaspoon, or to taste | ⅛ teaspoon, or to taste | ⅛ teaspoon, or to taste | ⅛ teaspoon, or to taste | ⅛ teaspoon, or to taste |
| **Unsalted butter, at room temperature** | ½ pound (2 sticks) | ½ pound (2 sticks) | ½ pound (2 sticks) | ½ pound (2 sticks) | 12 tablespoons (1½ sticks) |
| **Granulated sugar** | 2 cups | 2 cups | 2 cups minus 3 tablespoons | 2 cups minus 3 tablespoons | 1¾ cups |
| **Large eggs, at room temperature** | 4 | 5 | 5 | 5 | 5 |
| **Honey** | ¼ cup | ¼ cup | ⅓ cup | ⅓ cup | 3 tablespoons |
| **Vanilla extract** | 1 teaspoon | 1 teaspoon | 1 teaspoon | 1 teaspoon | 1 teaspoon |
| **Whole milk** | 1 cup | None | None | None | 1 cup plus 1 tablespoon |
| **Buttermilk** | None | 1 cup | 1 cup plus 2 tablespoons | 1¼ cups | None |

GINGER-HONEY ICING GLAZE (RECIPE FOLLOWS)

1. Position the rack and preheat the oven as indicated for your altitude in the chart above. Prepare the pan as directed.

2. Using the small holes of a box or flat metal or porcelain grater, or a Microplane, grate the fresh ginger. You need 3 tablespoons (or more, if you are a ginger fanatic). Lacking a grater, mince the ginger very fine with a knife. Put the grated ginger in a small bowl. Reserve 2 tablespoons of the chopped *candied* ginger for the garnish, and add the rest to the grated ginger, along with the lemon zest.

3. In a medium bowl, whisk together the sifted flour, baking powder, salt, and spices; if you like extra-hot flavors, add a double pinch of cayenne. Toss about 2 tablespoons of the flour mixture with the ginger–lemon zest to separate and coat the pieces. Set aside.

4. In the large bowl of an electric mixer, cream together the butter and sugar until well blended. Scrape down the bowl and beater. Beat in the eggs a couple at a time, then the honey and vanilla, beating well to blend. Scrape down the bowl again, then mix in the ginger–lemon zest mixture.

5. With the mixer on the lowest speed, gradually beat in the dry ingredients alternately with the milk or buttermilk. Once the batter is blended together, increase the speed and whip for about a minute, until smooth and creamy.

6. Scoop the batter into the prepared pan and smooth the top. Bake for the time indicated for your altitude in the chart above, or until the cake is golden brown, springy to the touch, and slightly cracked on top, and a cake tester inserted in the center comes out moist but clean. Cool the cake in its pan on a rack for 20 to 25 minutes.

7. Slide a knife between the cake and the pan sides to loosen it. Top the cake with another rack, a foil-covered cake disk, or a flat plate, and invert. Lift off the pan. Peel off the paper or foil, if used, and cool the cake completely.

8. Spread the glaze over the top of the cake and let it drip down the sides. While the glaze is still soft, sprinkle the top with the reserved chopped candied ginger.

## Ginger-Honey Icing Glaze
*(recipe is the same at all altitudes)*

**Makes** ½ cup, enough to coat one 10-inch Bundt or tube cake

1⅓ cups sifted confectioners' sugar
1¼ teaspoons ground ginger
¼ teaspoon ground cinnamon
2 tablespoons honey
3 tablespoons milk, or as needed
Pinch of salt
½ teaspoon fresh lemon juice

In a small bowl, whisk together all the ingredients until smooth and creamy. Add a drop more milk if necessary. Use the glaze as soon as it is made.

# Porterfield Pumpkin Bundt with Snow White Glaze

THIS IS the cake you need for every fall holiday—it is a big, attractive Bundt, with a moist crumb and a lightly spiced, not-too-sweet flavor. The pumpkin and oil keep the cake fresh even in high, dry mountain air. Topped with a white icing glaze and walnuts, it makes a gala presentation, and at every altitude it won high praise from taste-testers of all ages.

—⁓—

**General High Altitude Notes:** To strengthen the batter for the best rise at high altitudes, add one egg, reduce the sugar, and increase the flour. For more flavor, increase the salt and some of the spices. At sea level, the leavening is a combination of baking powder and baking soda; at 3,000 feet and above, I achieved a better rise with baking soda alone, decreasing it as the elevation increased. At sea level, I used orange juice for the liquid, but at 3,000 feet and above, I substituted buttermilk, in a slightly greater quantity, because it gives richer results while maintaining the needed acidity. Note that baking temperatures and times vary with the altitude.

**Special Equipment:** A 9½- to 10-inch (10- to 12-cup) Bundt or plain tube pan; baking parchment, wax paper, or aluminum foil; sifter; foil-covered 10-inch cardboard cake disk or flat plate; wooden skewer or cake tester

**Pan Preparation:** Generously coat the pan with butter-flavor nonstick vegetable spray or solid shortening, dust with flour, and tap out the excess flour. At 5,000 feet and above, line the greased pan with a ring of baking parchment, wax paper, or foil (see pages 31 or 34), then grease and flour it; tap out excess flour.

**Makes** one 10-inch Bundt or tube cake; serves 10 to 14

### High Notes
- *At 3,000 feet and above,* reduce the sugar and add one egg and a little flour. Replace the baking powder and soda combination with baking soda alone, and decrease the quantity as the elevation increases.
- *At 10,000 feet,* increase the spices for more flavor and reduce the oil.

| Ingredients | Sea Level | 3,000 feet | 5,000 feet | 7,000 feet | 10,000 feet |
|---|---|---|---|---|---|
| **Oven rack position, temperature, and baking time** | Rack in lower third of oven; bake at 350°F for 65 to 70 minutes | Rack in lower third of oven; bake at 375°F for 55 to 57 minutes | Rack in lower third of oven; bake at 375°F for 50 to 55 minutes | Rack in lower third of oven; bake at 375°F for 65 to 70 minutes | Rack in lower third of oven; bake at 375°F for 60 to 63 minutes |
| **Sifted all-purpose flour** | 3⅓ cups | 3⅓ cups plus 1 tablespoon | 3⅓ cups plus 2 tablespoons | 3½ cups | 3½ cups plus 1 tablespoon |
| **Baking powder** | 1½ teaspoons | None | None | None | None |
| **Baking soda** | ¼ teaspoon | 2 teaspoons minus ⅛ teaspoon | 1¾ teaspoons | 1½ teaspoons | 1⅛ teaspoons |
| **Salt** | ¾ teaspoon | 1 teaspoon | 1 teaspoon | 1 teaspoon | 1 teaspoon |
| **Ground cinnamon** | 2 teaspoons | 1½ teaspoons | 1½ teaspoons | 1½ teaspoons | 2½ teaspoons |
| **Ground nutmeg** | 1½ teaspoons | 1 teaspoon | 1 teaspoon | 1 teaspoon | 2 teaspoons |
| **Ground ginger** | ¾ teaspoon | ¾ teaspoon | ¾ teaspoon | ¾ teaspoon | 2 teaspoons |
| **Ground allspice or mace** | ½ teaspoon | ¼ teaspoon | ¼ teaspoon | ¼ teaspoon | 1 teaspoon |
| **Ground cloves** | ⅛ teaspoon | ⅛ teaspoon | ⅛ teaspoon | ⅛ teaspoon | ¼ teaspoon |
| **Granulated sugar** | 1½ cups | 1⅓ cups | 1⅓ cups | 1⅓ cups | 1¼ cups |
| **Dark brown sugar, packed** | 1¼ cups | 1 cup | 1 cup | 1 cup | 1 cup |
| **Canola or light olive oil** | 1 cup | 1 cup | 1 cup | 1 cup | ¾ cup |
| **Large eggs, at room temperature** | 5 | 6 | 6 | 6 | 6 |
| **Canned unsweetened pumpkin** | 2 cups | 2 cups | 2 cups | 2 cups | 2 cups |
| **Orange juice or milk** | ⅔ cup | None | None | None | None |
| **Buttermilk** | None | ¾ cup | 1 cup minus 2 tablespoons | 1 cup | 1 cup minus 2 tablespoons |

*(continued)*

| Ingredients | Sea Level | 3,000 feet | 5,000 feet | 7,000 feet | 10,000 feet |
|---|---|---|---|---|---|
| SNOW WHITE GLAZE (RECIPE FOLLOWS) | | | | | |

**1.** Position the rack and preheat the oven as indicated for your altitude in the chart above. Prepare the pan as directed.

**2.** In a medium bowl, whisk together the sifted flour, baking powder (if using), baking soda, salt, and spices. Set aside.

**3.** Add the granulated sugar to the large bowl of an electric mixer and crumble in the dark brown sugar, breaking up any clumps with your fingers. Add the oil and 2 eggs and beat until blended, then beat in the remaining eggs and the pumpkin. Scrape down the bowl and beater.

**4.** With the mixer on the lowest speed, alternately add the juice or buttermilk and the dry ingredients. When everything is blended, scrape down the bowl, then beat a few seconds longer until the batter is smooth and creamy.

**5.** Scoop the batter into the prepared pan. Bake for the time indicated for your altitude in the chart above, or until the cake has risen, is springy to the touch, and is cracked on top, and a cake tester inserted in the center comes out dry. Cool the cake in its pan on a rack for 20 to 25 minutes.

**6.** Slide a knife around the pan sides and the top of the tube to release the cake. Top the cake with a foil-covered cardboard cake disk or flat plate, invert, and lift off the pan. Peel off

the paper, if you used it. Cool the cake completely.

**7.** Spread the glaze on top of the cake, letting it drip down the sides. While the glaze is still soft, sprinkle on the nuts, if desired. The glaze hardens as it dries.

## Snow White Glaze
*(recipe is the same at all altitudes)*

If you want a vanilla-flavored glaze, add 1 teaspoon vanilla extract; for a maple flavor, add 1/2 teaspoon vanilla and 1/2 teaspoon maple extract.

**Makes** 1/2 cup

  1½ cups sifted confectioners' sugar
  2 tablespoons honey
  Scant pinch of salt
  2 to 3 drops fresh lemon juice
  1/4 teaspoon vanilla extract
  2 to 3 tablespoons milk or cream, or as needed
  Garnish: 1/4 cup chopped walnuts, optional

Whisk together all the ingredients until smooth and creamy. Add a drop more milk if necessary. The glaze should have a soft, just slightly runny (but not liquefied) consistency. Use the glaze as soon as it is prepared, top with nuts.

# Colorado Carrot Cake with Cream Cheese Frosting

THIS NOT-TOO-SWEET classic is everyone's favorite. Purists will want to add the Cream Cheese Frosting, but the cake is so rich that a light topping of powdered sugar is really enough.

I had great fun with this recipe, testing everything about it including its ability to fly. After I had moved into their mountain chalet, my Breckenridge, Colorado, hosts, Sandy and Skip Porterfield, returned to their Florida home. When I learned that Sandy was throwing a big birthday party for our mutual friend, Kit Johnson (who had so fortuitously introduced us), I decided to bake the 10,000-foot version of this recipe as a birthday cake to bring our "high altitude connection" full circle. I frosted the cake with the cream cheese icing, wrote "Happy Birthday" on top (with a little melted chocolate stirred into some of the cream cheese), and froze it overnight. Then I packed it in a carton along with ice packs, a box of candles, and a frozen Flourless Chocolate Espresso Truffle Cake (page 215) and sent them via FedEx overnight express. They arrived at Sandy's doorstep, in perfect condition, and just in time for the party.

I like to add chopped walnuts for additional texture, but you could also toss in ½ cup of sunflower seeds and/or currants or raisins.

---

**General High Altitude Notes:** This recipe works well at high altitudes, where it needs relatively few adjustments from the sea-level measurements. To strengthen the batter and add moisture, add extra eggs; for a brighter flavor, increase the spice quantities. At 7,000 feet and above, strengthen the batter by adding a little flour and cutting back on the sugar.

**Special Equipment:** A 9½- to 10-inch (10- to 12-cup) tube or Bundt pan; foil-covered 10-inch cardboard cake disk or flat plate; wooden skewer or cake tester

**Pan Preparation:** Generously coat the pan with solid shortening, dust with flour, and tap out the excess flour. At 5,000 feet and above, line the greased pan bottom with a ring of parchment paper, wax paper, or foil (see pages 30 or 34), then grease and flour the liner; tap out excess flour.

**Makes** one 10-inch tube or Bundt cake; serves 10 to 12

## High Notes

*At 3,000 feet and above,* add eggs and increase the spice quantities as the elevation increases. Adjust the oven temperature as noted and lower the rack to give the cake a little more heat.

*At 5,000 feet and above,* reduce the baking soda.

*At 7,000 feet,* reduce the sugar and add a little flour. Bake at 350°F instead of 375°F.

*At 10,000 feet,* add an egg plus a yolk, increase the flour, and reduce the sugar, oil, and leavening. Preheat the oven to 25 degrees higher than the actual baking temperature, then reduce the heat to 350°F when the cake is put into the oven.

| Ingredients | Sea Level | 3,000 feet | 5,000 feet | 7,000 feet | 10,000 feet |
|---|---|---|---|---|---|
| **Oven rack position, temperature, and baking time** | Rack in center; bake at 350°F for 40 to 45 minutes | Rack in lower third of oven; bake at 375°F for 50 to 52 minutes | Rack in lower third of oven; bake at 375°F for 45 to 50 minutes | Rack in lower third of oven; bake at 350°F for 35 to 40 minutes | Rack in lower third of oven; *preheat* to 375°F; *bake* at 350°F for 55 to 58 minutes |
| **Carrots, 8 to 10, peeled and grated (see Step 2)** | 3 cups (10 ounces) grated | 3 cups (10 ounces) grated | 3 cups (10 ounces) grated | 3 cups (10 ounces) grated | 3 cups (10 ounces) grated |
| **Walnuts, chopped medium-fine** | 1 cup (4 ounces) | 1 cup (4 ounces) | 1 cup (4 ounces) | 1 cup (4 ounces) | 1 cup (4 ounces) |
| **Sunflower seeds, optional** | 1/4 cup | 1/4 cup | 1/4 cup | 1/4 cup | 1/4 cup |
| **Canola or light olive oil** | 1 1/2 cups | 1 1/2 cups | 1 1/2 cups | 1 1/2 cups | 1 1/4 cups |
| **Granulated sugar** | 2 cups | 2 cups | 2 cups | 1 3/4 cups | 1 1/2 cups |
| **Large eggs, at room temperature** | 4 | 6 | 6 | 6 | 7 eggs, *plus* 1 yolk |
| **Vanilla extract** | 2 tablespoons | 2 tablespoons | 2 tablespoons | 2 tablespoons | 2 tablespoons |

*(continued)*

| Ingredients | Sea Level | 3,000 feet | 5,000 feet | 7,000 feet | 10,000 feet |
|---|---|---|---|---|---|
| **Wheat germ or oat or wheat bran** | ¼ cup | ¼ cup | ¼ cup | ¼ cup | 2 tablespoons |
| **All-purpose flour** | 2 cups | 2 cups | 2 cups | 2 cups plus 2 tablespoons | 2¼ cups |
| **Baking soda** | 2 teaspoons | 2 teaspoons | 1½ teaspoons | 1½ teaspoons | 1¼ teaspoons |
| **Salt** | 1 teaspoon | 1 teaspoon | 1 teaspoon | 1 teaspoon | 1 teaspoon |
| **Ground cinnamon** | 1½ teaspoons | 2 teaspoons | 2 teaspoons | 2 teaspoons | 2 teaspoons |
| **Ground nutmeg** | ½ teaspoon | ¾ teaspoon | ¾ teaspoon | ¾ teaspoon | 1 teaspoon |
| **Ground ginger** | ½ teaspoon | ½ teaspoon | ½ teaspoon | ¾ teaspoon | ¾ teaspoon |
| **Ground allspice** | ½ teaspoon | ½ teaspoon | ½ teaspoon | ½ teaspoon | ½ teaspoon |

CREAM CHEESE FROSTING (RECIPE FOLLOWS) OR CONFECTIONERS' SUGAR FOR DUSTING

**1.** Position the rack and preheat the oven as indicated for your altitude in the chart above. Prepare the pan as directed.

**2.** You can grate the carrots on a box grater or in a food processor fitted with the grating disk. If using the processor, remove the grated carrots and replace the grating disk with the regular steel cutting blade. Add the carrots and pulse 3 or 4 times just to shorten the grated pieces (but don't finely chop them).

Put the carrots in a bowl and add the chopped walnuts and sunflower seeds, if using.

**3.** In a large bowl, using a whisk, blend together the oil, sugar, eggs, vanilla, and wheat germ or bran. Set a strainer over the bowl and measure the flour, baking soda, salt, and spices into it. Stir/sift the dry ingredients onto the oil-egg mixture, and gently whisk until combined. Stir in the carrots and nuts.

**4.** Scoop the batter into the prepared pan and level the top. Bake for the time indicated for your altitude in the chart above, or until the top is springy to the touch and a cake tester inserted in the center comes out clean. Cool the cake in its pan on a wire rack for at least 20 minutes.

**5.** Slide a knife between the cake and the pan to loosen it. Top the cake with a flat plate or a foil-covered cardboard cake disk, invert, and lift off the pan. Peel off the paper, if you used it. Cool completely.

**6.** Frost the cake with the frosting or sift on a little confectioners' sugar.

## Cream Cheese Frosting
*(recipe is the same at all altitudes)*

**Makes** 2½ cups, enough to frost one 10-inch tube or Bundt cake

8 ounces Philadelphia regular cream cheese, at room temperature
8 tablespoons (1 stick) unsalted butter, at room temperature

Pinch of salt

1½ teaspoons vanilla extract

4 cups sifted confectioners' sugar, or as needed

In a food processor or the large bowl of an electric mixer, preferably with a paddle attachment, blend together the cream cheese and butter until very smooth and creamy.

Beat in the salt and vanilla. Gradually add the sugar, beating until smooth. The longer you beat, the softer the frosting will be; chill to harden if necessary in hot weather. (The frosting can be made a day in advance and refrigerated, covered; bring to room temperature and beat until smooth before using.)

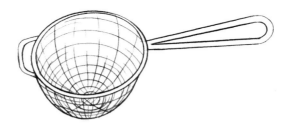

# El Dorado Cheesecake with Glazed Mango Topping

THIS CREAMY cheesecake with a simple nut-crumb crust is so named because it is rich, golden, and a treasure worthy of your discovery. It may not be precisely what Spanish explorers were seeking in sixteenth-century South America, but it took me a long time to get lucky and find the right combination of ingredients in "my" kitchen in El Dorado, Santa Fe. This is the ultimate cheesecake—luscious, sensuously creamy, and topped with glazed fresh mango slices.

Cheesecake is ubiquitous in New Mexico. My theory about why everyone makes it is first, because they can (see the high altitude notes below) and second, because cream really does soothe a pepper-ravaged tongue after a spicy meal. Soothing, however, is rarely the point. In fact, just to keep the burn going, many New Mexican pastry chefs add ground chile to their cheesecake batter. Or, if you want something completely different, you might try the creative approach I tasted at the Blue Corn Café & Brewery on Cerillos Drive in Santa Fe: Chimichanga Cheesecake, "a crispy cinnamon-sugar tortilla filled with creamy chocolate-marbled cheesecake topped with white chocolate and berry sauces."

Personally, I prefer a more classic cheesecake. I tested my cheesecakes with whole eggs and/or whipped egg whites, with and without added starch, and with sour cream inside or just on top. As you might guess, sharing the results made me hugely popular with El Dorado friends and neighbors. This final version (whole eggs, sour cream inside only, a touch of cornstarch) was the hands-down winner, unanimously selected by friends Nanscy Neiman and Bernie LeGette, ex–New Yorkers, who know from New York cheesecake and took their taste testing as seriously as they took the task of welcoming me into their delicious Santa Fe life.

Sweet ripe mangoes have a richly sensual, complex sweet-tart flavor that makes a marvelous topping for this cake. For a variation, you could use a mound of blueberries tossed with a few tablespoons of honey. Alternatively, if you'd like a Southwestern touch, top it with about 1½ cups of "bite-you-back" Chili-Cherry Preserves, made by La Carterra in Dixon, New Mexico (see Sources, page 329) or add a pinch (or more) of cayenne pepper to 1½ cups orange marmalade or apricot preserves, and garnish with finely julienned lemon or orange zest. Plan to add the mango topping or preserves about an hour before serving.

—⁘—

**General Cheesecake-Baking Tips:** The cake is best made a day in advance so the flavors mellow and the texture settles before serving. Bake the cheesecake on a jelly-roll pan for ease in handling. If the top cracks (it might, but just a little), you can just ignore it, because you will be covering it with fruit or preserves. Avoid beating too much air into the batter, because it increases the likelihood of cracking and alters the creamy texture; use the paddle attachment if your mixer has one. You can also mix the batter in a food processor, but don't overprocess the batter after adding the eggs, or you may incorporate too much air.

For a variation, try Tangerine Cheesecake, replacing the orange juice concentrate and zest with tangerine; or Lime Tequila Cheesecake, replacing the juice concentrate with limeade concentrate, omitting the orange extract, and adding 2 tablespoons tequila mix; for Fuzzy Navel Cheesecake (inspired by Letty Flatt, executive pastry chef at Deer Valley Resort in Park City, Utah), adding 3 tablespoons peach-flavored liqueur (schnapps), or to taste, to the basic recipe.

**General High Altitude Notes:** Compared to butter cakes, cheesecakes are relatively problem free at high altitudes because they don't have to

rise; however, the ingredients do have to set while maintaining a soft creamy texture, a feat best accomplished with moderate heat and a long, slow bake.

Cheesecake tops often crack as the steam escapes while the cake cools; at high altitudes, where everything cools faster than at sea level, cracks are more common. Since you will cover this one with fruit, though, cracks won't show; however, if they worry you, cover the cake with a plain cardboard cake disk as soon as it comes from the oven—the cardboard prevents rapid escape of steam, slowing down the cooling, as well as the cracking.

**Special Equipment:** A 9½- to 10-inch springform pan; jelly-roll pan; wax paper; grater; flat serving plate; aluminum foil; strainer

**Pan Preparation:** See Step 1.

**Makes** one 9½- to 10-inch cake; serves 12 to 14

**High Notes**
> *At 10,000 feet,* reduce the oven temperature and increase the baking time. Add one egg yolk and reduce sugar.

| Ingredients | Sea Level | 3,000 feet | 5,000 feet | 7,000 feet | 10,000 feet |
|---|---|---|---|---|---|
| **Oven rack position, temperature, and baking time** | Rack in center; bake at 350°F for 53 to 55 minutes | Rack in center; bake at 350°F for 53 to 55 minutes | Rack in center; bake at 350°F for 45 to 50 minutes | Rack in center; bake at 350°F for 38 to 45 minutes | Rack in center; bake at 325°F for 62 to 65 minutes |
| **Unsalted butter, at room temperature** | 1 tablespoon | 1 tablespoon | 1 tablespoon | 1 tablespoon | 1 tablespoon |
| **CRUMB CRUST** | | | | | |
| **Unsalted butter, melted and cooled** | 5 tablespoons | 5 tablespoons | 5 tablespoons | 5 tablespoons | 5 tablespoons |
| **Graham cracker crumbs** | 1 cup | 1 cup | 1 cup | 1 cup | 1 cup |
| **Very finely chopped pecans, almonds, or walnuts** | ½ cup (2 ounces) | ½ cup (2 ounces) | ½ cup (2 ounces) | ½ cup (2 ounces) | ½ cup (2 ounces) |
| **Granulated sugar** | 2 tablespoons | 2 tablespoons | 2 tablespoons | 2 tablespoons | 2 tablespoons |
| **CAKE** | | | | | |
| **Philadelphia regular cream cheese, at room temperature** | Four 8-ounce packages | Four 8-ounce packages | Four 8-ounce packages | Four 8-ounce packages | Four 8-ounce packages |
| **Granulated sugar** | 1¼ cups | 1¼ cups | 1¼ cups | 1¼ cups | 1 cup plus 2 tablespoons |
| **Sour cream** | 1 cup | 1 cup | 1 cup | 1 cup | 1 cup |
| **Cornstarch** | 2 tablespoons | 2 tablespoons | 2 tablespoons | 2 tablespoons | 2 tablespoons |
| **Salt** | ⅛ teaspoon | ⅛ teaspoon | ⅛ teaspoon | ¼ teaspoon | ¼ teaspoon |
| **Large eggs, at room temperature** | 4 | 4 | 4 | 4 | 4, *plus* 1 yolk |

(*continued*)

| Ingredients | Sea Level | 3,000 feet | 5,000 feet | 7,000 feet | 10,000 feet |
|---|---|---|---|---|---|
| **Frozen orange juice or lemonade concentrate, thawed** | 1/4 cup | 1/4 cup | 1/4 cup | 1/4 cup | 1/4 cup |
| **Orange extract** | 1 1/2 teaspoons | 1 1/2 teaspoons | 1 teaspoon | 1 teaspoon | 1 teaspoon |
| **Lemon extract** | 1/2 teaspoon | 1/2 teaspoon | 1/2 teaspoon | 1/2 teaspoon | 1/2 teaspoon |
| **Grated orange zest** | 1 1/2 tablespoons | 1 1/2 tablespoons | 1 1/2 tablespoons | 1 1/2 tablespoons | 1 1/2 tablespoons |
| MANGO TOPPING | | | | | |
| **Apricot preserves** | 1/2 cup | 1/2 cup | 1/2 cup | 1/2 cup | 1/2 cup |
| **2 large *ripe* mangoes (see Note, page 165)** | 1 1/2 cups slices | 1 1/2 cups slices | 1 1/2 cups slices | 1 1/2 cups slices | 1 1/2 cups slices |

**1.** Position the rack and preheat the oven as indicated for your altitude in the chart above. At 3,000 feet and above, place a jelly-roll pan on the baking rack to preheat (at sea level, just put the cake on the cold pan before setting it into the oven).

If you plan to serve and store this cake on the bottom of the springform pan, you can butter it directly, but if you plan to remove the cake from the pan bottom, cover the pan bottom with a generous square of aluminum foil, fasten the pan sides to the bottom, and fold the foil overhang flat underneath the pan. Spread the 1 tablespoon soft butter over the pan bottom and sides.

**2.** Make the crust: Put the melted butter in a small bowl and toss with the crumbs, nuts, and sugar. Press the crumbs evenly onto the pan bottom and about 1 1/2 inches up the sides. Set aside; or, in very hot weather, refrigerate.

**3.** If your mixer has a flat paddle, attach it. In the large mixer bowl, beat the cream cheese until very smooth and soft. Add the sugar and beat until creamy. Scrape down the bowl and beater. Beat in the sour cream, cornstarch, and salt. One at a time, beat in the eggs. Scrape down the bowl and beaters again. Beat in the juice concentrate, extracts, and zest. Scrape the bowl one last time to make sure the batter is smooth, but don't incorporate excess air.

**4.** Scoop the batter into the prepared pan and smooth the top. Set the cake in the oven on the jelly-roll pan and bake for the time indicated for your altitude in the chart above, or until the edges puff up, the top is a golden color with just a few cracks near the rim, and the cake center still looks soft—but not jiggly or fluid—when the side of the pan is tapped.

**5.** Remove the cake and set it on a wire rack in a draft-free location to cool. To prevent or slow cracking, cover the top with a cardboard cake disk. Cool completely (several hours), then refrigerate for at least several hours, or overnight, to allow the texture to firm up. Before topping the cake, run a thin knife blade between the cake and pan sides to loosen, then unhinge and remove the pan sides. Leave the cake on the pan bottom.

**6.** About 1 hour before serving, prepare the mango topping.

## Mango Topping
*(recipe is the same at all altitudes)*

½ cup apricot preserves
2 large ripe mangoes (each about 18 ounces)

**Makes** topping to cover one 9- to 10-inch cake

Stir the apricot preserves in a small pan over low heat until warm, then strain out the fruit chunks. Set aside.

Peel the mangoes. To slice the fruit, hold each mango on a narrow side, so the inner flat pit will be on edge, perpendicular to the table, and cut one thick slab of fruit from each side of the pit, holding the knife as close to the pit as you can. Lay each slab of mango flat and cut it into slices ⅛-inch thick. (The slices can be prepared a couple of hours ahead, covered with plastic wrap, and refrigerated.) Arrange the mango slices on top of the cake and brush on the slightly warm, strained apricot preserves. Refrigerate the cake until about 30 minutes before serving.

**Note:** Mangoes come in many varieties and sizes, but the type that is widely available in U.S. markets (*Mangifera indica*) is typically 3 to 5 inches long, oval or round, and green ripening to yellow gold or rose orange, mottled with green. When shopping, plan ahead, because mangoes are rarely ripe when in the store. Select fruit that is heavy for its size and beginning to show golden or reddish color. To ripen mangoes at home, set them on a window sill or in a paper bag (with a few holes poked in it) for several days, or until the sides give under gentle pressure. Use a vegetable peeler or paring knife to peel.

# Alpine Angel Cake with 7- to 15-Minute Icing

EAVENLY FOOD of the angels, this cake is divine: it rises like the Alps, has a slightly moist, tender crumb, and is not too sweet. I often serve it with a light sifting of confectioners' sugar on top ("snow on the Alps") and Blueberry-Honey Sauce (page 214), but for a party presentation you can frost it with the 7- to 15-Minute Icing. The basic recipe contains vanilla and (optional) almond extract, but you can substitute other flavors. To make Orange Angel Cake, replace the almond extract with orange extract plus 2 tablespoons grated orange zest, tossed with a little of the sugar-flour mixture in Step 3; add the zest when you fold in the whites. To make Coconut Angel Cake, use the vanilla and almond extract plus 1½ teaspoons coconut extract, and add ⅓ cup sweetened shredded coconut, tossed with a little of the sugar-flour mixture in Step 3; add the coconut when you fold in the whites.

To cool an angel cake, turn the pan upside down, either standing it on the little feet attached to the pan rim or hanging it over the neck of a bottle, so gravity can help stretch the fragile cell structure until it is cold and set; if you leave it right side up, the cake will collapse as it cools. (See "About Sponge Cakes and Egg Whites," page 110.)

---

**Note:** Superfine, or "bar," sugar is sold in the supermarket in 1-pound boxes (see page 38). This recipe calls for combination of confectioners' and superfine sugar because they will dissolve in the egg whites more quickly than regular granulated sugar (which also is heavier and will weigh down the batter). Instead of the combination, you can use all superfine sugar (1¼ cups). To prepare your own superfine sugar, whirl granulated sugar in the food processor until fine.

**General High Altitude Notes:** At altitudes above 2,500 feet, the trick with this cake is to under-beat the whites, just until they form soft, slightly droopy peaks; at this stage there is still room in them to expand when baked. If over-beaten to stiff peaks, the air cells, and the cake, will collapse when the cake cools. As the elevation increases, add flour to strengthen the cake's cellular structure and cream of tartar for acidity and to stabilize the whipped whites. To compensate for evaporation and a drier atmosphere, add a little water at 5,000 feet and above. The oven temperature must be carefully monitored because you need just enough heat to enable the whites to expand sufficiently and the starch to set the cell structure before the cake top overbrowns. If the oven is too hot, the top will glaze over before the interior batter rises and sets.

If your cake sinks, you can blame it on over-whipped whites and/or weak structure (not enough flour)—or the fact that you forgot to invert it while cooling.

**Special Equipment:** A 10 × 4-inch (16-cup) angel tube pan with a removable bottom; sifter; wax paper; flexible spatula or flat whisk; narrow-necked bottle (like a wine bottle) tall enough to hang the tube pan upside down on its neck (optional); foil-covered 10-inch cardboard cake disk or flat plate; serrated knife

**Pan Preparation:** None; do not grease the pan.

**Makes** one 10-inch tube cake; serves 10 to 12

**High Notes**

*At 3,000 feet* **and above,** add extra flour and cream of tartar. Raise the oven temperature and add flavor by increasing the extracts.

| Ingredients | Sea Level | 3,000 feet | 5,000 feet | 7,000 feet | 10,000 feet |
|---|---|---|---|---|---|
| **Oven rack position, temperature, and baking time** | Rack in center; bake at 325°F for 45 to 50 minutes | Rack in lower third of oven; bake at 375°F for 25 to 32 minutes | Rack in lower third of oven; bake at 375°F for 25 to 30 minutes | Rack in lower third of oven; bake at 375°F for 30 to 35 minutes | Rack in lower third of oven; bake at 350°F for 30 to 35 minutes |
| **Sifted cake flour** | 1 cup | 1 cup plus 1 tablespoon | 1 cup plus 2 tablespoons | 1 cup plus 2 tablespoons | 1¼ cups |
| **Sifted confectioners' sugar** | ½ cup | ½ cup | ½ cup | ½ cup | ½ cup |
| **Salt** | ½ teaspoon | ½ teaspoon | ½ teaspoon | ½ teaspoon | ½ teaspoon |
| **Large egg whites, at room temperature** | 1½ cups (10 to 13) | 1½ cups (10 to 13) | 1½ cups (10 to 13) | 1½ cups (10 to 13) | 1½ cups (10 to 13) |
| **Cream of tartar** | 1 teaspoon | 1½ teaspoons | 1½ teaspoons | 1½ teaspoons | 2 teaspoons |
| **Superfine sugar** | ¾ cup | ¾ cup | ¾ cup | ¾ cup | ¾ cup |
| **Vanilla extract** | 1 teaspoon | 1 teaspoon | 2 teaspoons | 2 teaspoons | 2 teaspoons |
| **Almond extract, optional** | ¾ teaspoon | 1 teaspoon | 1 teaspoon | 1 teaspoon | 2 teaspoons |
| **Water** | None | None | 2 tablespoons | 2 tablespoons | 2 tablespoons |

CONFECTIONERS' SUGAR OR 7- TO 15-MINUTE ICING (RECIPE FOLLOWS)

*Whipped Egg Whites*

*droopy peaks*

*stiff peaks*

**1.** Position the rack and preheat the oven as indicated for your altitude in the chart above. Prepare the pan as directed.

**2.** Sift the cake flour onto a piece of wax paper, then sift the confectioners' sugar and salt over it. Place the empty sifter over a bowl, gather up the edges of the wax paper, and tip the dry ingredients into the sifter, without shaking the sifter; let it sit over the bowl until needed.

**3.** Place the egg whites in the large bowl of the electric mixer and check the whites to make sure they no longer feel cold. Add the cream of tartar and whip on medium-high speed just until foamy. Gradually whip in the superfine sugar, increasing the mixer speed to high, but watch closely. As soon as you see beater tracks on top of the whites, stop the machine, lift the beater, and check the stiffness of the foam. At sea level, you want whites that will stand up in stiff peaks, but at 2,500 feet and above, you only want soft, droopy peaks (see sketch). If the whites look too soft, continue beating for just a few more seconds and check again; do not overbeat. The whites should be glossy and smooth.

**4.** With a flexible spatula, fold in the extract(s). Sift about one-third of the flour-sugar mixture onto the whites and fold it in, then slowly sift and fold in the rest (including any that fell into the other bowl) a little at a time. Fold with a very light touch, cutting through the center of the whites and down to the bowl bottom, then bringing the spatula up again toward you while giving the bowl a quarter turn, until all the dry ingredients are incorporated.

**5.** Scoop the batter gently into the pan and smooth the top. Cut through the batter once with the spatula to be sure there are no large air pockets. Bake for the time indicated for your altitude in the chart above, or until the cake is well risen and golden on top and a cake tester inserted in the center comes out clean. As soon as it is baked, invert the cake pan onto its feet or hang it upside down over the neck of a bottle, as shown on the following page, and let cool completely, several hours (or overnight).

**6.** To remove the cake from the pan, slide the blade of a long, thin knife between the cake and the pan sides, and then the central tube, to loosen it. Top the cake with a foil-covered cardboard disk or plate, invert, and lift off the pan. If your cake is stuck to the pan bottom, slide the knife between the pan and the bottom of the cake to release it. Top the cake with sifted confectioners' sugar or the icing, and cut with a serrated knife.

*Cooling cake on pan feet*

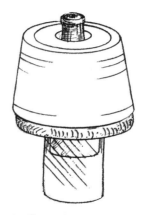

*Cooling cake over a bottle*

# 7- to 15-Minute Icing

You may remember this as 7-Minute Icing, which it is from sea level to about 5,000 feet. At higher elevations, the lower boiling point of the water means that it takes longer to heat the whites into a stiff, stable foam. Don't give up—keep whipping, and eventually it will work. You can vary the flavor by changing the extract.

**Special Equipment:** Double boiler; hand-held electric mixer

**Makes** 2½ cups, enough to frost a 10-inch tube cake

    2 large egg whites, at room temperature
    1½ cups superfine or granulated sugar
    ¼ cup plus 1 tablespoon lukewarm water
    2 teaspoons light corn syrup
    ¼ teaspoon cream of tartar
    1 teaspoon vanilla extract

Add water to the bottom of a double boiler one quarter to one third its depth and set over high heat until it comes to a rolling boil (this will take longer at high altitudes than at sea level). Meanwhile, stir together all the ingredients except the vanilla in the top of the double boiler, off the heat. Set a hand-held electric mixer next to the stove. At 7,000 feet and above, have a kettle of water boiling on the stove to replenish the water in the bottom pan if it evaporates. Peek into the bottom pan occasionally as you whip to see if there is enough water.

When the water boils, put the top pan in place and begin whipping the whites. Use medium-high speed for the first 5 minutes, then increase the speed to high and beat until the whites form a satiny foam that holds soft peaks and mounds on the beater, 2 to 7 minutes, depending on your altitude (the whites will be whipped again in the next step).

When the whites are ready, turn off the heat and set the top pan on a pot holder on the counter. Fold in the vanilla, then whip hard for an additional 1 to 3 minutes, until the whites form very stiff peaks on the beater tip. The icing will air-dry to a stiff outer surface, so use it as soon as it is made.

# Chocolate Sponge Roll with Hazelnut Toffee Cream

CHOCOLATE, HAZELNUT whipped cream, and toffee? This is the dessert of my dreams! One bite and you will be living the high life even if you aren't on a mountaintop. Use this recipe for a Bûche de Noël, the traditional Christmas Yule log cake. As an alternative to the Hazelnut Toffee Cream filling, fill and frost the roll with Mocha Buttercream Icing (page 123) or Bittersweet Chocolate Icing (page 119).

For an easy alternative filling, use a generous cup of raspberry preserves, and press ½ pint fresh raspberries into the jam. Serve with Raspberry Sauce (page 149). Note: Cocoa will rinse right out of a tea towel, but to make cleanup even easier, line the towel with paper towels before sifting on the cocoa. Be sure to leave the cake flat (not rolled) until completely cool to avoid compressing the structure; it could collapse as the steam tries to escape if rolled when hot. (See "About Sponge Cakes and Egg Whites," page 110.)

**General High Altitude Notes:** At 3,000 feet and above, improve the rise by reducing the sugar and cocoa and omitting the cornstarch and baking soda. Strengthen the batter, and increase the liquid, by adding 2 eggs. Increase the stability of the whipped whites and add acidity to the batter by adding cream of tartar. At 5,000 feet and above, use natural cocoa, such as regular Hershey's, which is more acidic than the Dutch-process cocoa; the acidity helps the cake to set quickly.

**Special Equipment:** A jelly-roll pan (10 × 15 × ½-inch); baking parchment or wax paper; 1 or 2 sifters (one for flour, one for cocoa); extra bowl for electric mixer (or a large mixing bowl); flexible spatula; icing spatula (optional); cotton tea towel at least 10 by 15

inches; wooden skewer or cake tester; serrated knife

**Pan Preparation:** Coat the the pan with butter-flavor nonstick vegetable spray or solid shortening, then line with wax paper or baking parchment, grease the paper, and dust with flour; tap out the excess flour.

**Makes** one 10-inch cake roll; serves 10 to 12

**High Notes**

*At 3,000 feet and above,* reduce the sugar and cocoa and omit the cornstarch and baking soda. Add 2 eggs and cream of tartar.

*At 5,000 feet and above,* replace the Dutch-process cocoa with the more acidic natural cocoa. Add a little more salt to improve the flavor.

| Ingredients | Sea Level | 3,000 feet | 5,000 feet | 7,000 feet | 10,000 feet |
|---|---|---|---|---|---|
| **Oven rack position, temperature, and baking time** | Rack in center; bake at 350°F for 12 to 15 minutes | Rack in center; bake at 375°F for 7 to 8 minutes | Rack in center; bake at 375°F for 5 to 7 minutes | Rack in lower third of oven; bake at 375°F for 9 to 10 minutes | Rack in center; bake at 350°F for 9 to 10 minutes |
| **Sifted cake flour** | ¼ cup plus 1 tablespoon | ¼ cup | ¼ cup | ¼ cup | ¼ cup plus 1 tablespoon |
| **Sifted cornstarch** | 2 tablespoons | None | None | None | None |
| **Sifted Dutch-process cocoa** | ⅓ cup | ¼ cup | None | None | None |
| **Sifted natural cocoa, such as Hershey's regular** | None | None | ¼ cup | ¼ cup | ¼ cup |
| **Salt** | ⅛ teaspoon | ⅛ teaspoon | ¼ teaspoon | ¼ teaspoon | ¼ teaspoon |
| **Baking powder** | ½ teaspoon | ½ teaspoon | ½ teaspoon | ½ teaspoon | ¼ teaspoon + ⅛ teaspoon |
| **Baking soda** | ¼ teaspoon | None | None | None | None |
| **Large eggs, separated, at room temperature** | 4 | 6 | 6 | 6 | 6 |
| **Cream of tartar** | None | ¼ teaspoon | ¼ teaspoon | ¼ teaspoon | 1 teaspoon |
| **Granulated sugar, divided** | ½ cup plus ¼ cup | ¼ cup plus ¼ cup | 3 tablespoons + 3 tablespoons | 3 tablespoons + 3 tablespoons | 3 tablespoons + 3 tablespoons |
| **Vanilla extract** | 1 teaspoon | 1 teaspoon | ½ teaspoon | ½ teaspoon | ½ teaspoon |
| **Cocoa for unmolding cake** | ⅓ cup | ⅓ cup | ⅓ cup | ⅓ cup | ⅓ cup |

HAZELNUT TOFFEE CREAM (RECIPE FOLLOWS)

1. Position the rack and preheat the oven as indicated for your altitude in the chart above. Prepare the pan as directed.

2. Sift together the flour, cornstarch (if using), cocoa, salt, baking powder, and baking soda (if using) into a medium bowl. Set aside.

3. Put the egg whites in the large bowl of an electric mixer. Check the whites to make sure they no longer feel cold. Add the cream of tartar, if using, and whip the whites on medium speed just until foamy. Gradually whip in the first measure of sugar, increasing the speed to high, but watch closely: As soon as you see beater tracks on top of the whites, stop the machine, lift the beater, and check the stiffness of the foam. At sea level, you want whites that stand up in stiff peaks, but at 2,500 feet and above, you only want soft, droopy peaks (see sketch). If the whites are too soft, continue beating for just a few more seconds and check again; do not overbeat. The whites should be glossy and smooth.

Remove the bowl from the mixer stand, scrape the beater into the bowl, and return the beater (without washing) to the mixer to use again. Or, if you have only one mixer bowl, scrape the whites into another large bowl so you can reuse the first bowl without washing it. Set the whites aside.

4. Using the mixer, whip the yolks with the vanilla and the remaining granulated sugar until thick and light colored. Stop the machine and scrape down the bowl and beater. Continue to whip the yolks until they form a flat ribbon falling back upon itself when the beater is lifted. (At sea level, this takes about 3 minutes with a KitchenAid mixer on speed #8; with other mixers and at higher altitudes, it can take 6 to 7 minutes or longer.) Remove the bowl from the mixer stand.

5. With a flexible spatula or flat whisk, fold about one-third of the whipped whites into the yolks to soften and lighten them, then sprinkle about ¼ cup of the flour-cocoa mixture onto the batter and fold them together. Fold with a light touch, cutting through the center of the batter and down to the bowl bottom, then bringing the spatula up again toward you while giving the bowl a quarter turn. Repeat, alternately folding in the remaining whipped whites with all the flour-cocoa mixture; don't worry if you see a few streaks of white.

6. Scoop the batter out onto the prepared pan and, using a rubber spatula or icing spatula, spread it out to the edges. Bake for the time indicated for your altitude in the chart above, or just until the top is springy to the touch and the edges are beginning to pull away from the pan sides; a cake tester inserted in the center should come out clean. Do not overbake, or the cake will be dry.

7. While the cake bakes, spread a tea towel out on a flat surface. Cover it with paper towels

*Whipped Egg Whites*

*droopy peaks*

*stiff peaks*

if you wish, then sift the ⅓ cup cocoa over the top, making a 10 × 15-inch rectangle.

**8.** As soon as the cake is baked, invert the pan over the sifted cocoa. Lift off the pan and peel off the paper. Use a serrated knife to slice a scant ⅛-inch-wide strip of crisp edging from the cake (sketch a, below). Leave the cake flat and cool it completely.

**9.** When the cake has cooled, fold one short end of the towel over a short end of the cake, then roll them together (b). Set the roll seam side down on a wire rack or plate until ready to fill it.

**10.** To fill the cake, unroll it and spread on the hazelnut cream (c). Reroll the cake, using the end of the towel to lift and push it as you roll (d). Set the cake seam side down and, if you wish, sift on a little more cocoa. Cut the cake with a serrated knife or refrigerate the cream-filled cake until ready to serve.

# Hazelnut Toffee Cream
*(recipe is the same at all altitudes)*

To whip cream quickly, use a chilled bowl and beater. To crush the toffee candy, break the bars into a strong plastic bag and crush them with a rolling pin or hammer until the pieces are in ¼- to ⅛-inch bits.

**Makes** 1½ cups, enough to fill one cake roll (serve any leftover cream on the side)

> ¼ cup canned roasted hazelnut praline paste (available from American Almond Products; see Sources, page 329), or ¾ teaspoon hazelnut (or almond) extract (see Sources) plus 2 tablespoons Frangelico (hazelnut) liqueur
> ¾ cup chilled heavy cream (36 to 40% butterfat)
> 2 tablespoons granulated sugar
> ½ teaspoon vanilla extract
> ⅓ to ½ cup finely chopped chocolate-covered toffee candy (two 1.4-ounce Skor bars or two 1³⁄₁₆-ounce Heath bars)

If using praline paste, measure about 3 table-spoons of the cream into a small bowl and stir/whisk in the paste until the mixture is smooth and soft. Set aside.

Using a chilled bowl and beater, whip the remaining cream (or all of it, if not using praline paste) just until soft peaks form. Add the sugar, vanilla, and hazelnut extract and liqueur, if using. Use a whisk to blend and whip for a few seconds longer, until the cream holds its shape in peaks but is not too stiff. Fold in the crushed toffee, along with the praline cream, if using.

*a*

*c*

*b*

*d*

# Four-Layer Orange Sponge Cake with Tangerine Mousse Filling

THIS SPONGE cake is a necessity for any baker's repertoire because it is so versatile. It is related to the French sponge cake known as *génoise*. It has a fine grain and tender crumb and can be split into four flexible (rather than fragile) layers. Compared to a butter cake, the texture of the sponge is slightly dry and benefits from a liberal, very Gallic splash of liqueur, which soaks in to enhance the flavor. If you wish, use an orange liqueur such as Grand Marnier, Mandarin tangerine liqueur, or Triple Sec, or use peach schnapps. For a do-ahead gala summer dessert, fill the layers with the Tangerine (or Strawberry or Raspberry) Mousse, and sift confectioners' sugar on top. This cake was the hit of a dessert buffet I made (including four other "test" cakes) for an August party at the home of my Santa Fe cousin, Bessy Berman. (See "About Sponge Cakes and Egg Whites," page 110.)

**General High Altitude Notes:** This cake is leavened entirely by the air whipped into the eggs. At 2,500 feet and above, the trick is to underbeat the whites, just until they form soft, slightly droopy peaks. At this stage there is still room in them to expand when baked. If overbeaten, to stiff peaks, the air cells, and the cake, will collapse when the cake cools. Be sure to put the cake into the oven as soon as it is ready, or the air cells will start to deflate.

*At 3,000 feet and above,* strengthen the structure by reducing the sugar. Cut out some of the butter and replace it with a large egg plus a yolk (yolks contain all the fat of the egg), which will add richness, liquid, strength, and flexibility. To improve the rise, cut back on the flour slightly; add flavor with more salt and extract.

*At 5,000 feet and above,* add extra liquid to compensate for evaporation at high altitudes.

*At 10,000 feet,* strengthen the batter with a little extra flour. Increase the cream of tartar to stabilize the whites and add acidity, which helps the cake set faster.

**Special Equipment:** Two 9 × 1½- or 2-inch round cake pans; baking parchment or wax paper (optional); sifter; extra bowl for electric mixer (or a large mixing bowl); flexible spatula; two foil-covered 10-inch cardboard cake disks or flat plates; wooden skewer or cake tester; serrated knife; icing spatula (optional)

**Pan Preparation:** Coat the pans with butter-flavor nonstick vegetable spray or solid shortening, dust with flour, and tap out the excess flour. At 5,000 feet and above, line the greased pans with baking parchment or wax paper, then grease and flour the paper; tap out the excess flour.

**Makes** one 4-layer 9-inch cake; serves 10 to 12

### High Notes

*At 3,000 feet and above,* reduce the sugar, butter, and flour. Add one egg plus one yolk.

*At 5,000 feet and above,* add more liquid.

*At 10,000 feet,* add more flour and cream of tartar.

| Ingredients | Sea Level | 3,000 feet | 5,000 feet | 7,000 feet | 10,000 feet |
| --- | --- | --- | --- | --- | --- |
| **Oven rack position, temperature, and baking time** | Rack in center; bake at 375°F for 20 to 27 minutes | Rack in center; bake at 375°F for 20 to 24 minutes | Rack in center; bake at 375°F for 17 to 20 minutes | Rack in lower third of oven; bake at 350°F for 15 to 17 minutes | Rack in lower third of oven; bake at 350°F for 15 to 18 minutes |
| **Sifted cake flour** | 1½ cups plus 1 tablespoon | 1⅓ cups plus 1 tablespoon | 1¼ cups plus 1 tablespoon | 1¼ cups | 1⅓ cups plus 1 tablespoon |
| **Salt** | Pinch | ½ teaspoon | ½ teaspoon | ½ teaspoon | ½ teaspoon |
| **Large eggs, separated, at room temperature** | 6 | 7 | 7 | 7 | 7 |
| **Cream of tartar** | ½ teaspoon | ½ teaspoon | ½ teaspoon | ½ teaspoon | 1 teaspoon |
| **Granulated sugar, divided** | ½ cup plus ½ cup | 6 tablespoons + 6 tablespoons | 6 tablespoons + 6 tablespoons | 6 tablespoons + 6 tablespoons | 6 tablespoons + 6 tablespoons |
| **Large egg yolk, at room temperature** | None | 1 | 1 | 1 | 1 |
| **Vanilla extract** | 1 teaspoon | 1 teaspoon | 1 teaspoon | 1 teaspoon | 1 teaspoon |
| **Orange extract** | 1 teaspoon | 1 teaspoon | 1 teaspoon | 1 teaspoon | 1 teaspoon |
| **Lemon extract** | 1 teaspoon | 1 teaspoon | 1 teaspoon | 1 teaspoon | 1 teaspoon |
| **Grated orange zest** | 2 tablespoons | 2 tablespoons | 2 tablespoons | 2 tablespoons | 2 tablespoons |
| **Grated lemon zest** | 1 teaspoon | 1 teaspoon | 1 teaspoon | 1 teaspoon | 1 teaspoon |

*(continued)*

| Ingredients | Sea Level | 3,000 feet | 5,000 feet | 7,000 feet | 10,000 feet |
|---|---|---|---|---|---|
| **Fresh orange or lemon juice** | None | None | 3 tablespoons | 3 tablespoons | 3 tablespoons |
| **Unsalted butter, melted and cooled** | 6 tablespoons | 3 tablespoons | 3 tablespoons | 3 tablespoons | 3 tablespoons |
| TANGERINE MOUSSE (RECIPE FOLLOWS) | | | | | |
| CONFECTIONERS' SUGAR | | | | | |

**1.** Position the rack and preheat the oven as indicated for your altitude in the chart above. Prepare the pans as directed.

**2.** Sift the flour and salt into a small bowl. Set aside.

**3.** Put the egg whites into the large bowl of the electric mixer and check the whites to make sure they are no longer cold. Add the cream of tartar and whip on medium speed just until foamy. Gradually whip in half the sugar (½ cup at sea level, 6 tablespoons at all other altitudes), increasing the mixer speed to high, but watch closely: As soon as you start to see beater tracks on top of the whites, stop the machine, lift the beater, and check the stiffness of the foam. At sea level, you want whites that stand up in stiff peaks, but at 2,500 feet and above, you only want a soft, droopy peak (see sketch). If the whites look too soft, continue beating for just a few more seconds and check

again; do not overbeat. The whites should be glossy and smooth. Remove the bowl from the mixer stand, scrape the beater into the bowl, and return the beater to the mixer (without washing) to use again. Or, if you have only one mixer bowl, scrape the whites into another large bowl so you can reuse the first bowl without washing it. Set the whites aside.

**4.** Using the mixer, whip the yolks with the remaining sugar until thick and light colored. Stop the machine and scrape down the bowl and beater. Add the extracts, grated zests, and juice, if using, and whip on high speed until the yolks form a flat ribbon falling back on itself when the beater is lifted; this can take 3 to 7 minutes, depending upon the type of mixer and the altitude. Remove the bowl from the mixer stand.

**5.** Using a flexible spatula, fold about a cup of the whipped whites into the yolk mixture to

*Whipped Egg Whites*

*droopy peaks*

*stiff peaks*

lighten it, then alternately fold in the flour and the remaining whites. Fold with a light touch, cutting through the center of the batter and down to the bowl bottom, then bringing the spatula up again toward you while giving the bowl a quarter turn, until all the dry ingredients are incorporated. Don't worry if you see some streaks of white in the batter.

**6.** Scoop about 1 cup of the batter into a medium bowl and fold in the melted and cooled butter. Fold the butter mixture back into the batter.

**7.** Scoop the batter into the prepared pans. Bake for the time indicated for your altitude in the chart above, or until the cake is risen, a pale golden color and springy to the touch, and a cake tester inserted in the middle comes out clean. Cool the layers in the pans on a wire rack for about 10 minutes.

**8.** Run a knife between the pan sides and the layers to release them. Cover each layer with a flat plate or foil-covered cardboard cake disk, invert, and lift off the pans. Peel off the paper, if you used it. Cool the layers completely.

**9.** To make 4 layers, use a long serrated knife to split each layer in half horizontally (see sketch below) then slide a foil-covered disk between the split layers and lift up the top half onto the disk. If not ready to assemble the cake, double-wrap each layer in plastic wrap, and place together in a plastic bag or wrap in foil (this is especially important at 3,000 feet and above, when dry atmosphere and quick evaporation cause cakes to stale quickly).

**10.** If you wish, before filling the cake with the mousse, you can sprinkle some fruit-flavored liqueur (see the recipe introduction) on the cut surface of each layer. Spread the mousse between the layers. Refrigerate the cake until about 30 minutes before serving, then sift on a little confectioners' sugar.

## Tangerine Mousse
*(recipe is the same at all altitudes)*

Frozen tangerine juice concentrate gives this mousse its flavor, but you can also make it with fresh ripe (or frozen) strawberries or raspberries. Use the mousse as a cake filling, or serve it by itself in long-stemmed glasses, garnished with sprigs of mint or berries. Note: The mousse takes about 3 hours to set up before you can use it, so plan ahead. You can make the mousse 1 or 2 days before you need it; cover and refrigerate. To speed the whipping of the cream, chill a bowl and the beater in the refrigerator.

To make Strawberry or Raspberry Mousse, replace the tangerine juice concentrate and the ¾ cup orange juice or water with 1 cup berry puree; use 2 to 4 tablespoons sugar, depending on the sweetness of the puree. Omit the tangerine liqueur and grated zest, or substitute raspberry liqueur (Chambord) or eau-de-vie (framboise) or Grand Marnier.

**Special equipment:** A medium metal bowl; larger metal bowl (optional)

**Makes** about 4 cups, enough to fill a 3- or 4-layer cake; serves 6 to 8 on its own

1 tablespoon unflavored gelatin

¼ cup cold water or orange juice

½ cup water or orange juice, brought to a boil

1½ tablespoons fresh lemon juice

⅓ cup granulated sugar

Pinch of salt

One 6-ounce can frozen tangerine juice concentrate, stirred into ¾ cup orange juice or water

Grated zest of 2 tangerines or 1 orange

3 tablespoons Mandarin (tangerine) liqueur or other orange-flavored liqueur, optional

¾ cup chilled heavy cream (36 to 40% butterfat)

Sprinkle the gelatin over the ¼ cup cold water or juice in a large saucepan and set aside for 2 to 3 minutes, until the gelatin softens.

Stir in the ½ cup boiling water or juice, and stir until the gelatin is completely dissolved.

Stir in the lemon juice, sugar, salt, tangerine juice concentrate mixture, and zest. Place the pan over medium heat and stir until the sugar is dissolved. Add the liqueur, if using, and transfer the mixture to a metal bowl.

To thicken the mousse, you can either refrigerate it for about 45 minutes, stirring occasionally, or speed the process by setting the bowl in a larger bowl of ice water: stir on and off for 10 to 15 minutes, until the mousse feels thick, mounds on the spoon, and looks like soft pudding. Remove the mousse from the ice water before it sets hard; if it gets too stiff, stir it over a pan of very warm water for a couple of minutes to soften, stirring occasionally.

Using a chilled bowl and beater, whip the cream until soft peaks form, then fold it into the partially thickened tangerine mousse. Scoop the mousse into a bowl (or directly into serving dishes, if serving it by itself). Cover and refrigerate for at least 3 hours, or overnight, to set, before spreading between the cake layers or serving.

# Wilton Walnut Torte

THIS IS a basic Austrian *nusstorte*, in which toasted nuts and bread crumbs replace flour. It is baked in a thin sheet, then sliced into four narrow strips and filled and stacked into an elegant bar-shaped cake. You can give it a plain or fancy finish, depending on the occasion. The simplest solution is to spread preserves between the layers and top the cake with sifted confectioners' sugar. Alternatively, you can add fresh berries to the preserves between the layers and frost the sides with sweetened whipped cream or ½ recipe Mocha Buttercream Icing (page 123), then coat them with ¾ cup chopped toasted walnuts, pressing them onto the icing with the palm of your hand. Spread ½ cup slightly warmed (and then strained) raspberry or apricot jam on top. Other filling ideas: Hazelnut Toffee Cream (page 173) or Nutella (a jarred chocolate-hazelnut spread available in many supermarkets and in gourmet food stores), or try slightly softened coffee or butter pecan ice cream (freeze the cake after filling). Don't try to roll this cake; it is not flexible and will crack. (See "About Sponge Cakes and Egg Whites," page 110.)

You will need fresh bread crumbs for this recipe. Cut the crusts from 3 or 4 slices of white or whole-wheat bread, tear them into pieces, and whirl in the food processor to make fine crumbs. Measure out ⅔ cup, lightly packed; freeze any leftovers in a plastic bag. For the lightest cake texture, grind the nuts in a hand-held rotary nut mill (see sketch, page 33, to make a sawdust-like powder). Lacking a mill, finely chop the nuts in a food processor, along with the cornstarch, to prevent caking.

**General High Altitude Notes:** At sea level, this cake is leavened entirely by air whipped into the eggs; above sea level, I add some baking powder to guarantee a good rise, although whipped egg foam is still the primary leavening. At 2,500 feet and above, the trick is to underbeat the whites, just until they form soft, slightly droopy peaks. At this stage there is still room in them to expand when baked. If over-beaten to stiff peaks, the air cells, and the cake, will collapse the cake cools. Be sure to put the cake into the oven as soon as it is ready, or the air cells will start to deflate.

At 3,000 feet and above, add baking powder to ensure a good rise. Also increase the cream of tartar to add stability to whipped whites and acidity to the batter so it will set quickly. For the best flavor, increase the extracts and lemon juice.

**Special Equipment:** Rotary nut mill or food processor; jelly-roll pan (10 × 15 × ½-inch); baking parchment or wax paper; sifter; extra bowl for electric mixer (or a large mixing bowl); flexible spatula; icing spatula (optional); cotton tea towel at least 10 by 15 inches; wooden skewer or cake tester; serrated knife; stiff cardboard cut into a 4½ × 11-inch rectangle and covered with aluminum foil or a long flat rectangular serving platter

**Pan Preparation:** Coat the pan with butter-flavor nonstick vegetable spray or solid shortening, line with wax paper or baking parchment, grease the paper, and dust with flour; tap out the excess flour.

**Makes** one 3½ × 9 × 1½-inch-high torte; serves 6 to 8

**High Notes**

At 3,000 feet and above, adjust baking powder as noted and add cream of tartar.

At 7,000 feet and above, reduce the baking powder.

At 10,000 feet, add more cream of tartar.

| Ingredients | Sea Level | 3,000 feet | 5,000 feet | 7,000 feet | 10,000 feet |
|---|---|---|---|---|---|
| **Oven rack position, temperature, and baking time** | Rack in center; bake at 350°F for 12 to 15 minutes | Rack in center; bake at 350°F for 15 to 17 minutes | Rack in center; bake at 350°F for 13 to 15 minutes | Rack in center; bake at 350°F for 18 to 22 minutes | Rack in center; bake at 350°F for 18 to 22 minutes |
| **Walnuts** | 2 cups (8 ounces) | 2 cups (8 ounces) | 2 cups (8 ounces) | 2 cups (8 ounces) | 2 cups (8 ounces) |
| **Cornstarch, sifted** | ⅓ cup | ⅓ cup | ⅓ cup | ⅓ cup | ⅓ cup |
| **Fresh bread crumbs, packed** | ⅔ cup (1¼ ounces) | ⅔ cup (1¼ ounces) | ⅔ cup (1¼ ounces) | ⅔ cup (1¼ ounces) | ⅔ cup (1¼ ounces) |
| **Baking powder** | None | ¾ teaspoon | ¾ teaspoon | ½ teaspoon | ¼ teaspoon |
| **Large eggs, separated, at room temperature** | 6 | 6 | 6 | 6 | 6 |
| **Cream of tartar** | ⅛ teaspoon | ¼ teaspoon | ¼ teaspoon | ¼ teaspoon | ½ teaspoon |

(continued)

| Ingredients | Sea Level | 3,000 feet | 5,000 feet | 7,000 feet | 10,000 feet |
|---|---|---|---|---|---|
| **Salt** | ¼ teaspoon | ¼ teaspoon | ¼ teaspoon | ¼ teaspoon | ¼ teaspoon |
| **Granulated sugar, divided** | ¼ cup plus ½ cup | ¼ cup plus ½ cup | ¼ cup plus ½ cup | ¼ cup plus ½ cup | ¼ cup plus ½ cup |
| **Ground cinnamon** | Pinch | Pinch | Pinch | Pinch | Pinch |
| **Almond extract** | ¼ teaspoon | ½ teaspoon | ½ teaspoon | ½ teaspoon | ½ teaspoon |
| **Vanilla extract** | ½ teaspoon | 1 teaspoon | 1 teaspoon | 1 teaspoon | 1 teaspoon |
| **Fresh lemon juice** | None | 1 teaspoon | 1 teaspoon | ½ teaspoon | ½ teaspoon |
| **Confectioners' sugar for unmolding cake** | ⅓ cup | ⅓ cup | ⅓ cup | ⅓ cup | ⅓ cup |
| **FILLING** | | | | | |
| **Apricot or raspberry preserves** | 1 cup | 1 cup | 1 cup | 1 cup | 1 cup |
| **TOPPING** | | | | | |
| **Confectioners' sugar** | ½ cup | ½ cup | ½ cup | ½ cup | ½ cup |

1. Position the rack as indicated for your altitude in the chart above, and preheat the oven to 325°F. Prepare the pan as directed.

To toast walnuts, spread them in a shallow pan and toast in the oven for 5 to 15 minutes (longer at higher elevations), shaking them a few times, until they darken very slightly in color and are aromatic. Let cool. Increase the oven temperature to 350°F.

2. If you have a rotary nut mill, grind the toasted nuts to a fine powder over a bowl, picking out any big chunks that fall through the cracks. Measure 2 cups of ground nuts and place in a medium bowl. Lacking a nut mill, combine the toasted nuts with the cornstarch in a food processor and finely chop. Transfer to a medium bowl. Add the cornstarch (if not already blended in), bread crumbs, and baking powder, if using, to the nuts.

3. Put the egg whites in the large bowl of an electric mixer, and check to make sure the whites no longer feel cold. Add the cream of tartar and salt and whip on medium speed just until foamy. Gradually whip in ¼ cup of the sugar, increasing the mixer speed to high, but watch closely. As soon as you start to see beater tracks on top of the whites, stop the machine, lift the beater, and check the stiffness of the foam. At sea level, you want whites that stand up in stiff peaks, but at 2,500 feet and above, you only want soft, droopy peaks (see sketch, page 176). If the whites look too soft, continue beating for just a few more seconds and check again; do not overbeat. The whites should be glossy and

smooth. Remove the bowl from the mixer stand, scrape the beater into the bowl, and return the beater to the mixer (without washing) to use again. Or, if you have only one mixer bowl, scrape the whites into another large bowl, so you can reuse the first bowl without washing it. Set the whipped whites aside.

**4.** Using the mixer, whip the yolks with the remaining ½ cup sugar until thick and light colored. Stop the machine and scrape down the bowl and beater. Whip on high speed until the yolks form a flat ribbon falling back on itself when the beater is lifted; this can take 3 to 7 minutes or longer, depending upon the type of mixer. Add the cinnamon, extracts, and lemon juice, if using. Remove the bowl from the mixer stand.

**5.** Using a flexible spatula, fold about a cup of the whipped whites into the yolk mixture to lighten it, then alternately fold in the nut mixture and the remaining whites. Fold with a light touch, cutting through the center of the batter and down to the bottom of the bowl, then bring the spatula up again toward you while giving the bowl a quarter turn, until all the dry ingredients are incorporated.

**6.** Scoop the batter out onto the prepared pan and use a flexible spatula or icing spatula to spread it in an even layer out to the pan edges. Bake for the time indicated for your altitude in the chart above, or until the top is golden and feels springy to the touch and the edges are just beginning to pull away from the pan sides; a cake tester inserted in the center should come out clean. Do not overbake; the cake will be dry.

**7.** While the cake bakes, spread a tea towel out on a flat surface and sift the confectioners' sugar over it, making a 10 × 15-inch rectangle.

**8.** As soon as the cake is baked, invert the pan over the sugared area on the towel. Lift off the pan and peel off the paper. Leave the cake flat on the towel to cool completely.

**9.** Using a serrated knife, cut the cake crosswise into 4 equal strips, each about 3¼ by 9¼ inches, as shown. Spread a dab of preserves in the center of the foil-covered cardboard base and set one of the cake strips in place. Spread about ⅓ cup preserves over the layer, add another layer, and repeat. Sift a heavy coating of confectioners' sugar over the top layer (or see the recipe introduction for other ideas). To serve, cut into crosswise slices using the serrated knife.

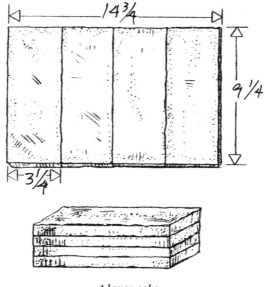

*4-layer cake*

# Boulder Blitz Torte

THIS CAKE is the original "twofer," butter cake and meringue layers baked on top of each other in the same pans; for a bonus, one meringue layer forms the cake top: Simply covered with cinnamon sugar and almonds, it looks spectacular and needs no further decoration. The result is delightful in your mouth, with the tender buttery cake crumb contrasting with the crisp sugary meringue and nuts. My favorite filling is Hazelnut Toffee Cream (page 173, whipped cream with crushed toffee), but this is also good with vanilla pastry cream (in a pinch, you could even use packaged cooked-style vanilla pudding flavored with added almond extract) and sliced ripe peaches or nectarines. If using the cream, prepare and fill the cake no more than about one hour before serving (the crushed toffee can be prepared in advance).

In Germany and Austria, where it originated, this cake is also known as Blitz Kuchen. The name, I believe, refers to the fact that you make two cakes at once as quick as lightning (*blitz* in German).

Don't bake this recipe on a rainy or humid day, or the meringue will soften. Be sure to use sliced almonds (available in supermarkets), not slivered almonds, which look like matchsticks. The eggs are separated; the yolks go into the butter cake and the whites make the meringue.

**General High Altitude Notes:** At 3,000 feet and above, use buttermilk instead of whole milk, because its acidity helps the cake set more quickly. Increase the quantity of buttermilk as the altitude increases to compensate for evaporation.

From 3,000 to 7,000 feet, use all-purpose flour, which has a little more protein than cake flour and adds to cake strength.

At 2,500 feet and above, the trick with this cake is to underbeat the whites, just until they form soft, slightly droopy peaks. At this stage, there is still room in them to expand when baked. If overbeaten to stiff peaks, the air cells may collapse when the cake cools. At 3,000 feet and above, reduce baking powder.

**Special Equipment:** Two 8 × 1½-inch round cake pans (9-inch pans make too-thin layers); baking parchment or wax paper; 3 foil-covered 9-inch cardboard cake disks or flat plates; wooden skewer or cake tester

**Pan Preparation:** Coat the pans with butter-flavor nonstick vegetable spray or solid shortening, dust with flour, and tap out the excess flour. At 5,000 feet and above, line the greased pans with wax paper or baking parchment, then grease and flour the paper; tap out the excess flour.

**Makes** one 2-layer 8-inch cake; serves 8 to 10

### High Notes

*At 3,000 feet and above,* use type of flour noted in chart. Replace the whole milk with buttermilk.

*From 3,000 to 5,000 feet,* bake in the center of the oven, but raise the temperature 25 degrees and cut time.

*At 7,000 feet and above,* place the rack lower in the oven to expose the cake to more heat, but reduce the temperature to 350°F and bake a little longer.

*At 10,000 feet,* use cake flour for the best texture, but increase the amount to strengthen the cake. Reduce the sugar and butter.

| Ingredients | Sea Level | 3,000 feet | 5,000 feet | 7,000 feet | 10,000 feet |
|---|---|---|---|---|---|
| **Oven rack position, temperature, and baking time** | Rack in center; bake at 350°F for 30 to 35 minutes | Rack in center; bake at 375°F for 18 to 23 minutes | Rack in center; bake at 375°F for 20 to 24 minutes | Rack in lower third of oven; bake at 350°F for 30 to 35 minutes | Rack in lower third of oven; bake at 350°F for 30 to 35 minutes |
| **TOPPING** | | | | | |
| **Granulated Sugar** | 1 tablespoon | 1 tablespoon | 1 tablespoon | 1 tablespoon | 1 tablespoon |
| **Ground cinnamon** | 1 teaspoon | 1 teaspoon | 1 teaspoon | 1 teaspoon | 1 teaspoon |
| **Sliced almonds (not slivered)** | ⅓ cup (1 ounce) | ⅓ cup (1 ounce) | ⅓ cup (1 ounce) | ⅓ cup (1 ounce) | ⅓ cup (1 ounce) |
| **BUTTER CAKE LAYER** | | | | | |
| **Sifted cake flour** | 1 cup | None | None | None | 1 cup plus 3 tablespoons |
| **Sifted all-purpose flour** | None | 1 cup | 1 cup | 1 cup | None |
| **Baking powder** | 1 teaspoon | 1 teaspoon minus a pinch | ¾ teaspoon | ¾ teaspoon | ½ teaspoon |
| **Salt** | ⅛ teaspoon | ⅛ teaspoon | ⅛ teaspoon | ⅛ teaspoon | ⅛ teaspoon |

*(continued)*

| Ingredients | Sea Level | 3,000 feet | 5,000 feet | 7,000 feet | 10,000 feet |
|---|---|---|---|---|---|
| **Unsalted butter, at room temperature** | 8 tablespoons (1 stick) | 8 tablespoons (1 stick) | 8 tablespoons (1 stick) | 8 tablespoons (1 stick) | 6 tablespoons (¾ stick) |
| **Granulated sugar** | ½ cup | ½ cup | ½ cup | ½ cup | ⅓ cup plus 1 tablespoon |
| **Large egg yolks, at room temperature** | 4 | 4 | 4 | 4 | 4 |
| **Vanilla extract** | 1 teaspoon | 1 teaspoon | 1 teaspoon | 1 teaspoon | 1 teaspoon |
| **Almond extract** | 1 teaspoon | 1 teaspoon | 1 teaspoon | 1 teaspoon | 1 teaspoon |
| **Whole milk** | ⅓ cup | None | None | None | None |
| **Buttermilk** | None | ⅓ cup plus 1 tablespoon | ⅓ cup plus 2 tablespoons | ⅓ cup plus 2 tablespoons | ½ cup |
| **MERINGUE CAKE LAYER** | | | | | |
| **Large egg whites, at room temperature** | 4 (½ cup) | 4 (½ cup) | 4 (½ cup) | 4 (½ cup) | 4 (½ cup) |
| **Cream of tartar** | ¼ teaspoon | ¼ teaspoon | ¼ teaspoon | ¼ teaspoon | ½ teaspoon |
| **Superfine or granulated sugar** | 1 cup | 1 cup | 1 cup | 1 cup | 1 cup |

**FILLING: HAZELNUT TOFFEE CREAM (PAGE 173)**

**1.** Position the rack and preheat the oven as indicated for your altitude in the chart above. Prepare the pans as directed.

Stir together the topping sugar and cinnamon in a small bowl. Put the sliced almonds in another small bowl. Set aside.

**2.** Prepare the butter cake layer: In a medium bowl, whisk together the sifted flour, baking powder, and salt.

**3.** In the large bowl of an electric mixer, cream together the butter and sugar until well blended. Scrape down the bowl and beater. Beat in the egg yolks two at a time, and then the extracts. Scrape the bowl again, and beat well to blend. Don't worry if the batter looks curdled—the flour will bring it together.

**4.** With the mixer on the lowest speed, slowly add the dry ingredients, alternating with the milk or buttermilk. Once the batter is blended together, increase the speed and whip for about a minute, until smooth and creamy. Divide the batter evenly between the prepared pans and smooth the tops. It will not look very thick, but that is okay. Set the pans aside on the counter.

**5.** Prepare the meringue layer: Put the egg whites in the clean mixer bowl and check to make sure they no longer feel cold. Add the cream of tartar and whip on medium speed just until foamy. Gradually whip in the sugar, increasing the mixer speed to high, but watch closely: As soon as you start to see beater tracks on top of the whites, stop the machine, lift the beater, and check the stiffness of the foam. At sea level, you want stiffly beaten whites that stand up in *nearly* stiff peaks, but at 2,500 feet and above, you only want soft, droopy peaks (see sketch). If the whites look too soft, continue beating for just a few more seconds and check again; do not overbeat. The whites should be glossy and smooth.

**6.** Divide the meringue evenly between the cake pans, spreading it over the butter cake batter. Use the spatula or the back of a spoon to pull the meringue up into peaks or points all over (it's okay if they droop slightly). Sprinkle the cinnamon sugar and then the sliced almonds evenly over the meringue layers.

**7.** Bake for the time indicated for your altitude in the chart above, or until the meringue tops are a darkened ivory color (not brown) and feel very crisp on top (the inside of the meringue will stay a little soft). The cake will be starting to shrink from the pan sides, and a cake tester inserted in the middle should come out moist (from the meringue) but not show any wet batter. Cool the layers in the pans on a wire rack for about 10 minutes.

**8.** Decide which of the meringue layers is the prettiest and should be the top of the cake; the loser will be upside down on the bottom, and the two butter layers will be in the middle with filling between. Run a knife between the cakes and pan sides to loosen, then top each layer with a foil-covered cardboard cake disk or flat plate and invert gently (don't worry if a little cinnamon sugar falls off). Lift off the pans and peel off the paper, if you used it. Top the best layer with another plate or foil-covered disk and invert again, so the meringue top is facing up. Cool the layers completely (while you prepare the filling).

**9.** To assemble the cake, spread the filling on the butter cake layer that is facing up. Use a broad spatula or pancake turner to help lift up the top layer, and place it—best meringue side up—on top of the filling. Do not ice the cake sides. Refrigerate the cake until ready to serve.

*Whipped Egg Whites*

*droopy peaks*

*stiff peaks*

# Passover Mocha Sponge Cake

THIS TALL cocoa-flavored sponge cake reminds me of a chocolate angel food cake—it's not too sweet and has a light tender crumb. It will be the hit of the party if you take it to a Passover Seder. Serve it with fresh fruit and Raspberry Sauce (page 149) or the Ultimate Chocolate Sauce (page 260). This recipe uses potato starch instead of flour, so it is suitable for wheatless diets. Potato starch is sold in most supermarkets and natural food stores, but don't confuse it with potato *flour*, a different product that will not work in this cake (see page 37 and Sources, page 329).

Grated chocolate gives this cake extra flavor; use the medium holes of a box or flat grater or (most easily) use a Microplane grater. (See "About Sponge Cakes and Egg Whites," page 110.)

**General High Altitude Notes:** At 2,500 feet and above, the trick with this cake is to underbeat the whites, just until they form soft, slightly droopy peaks. At this stage there is still room in them to expand when baked. If overbeaten to stiff peaks, the air cells, and the cake, will collapse when the cake cools. Oven temperature must be carefully monitored because you need just enough heat to allow the whites to expand sufficiently and the starch to set the cell structure before the cake top overbrowns; if the oven is too hot, the top glazes over before the interior batter rises and sets.

As the elevation increases, add extra cocoa to strengthen the cake's cellular structure and add cream of tartar for acidity and to stabilize the whipped whites. To compensate for evaporation and dry atmosphere, add extra coffee at 3,000 feet and above. This recipe uses natural cocoa, such as Hershey's regular, because it is more acidic than Dutch-process cocoa, and acidity helps the cake to set quickly.

High altitude tests on this cake were quite stable until I reached 10,000 feet. To all outward appearances, it was baked, but as I unmolded it from the pan, it slumped into a wet mess—apparently the inner batter was neither strong enough nor hot enough to set up. After several trials, my solution was to increase the starch, including the cocoa, to strengthen the structure. Because potato starch contains no gluten, reducing the sugar has little effect on the cake's strength.

**Special Equipment:** A 10 × 4-inch angel food tube pan, preferably with a removable bottom; sifter; wax paper; grater; flexible spatula or flat whisk; tall narrow-necked bottle (like a wine bottle) large enough to hang the tube pan upside down on its neck; foil-covered 10-inch cardboard cake disk or flat plate; long, thin-bladed knife; wooden skewer or cake tester; serrated knife

**Pan Preparation:** Do not grease the pan; if using a one-piece tube pan, line it with a ring of wax paper or baking parchment (see pages 30–31).

**Makes** one 10-inch tube cake; serves 12 to 14

## High Notes

*At 3,000 feet and above,* add more cocoa, cinnamon, salt, cream of tartar, coffee, and another egg. Reduce the sugar.

*At 5,000 feet and above,* add another egg.

*At 10,000 feet,* increase the potato starch, cocoa, and cream of tartar. Reduce the oven temperature and bake longer.

| Ingredients | Sea Level | 3,000 feet | 5,000 feet | 7,000 feet | 10,000 feet |
|---|---|---|---|---|---|
| **Oven rack position, temperature, and baking time** | Rack in center; bake at 350°F for 55 to 60 minutes | Rack in lower third of oven; bake at 375°F for 35 to 38 minutes | Rack in lower third of oven; bake at 375°F for 35 to 38 minutes | Rack in lower third of oven; bake at 375°F for 35 to 38 minutes | Rack in lower third of oven; bake at 350°F for 42 to 45 minutes |
| **Sifted potato starch** | 1 cup | 1 cup | 1 cup | 1 cup | 1 cup plus 3 tablespoons |
| **Natural cocoa, such as Hershey's regular** | 2 tablespoons | 3 tablespoons | 3 tablespoons | 3 tablespoons | ¼ cup plus 1 tablespoon |
| **Ground cinnamon** | Pinch | ⅛ teaspoon | ¼ teaspoon | ¼ teaspoon | ¼ teaspoon |
| **Large eggs, separated, at room temperature** | 8 | 9 | 10 | 10 | 10 |
| **Salt** | ¼ teaspoon | ¾ teaspoon | ¾ teaspoon | ¾ teaspoon | ¾ teaspoon |
| **Cream of tartar** | ½ teaspoon | ¾ teaspoon | ¾ teaspoon | ¾ teaspoon | 1¼ teaspoons |
| **Granulated sugar, divided** | ¾ cup plus ¾ cup | ¾ cup plus ½ cup | ¾ cup plus ½ cup | ¾ cup plus ½ cup | ¾ cup plus ½ cup |
| **Vanilla extract** | 1 teaspoon | 1 teaspoon | 1 teaspoon | 1 teaspoon | 1 teaspoon |

*(continued)*

| Ingredients | Sea Level | 3,000 feet | 5,000 feet | 7,000 feet | 10,000 feet |
|---|---|---|---|---|---|
| **Strong coffee or espresso, or instant coffee powder plus hot water** | ¼ cup, *or* 1 tablespoon powder dissolved in ¼ cup water | ⅓ cup, *or* 1 tablespoon powder dissolved in ⅓ cup water | ⅓ cup, *or* 1 tablespoon powder dissolved in ⅓ cup water | ⅓ cup, *or* 1 tablespoon powder dissolved in ⅓ cup water | ⅓ cup, *or* 1 tablespoon powder dissolved in ⅓ cup water |
| **Semisweet chocolate, grated** | 1½ ounces | 1½ ounces | 1½ ounces | 1½ ounces | 1½ ounces |
| **TOPPING** | | | | | |
| **Confectioners' sugar or cocoa** | 2 tablespoons | 2 tablespoons | 2 tablespoons | 2 tablespoons | 2 tablespoons |

**1.** Position the rack and preheat the oven as indicated for your altitude in the chart above. At 10,000 feet, remove the upper rack from the oven, because the cake rises so much that it may bump into it. Prepare the pan if necessary (see above).

**2.** Sift together the potato starch, cocoa, and cinnamon into a bowl. Set aside.

**3.** Put the egg whites in the large bowl of the electric mixer and check to make sure they no longer feel cold. Add the salt and cream of tartar and whip on medium speed just until foamy. Gradually whip in ¾ cup of the sugar, increasing the mixer speed to high, but watch closely: As soon as you start to see beater tracks

on top of the whites, stop the machine, lift the beater, and check the stiffness of the foam. At sea level, you want whites that stand up in stiff peaks, but at 2,500 feet and above, you only want soft, droopy peaks (see sketch). If the whites look too soft, continue beating for just a few more seconds and check again; do not over-beat. The whites should be glossy and smooth. Remove the bowl from the mixer stand, scrape the beater into the bowl, and return the beater to the mixer (without washing) to use again. Or, if you have only one mixer bowl, scrape the whites into another large bowl, so you can reuse the mixer bowl without washing it. Set the whites aside.

*Whipped Egg Whites*

*droopy peaks*

*stiff peaks*

**4.** Using the mixer, whip the yolks with the remaining sugar until thick and light colored. Stop the machine and scrape down the bowl and beater. Add the vanilla and, on very low speed, beat in the coffee. Whip on high speed for 2 full minutes. Remove from the mixer stand.

**5.** Using a flexible spatula, fold about half the cocoa mixture into the yolk batter, then alternately fold in the whipped whites, the remaining cocoa mixture, and the grated chocolate. Fold with a light touch, cutting through the center of the batter and down to the bowl bottom, then bringing the spatula up again toward you while giving the bowl a quarter turn, until all the dry ingredients are incorporated. Don't worry if you see some streaks of white in the batter.

**6.** Scoop the batter into the pan. Bake for the time indicated for your altitude in the chart above, or until the cake is well risen and springy to the touch, and a cake tester inserted in the center comes out clean. As soon as the cake is done, invert the pan onto its feet or hang the pan upside down over the neck of a bottle (see sketch). Leave upside down until completely cool, several hours (or overnight).

**7.** To remove the cake from the pan, slide the blade of a long, thin knife between the cake and the pan sides, then run the knife around the center tube. Top the cake with a foil-covered cardboard disk or plate and invert, giving the pan a sharp downward shake. Lift off the pan. If the cake is stuck to the pan's removable bottom, slide the knife between the pan and the bottom of the cake to release it. Or peel off the paper, if you used it and it stuck to the cake.

**8.** Just before serving, top the cake with a little sifted confectioners' sugar or cocoa. Cut with a serrated knife, and serve with fresh fruit or sauce of your choice, if desired.

*Cooling cake on pan feet*

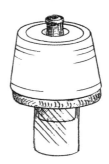

*Cooling cake over a bottle*

# Sour Cream Streusel Coffee Cake

A FAVORITE AT all our family gatherings, this rich, moist cake ribboned with crunchy cinnamon-nut crumbs begs to be dunked into a mug of hot coffee. The recipe is tried, true, and reliable at every altitude (when you follow the adjustments given).

The cake lends itself to creative flavor variations: try adding a teaspoon of almond extract, or blending the vanilla with a half-teaspoon each of almond and lemon extract. To make Chocolate Chip Coffee Cake (at any altitude), change the topping-filling crumb mixture to ½ cup sugar, 1 teaspoon cinnamon, 2 teaspoons unsweetened cocoa, ½ cup chopped nuts, and ½ cup mini–chocolate chips; add to the cake batter 3 tablespoons canola oil and 1 cup (6 ounces) mini–chocolate chips.

**General High Altitude Notes:** This cake has a dense, heavy batter; if the heat is too high it tends to crust over on top before the interior batter is set. Note the baking temperatures and times indicated in the recipe change at different altitudes for optimal results.

**Special Equipment:** 9- to 9½-inch (10- to 12-cup capacity) Bundt or tube pan; 2 flat plates or cardboard cake disks covered with aluminum foil; wooden skewer or cake tester

**Pan Preparation:** Very generously coat pan with butter or solid shortening, then dust with flour; tap out excess flour. Take special care to add extra shortening in decorative indentations of a Bundt pan. Note: You can also coat pan with nonstick vegetable spray, but it tends to puddle in the bottom of a Bundt pan.

**Makes** 14 to 16 servings

**High Notes**
*At 3,000 feet and above,* reduce sugar and leavening and add an egg.
*At 5,000 feet and above,* add liquid.
*At 7,000 feet and above,* lower baking temperature from 375°F to 350°F but increase baking time.
*At 10,000 feet,* strengthen the batter with a little more flour.

| Ingredients | Sea Level | 3000 feet | 5000 feet | 7000 feet | 10,000 feet |
|---|---|---|---|---|---|
| Oven rack position, temperature, and baking time | Rack in center; bake at 350°F for 50 to 55 minutes | Rack in lower third of oven; bake at 375°F for 42 to 45 minutes | Rack in lower third of oven; bake at 375°F for 45 to 50 minutes | Rack in lower third of oven; bake at 350°F for 50 to 55 minutes | Rack in lower third of oven; bake at 350°F for 55 to 58 minutes |

**TOPPING-FILLING CRUMB MIXTURE**

| Ingredients | Sea Level | 3000 feet | 5000 feet | 7000 feet | 10,000 feet |
|---|---|---|---|---|---|
| Chopped walnuts | ³/₄ cup (3 ounces) | ³/₄ cup (3 ounces) | ³/₄ cup (3 ounces) | ³/₄ cup (3 ounces) | ³/₄ cup (3 ounces) |
| Granulated sugar | ¹/₃ cup | ¹/₃ cup | ¹/₃ cup | ¹/₃ cup | ¹/₃ cup |
| Cinnamon | ³/₄ teaspoon | ³/₄ teaspoon | ³/₄ teaspoon | ³/₄ teaspoon | ³/₄ teaspoon |

**CAKE**

| Ingredients | Sea Level | 3000 feet | 5000 feet | 7000 feet | 10,000 feet |
|---|---|---|---|---|---|
| Sifted all-purpose flour | 3 cups | 3 cups | 3 cups | 3 cups | 3 cups plus 3 tablespoons |
| Baking powder | 1¹/₂ teaspoons | 1¹/₂ teaspoons | 1 teaspoon | 1 teaspoon | 1 teaspoon |
| Baking soda | 1 teaspoon | ¹/₂ teaspoon | ¹/₂ teaspoon | ¹/₂ teaspoon | ¹/₂ teaspoon |
| Salt | 1 teaspoon | 1 teaspoon | 1 teaspoon | 1 teaspoon | 1 teaspoon |
| Unsalted butter, softened | ³/₄ cup (1¹/₂ sticks) | ³/₄ cup (1¹/₂ sticks) | ³/₄ cup (1¹/₂ sticks) | ³/₄ cup (1¹/₂ sticks) | ³/₄ cup (1¹/₂ sticks) |
| Granulated sugar | 1¹/₂ cups | 1¹/₃ cups | 1¹/₄ cups | 1¹/₄ cups | 1¹/₃ cups |
| Large eggs, at room temperature | 4 | 5 | 5 | 5 | 5 |
| Sour cream | 1¹/₂ cups | 1¹/₂ cups | 1¹/₂ cups | 1¹/₂ cups | 1¹/₂ cups |
| Milk or buttermilk | None | None | 3 tablespoons | ¹/₃ cup | ¹/₃ cup |
| Vanilla extract | 2 teaspoons | 2 teaspoons | 2 teaspoons | 2 teaspoons | 2 teaspoons |

**1.** Position the rack and preheat the oven as indicated for your altitude in the chart above. Prepare the pan as directed above, taking special care to generously greasing any indentations in a decorative Bundt pan.

**2.** Prepare the topping-filling crumb mixture: In a small bowl, toss together all the topping ingredients. Set aside.

**3.** In a medium bowl, whisk together the flour, baking powder, baking soda, and salt. In the large bowl of an electric mixer, or in a large bowl using a wooden spoon, cream together the butter and sugar until well blended. Scrape down the bowl and beater. Beat in the eggs a couple at a time, along with the sour cream, milk or buttermilk (if using), and vanilla. Beat well to blend, then scrape down bowl and beater.

**4.** With the beater on the lowest speed, slowly add the dry ingredients, stirring just to incorporate them completely, but don't over-beat. Scrape down the bowl again, then beat another few seconds. The batter should be smooth, thick, and creamy.

**5.** Sprinkle about half the crumb mixture onto the bottom of the prepared baking pan. Spoon about half the batter over the crumbs, sprinkle on the remaining crumbs, then cover with the remaining batter and smooth the top. Bake as indicated for your altitude in the chart above, or until the cake is well-risen, golden-brown, and a cake tester in the center comes out clean or with just a few moist crumbs. The top will feel springy to your finger when lightly pressed. Cool the cake in its pan on a wire rack for no less than 20 minutes to release steam.

**6.** Run the tip of a paring knife between the rim of the pan and the cake to loosen it. Top with a flat plate or foil-covered cardboard disk, invert, and lift off the baking pan. The crumb topping will now be decorating the cake top.

# Taos Lemon Sponge Roll with Light Lemon Curd Filling

THIS MOIST, tender sponge cake is rolled around a creamy lemon or orange curd to make a delightful, highly flavorful dessert—a perfect finish for a gala dinner, light lunch, or afternoon tea. Serve it with Blueberry-Raspberry Sauce (page 149) and garnish it with fresh berries or organic nasturtium blossoms. For an easy alternative filling, use a generous cup of orange marmalade (spiked with Grand Marnier, if you wish) or pineapple or blackberry preserves mixed with fresh berries. (See "About Sponge Cakes and Egg Whites," page 110.)

This delectable cake will always remind me of a glorious summer day I shared with friends Carol Anthony and Jane Reid exploring the mountains north of Santa Fe. We visited Echo Cave (which really works) and wandered through Georgia O'Keeffe's dazzling scenery around Ghost Ranch. By late afternoon, as the falling sun began to turn the mountain shadows a unique shade of purple while it brushed the rest of the world with gold, the three of us sat around a little blue table outside a Taos café drinking Champagne and sampling the house specialty, lemon sponge roll.

---

**General High Altitude Notes:** At 3,000 feet and above, add an extra egg yolk for tenderness and flexibility. As the altitude increases, reduce the cornstarch, so the batter is less dry. Add lemon juice to enhance the flavor and add acidity, which helps batter set up quickly. Increase the juice to compensate for evaporation at highest altitudes. At 10,000 feet, strengthen the batter by cutting back on the sugar and adding a little flour.

**Special Equipment:** A jelly-roll pan (10 × 15 × ½-inch); baking parchment or wax paper; sifter; extra bowl for electric mixer (or another large bowl); flexible spatula; icing spatula (optional); cotton tea towel at least 10 by 15 inches; wooden skewer or cake tester; serrated knife

**Pan Preparation:** Coat the pan with butter-flavor nonstick vegetable spray or solid shortening, line with wax paper or baking parchment, grease the paper, and dust with flour; tap out the excess flour.

**Makes** one 10-inch cake roll; serves 10 to 12

## High Notes

*At 3,000 feet and above,* and an egg yolk and lemon juice. Reduce the cornstarch.

*At 7,000 feet and above,* increase the lemon extract.

*At 10,000 feet,* reduce the sugar and add more flour.

| Ingredients | Sea Level | 3,000 feet | 5,000 feet | 7,000 feet | 10,000 feet |
|---|---|---|---|---|---|
| **Oven rack position, temperature, and baking time** | Rack in center; bake at 350°F for 10 to 12 minutes | Rack in center; bake at 350°F for 10 to 12 minutes | Rack in center; bake at 350°F for 10 to 12 minutes | Rack in center; bake at 350°F for 11 to 12 minutes | Rack in center; bake at 350°F for 12 minutes |
| **Sifted cake flour** | ½ cup | ½ cup plus 1 tablespoon | ½ cup | ½ cup | ½ cup plus 2 tablespoons |
| **Sifted cornstarch** | ¼ cup | 3 tablespoons | 2 tablespoons | 2 tablespoons | None |
| **Large eggs, separated, at room temperature** | 4 | 4 | 4 | 4 | 4 |
| **Salt** | ⅛ teaspoon | ⅛ teaspoon | ⅛ teaspoon | ⅛ teaspoon | ⅛ teaspoon |
| **Cream of tartar** | ½ teaspoon | ½ teaspoon | ½ teaspoon | ½ teaspoon | ¾ teaspoon |
| **Granulated sugar, divided** | 6 tablespoons plus ¼ cup | 6 tablespoons plus ¼ cup | 6 tablespoons plus ¼ cup | 6 tablespoons plus ¼ cup | ¼ cup plus ¼ cup |
| **Large egg yolk** | None | 1 | 1 | 1 | 1 |
| **Vanilla extract** | ¾ teaspoon | ½ teaspoon | ½ teaspoon | ½ teaspoon | ½ teaspoon |
| **Lemon extract** | 1 teaspoon | 1 teaspoon | 1 teaspoon | 1½ teaspoons | 1½ teaspoons |
| **Grated lemon zest** | 1 tablespoon | 2 tablespoons | 2 tablespoons | 2 tablespoons | 2 tablespoons |
| **Fresh lemon juice** | None | 2 tablespoons | 2 tablespoons | 2 tablespoons | 1 tablespoon |

(*continued*)

| Ingredients | Sea Level | 3,000 feet | 5,000 feet | 7,000 feet | 10,000 feet |
| --- | --- | --- | --- | --- | --- |
| Confectioners' sugar for unmolding cake | ⅓ cup | ⅓ cup | ⅓ cup | ⅓ cup | ⅓ cup |

LIGHT LEMON CURD FILLING (RECIPE FOLLOWS)

**1.** Position the rack and preheat the oven as indicated for your altitude in the chart above. Prepare the pan as directed.

**2.** Sift or whisk together the flour and cornstarch (if using) to blend them well.

**3.** Put the egg whites in the large bowl of an electric mixer and check to make sure they no longer feel cold. Add the salt and cream of tartar and whip on medium speed just until foamy. Gradually whip in the 6 tablespoons sugar (or ¼ cup if you are at 10,000 feet), increasing the mixer speed to high, but watch closely: As soon as you see beater tracks on top of the whites, stop the machine, lift the beater, and check the stiffness of the foam. At sea level, you want whites that stand up in stiff peaks, but at 2,500 feet and above, you only want soft, droopy peaks (see sketch, page 189). If the whites look too soft, continue beating for just a few more seconds and check again; do not overbeat. The whites should be glossy and smooth.

**4.** Remove the bowl from the mixer stand, scrape the beater into the bowl, and return it to the mixer (without washing) to use again. Or, if you have only one mixer bowl, scrape the whites into another large bowl so you can reuse the mixer bowl without washing it. Set the whipped whites aside.

**5.** Using the mixer, whip all the egg yolks with the remaining ¼ cup sugar until thick and light colored. Stop the machine and scrape down the bowl and beater a couple of times.

Add the vanilla, lemon extract, grated zest, and juice, if using. Whip the yolks until they form a flat ribbon falling back upon itself when the beater is lifted. At sea level, this takes about 3 minutes with the KitchenAid on speed #8; with other mixers and at higher altitudes, it can take 6 to 7 minutes or longer.

**6.** Spoon about 3 tablespoons of the flour mixture onto the batter and fold together. Repeat, gradually folding in all the flour mixture along with previously whipped whites; fold with a light touch, cutting through the center of the batter and down to the bowl bottom, and then bringing the spatula up again toward you while giving the bowl a quarter turn.

**7.** Scoop the batter out onto the prepared pan and spread it out to the pan edges, using a rubber spatula or icing spatula. Bake for the time indicated for your altitude in the chart above, or just until the top is golden and feels springy to the touch, and the edges are just beginning to pull away from the pan sides. Do not overbake, or the cake will be dry.

**8.** While the cake bakes, spread a tea towel out on a flat surface and sift the ⅓ cup confectioners' sugar over it, making a 10 × 15-inch rectangle.

**9.** As soon as the cake is baked, invert the pan over the sugared area on the towel. Lift off the pan and peel off the paper. Use a serrated knife to slice a scant ⅛-inch-wide strip of crisp edging from all around the cake, so it

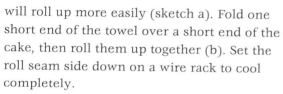

will roll up more easily (sketch a). Fold one short end of the towel over a short end of the cake, then roll them up together (b). Set the roll seam side down on a wire rack to cool completely.

**10.** When the cake is cool, unroll it and spread on the lemon curd (c). Reroll using the end of the towel to lift and push the cake as it rolls up (d). Set the cake seam side down on a platter and sift confectioners' sugar over the top. Cut the cake with a serrated knife. (Store leftovers in the refrigerator; if the cake is filled with preserves, refrigeration is unnecessary.)

# Light Lemon Curd Filling

*(recipe is basically the same at all altitudes, but the curd takes longer to come to a boil and thicken at higher altitudes)*

This lightened curd has a rich taste and creamy texture, but compared to a classic curd made with six egg yolks, much less fat and no cholesterol because it is thickened with cornstarch, like a pudding. You can make the curd a day or two in advance, cover, and refrigerate. To make Orange Curd, omit the lemon juice, increase the orange juice to 1 cup, and replace the lemon zest with orange zest.

**Makes** about 1 cup, enough to fill one cake roll (double the recipe to fill a 3-layer 8- or 9-inch cake)

> ½ cup granulated sugar
> 1½ tablespoons cornstarch
> 1 teaspoon all-purpose flour
> Pinch of salt
> ¾ cup orange juice
> Grated zest of ½ lemon (about 1½ teaspoons)
> ¼ cup fresh lemon juice
> 2 tablespoons heavy cream

In a 2-quart nonreactive saucepan (off the heat) whisk together the sugar, cornstarch, flour, and salt. Slowly whisk in the orange juice, lemon zest, and lemon juice, blending until there are no lumps. Set the pan over medium-high heat and stir with a wooden spoon for about 1 minute, then raise the heat to high and stir constantly, bringing the mixture to a full bubbling boil. Still stirring and making sure to reach into the pan corners, boil for 1 full minute (or longer at high altitudes), until the mixture is smooth and thick enough to generously coat the back of a spoon. Beat in the cream and set aside to cool before using, or refrigerate until ready to use.

# McCall Mocha Chiffon Cake
# with Champagne Sabayon Sauce

CHIFFON CAKES are related to angel food cakes but are richer because they contain both egg yolks and oil. Like their culinary cousins, chiffon cakes are baked in a tall tube pan and have a light, tender crumb and dramatic high rise. The flavor of this mocha version is a mellow balance between chocolate and coffee, but if you prefer plain chocolate, omit the coffee. The cake is complemented by either Raspberry Sauce (page 149) or Apricot-Orange Sauce (page 207), but my favorite is a divinely rich indulgence, Champagne Sabayon Sauce. This cake was a favorite of the medical staff who taste-tested my desserts at McCall Memorial Hospital in McCall, Idaho (see page 9).

A chiffon cake is cooled by hanging the pan upside down over the neck of a tall bottle so gravity can stretch the fragile cell structure until it cools and sets; if cooled right side up, the cake could collapse onto itself. (See "About Sponge Cakes and Egg Whites," page 110.)

**General High Altitude Notes:** At 2,500 feet and above, the trick with this cake is to underbeat the whites, just until they form soft, slightly droopy peaks. At this stage there is still room in them to expand when baked. If overbeaten to stiff peaks, the air cells, and the cake, will collapse when the cake cools. Monitor the oven temperature, because you need just enough heat to allow the whites to expand sufficiently and the starch to set the cell structure before the cake top overbrowns; if the oven is too hot, the top of the cake will crust over before the interior batter rises and sets.

As the elevation increases, adjust the leavening. At 5,000 feet and above, strengthen the batter with extra flour. Replace the Dutch-process

cocoa with more acidic natural cocoa, add a tiny bit of baking soda to enhance the cocoa's color, and adjust leavening. To compensate for evaporation and dry atmosphere, add a little more water. At 7,000 feet, add cream of tartar for acidity and to stabilize the whipped whites. At 10,000 feet, strengthen the cake structure by reducing the sugar and adding a whole egg, which also supplies moisture. Since both cocoa and flour are drying, add corn syrup for a more moist crumb.

**Special Equipment:** A 10 × 4-inch tube pan, preferably with a removable bottom; sifter; wax paper; flexible spatula or flat whisk; tall narrow-necked bottle (like a wine bottle) large enough to hang the tube pan upside down from its neck; foil-covered 10-inch cardboard cake disk or flat plate; wooden skewer or cake tester; long thin-bladed knife; serrated knife

**Pan Preparation:** Do not grease the pan; if using a one-piece tube pan, line it with a ring of wax paper or baking parchment (see pages 30–31).

**Makes** one 10-inch tube cake; serves 14 to 16

## High Notes

*At 5,000 feet and above,* add more flour and replace the Dutch-process cocoa with natural cocoa. Add baking soda and decrease the baking powder.

*At 7,000 feet and above,* return the oven temperature to 325°F so the cake top does not crust over before the interior batter bakes through.

*At 10,000 feet,* reduce the sugar, add an egg and corn syrup, and increase the cream of tartar.

| Ingredients | Sea Level | 3,000 feet | 5,000 feet | 7,000 feet | 10,000 feet |
|---|---|---|---|---|---|
| **Oven rack position, temperature, and baking time** | Rack in center; bake at 325°F for 65 to 70 minutes | Rack in lower third of oven; bake at 350°F for 45 to 47 minutes | Rack in lower third of oven; bake at 350°F for 40 to 45 minutes | Rack in lower third of oven; bake at 325°F for 40 to 45 minutes | Rack in lower third of oven; bake at 325°F for 45 to 50 minutes |
| **Large eggs, separated, at room temperature** | 6 | 6 | 6 | 6 | 7 |
| **Cream of tartar** | ½ teaspoon | ½ teaspoon | ½ teaspoon | ¾ teaspoon | 1 teaspoon |
| **Granulated sugar, divided** | ¾ cup plus ¾ cup | ¾ cup plus ¾ cup | ¾ cup plus ¾ cup | ¾ cup plus ¾ cup | ¾ cup plus ½ cup |
| **Sifted cake flour** | 1¾ cups | 1¾ cups | 2 cups minus 2 tablespoons | 2 cups | 2 cups |
| **Sifted Dutch-process cocoa** | ½ cup | ½ cup | None | None | None |
| **Sifted natural cocoa, such as Hershey's regular** | None | None | ½ cup | ½ cup | ½ cup |
| **Instant coffee powder or instant espresso powder** | 1 tablespoon coffee powder or 2 teaspoons espresso powder | 1½ tablespoons coffee powder or 2 teaspoons espresso powder | 1½ tablespoons coffee powder or 2 teaspoons espresso powder | 1½ tablespoons coffee powder or 2 teaspoons espresso powder | 1½ tablespoons coffee powder or 2 teaspoons espresso powder |

(*continued*)

| Ingredients | Sea Level | 3,000 feet | 5,000 feet | 7,000 feet | 10,000 feet |
|---|---|---|---|---|---|
| **Baking powder** | 1 tablespoon | 2½ teaspoons | 2¼ teaspoons | 2⅛ teaspoons | 2¼ teaspoons |
| **Baking soda** | None | None | ⅛ teaspoon | ⅛ teaspoon | Pinch |
| **Salt** | ½ teaspoon | ½ teaspoon | ½ teaspoon | ½ teaspoon | ½ teaspoon |
| **Ground cinnamon** | Pinch | Pinch | Pinch | Pinch | Pinch |
| **Water** | ¾ cup | ¾ cup | 1 cup minus 2 tablespoons | 1 cup minus 2 tablespoons | 1 cup minus 2 tablespoons |
| **Canola oil** | ½ cup | ½ cup | ½ cup | ½ cup | ⅓ cup plus 1 tablespoon |
| **Vanilla extract** | 1 teaspoon | 1 teaspoon | 1 teaspoon | 1 teaspoon | 1 teaspoon |
| **Dark corn syrup** | None | None | None | None | 2 tablespoons |
| **TOPPING (OPTIONAL)** | | | | | |
| **Cocoa or confectioners' sugar** | 2 tablespoons | 2 tablespoons | 2 tablespoons | 2 tablespoons | 2 tablespoons |
| **CHAMPAGNE SABAYON SAUCE (RECIPE FOLLOWS)** | | | | | |

1. Position the rack and preheat the oven as indicated for your altitude in the chart above. Line the one-piece tube pan as directed, if using.

2. Put the egg whites into the large bowl of an electric mixer and check to make sure they no longer feel cold. Add the cream of tartar and whip on medium speed just until foamy. Gradually whip in ¾ cup of the sugar, increasing the mixer speed to high, but watch closely: As soon as you start to see beater tracks on top of the whites, stop the machine, lift the beater, and check the stiffness of the foam. At sea level, you need whites that stand up in nearly stiff peaks, but at 2,500 feet and above, you only want soft, droopy peaks (see sketch, following page). If the whites look too soft, continue beating for just a few more seconds and check again; do not overbeat. The whites should be glossy and smooth. Scrape the whites from the beater into the bowl.

3. In a large bowl, whisk together the flour, cocoa, coffee powder, baking powder, baking soda (if using), salt, cinnamon, and the remaining ¾ cup (½ cup at 10,000 feet) sugar. Make a well in the center of the dry ingredients and add the egg yolks, water, oil, vanilla, and corn syrup (if using). With a whisk, working in the center first, blend together all the wet ingredients, then gradually pull in the flour mixture, whisking or stirring hard with a spoon to blend everything together.

Fold in the whipped whites in 3 or 4 additions. Fold with a light touch, cutting through the center of the batter and down to the bowl bottom, then bringing the spatula up again toward you while giving the bowl a quarter

*Whipped Egg Whites*

*droopy peaks*

*stiff peaks*

turn, until all the whites are incorporated. Don't worry if you see some white streaks.

**4.** Scoop the batter gently into the baking pan and cut through it once with a knife to remove any large air pockets; smooth the top. Bake for the time indicated for your altitude in the chart above, or until the cake is well risen and springy to the touch and a cake tester inserted in the center comes out clean.

**5.** As soon as the cake is baked, invert the pan onto its own feet or hang it upside down over the neck of a bottle (see sketch, page 190). Leave upside down until the cake is completely cool, several hours (or overnight).

**6.** To remove the cake from the pan, slide the blade of a long, thin knife between the cake and the pan sides to loosen it, then slide it around the central tube. Top the cake with a foil-covered cardboard disk or plate and invert. Lift off the pan, or if your cake is stuck to the removable pan bottom, slide the knife between the pan and the bottom of the cake to release it. Or peel off the paper, if you used it and it stuck to the cake. You may wish to invert the cake again, so the prettier surface (the baked top) faces up.

**7.** Just before serving, sift a little cocoa or confectioners' sugar on the top, if you wish. Cut the cake with a serrated knife, and serve with the sauce.

# Champagne Sabayon Sauce
*(recipe is the same at all altitudes)*

Sabayon (*zabaglione* in Italian), is a French wine custard sauce prepared by whipping egg yolks, sugar, and wine together over heat. Use Champagne if you have it, or substitute Marsala (for the classic Italian version) or any dry white wine. My friend Stacy Pearl made a great variation by combining 3/4 cup chenin blanc (white wine) and 1/4 cup Triple Sec.

At high altitudes, water takes longer to boil than at sea level, so the yolk mixture will take longer to get hot and thicken. Don't give up, just keep beating; it will work. At 5,000 to 7,000 feet, the trick is to bring the water in the bottom of the double boiler to a full boil (instead of a simmer) before setting the yolk mixture over it—but then begin to whip it at once so the eggs don't poach. At 10,000 feet, to get sufficient heat, you may need to put the pan directly over medium heat for the first 5 minutes of whipping; keep water boiling in the bottom of the double boiler so you can switch over and set the yolk mixture over the boiling water occasionally to prevent the mixture from scorching. Serve the sauce warm or chill it (which will reduce the volume slightly) by beating over an ice water bath.

**Special Equipment:** A 1½ to 2-quart double boiler (or pot with metal bowl set above it); hand-held electric mixer; large metal bowl (optional); instant-read thermometer (optional)

**Makes** 4 cups (warm) or about 3½ cups (chilled)

 8 large egg yolks
 ½ cup granulated sugar
 1 cup Champagne or other wine

If you plan to serve the sabayon cold, set a bowl of ice water near the stove, along with the measured wine, your electric mixer, and an instant-read thermometer, if you have one.

Put the yolks in the top of the double boiler and set aside. Put 2 to 3 inches of water in the bottom of a double boiler, cover, and bring to a boil.

Once the water is boiling, whisk the sugar into the yolks, beating hard (don't let the yolks and sugar sit together without beating, or the yolks will harden). Set the mixture over (not touching) the boiling water (use a gentle boil at sea level) and begin whipping at once. The mixture will gradually begin to foam and then, after 2 to 4 minutes, expand in volume. At this point, gradually drizzle in the wine while continuing to whip constantly. At sea level to 3,000 feet, you can reduce the heat slightly to simmer; at 5,000 feet or above, leave it high enough to keep the water boiling hard. After 6 to 8 minutes (longer at 10,000 feet), the sabayon should have tripled in volume and be thick enough to heavily coat the back of a spoon; it will register 142° to 145°F on the instant-read thermometer.

Serve warm, or cold. To chill, be sure the sabayon is in a (shockproof) metal bowl, set it in the ice water bath, and whip until cool.

# Orange Chiffon Cake with Apricot-Orange Sauce

A PERFECT WARM-WEATHER dessert, this flavorful yellow tube cake has a delicate, moist crumb that pairs wonderfully with fresh berries and the tangy Apricot-Orange Sauce. (See "About Sponge Cakes and Egg Whites," page 110.) In my mind, this recipe will always be connected to Santa Fe. I had been testing chiffon cakes and sauces there for several days, and I needed to take time off. I called my good friend Lorraine Schechter, who is always enthusiastic about showing me around her beloved New Mexican mountains, and we met early the next morning. It was a perfect-as-usual Santa Fe day, clear cobalt sky, cool but sunny air, and we set off for our favorite destination, Santa Fe's irresistibly tempting flea market, where my most unusual find was a display of clocks made out of shellacked, golden, home-baked fry breads.

Our afternoon drive took us northeast, into mauve- and madder-hued mountains striped with silver and terra-cotta bands, giving them a definite layer-cake look. We wound our way through the tiny trading post of Las Trampas, past valleys of cottonwood trees and across sandy hills dappled with juniper and dusty blue sage. When we finally reached the little village of Dixon, it was a memorable moment: first, because we found ice-cold lemonade when we really needed it, and second, because we discovered a gift shop selling the amazing spiced jams of Sylvia Vergara. A legend in that tiny town, Sylvia is an artist, flamenco dancer, and poet turned cook, now producing a commercial line of syrups, vinegars, and fruit preserves (see Sources, page 329). Her magic, at least the part she will discuss, involves stirring up big batches of sugared fruits (wild cherry, lemon marmalade, plum, wild mint–lemon) infused with spicy blends of red or flame-roasted green chiles. In the shop, we tasted a few tantalizing samples and bought one of each. Sylvia suggested spreading her jam on cream cheese–topped crackers, but I was already thinking about a jelly-roll filling, cheesecake topping, and this chiffon cake sauce.

**Note:** The amount of grated zest you get from an orange depends upon its size as well as the type of grater used. I used the Microplane grater (page 32), which yields more than a box grater. Two oranges should give you 2 tablespoons grated zest; for the 2½ tablespoons used above 7,000 feet, you may need to use another orange.

—⟋⟋⟋⟋—

**General High Altitude Notes:** At 2,500 feet and above, the trick with this cake is to underbeat the whites, just until they form soft, slightly droopy peaks. At this stage there is still room in them to expand when baked. If overbeaten to stiff peaks, the air cells, and the cake, will collapse when the cake cools.

As the elevation increases, add extra flour or change from cake flour to all-purpose flour to strengthen the cake's cellular structure. Add cream of tartar for more acidity and to stabilize the whipped whites. To compensate for evaporation and dry atmosphere, add a little more liquid, in the form of lemon juice, at 3,000 feet and above. Monitor the oven temperature carefully, because you need just enough heat to allow the whites to expand sufficiently and the starch to set the cell structure before the cake top overbrowns; if the oven is too hot, the top glazes over before the interior batter rises and sets.

**Special Equipment:** A 10 × 4-inch tube pan, preferably with a removable bottom; sifter; wax paper; flexible spatula or flat whisk; tall narrow-necked bottle (like a wine bottle) large enough to hang the tube pan upside down on its neck; foil-covered 10-inch cardboard cake disk or flat plate; long thin-bladed knife; serrated knife

**Pan Preparation:** Do not grease the pan; if using a one-piece tube pan, line it with a ring of wax paper or baking parchment (see page 30).

**Makes** one 10-inch tube cake; serves 14 to 16

**High Notes**

At **3,000 feet and above,** add lemon juice. Increase the oven temperature and bake for a shorter time.

At **5,000 feet and above,** position the rack in the lower third of the oven. Add a little more flour.

At **7,000 feet and above,** strengthen the batter by switching to all-purpose flour, which contains more protein than cake flour (but still gives a tender crumb). Add more lemon juice, grated orange zest, and extract. Return the oven temperature to 325°F but lower the rack to give the cake more heat, and bake it longer.

At **10,000 feet,** reduce the sugar and oil and add another egg, cream of tartar, and corn syrup.

| Ingredients | Sea Level | 3,000 feet | 5,000 feet | 7,000 feet | 10,000 feet |
|---|---|---|---|---|---|
| **Oven rack position, temperature, and baking time** | Rack in center; bake at 325°F for 65 to 70 minutes | Rack in center; bake at 350°F for 40 to 43 minutes | Rack in lower third of oven; bake at 350°F for 35 to 40 minutes | Rack in lower third of oven; bake at 325°F for 45 to 50 minutes | Rack in lower third of oven; bake at 325°F for 45 to 50 minutes |
| **Large eggs, separated, at room temperature** | 6 | 6 | 6 | 6 | 7 |
| **Cream of tartar** | ½ teaspoon | ½ teaspoon | ½ teaspoon | ½ teaspoon | 1 teaspoon |
| **Granulated sugar, divided** | ¾ cup plus ¾ cup | ¾ cup plus ¾ cup | ¾ cup plus ¾ cup | ¾ cup plus ¾ cup | ¾ cup plus ½ cup |
| **Sifted cake flour** | 2½ cups | 2½ cups plus 1 tablespoon | 2½ cups plus 1 tablespoon | None | None |
| **Sifted all-purpose flour** | None | None | None | 2½ cups plus 1 tablespoon | 2½ cups plus 2 tablespoons |
| **Baking powder** | 1 tablespoon | 1 tablespoon | 1 tablespoon | 1 tablespoon | 2¼ teaspoons |
| **Salt** | ½ teaspoon | ½ teaspoon | ½ teaspoon | ½ teaspoon | ½ teaspoon |
| **Grated orange zest** | 2 tablespoons | 2 tablespoons | 2 tablespoons | 2½ tablespoons | 2½ tablespoons |
| **Fresh orange juice** | ¾ cup | ¾ cup | ¾ cup | ¾ cup | ¾ cup |
| **Fresh lemon juice** | None | 2 tablespoons | 2 tablespoons | ¼ cup | ¼ cup |
| **Canola oil** | ½ cup | ½ cup | ½ cup | ½ cup | ⅓ cup plus 1 tablespoon |
| **Vanilla extract** | 1 teaspoon | 1 teaspoon | 1 teaspoon | 1 teaspoon | 1 teaspoon |
| **Orange extract** | 1½ teaspoons | 1½ teaspoons | 1½ teaspoons | 2 teaspoons | 2 teaspoons |
| **Light corn syrup** | None | None | None | None | 2 tablespoons |

APRICOT-ORANGE SAUCE (RECIPE FOLLOWS)

1. Position the rack and preheat the oven as indicated for your altitude in the chart above. Prepare the pan as directed.

2. Put the egg whites into the large bowl of an electric mixer and check to make sure they are no longer cold. Add the cream of tartar and whip on medium speed just until foamy. Gradually whip in ¾ cup of the sugar, increasing the mixer speed to high, but watch closely: As soon as you start to see beater tracks on top of the whites, stop the machine, lift the beater, and check the stiffness of the foam. At sea level, you want whites that stand up in nearly stiff peaks, but at 2,500 feet and above, you only want soft, droopy peaks (see sketch, following page). If the whites look too soft, continue beating for just a few more seconds and check again; do not over-beat. The whites should be glossy and smooth.

Scrape the whites from the beater back into the bowl and set aside.

3. In a large bowl, whisk together the flour, baking powder, salt, and the remaining ¾ cup (or ½ cup at 10,000 feet) sugar. Make a well in the center of the dry ingredients and add the yolks, zest, juices, oil, and extracts; at 10,000 feet, add the corn syrup. With a whisk, working in the center first, blend together all the wet ingredients, then gradually pull in the flour mixture, whisking or stirring hard with a spoon to blend everything together.

4. Fold in the whites in 3 or 4 additions. Fold with a light touch, cutting through the center of the batter and down to the bowl bottom, then bringing the spatula up again toward you while giving the bowl a quarter turn, until all the whites are incorporated. Don't worry if you see some white streaks.

5. Scoop the batter gently into the baking pan. Cut through it once with a knife to remove any large air pockets, and smooth the top. Bake for the time indicated for your altitude in the chart above, or until the cake is well risen and springy to the touch and a cake tester inserted in the center comes out clean.

6. As soon as the cake is baked, invert the pan onto its feet or hang it upside down over the neck of a bottle (see sketch, following page). Leave upside down until completely cool, several hours (or overnight).

7. To remove the cake from the pan, slide the blade of a long, thin knife between the cake and the pan sides to loosen it, then slide it

When I was testing recipes in Mammoth, California (about 9,000 feet), I had to make many changes to allow for the altitude. I raised the oven temperature about twenty-five degrees and cooked things much longer, but the most surprising adjustment was in taste: my sea-level sauces were suddenly so bland that I had to keep tasting over and over and adding more salt.

—Martha Rose Shulman, cookbook author, *Ready When You Are*

*Cooling cake on pan feet*

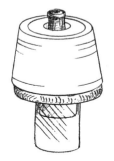

*Cooling cake over a bottle*

around the central tube. Top the cake with a foil-covered cardboard disk or plate and invert. Lift off the pan. If your cake is stuck to the removable pan bottom, slide the knife between the pan and the bottom of the cake to release it. Or peel off the paper, if you used it and it stuck to the cake. You may wish to invert the cake again so the prettier surface (the baked top) faces up.

**8.** Cut the cake with a serrated knife and serve with the sauce.

# Apricot-Orange Sauce
*(recipe is the same at all altitudes)*

This colorful, tangy sauce adds sparkle to any sponge cake (as a bonus, it is fat- and cholesterol-free). It is also delicious over vanilla ice cream or orange sorbet, and it couldn't be easier to prepare. To give the sauce a Southwestern kick, add some pure ground red chile or roasted New Mexican green chile, to taste. If you have time to plan ahead, use one of Sylvia Vergara's chile-spiked preserves (see Sources, page 329) instead of regular apricot preserves and omit the liqueur.

**Makes** about 1¾ cups

> 1 cup apricot preserves
> ½ cup fresh orange juice
> ¼ cup Grand Marnier or other citrus-flavored liqueur, or rum, optional

Place the preserves and juice in a small saucepan over medium heat and stir together until smooth. Remove from the heat and stir in the liqueur or other spirits, if using. Serve warm or at room temperature.

*Whipped Egg Whites*

*droopy peaks*

*stiff peaks*

# Reduced-Fat Chocolate Dream Cake

YOU REALLY can have your cake and eat it, too, with this recipe—rich and chocolatey (with both cocoa and melted semisweet chocolate), it has a moist tender crumb *and* just half the fat of a classic buttermilk chocolate cake. Garnish it with ripe strawberries and serve it at your next party. If you don't tell, your guests will never guess that it has only 26 percent calories from fat, 241 calories, and 8 grams of fat per serving. For a fat-free icing for the layer cake, use 7- to 15-Minute Icing (page 169).

**General High Altitude Notes:** To develop this reduced-fat recipe, I replaced part of the fat in a classic (buttery) chocolate cake with a blend of yogurt, corn syrup, and applesauce. This recipe can be baked in layers or a tube pan from sea level to about 8,500 feet. Above that, it will sink in layer pans but rise beautifully if baked in a tube pan, which delivers heat to the center of the heavy, wet batter. Above 5,000 feet, the cake tends to stick to the pan, so it should be lined with paper for easy release. This recipe uses cake flour because it contains less protein than all-purpose and takes less fat to tenderize it. Yogurt adds moisture, flavor, and acidity.

**Special Equipment:** Two 8- or 9-inch round cake pans or one 9-inch (10- to 12-cup) tube or Bundt pan; baking parchment, wax paper, or aluminum foil; 2 foil-covered 9-inch cardboard cake disks or flat plates (or one if using a tube pan)

**Pan Preparation:** Generously coat the pan(s) with solid shortening, then dust with sifted cocoa and tap out the excess cocoa. At 5,000 feet and above, line the pan(s) with baking parchment, wax paper, or foil (see page 31 or page 34) pressing it into the greased pan, and grease and flour the liner; tap out the excess flour.

**Makes** one 2-layer 8- or 9-inch cake; serves 12 to 14; or one 9-inch tube cake; serves 12

**High Notes**

*At 3,000 feet and above,* increase the flour and yogurt and cut back a little on the sugar.

*At 5,000 feet and above,* use the more acidic natural cocoa rather than alkali Dutch-process cocoa.

*At 10,000 feet,* bake in a tube pan. Reduce the corn syrup and applesauce, and add a little more yogurt.

| Ingredients | Sea Level | 3,000 feet | 5,000 feet | 7,000 feet | 10,000 feet |
| --- | --- | --- | --- | --- | --- |
| **Oven rack position, temperature, and baking time** | Rack in center; bake at 325°F: layers for 25 to 28 minutes, tube pan for 40 to 45 minutes | Rack in center; bake at 375°F: layers for 22 to 28 minutes, tube pan for 30 to 35 minutes | Rack in center; bake at 375°F: layers for 22 to 25 minutes, tube pan for 30 to 33 minutes | Rack in lower third of oven; bake at 350°F: layers for 25 to 28 minutes, tube pan for 30 to 35 minutes | Rack in center; bake tube at 350°F for 30 to 32 minutes |
| **Semisweet chocolate, chopped** | 2 ounces | 2 ounces | 2 ounces | 2 ounces | 2 ounces |
| **Sifted cake flour** | 1 cup | 1 cup plus 1 tablespoon | 1 cup plus 1 tablespoon | 1 cup plus 1 tablespoon | 1 cup plus 2 tablespoons |
| **Dutch-process cocoa** | ¾ cup | ¾ cup | None | None | None |
| **Natural cocoa, such as Hershey's regular** | None | None | ¾ cup | ¾ cup | ¾ cup |
| **Salt** | ¼ teaspoon | ½ teaspoon | ½ teaspoon | ½ teaspoon | ½ teaspoon |
| **Baking powder** | ½ teaspoon | ½ teaspoon | ¼ teaspoon | ¼ teaspoon | ¼ teaspoon |
| **Baking soda** | ¼ teaspoon | None | ¼ teaspoon | ⅛ teaspoon | ⅛ teaspoon |
| **Large eggs, at room temperature** | 2 | 2 | 2 | 2 | 2 |
| **Large egg whites, at room temperature** | 3 | 3 | 3 | 3 | 3 |
| **Plain or vanilla nonfat yogurt, top liquid poured off** | 2 tablespoons | 3 tablespoons | 3 tablespoons | 3 tablespoons | ¼ cup |
| **Granulated sugar** | 1¼ cups | 1¼ cups minus 1 tablespoon | 1¼ cups minus 1 tablespoon | 1¼ cups minus 1 tablespoon | 1 cup plus 2 tablespoons |
| **Dark corn syrup** | ¾ cup | ¾ cup | ¾ cup | ¾ cup | ½ cup plus 2 tablespoons |

*(continued)*

| Ingredients | Sea Level | 3,000 feet | 5,000 feet | 7,000 feet | 10,000 feet |
|---|---|---|---|---|---|
| **Canola oil** | ¼ cup | ¼ cup | ¼ cup | ¼ cup | ¼ cup |
| **Applesauce** | ¾ cup | ¾ cup | ¾ cup | ¾ cup | ½ cup plus 2 tablespoons |
| **Vanilla extract** | 1 tablespoon | 1 tablespoon | 1 tablespoon | 1 tablespoon | 1 tablespoon |
| LAYER CAKE FILLING | | | | | |
| **Apricot or raspberry preserves** | 1 cup | 1 cup | 1 cup | 1 cup | 1 cup |
| TOPPING (OPTIONAL) | | | | | |
| **Cocoa or confectioners' sugar** | 3 tablespoons | 3 tablespoons | 3 tablespoons | 3 tablespoons | 3 tablespoons |

**1.** Position the rack and preheat the oven as indicated for your altitude in the chart above. Prepare the pan(s) as directed.

**2.** Put the chocolate in the top of a double boiler set over simmering (at sea level to 5,000 feet) or boiling (at 5,000 feet and above) water and heat, stirring occasionally, until smooth; or melt the chocolate in the microwave (see page 35). Remove from heat and set aside to cool.

**3.** In a medium bowl, whisk together the flour, cocoa, salt, baking powder, and baking soda (if using).

**4.** In a large bowl, whisk together the whole eggs, extra whites, yogurt, sugar, corn syrup, oil, applesauce, and vanilla. Slowly stir in the dry ingredients, blending just until smooth; don't overbeat. Scrape in the melted chocolate and beat well; the batter will be quite runny.

**5.** Pour the batter into the prepared pan(s). Bake for the time indicated for your altitude in the chart above, or until the top of the cake feels springy to the touch and a cake tester inserted in the center comes out clean; don't overbake, or the cake will be dry.

**6.** Cool the cake in its pan(s) on a wire rack: layers for about 10 minutes, tube pan for about 15 to 20 minutes.

**7.** Run a knife around the pan sides, and around the top of the tube, if you used a tube pan, to loosen the cake. Top with a plate or foil-covered cardboard cake disk and invert. Remove the pan(s), and peel off the paper, if you used it. Cool the cake completely.

**8.** Spread the preserves between the layers. Sift a little cocoa or confectioners' sugar on top of the filled layers or the tube cake, if desired. Serve with fresh berries, and cut with a serrated knife.

# Reduced-Fat Orange Tube Cake with Blueberry-Honey Sauce

THIS IS a moderately sweet cake with a strong orange flavor and a tender, moist crumb. Serve it plain for afternoon tea or a midnight snack, or dress it up with the Blueberry-Honey Sauce, and it's fit for a party. If you don't mention that it is reduced in fat, no one will ever guess. The delicious numbers now are only 225 calories, 12 percent calories from fat, and 3 grams of fat per serving. See Note, page 204, about grated zest.

**General High Altitude Notes:** To reduce the fat and cholesterol, I adapted a butter cake recipe, replacing one cup of the fat with a blend of corn syrup, applesauce, and oil, and substituting egg whites for some eggs. This recipe must be baked in a tube pan to allow the heat to reach the center of the batter, facilitating a good rise. Cake flour is used because it contains less protein than all-purpose and thus takes less fat to tenderize it. As the altitude increases, the batter is strengthened by dropping the cornstarch used at sea level, adding flour, and cutting back on the sugar. From 5,000 to 7,000 feet, add liquid to replace that lost to evaporation. At 3,000 feet, the sea-level combination of baking powder and baking soda is replaced by baking powder alone in order to retain more acidity in the batter; the cream of tartar is also increased to add acidity. The baking powder is increased up to 5,000 feet, then slightly reduced as the altitude rises.

**Special Equipment:** A 9-inch (8-cup) Bundt or tube pan, preferably nonstick; wooden skewer or cake tester; serrated knife; foil-covered 10-inch cardboard cake disk or flat plate

**Pan Preparation:** Generously coat the pan with butter-flavor nonstick vegetable spray or solid shortening, dust with flour (especially the sides of the tube), and tap out the excess flour.

**Makes** one 9-inch tube cake; serves 10

### High Notes

*At 3,000 feet and above,* omit the cornstarch and add flour. Omit the baking soda and increase the baking powder. Cut the sugar slightly and add more oil.

*At 5,000 feet to 7,000 feet,* add a little more liquid.

*At 10,000 feet and above,* add more flour. Reduce the baking powder and sugar, and use the same amount of liquid as at sea level.

| Ingredients | Sea Level | 3,000 feet | 5,000 feet | 7,000 feet | 10,000 feet |
|---|---|---|---|---|---|
| Oven rack position, temperature, and baking time | Rack in center; bake at 350°F for 35 to 45 minutes | Rack in center; bake at 375°F for 30 to 35 minutes | Rack in lower third of oven; bake at 375°F for 32 to 36 minutes | Rack in lower third of oven; bake at 350°F for 32 to 36 minutes | Rack in center; bake at 350°F for 30 to 35 minutes |
| Sifted cake flour | 1½ cups | 1½ cups plus 2 tablespoons | 1¾ cups | 1¾ cups | 2 cups minus 2 tablespoons |
| Cornstarch | ¼ cup | None | None | None | None |
| Baking powder | 1 teaspoon | 1½ teaspoons | 1½ teaspoons | 1¼ teaspoons | ¾ teaspoon |
| Baking soda | ½ teaspoon | None | None | None | None |
| Salt | ¼ teaspoon | ½ teaspoon | ½ teaspoon | ½ teaspoon | ½ teaspoon |
| Granulated sugar, divided | ¾ cup plus ¼ cup | ½ cup plus ¼ cup plus 2 tablespoons | ½ cup plus ¼ cup plus 2 tablespoons | ½ cup plus ¼ cup plus 2 tablespoons | ½ cup plus ⅓ cup |
| Canola oil | 2 tablespoons | 3 tablespoons | 3 tablespoons | 3 tablespoons | 3 tablespoons |
| Dark or light corn syrup | ⅓ cup | ⅓ cup | ⅓ cup | ⅓ cup | ⅓ cup |
| Orange juice | ½ cup | ½ cup | ½ cup plus 1 tablespoon | ½ cup plus 1 tablespoon | ½ cup |
| Applesauce | ½ cup | ½ cup | ½ cup | ½ cup | ½ cup |
| Vanilla extract | ½ teaspoon | ½ teaspoon | ½ teaspoon | ½ teaspoon | ½ teaspoon |
| Orange extract | 1½ teaspoons | 1½ teaspoons | 1½ teaspoons | 1½ teaspoons | 1½ teaspoons |
| Grated orange zest | 2 tablespoons | 2 tablespoons | 2 tablespoons | 2 tablespoons | 2 tablespoons |
| Large egg whites, at room temperature | 3 | 3 | 3 | 3 | 3 |
| Cream of tartar | Pinch | ½ teaspoon | ½ teaspoon | ½ teaspoon | ¾ teaspoon |
| TOPPING | | | | | |
| Confectioners sugar, optional | 2 tablespoons | 2 tablespoons | 2 tablespoons | 2 tablespoons | 2 tablespoons |

BLUEBERRY-HONEY SAUCE (RECIPE FOLLOWS)

1. Position the rack and preheat the oven as indicated for your altitude in the chart above. Prepare the pan as directed.

2. In a large bowl, whisk together the flour, cornstarch (if using), baking powder, baking soda (if using), and salt. Stir in the first amount of sugar (¾ cup at sea level, ½ cup at 3,000 feet and above).

3. In a small saucepan, combine the oil, corn syrup, and fruit juice and stir over medium heat just until well blended and smooth. Remove and cool.

4. Make a well in the center of the flour mixture and pour in the cooled corn syrup mixture. Whisk to blend, then whisk in the applesauce, extracts, and grated zest.

5. Put the egg whites into the large bowl of an electric mixer and check to make sure they no longer feel cold. Add the cream of tartar and whip on medium speed just until foamy. Gradually whip in the remaining sugar, increasing the mixer speed to high, but watch closely: As soon as you start to see beater tracks on top of the whites, stop the machine, lift the beater, and check the stiffness of the foam. At sea level, you need whites that stand up in nearly stiff peaks, but at 2,500 feet and above, you only want a soft, droopy peaks (see sketch). If the whites look too soft, continue beating for just a few more seconds and check again; do not over-beat. The whites should be glossy and smooth. Scrape the whites from the beater into the bowl.

6. Stir about 1 cup of the whipped whites into the orange batter just to lighten it, then fold in the remaining whites in several additions. Fold with a light touch, cutting through the center of the batter and down to the bowl bottom, then bring the spatula up again toward you while giving the bowl a quarter turn, until all the whites are incorporated. Don't worry if you see some streaks.

7. Scoop the batter gently into the prepared pan and smooth the top. Bake for the time indicated for your altitude in the chart above, or until the cake feels springy to the touch and a cake tester inserted in the center comes out clean. Cool the cake in its pan on a wire rack for about 10 minutes.

8. Run a knife between the cake and the pan sides, and then around the rim of the tube to loosen it. Top with a foil-covered cardboard cake disk or plate and invert. Remove the pan and cool the cake completely.

9. Just before serving, top the cake with a light sifting of confectioners' sugar, if desired. Cut with a serrated knife, and serve with the sauce.

*Whipped Egg Whites*

*droopy peaks*

*stiff peaks*

# Blueberry-Honey Sauce

*(recipe is the same at all altitudes)*

This sweet-tart sauce has a rich fresh flavor and a deep blue color that complements any angel food or sponge cake.

**Makes** 2 cups

  2 cups fresh blueberries, picked over and
    rinsed, or 2 cups frozen berries, any ice
    particles removed
  ½ cup plus 2 tablespoons fresh orange juice
  ¼ to ⅓ cup honey (to taste)
  Grated zest of ½ lemon
  1 tablespoon fresh lemon juice, or to taste
  Pinch of ground nutmeg
  1 tablespoon cornstarch

In a medium heavy-bottomed saucepan, combine the berries, ½ cup of the orange juice, ¼ cup honey, the lemon zest and juice, and nutmeg. Bring to a boil over high heat and boil, bubbling, for 3 to 4 minutes, stirring and mashing some (not all) of the fruit to release juice. Remove from the heat.

Dissolve the cornstarch in the remaining 2 tablespoons orange juice, and stir into the berry mixture. Set the pan back over high heat and bring to a full rolling boil, stirring, then boil, stirring, until the sauce thickens, is no longer cloudy, and coats the back of a spoon (about 1 minute at sea level, several minutes at higher altitudes). Taste and adjust the flavor with more honey or lemon juice if needed. Serve warm or at room temperature.

When I bake at home in Missoula, Montana (3,300 feet), I need to make several changes to sea-level recipes to get them to work. I often add an extra egg, use buttermilk whenever I can, underbeat egg whites, and cut the amount of baking soda in half in my Devil's Food Cake. My most unusual trick, however, is to start baking a "puff" (sponge, angel, or chiffon) cake in a cold oven. I learned this method, applied to angel food cake, from the *Butte* [Montana, 5,500 feet] *Heritage Cookbook*, published in the 1970s, and since then it's become my favorite technique for all egg white–risen cakes. I prepare the batter in the usual way (but underbeat the whites slightly), set the pan in the cold oven, then turn the heat to 350°F—or the recommended temperature—and set a timer for the regular time; at the end, the cake has risen and baked perfectly!

—Greg Patent, cookbook author, *Baking in America*

# Flourless Chocolate Espresso Truffle Cake

THIS RECIPE remains my favorite of all the cakes I've baked for all my books. I love it warm from the oven when it is as soft as a just-set pudding, and I like it even better chilled—or straight from the freezer—when it has the consistency of a velvety truffle. Easy and quick to put together, it is totally reliable, even when frozen and shipped across the country (page 157).

You will see that the measurements for this recipe do not change with the altitude. Since this cake is closer to a custard or cheesecake than a layer cake, you avoid high altitude leavening and rising problems. The only altitude tricks are in the baking technique and in monitoring the heat (baking temperature, time, and oven rack placement) to be sure the batter gets hot enough inside to set.

The quality of the chocolate determines the taste of the cake, but you don't need to use an exotic brand. I like Baker's bittersweet (sold in a bright purple box in the supermarket) as well as Callebaut or Lindt Excellence. I use Medaglia d'Oro instant espresso coffee, available in supermarkets and gourmet food shops, but you can substitute 1 tablespoon regular instant coffee. Or, for a different flavor, omit the coffee and use 2 teaspoons hazelnut or orange extract or 1 teaspoon peppermint extract.

The cake needs no decoration, unless you want to melt some white chocolate and pipe a greeting. For a party presentation, I like to press toasted sliced almonds (not to be confused with matchstick-like slivered almonds) onto the sides of the warm cake; as an alternative, you can pipe a border of whipped cream around the edge of the cooled cake just before serving.

If you don't have a food processor, you can prepare the batter in a double boiler: melt the chocolate with the butter. Whisk in the separately cooked sugar-water-coffee syrup, then whisk in lightly beaten eggs. Pour the batter into the prepared pan and bake as directed.

**General High Altitude Notes:** To keep the cake texture creamy, this cake is baked like a custard, in a water bath, which guarantees gentle heat. At sea level, you can simply pour boiling water into the larger water bath pan just before baking the cake. At 3,000 feet and above, however, water takes longer to boil and evaporates more quickly. To get enough heat to the center of the batter to bake it properly, you must put a baking pan of just-boiled water in the oven to keep it very hot while you prepare the batter. By the time the batter is made, this water will be hot enough to transmit sufficient heat. Also, be sure to keep a kettle of extra water boiling during the baking time, to replace any that evaporates (usually necessary only at 10,000 feet). If, by accident, a drop of water touches the cake's surface, you can wick it off with the corner of a tissue or paper towel.

**Special Equipment:** A 9 × 1½-inch round cake pan; wax paper or baking parchment; roasting pan large enough to hold the cake pan (approxi-mately 10 × 14 × 2 inches); small saucepan (preferably with a pouring spout); 2-cup measure or medium bowl; food processor; large frying pan (optional); 2 foil-covered 9-inch cardboard cake disks or flat plates; plastic wrap

**Pan Preparation:** Coat the pan with butter or solid shortening and line the bottom with wax paper or baking parchment.

**Makes** one 9-inch cake; serves 10 to 12

**High Notes**

*At 3,000 feet and above,* place the roasting pan in the oven and add about ½ inch of boiling water before you begin to make the batter.

*At 5,000 feet and above,* preheat the oven to 25 degrees higher than the baking temperature to get the water bath hot enough. Reduce the heat by 25 degrees as soon as you set the cake pan in the water bath in the oven.

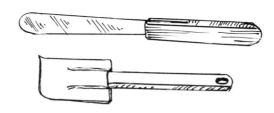

| Ingredients | Sea Level | 3,000 feet | 5,000 feet | 7,000 feet | 10,000 feet |
|---|---|---|---|---|---|
| **Oven rack position, temperature, and baking time** | Rack in lower third of oven; bake at 350°F for 30 to 38 minutes | Rack in lower third of oven; bake at 350°F for 28 to 30 minutes | Rack in lower third of oven; *preheat* oven to 375°F; *bake* at 350°F for 25 to 28 minutes | Rack in center; *preheat* oven to 375°F; *bake* at 350°F for 25 to 33 minutes | Rack in center; *preheat* oven to 375°F; *bake* at 350°F for 25 to 30 minutes |
| **Semisweet or bittersweet chocolate, coarsely chopped** | 8 ounces | 8 ounces | 8 ounces | 8 ounces | 8 ounces |
| **Water** | ½ cup | ½ cup | ½ cup | ½ cup | ½ cup |
| **Granulated sugar** | 1 cup | 1 cup | 1 cup | 1 cup | 1 cup |
| **Instant espresso powder** | 2 teaspoons | 2 teaspoons | 2 teaspoons | 2 teaspoons | 2 teaspoons |
| **Unsalted butter, at room temperature, cut into tablespoons** | ½ pound (2 sticks) | ½ pound (2 sticks) | ½ pound (2 sticks) | ½ pound (2 sticks) | ½ pound (2 sticks) |
| **Large eggs, at room temperature** | 4 | 4 | 4 | 4 | 4 |
| **GARNISH (OPTIONAL)** | | | | | |
| **Sliced almonds** | 1 cup (3½ ounces) | 1 cup (3½ ounces) | 1 cup (3½ ounces) | 1 cup (3½ ounces) | 1 cup (3½ ounces) |

**1.** Position the rack and preheat the oven as indicated for your altitude in the chart above. At 3,000 feet and above, place the roasting pan in the oven and pour in boiling water to a depth of no more than ½ inch. (At sea level, you can prepare the water bath when the batter is ready.) Prepare the cake pan as directed.

**2.** Put the chocolate in the bowl of a food processor and process for about 1 minute, until reduced to a fine powder. (Leave the chocolate in the bowl.)

**3.** In a small saucepan, stir together the water, sugar, and espresso powder over medium heat until the sugar and coffee dissolve. Then bring the syrup to the point where you see little bubbles around the edges—just *before* it reaches a full boil (it can boil over easily, so watch carefully); this can take 3 to 4 minutes at sea level, or longer at higher altitudes. Remove from the heat.

**4.** With the processor running, slowly pour the hot sugar syrup through the feed tube onto the powdered chocolate, then process for about 10 seconds to melt all the chocolate. Stop the machine and scrape down the bowl with a flexible spatula, then pulse for a few more seconds.

**5.** With the machine running, add the bits of soft butter through the feed tube 2 at a time, letting them melt completely (about 20 seconds) before adding more. When all the butter has been added, pulse several times, then turn off the machine and again scrape down the bowl; make sure all the butter has melted and the mixture is smooth.

**6.** Break the eggs into a 2-cup measure or a bowl and beat lightly with a fork, then slowly pour them through the feed tube onto the chocolate, pulsing every few seconds to blend; pulse 8 to 12 times, just enough to incorporate all the eggs without beating in excess air.

**7.** Scrape the batter into the prepared pan and smooth the top. At sea level, set the cake in the roasting pan, place both on the oven shelf, and then reach in with the kettle and carefully pour boiling water into one corner of the pan, just to a depth of about ½ inch (just under the halfway mark of the side of the cake pan). At 3,000 feet and above, carefully set the cake pan in the middle of the roasting pan of preheated water.

**8.** Bake the cake for the time indicated for your altitude in the chart above, or *just* until the batter no longer sticks to your fingertip when you touch the top of the cake, which will have lost its wet look and feel firm or slightly rubbery to the touch. Remove both pans from the oven (take care not to let water splash) and set them on a heatproof surface. Lift out the cake pan and set it on a wire rack to cool for 20 to 30

minutes, until the pan bottom feels just comfortably warm to the touch.

**9.** While the cake cools, if using almonds, toast them in a large frying pan over medium heat, turning and stirring frequently, until aromatic and golden brown. Remove and set aside to cool.

**10.** When the cake has cooled and is beginning to pull away from pan sides, run a knife between the cake and pan side to loosen it. (If your cake has unexpectedly gotten cold in the pan, you can set it over very low heat for a couple of seconds, just to warm the pan and melt the coating inside.) Top the cake with a generous sheet of plastic wrap (don't use foil for this task—it would stick to the cake and mar its surface) that overhangs the pan sides by a couple of inches. Top the plastic with a foil-covered cake disk or flat plate and invert the pan with a gentle downward shake: the cake will slide out. Lift off the pan and peel off the paper. Center a second plate or foil-covered disk over the cake, invert again, and remove the top plate or disk. Slowly peel off the plastic wrap; the surface should be unmarked.

**11.** To decorate the cake sides with almonds, place the cake on a wire rack, over a large tray or jelly-roll pan, to catch dropped nuts. Pick up the toasted nuts in your fingers and press them onto the cake sides, working all around the cake. (If the cake has cooled too much for the nuts to stick, melt a little chopped chocolate and spread it onto the cake sides with a knife as you stick on the nuts.) Serve right away or cool the cake completely, then refrigerate it until about 30 minutes before serving.

**Note:** To freeze the cake, chill it until it is hard, then double-wrap airtight in plastic wrap, and store in a heavy-duty self-sealing plastic bag.

# Cookies

## Baking Cookies at High Altitudes

As a general rule, cookies are among the easiest things to bake at high altitudes. Some sea-level recipes work without adjustment, so it is best to bake a trial batch before making any changes. As you will see from the recipes in this chapter, my adjustments are minimal, but they were arrived at after many trials with differing variables.

The biggest problem when baking cookies at high altitudes is that the batter spreads out too much. As you rise in elevation and atmospheric pressure decreases, cookies tend to spread, getting bigger, thinner, and tougher or overcrisp. Liquids evaporate faster at high altitudes, leaving higher concentrations of sugar and fat, which can alter a cookie's texture. According to tests done by the Department of Food Science and Nutrition at Colorado State University, the "overspread" of cookies was under 10 percent at between sea level and 5,000 feet but up to 30 percent from 5,000 to 7,000 feet. Those tests were done for commercial bakers, who are more concerned with uniform cookie size than home bakers, but we all want cookies to have the best possible texture, taste, and appearance.

In my own cookie tests, I first saw the need for adjustments at around 3,000 feet, when flavor was less pronounced than I was used to at sea level. To brighten the taste, I added a little more salt or more of the extracts. With a few cookies, I found a tendency to overspread, and I corrected for it by raising the oven temperature by 25 degrees. At 5,000 feet and above, I needed to make more changes as the spread grew and occasionally the texture was not right. I added a little flour and/or reduced the sugar to slow down the tendency to spread.

Chocolate chip cookies are usually the easiest to make and the most reliable, but at 10,000 feet, I had a lot of trouble trying to get the right texture: tender but crisp-chewy. My sea-level recipe spread way too much, and the cookies had a tough, coarse texture. I tried adding more flour (they got tougher), reducing the sugar (they spread less but lacked taste), and cutting back on butter (they were too dry). I also played with different proportions of butter (which is about 81 percent fat plus water and dry milk solids, with a melting point of around 92°F) and Crisco (100 percent fat, melting point of 110° to 120°F). Since Crisco melts more slowly than butter, it reduced spreading, and it made thicker, chewier cookies, but they had lost their great taste; using half Crisco and half butter didn't completely solve the problem. I reduced the baking soda, without notable success. Finally, I phoned Utah pastry chef Letty Flatt, who discusses high altitude cookies in her cookbook *The Chocolate Snowball* (Three Forks, 1999). She offered her solution: use sea-level measurements except for more flour, and bake at a lower temperature for a longer time. It worked. According to food chemist Shirley Corriher, the extra flour "dilutes" the sugar crystallization and keeps the cookies tender. The lower temperature lets the cookies bake without hardening too much. I still like to underbake them slightly so they are not totally crunchy.

If you think adjustments are necessary with some of your own recipes, consider the following: To control spread by strengthening the batter, add a little flour or cut down the sugar. To improve overall quality and limit spread, slightly reduce the baking powder, baking soda, or cream of tartar as the altitude increases. Or, raise the oven temperature 15 to 25 degrees and (perhaps) cut the baking time. In some cases,

though, it helps to reduce oven temperature and lengthen baking time. Don't look for a pattern in baking temperatures and times in the recipe charts; I tried to find the best results at each elevation, and these vary. For a thicker or chewier cookie, replace 2 or 3 tablespoons of the butter with an equal amount of Crisco (don't replace all the butter).

If the texture is too dry, you can add a little liquid or another egg yolk or a little light or dark corn syrup. Egg yolk and corn syrup both add liquid as well as contribute emulsifiers, moisturizing and softening the crumb and countering the dryness of flour caused by excess evaporation at high altitudes.

To store cookies at high altitudes, especially in dry mountain air, be aware that cookies can dry out almost as soon as they are baked. Once cooled, they should be placed in an airtight plastic container or wrapped in plastic wrap, then put in a self-sealing plastic bag. Fragile or decorated cookies can be boxed or set on a cardboard support before wrapping air-tight.

Unbaked cookie dough can be double-wrapped airtight and frozen for up to a month without losing flavor. I like to freeze dough in small batches so I can bake up a few fresh cookies whenever I want them. If you are baking dough that is still frozen, increase the baking time slightly.

# Old-Fashioned Sugar Cookies

THESE CRISP, buttery, cut-out cookies bring out the kid in anyone who tastes them.

They can be plain or fancy. If you are in a holiday hurry, simply cut the rolled dough into circles with the rim of a glass dipped in flour, or slice them into squares or diamonds, brush on a little milk or egg glaze, and sprinkle with sugar. For a creative extravaganza, use your most imaginative cookie cutters, make the Sugar Cookie Icing (below), and consider the cookies a blank canvas for your sweetest artistic skills.

To make hanging Christmas tree ornaments, roll the dough a tiny bit thicker than usual (for strength) and poke a hole in the top of each cookie with a drinking straw or toothpick before baking. Instead of using commercial coloring, you can make natural icing colors using a few drops of seedless raspberry jam (pink) or frozen orange juice concentrate (yellow).

**General High Altitude Notes:** I tested this recipe using both all-purpose flour, which is moderately strong, and cake flour, which is softer and contains less protein. Theoretically, cake flour makes a more tender cookie, but at high elevations, cake flour made this dough too soft, so that it needed extra flour or chilling to get to the right consistency and then spread too much when baked. My flour preference, at every altitude, is all-purpose; when you roll thin cookies, they will be perfectly tender.

**Special Equipment:** Cookie sheets (not insulated); baking parchment or Silpats or other nonstick baking mats (optional); paddle for electric mixer (optional); sifter; rolling pin; wax paper; cookie cutters; pastry brush

**Pan Preparation:** Line the cookie sheets with baking parchment or nonstick baking mats or lightly coat with butter.

**Makes** about 50 to 55 cookies (2-inch diameter); recipe can be doubled

**High Notes**
  *At 3,000 feet and above,* reduce the baking powder slightly and add more extract.
  *At 10,000 feet,* omit one egg, slightly reduce the flour in the dough (but continue to use it on the rolling pin and counter), and add a little cream of tartar.

| Ingredients | Sea Level | 3,000 feet | 5,000 feet | 7,000 feet | 10,000 feet |
|---|---|---|---|---|---|
| **Oven rack position, temperature, and baking time** | Divide oven into thirds; bake at 350°F for 8 to 12 minutes | Divide oven into thirds; bake at 350°F for 8 to 12 minutes | Divide oven into thirds; bake at 350°F for 8 to 12 minutes | Divide oven into thirds; bake at 350°F for 8 to 12 minutes | Divide oven into thirds; bake at 350°F for 12 to 15 minutes |
| **Unsalted butter, at room temperature** | 12 tablespoons (1½ sticks) | 12 tablespoons (1½ sticks) | 12 tablespoons (1½ sticks) | 12 tablespoons (1½ sticks) | 12 tablespoons (1½ sticks) |
| **Granulated sugar** | 1 cup | 1 cup | 1 cup | 1 cup | 1 cup |
| **Large egg(s), at room temperature** | 2 | 2 | 2 | 2 | 1 |
| **Vanilla or almond extract** | 1 teaspoon | 2 teaspoons | 2 teaspoons | 2 teaspoons | 2 teaspoons |
| **All-purpose flour, plus extra for rolling out** | 2¾ cups | 2¾ cups | 2¾ cups | 2¾ cups | 2½ cups plus 2 tablespoons |
| **Baking powder** | 1 teaspoon | 1 teaspoon minus ⅛ teaspoon | ¾ teaspoon | ¾ teaspoon | ½ teaspoon |
| **Salt** | 1 teaspoon | 1 teaspoon | 1 teaspoon | 1 teaspoon | 1 teaspoon |
| **Cream of tartar** | None | None | None | None | ¼ teaspoon |
| GLAZE (OPTIONAL) | | | | | |
| **Egg white or whole egg, beaten** | 1 | 1 | 1 | 1 | 1 |
| **Water** | 1 teaspoon | 1 teaspoon | 1 teaspoon | 1 teaspoon | 1 teaspoon |

DECORATIONS (OPTIONAL) Finely chopped nuts, colored granulated or coarse sugar, cinnamon, silver dragees, etc.

SUGAR COOKIE ICING (RECIPE FOLLOWS; OPTIONAL)

1. Position the racks and preheat the oven as indicated for your altitude in the chart above. Prepare the cookie sheets as directed.

2. In the large bowl of an electric mixer, preferably with a paddle attachment, cream the butter and sugar until well blended. Beat in the egg(s) and vanilla, then scrape down the bowl and beater. Remove the bowl from the mixer stand.

3. Place a sifter over the bowl and measure the flour, baking powder, salt, and cream of tartar into it. Stir/sift the dry ingredients onto the egg mixture, then beat with a sturdy spoon or the electric mixer on the lowest speed until well incorporated. Form the dough into a ball. If it feels too sticky, add 1 or 2 more tablespoons flour, until it is easier to handle. (In very hot weather, if the dough still feels too soft, divide it into four pieces, shape into flat disks, and refrigerate in a plastic bag until firm.)

4. Work with about one-third to one-half of the dough at a time and keep the rest in the refrigerator. For ease in handling, using a lightly floured rolling pin, roll out each portion of the dough about ⅛-inch thick on a piece of baking parchment or on a Silpat or other baking mat fitted to a cookie sheet. Dip the cookie cutters in flour to prevent sticking, and then cut out shapes. Leave about ½ to ¾ inch space between each cut shape. Use the tip of a knife to help lift and peel away the between-cookie bits, leaving the cookies in place. If you want to make hanging cookies, use a drinking straw or toothpick to poke a hole in the top of each cookie. Slide the parchment or other liner with the cut-out cookies onto a cookie sheet. Gather the dough scraps together, reroll, and cut out more cookies.

Alternatively, roll out the dough on a lightly floured counter, cut out the cookies, and use a broad spatula to transfer them to a prepared cookie sheet.

5. If desired, brush each cookie with a little egg glaze (egg white makes a clear glaze, whole egg gives a golden color) and sprinkle with finely chopped nuts, cinnamon, or sugar, if desired. Or you can decorate the cookies with icing after baking and cooling.

6. Bake the cookies for the time indicated for your altitude in the chart above, or until they look slightly golden around the edges. If baking seems uneven, rotate the pans back to front in the oven halfway through the baking time. Cool the cookies on a wire rack. If the cookies were baked on parchment or a baking mat, simply slide it off the cookie sheet onto the wire rack to cool. If you poked hanging holes in the cookies, repoke them now to widen any holes that may have closed up during baking.

7. If using the icing, mix it while the cookies cool. When the cookies are completely cooled, spread on the icing with a butter knife. Or put some of each color in a plastic bag, seal the top(s), and cut a tiny hole in one corner of each bag with scissors. If you want a carefully controlled fine line, drop a metal decorating tip into the corner of the plastic bag *before* adding the icing. Squeeze the icing out of the bag to make designs (after use, discard the bag; be sure to save the metal tip, if you used it). Leave the decorated cookies on the wire racks to air-dry the icing. At sea level, this can take an hour or more; at higher altitudes, the icing will dry more quickly. When the icing is hard, store the cookies in an airtight container, separated by layers of wax paper or plastic wrap.

## Sugar Cookie Icing
*(recipe is the same at all altitudes)*

**Special Equipment:** Small cups or bowls; pint-size self-sealing plastic bags and scissors; #5 or #6 plain decorating tips (optional)

**Makes** ¾ cup (recipe can be doubled)

2 tablespoons unsalted butter, melted and
   cooled
2 cups sifted confectioners' sugar
1 teaspoon vanilla extract or fresh lemon juice
2 to 3 tablespoons milk or water, as needed
Food coloring (liquid, powder, or paste; see
   Sources, page 329), optional

Combine the butter, sifted sugar, and vanilla
or lemon juice in a medium bowl and beat with
an electric mixer until smooth. Add enough
milk or water a drop at a time to make the icing
smooth enough to spread. If desired, put a couple of tablespoons of plain icing in each of several cups and stir a scant drop of color into
each, then add more color a tiny bit at a time if
necessary. Cover unused icing (especially at
high altitudes) with plastic wrap, to prevent it
from drying out.

# Sun Valley Peanut Butter Butter Cookies

NOTHING MAKES me reach for a cold glass of milk faster than these tender, sweet-salty cookies. Share them with friends, and you will feel like a kid on the back porch on a summer day. Use the tines of a table fork to press the classic crosshatch design on top.

In hot weather, if the room temperature exceeds 75°F, the batter may be very soft. Resist the temptation to add extra flour; instead, spread the batter out in a flat baking pan and refrigerate it for about 1 hour, or until firm, before shaping and baking.

I usually use commercial chunky peanut butter for these cookies, but organic all-natural peanut butter also works well if you stir it to blend in any separated oil before adding it to the batter.

---

**General High Altitude Notes:** As the altitude increases, decrease the sugar and leavening and add a little more flavoring.

**Special Equipment:** Cookie sheets (not insulated); baking parchment or Silpat or other nonstick baking mat (optional); flat paddle attachment for electric mixer (optional)

**Pan Preparation:** Line the cookie sheets with baking parchment or nonstick baking mats or lightly coat with butter.

**Makes** about 48 cookies (2-inch diameter)

| Ingredients | Sea Level | 3,000 feet | 5,000 feet | 7,000 feet | 10,000 feet |
|---|---|---|---|---|---|
| **Oven rack position, temperature, and baking time** | Divide oven in thirds; bake at 350°F for 12 to 15 minutes | Rack in center; bake at 375°F for 10 to 12 minutes | Rack in center; bake at 375°F for 10 to 12 minutes | Rack in center; bake at 375°F for 12 to 15 minutes | Rack in center; bake at 350°F for 12 to 15 minutes |
| **Unsalted butter, at room temperature** | 8 tablespoons (1 stick) | 8 tablespoons (1 stick) | 8 tablespoons (1 stick) | 8 tablespoons (1 stick) | 8 tablespoons (1 stick) |
| **Granulated sugar** | ¼ cup plus 2 tablespoons | ⅓ cup | ⅓ cup | ⅓ cup | ⅓ cup |
| **Dark brown sugar, packed** | ¼ cup plus 2 tablespoons | ⅓ cup | ⅓ cup | ⅓ cup | ⅓ cup |
| **Large egg, at room temperature** | 1 | 1 | 1 | 1 | 1 |
| **Vanilla extract** | 1 teaspoon | 1 teaspoon | 1 teaspoon | 2 teaspoons | 2 teaspoons |
| **Peanut butter, preferably chunky-style** | 1 cup | 1 cup | 1 cup | 1 cup | 1 cup |
| **All-purpose flour** | 1¼ cups | 1¼ cups | 1¼ cups | 1¼ cups | 1¼ cups |
| **Baking soda** | ¼ teaspoon | Scant ¼ teaspoon | Scant ¼ teaspoon | ⅛ teaspoon | ⅛ teaspoon |
| **Salt** | ½ teaspoon | ½ teaspoon | ½ teaspoon | ½ teaspoon | ½ teaspoon |
| **TOPPING** | | | | | |
| **Granulated sugar** | ½ cup | ½ cup | ½ cup | ½ cup | ½ cup |

**1.** Position the rack and preheat the oven as indicated for your altitude in the chart above. Prepare the cookie sheets as directed.

**2.** In a large bowl with a sturdy spoon, or in the bowl of an electric mixer, preferably with a paddle attachment, beat together the butter and both sugars until smooth and well blended. Scrape down the bowl. Beat in the egg, vanilla, and peanut butter and scrape down the bowl again.

**3.** Place a sifter over the bowl and measure the flour, baking soda, and salt into it. Stir/sift the dry ingredients onto the peanut butter mixture, then slowly beat everything together.

**4.** Place the topping sugar in a small bowl or cup. To make each cookie, scoop up a heaping teaspoon of dough and roll it into a ball in your hand, then dip the top of the ball into the sugar, and set it, sugar up, on the prepared cookie sheets, spacing the balls about 1 inch apart. With the tines of a table fork, press a crosshatch pattern into the top of each sugared dough ball (see sketch), flattening the cookies to about ¼-inch thick.

**5.** Bake the cookies for the time indicated for your altitude in the chart above, or until they begin to color slightly on top and turn golden brown around the edges. Watch carefully, because they can quickly overbrown on the bottom.

**6.** If the cookies were baked on baking parchment or a nonstick mat, simply slide it onto a wire rack for the cookies to cool. Otherwise, transfer the cookies to a rack to cool completely. When cooled, store in an airtight container.

# Jughandle Gingersnaps

THIS SPICE cookie comes from Sweden, where it is called *pepparkakor* and traditionally cut into pig, horse, and rooster shapes decorated with royal icing. The gingersnap cookies are crisp and assertively spiced, and the dough is easy to cut into your favorite shapes for everyday or holiday treats. For Chanukah, make dreidles or six-pointed stars; for Christmas, cut out teddy bears, trees, and angels. To make hanging Christmas tree ornaments, roll out the dough a tiny bit thicker than usual and poke a hole in the top of each cookie with a drinking straw or toothpick before baking.

To measure molasses easily, first grease the measuring cup with nonstick spray. Grown-ups will enjoy the sophisticated variation for Double Ginger Cookies. I discovered another unusual gingersnap treat at Mollie MacDuff's, a little bakery-café on the main street of Fairplay, Colorado. Baker/owner David Fair turns out a variety of baked goods but his imagination is over-the-top (elevation: 9,970 feet) with his Gingersnap Cookie Dessert: The cookies are topped by homemade cinnamon ice cream and shaved pickled ginger (the type used on sushi)!

---

**General High Altitude Notes:** To prevent the cookies from overspreading at 3,000 feet and above, add a little more flour and reduce the baking soda slightly as the elevation increases. To improve the flavor, add a little more salt.

**Special Equipment:** Cookie sheets; baking parchment or Silpat or other nonstick baking mats (optional); flat paddle for electric mixer (optional); sifter; rolling pin; wax paper; cookie cutters; pastry brush; for hanging holes: drinking straw or toothpick

**Pan Preparation:** Line the cookie sheets with baking parchment or nonstick baking mats or lightly coat with butter or nonstick vegetable spray.

**Makes** about 50 cookies (3-inch diameter) or 30 figures (5-inches tall)

| Ingredients | Sea Level | 3,000 feet | 5,000 feet | 7,000 feet | 10,000 feet |
|---|---|---|---|---|---|
| **Oven rack position, temperature, and baking time** | Divide oven in thirds; bake at 350°F for 8 to 10 minutes | Divide oven in thirds; bake at 350°F for 8 to 10 minutes | Divide oven in thirds; bake at 350°F for 10 to 12 minutes | Divide oven in thirds; bake at 350°F for 8 to 10 minutes | Divide oven in thirds; bake at 350°F for 10 to 12 minutes |
| **Unsalted butter, at room temperature** | 8 tablespoons (1 stick) | 8 tablespoons (1 stick) | 8 tablespoons (1 stick) | 8 tablespoons (1 stick) | 8 tablespoons (1 stick) |
| **Dark brown sugar, packed** | ½ cup | ½ cup | ½ cup | ½ cup | ½ cup |
| **Molasses** | ½ cup | ½ cup | ½ cup | ½ cup | ½ cup |
| **Large egg, at room temperature** | 1 | 1 | 1 | 1 | 1 |
| **All-purpose flour, plus extra for rolling out** | 3 cups, or as needed | 3 cups plus 1 tablespoon, or as needed | 3 cups plus 1 tablespoon, or as needed | 3 cups plus 1 tablespoon, or as needed | 3¼ cups, or as needed |
| **Salt** | ½ teaspoon | ¾ teaspoon | ¾ teaspoon | 1 teaspoon | 1 teaspoon |
| **Baking soda** | ½ teaspoon | Scant ½ teaspoon | Scant ½ teaspoon | Scant ½ teaspoon | ¼ teaspoon + ⅛ teaspoon |
| **Ground cloves** | 1 teaspoon | 1 teaspoon | 1 teaspoon | 1 teaspoon | 1 teaspoon |
| **Ground cinnamon** | 1 teaspoon | 1 teaspoon | 1 teaspoon | 1 teaspoon | 1 teaspoon |
| **Ground nutmeg** | ½ teaspoon | ½ teaspoon | ½ teaspoon | ½ teaspoon | ½ teaspoon |
| **Ground allspice or cardamom** | ½ teaspoon | ½ teaspoon | ½ teaspoon | ½ teaspoon | ½ teaspoon |
| **Ground ginger** | 2½ teaspoons | 2½ teaspoons | 2½ teaspoons | 2½ teaspoons | 2½ teaspoons |

ROYAL ICING (RECIPE FOLLOWS)

**1.** Position the racks and preheat the oven as indicated for your altitude in the chart above. Prepare the cookie sheets as directed.

**2.** In a large bowl, using a sturdy spoon, or in the bowl of an electric mixer, preferably fitted with a paddle attachment, cream together the butter and brown sugar until very soft and well blended, without lumps. Beat in the molasses and egg. Scrape down the bowl.

**3.** Set a sifter over the bowl and measure the flour, salt, baking soda, and spices into it. Stir/sift them onto the ingredients below, then beat slowly until thoroughly mixed. If the dough feels sticky to the touch, add a tablespoon more flour (up to 4 tablespoons maximum), until the dough is no longer tacky but still soft and pliable. In very hot weather, you may have to chill dough to stiffen it more, but resist adding any extra flour.

4. Work with about one third to one half of the dough at a time and keep the rest in the refrigerator. For ease in handling, place the dough on a piece of baking parchment or a Silpat fitted to a cookie sheet and with a lightly floured rolling pin, roll the dough about 1/8-inch thick (slightly thicker if cookies will be hanging). Dip the cookie cutters in flour to prevent sticking, then cut out shapes, leaving about 1/2 inch between each cut shape. Use the tip of a knife to help lift and peel away the between-cookie dough scraps, leaving the cookies in place. Slide the liner with the cookies onto a cookie sheet. Gather the scraps together, reroll, and cut more shapes on another sheet of baking parchment or another baking mat. Alternatively, you can roll out the dough on a lightly floured counter, cut out the cookies, and use a broad spatula to transfer them to a prepared cookie sheet.

To make hanging cookies, use a drinking straw or toothpick to poke a hole in the top of each cookie. If you have cut out gingerbread men or women, you can press on bits of slivered nuts or raisins or chocolate chips for facial features and buttons (or decorate with icing after baking).

5. Bake the cookies for the time indicated for your altitude in the chart above, or until they are a slightly darker golden brown around the edges. If baking seems uneven, rotate the pans back to front in the oven halfway through the baking time. Cool the cookies on a wire rack; if they were baked on parchment or a baking mat, simply slide it off the cookie sheet

onto the wire rack to cool. Use a straw or toothpick to widen the precut hanging holes while the cookies are still warm. Cool completely.

6. When the cookies are completely cold, spread on the icing with a butter knife. Or put it in a plastic bag, seal the top, and cut a tiny hole in one corner with scissors. If you want a carefully controlled fine line, drop a metal decorating tip into the corner of the plastic bag *before* adding the icing. Squeeze the icing out of the bag to draw designs (after use, discard the bag; be sure to save the metal tip, if you used it). Leave the decorated cookies on the wire rack to air-dry. At sea level, this can take an hour or more; at higher altitudes, the icing will dry more quickly. When the icing is hard, store the cookies in an airtight container, separated by layers of wax paper or plastic wrap.

## Double Ginger Cookies

Prepare the recipe as above, but add 1 to 2 tablespoons of grated fresh ginger (or to taste) along with the egg and molasses. Roll the cookies as thin as possible, brush with egg glaze, and sprinkle with granulated sugar and finely chopped candied ginger.

**Makes** about 50 cookies

## Royal Icing

*Select one of the versions below. Meringue powder is sold in supermarkets or by mail order; see Sources, page 329.*

Royal icing air-hardens very quickly at sea level and even more quickly at higher elevations. Keep the bowl or cups of icing covered at all times with plastic wrap or a damp towel. You may need to add a few drops more water after the icing stands for a period of time.

**Special Equipment:** Pint-size self-sealing plastic bags; scissors; #5 or #6 plain decorating tips (optional)

**Makes** 2 cups

### Meringue Powder Icing

3 tablespoons meringue powder

¼ cup plus 2 tablespoons warm water, or as needed

One 1-pound box confectioners' sugar, sifted

### Classic Royal Icing (uncooked egg whites)

2 large egg whites, at room temperature

⅛ teaspoon cream of tartar

⅛ teaspoon salt

3½ cups sifted confectioners' sugar, or as needed

2 tablespoons fresh lemon juice, or as needed

*To make the meringue powder icing*, whisk together the powder and warm water in a large bowl, then let sit for 3 to 4 minutes so the powder absorbs the liquid. Add the sifted sugar and beat slowly with an electric mixer on the lowest speed until the icing is smooth and the consistency of softly whipped cream, making soft peaks. Add 1 to 2 more teaspoons warm water if the icing is too stiff to spread.

*To make the classic royal icing*, combine all the ingredients in a large bowl and beat with an electric mixer on the lowest speed until the icing is smooth and thick. Adjust the consistency by adding more sugar or liquid until spreadable.

We Deer Valley bakers are used to the peculiarities of high altitude baking: our kitchens are at 7,200, 8,100, and 8,500 feet. Because our kitchens are at such celestial heights, we adapt. My pastry chefs and I use the word *altitude* as a verb. If someone has a failed recipe, my first response is, "Did you altitude it?" The translation: to adjust formulas and/or techniques to compensate for decreased air pressure and humidity.

—Letty Flatt, Executive Pastry Chef, Deer Valley Resorts, Park City, Utah, cookbook author, *Chocolate Snowball*

# Danish Oat Cookies

THIS IS my favorite cookie. The taste of sweet butter blends in crisp perfection with the nutty flavor of toasted oats to make this Denmark's answer to America's sweet/salty potato chip. Danish bakers make these traditional *Havresmaakager* for Christmas and say they bring a special protective blessing into your home. I defy you to eat just one.

**General High Altitude Notes:** The ingredients are the same at any altitude, but baking temperatures and times vary. The point is to bake the cookies long enough to toast the oats without overbaking or burning them. The batter spreads as the cookies bake, so don't place them too close to each other. The cookies are easier to handle and less fragile when not made too large.

**Special Equipment:** Cookie sheets (not insulated); baking parchment or Silpats or other nonstick baking mats; flat paddle attachment for electric mixer (optional)

**Pan Preparation:** Line the cookie sheets with baking parchment or nonstick baking mats.

**Makes** 55 to 60 cookies (2-inch diameter)

| Ingredients | Sea Level | 3,000 feet | 5,000 feet | 7,000 feet | 10,000 feet |
|---|---|---|---|---|---|
| **Oven rack position, temperature, and baking time** | Divide oven in thirds; bake at 350°F for 10 to 15 minutes | Divide oven in thirds; bake at 350°F for 10 to 12 minutes | Divide oven in thirds; bake at 350°F for 10 to 11 minutes | Divide oven in thirds; bake at 350°F for 12 to 15 minutes | Divide oven in thirds; bake at 325°F for 12 to 15 minutes |
| **Unsalted butter, melted and cooled** | ½ pound (2 sticks) | ½ pound (2 sticks) | ½ pound (2 sticks) | ½ pound (2 sticks) | ½ pound (2 sticks) |
| **Granulated sugar** | ¾ cup | ¾ cup | ¾ cup | ¾ cup | ¾ cup |
| **Large egg, at room temperature** | 1 | 1 | 1 | 1 | 1 |
| **Vanilla extract** | 1 teaspoon | 1 teaspoon | 1 teaspoon | 1 teaspoon | 1 teaspoon |

*(continued)*

| Ingredients | Sea Level | 3,000 feet | 5,000 feet | 7,000 feet | 10,000 feet |
|---|---|---|---|---|---|
| Old-fashioned rolled oats | 2 cups | 2 cups | 2 cups | 2 cups | 2 cups |
| Toasted wheat germ | ½ cup | ½ cup | ½ cup | ½ cup | ½ cup |
| All-purpose flour | ½ cup | ½ cup | ½ cup | ½ cup | ½ cup |
| Salt | ½ teaspoon | ½ teaspoon | ½ teaspoon | ½ teaspoon | ½ teaspoon |

**1.** Position the rack and preheat the oven as indicated for your altitude in the chart above. Prepare the cookie sheets as directed.

**2.** In a large bowl, using a sturdy spoon, or in the bowl of an electric mixer, preferably with a paddle attachment, beat together the melted butter and sugar. Beat in the egg and vanilla, then beat in the oats, wheat germ, flour, and salt. The dough will be quite soft.

**3.** Drop the dough by the teaspoonful about 1½ inches apart on the prepared cookie sheets. Bake the cookies for the time indicated for your altitude in the chart above, or until the tops turn a golden color and the edges darken to a rich golden brown; the longer the baking time, the crunchier the cookie (but beware of burning). If baking seems uneven, rotate the pans back to front in the oven halfway through the baking time.

**4.** Cool the cookies on a wire rack—they are very fragile while still hot, so let them cool a few minutes before moving them, then simply slide the parchment or baking mat off the cookie sheet onto the wire rack to cool. Store the cooled cookies in an airtight container.

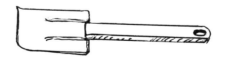

# Trout Dale Oatmeal-Raisin Cookies

T HESE COOKIE jar classics are crunchy but with a little chew, the taste a buttery blend of nutty toasted oats and sweet raisins. . . . What more could you ask for? Take them on picnics and pack them in kids' lunch boxes.

The longer you bake these cookies, the more crisp they will be; I prefer them baked the minimum time so they remain a little chewy. To personalize the recipe, instead of (or in addition to) the raisins, you can add ¾ to 1 cup dried cranberries, dried cherries, cut-up dried apricots, chocolate-coated raisins (see Sources, page 329), or chopped nuts.

**General High Altitude Notes:** To prevent the cookies from overspreading as the altitude increases, add more flour and reduce the leavening and sugar. To improve the flavor, add more salt and vanilla.

**Special Equipment:** Cookie sheets (not insulated); baking parchment or Silpat or other nonstick baking mats (optional); flat paddle attachment for electric mixer (optional)

**Pan Preparation:** Line the cookie sheets with baking parchment or nonstick mats or coat with butter or nonstick vegetable spray.

**Makes** 55 to 60 cookies (2-inch diameter)

| Ingredients | Sea Level | 3,000 feet | 5,000 feet | 7,000 feet | 10,000 feet |
|---|---|---|---|---|---|
| **Oven rack position, temperature, and baking time** | Divide oven into thirds; bake at 350°F for 12 to 16 minutes | Rack in center; bake at 350°F for 12 to 13 minutes | Rack in center; bake at 350°F for 13 to 15 minutes | Rack in center; bake at 350°F for 10 to 12 minutes | Rack in center; bake at 350°F for 12 to 15 minutes |
| **All-purpose flour** | 1½ cups | 1½ cups | 1½ cups plus 1½ tablespoons | 1½ cups plus 1 tablespoon | 1½ cups plus 2 tablespoons |
| **Baking soda** | ½ teaspoon | ½ teaspoon | Generous ¼ teaspoon | ¼ teaspoon | ¼ teaspoon |
| **Salt** | 1 teaspoon | 1 teaspoon | Generous 1 teaspoon | Generous 1 teaspoon | ¾ teaspoon |

*(continued)*

| Ingredients | Sea Level | 3,000 feet | 5,000 feet | 7,000 feet | 10,000 feet |
|---|---|---|---|---|---|
| **Ground cinnamon** | ½ teaspoon | ½ teaspoon | ½ teaspoon | ½ teaspoon | ½ teaspoon |
| **Unsalted butter, at room temperature** | ½ pound (2 sticks) | ½ pound (2 sticks) | ½ pound (2 sticks) | ½ pound (2 sticks) | ½ pound (2 sticks) |
| **Granulated sugar** | 1 cup | ¾ cup | ¾ cup | ¾ cup | ¾ cup plus 2 tablespoons |
| **Dark brown sugar, packed** | ½ cup | ½ cup | ½ cup | ½ cup | ½ cup |
| **Large eggs, at room temperature** | 2 | 2 | 2 | 2 | 2 |
| **Vanilla extract** | 1 teaspoon | 1 teaspoon | 1½ teaspoons | 1½ teaspoons | 2 teaspoons |
| **Old-fashioned rolled oats** | 3 cups | 3 cups | 3 cups | 3 cups | 3 cups |
| **Raisins** | 1 (6 ounces) cup | 1 (6 ounces) cup | 1 (6 ounces) cup | 1 (6 ounces) cup | 1 (6 ounces) cup |

**1.** Position the rack and preheat the oven as indicated for your altitude in the chart above. Prepare the cookie sheets as directed.

**2.** In a medium bowl, whisk together the flour, baking soda, salt, and cinnamon.

**3.** In a large bowl, using a sturdy spoon, or in the bowl of an electric mixer, preferably with a paddle attachment, beat the butter until soft and creamy, then beat in both sugars. Scrape down the bowl and beater, if using, and beat until smooth. Beat in the eggs and vanilla, and scrape down the bowl again.

**4.** Stirring slowly, or with the mixer on the lowest speed, gradually work in the flour mixture, then the oats and raisins. The dough will feel very stiff. (You can make the dough ahead, cover, and refrigerate for several hours.)

**5.** Drop the dough onto the prepared cookie sheets by the heaping tablespoon, placing the cookies about 2 inches apart. Bake for the time indicated for your altitude in the chart above, or until the cookies are golden brown; the longer they bake, the crisper they will be.

**6.** Cool the cookies on a wire rack. If the cookies were baked on parchment or a baking mat, simply slide it off the cookie sheet onto the wire rack to cool. When the cookies are completely cool, store them in an airtight container.

# Black-and-White Chocolate Chip Cookies

W HO CAN resist the classic buttery taste, generous hits of rich dark and white chocolate, crunchy nuts, and slightly chewy center? I had some of my biggest raves in Denver, from Emma, age ten, and Preston, age eight, children of my good friends Tracy and Randy Spalding, who generously shared their home and kitchen with me for testing on several occasions. One afternoon after school, Preston helped me bake, and another time the whole family visited me in Breckenridge for a day of sightseeing and taste testing. They took home samples of many cookies (some baked, some doughs still frozen) to fill lunch boxes and share with other kids at school.

White chocolate chips add extra sweetness to these classic cookies; to balance this, you can substitute chopped bittersweet (not unsweetened) chocolate for the semisweet chips if you wish or, as I have done, throw in a handful of dried cranberries. For best results, use a fine-quality white chocolate such as Lindt Swiss White confectionery bar or Guittard Vanilla Milk Chips or Ghirardelli Classic White Chips (sold in supermarkets, or see Sources, page 329).

**General High Altitude Notes:** This recipe gave predictable results until I reached 10,000 feet in Colorado (see page 219). Suddenly they spread way too much and had entirely the wrong texture. I made many changes before arriving at a good solution: add flour, reduce the temperature, and bake longer.

**Special Equipment:** Cookie sheets (not insulated); baking parchment or Silpat or other nonstick baking mat (optional); flat paddle attachment for electric mixer (optional)

**Pan Preparation:** Line the cookie sheets with baking parchment or nonstick mats or lightly coat with butter or nonstick vegetable spray.

**Makes** 55 to 60 cookies (2½- to 3-inch diameter)

**High Notes**

*At 3,000 feet,* leave the ingredients as written for a flat crisp cookie, or add 1 tablespoon flour and replace 2 tablespoons of the butter with Crisco for a fatter, slightly chewy cookie.

*At 7,000 feet and above,* reduce the oven temperature and cut down the sugar to prevent overspread. Increase the flavor by adding more vanilla.

**At 10,000 feet,** again to prevent overspreading, add more flour, reduce the oven temperature an additional 25 degrees, bake only on the lower oven rack, and increase the baking time.

| Ingredients | Sea Level | 3,000 feet | 5,000 feet | 7,000 feet | 10,000 feet |
|---|---|---|---|---|---|
| **Oven rack position, temperature, and baking time** | Divide oven in thirds; bake at 375°F for 10 to 11 minutes | Divide oven in thirds; bake at 375°F for 10 to 12 minutes | Rack in center; bake at 375°F for 9 to 10 minutes | Rack in center; bake at 350°F for 8 to 10 minutes | Rack in lower third; bake at 325°F for 14 to 15 minutes |
| **All-purpose flour** | 2¼ cups | 2¼ cups | 2¼ cups | 2¼ cups | 3 cups |
| **Baking soda** | 1 teaspoon | 1 teaspoon | 1 teaspoon | 1 teaspoon | 1 teaspoon |
| **Salt** | 1 teaspoon | 1 teaspoon | 1 teaspoon | 1 teaspoon | 1 teaspoon |
| **Unsalted butter, at room temperature** | ½ pound (2 sticks) | ½ pound (2 sticks) | ½ pound (2 sticks) | ½ pound (2 sticks) | ½ pound (2 sticks) |
| **Granulated sugar** | ¾ cup | ¾ cup | ¾ cup | ¾ cup minus 2 tablespoons | ¾ cup minus 2 tablespoons |
| **Dark brown sugar, packed** | ¾ cup | ¾ cup | ¾ cup | ¾ cup | ¾ cup |
| **Large eggs, at room temperature** | 2 | 2 | 2 | 2 | 2 |
| **Vanilla extract** | 1 teaspoon | 1 teaspoon | 1 teaspoon | 1½ teaspoons | 2 teaspoons |
| **Semisweet chocolate chips or coarsely chopped chocolate** | 1 cup (6 ounces) | 1 cup (6 ounces) | 1 cup (6 ounces) | 1 cup (6 ounces) | 1 cup (6 ounces) |
| **White chocolate chips or coarsely chopped chocolate** | 1 cup (6 ounces) | 1 cup (6 ounces) | 1 cup (6 ounces) | 1 cup (6 ounces) | 1 cup (6 ounces) |
| **Pecans or walnuts, broken, optional** | 1 cup (4 ounces) | 1 cup (4 ounces) | 1 cup (4 ounces) | 1 cup (4 ounces) | 1 cup (4 ounces) |

**1.** Position the rack and preheat the oven as indicated for your altitude in the chart above. Prepare the pans as directed.

**2.** In a medium bowl, whisk together the flour, baking soda, and salt.

**3.** In a large bowl, using a sturdy spoon, or the bowl of an electric mixer, preferably with a paddle attachment, beat the butter until soft and creamy, then beat in both sugars. Scrape down the bowl and beater, if using, and mix until smooth. Beat in the eggs and vanilla. Stirring slowly, or with the mixer on the lowest speed, gradually beat in the flour mixture, then stir in the chips or chopped chocolate, and nuts, if using.

**4.** Drop the batter by the rounded teaspoon about 2 inches apart on the prepared cookie sheets. Bake for the time indicated for your altitude in the chart above, or until golden brown. Don't overbake, or the cookies will be too dry and crisp when cooled; it is better to underbake them slightly so the centers will be a little chewy.

**5.** Cool the cookies on a wire rack. If they were baked on parchment or a nonstick mat, simply slide it off the cookie sheet onto the wire rack to cool. When they are completely cooled, store the cookies in an airtight container.

# Mexican Wedding Cookies

**M**ELT-IN-YOUR-MOUTH BUTTER-NUT cookies coated with powdered sugar are familiar in many countries, though they go by many different names. In Mexico, they are *pastelitos de boda* (bride's little cakes), traditionally served at weddings; in Greece, *kourambiedes*, sometimes flavored with rose water or brandy or topped with a whole clove for Christmas; in Austria, *Butterhörnchen* (butter horns); and in the United States, butterballs or snowballs.

Cake flour, which has less protein and is softer than all-purpose, will make a slightly more tender cookie, but either type will work. The flavor of the cookie can be changed by using different nuts; if substituting toasted and finely chopped hazelnuts, use ½ teaspoon hazelnut extract in place of the almond extract. In very hot weather, the dough may feel too soft to mold and should be refrigerated until firm; resist the temptation to stiffen the dough by adding more flour, which would make tough cookies.

---

**General High Altitude Notes:** These cookies will dry out quickly at high altitudes and should be stored in an airtight container as soon as they are completely cooled.

**Special Equipment:** Cookie sheets (not insulated); baking parchment or Silpats or other nonstick mats; flat paddle attachment for electric mixer (optional); wax paper; sifter

**Pan Preparation:** Line the cookie sheets with baking parchment or nonstick mats or leave ungreased.

**Makes** about 40 cookies (1- to 1¼-inch diameter)

**High Notes**
*At 3,000 feet and above,* increase the salt and extract for additional flavor.
*At 7,000 feet and above,* stiffen the batter by adding a little more confectioners' sugar.

| Ingredients | Sea Level | 3,000 feet | 5,000 feet | 7,000 feet | 10,000 feet |
|---|---|---|---|---|---|
| **Oven rack position, temperature, and baking time** | Divide the oven into thirds; bake at 350°F for 15 to 20 minutes | Divide the oven into thirds; bake at 350°F for 15 to 20 minutes | Divide the oven into thirds; bake at 350°F for 15 to 20 minutes | Divide the oven into thirds; bake at 350°F for 15 to 20 minutes | Divide the oven into thirds; bake at 350°F for 15 to 17 minutes |
| **Unsalted butter, at room temperature** | ½ pound (2 sticks) | ½ pound (2 sticks) | ½ pound (2 sticks) | ½ pound (2 sticks) | ½ pound (2 sticks) |
| **Sifted cake or all-purpose flour** | 2½ cups | 2½ cups | 2½ cups | 2½ cups | 2½ cups |
| **Sifted confectioners' sugar** | ½ cup | ½ cup | ½ cup | ½ cup plus 2 tablespoons | ½ cup plus 2 tablespoons |
| **Salt** | ½ teaspoon | Generous ½ teaspoon | Generous ½ teaspoon | Generous ½ teaspoon | Generous ½ teaspoon |
| **Finely chopped walnuts, almonds, or pecans** | 1 cup (4 ounces) | 1 cup (4 ounces) | 1 cup (4 ounces) | 1 cup (4 ounces) | 1 cup (4 ounces) |
| **Vanilla extract** | 1 teaspoon | 2 teaspoons | 2 teaspoons | 2 teaspoons | 2 teaspoons |
| **Almond extract** | ½ teaspoon | ¾ teaspoon | ¾ teaspoon | ¾ teaspoon | ¾ teaspoon |
| **Sifted confectioners' sugar for rolling and storing cookies** | 2 cups, or as needed | 2 cups, or as needed | 2 cups, or as needed | 2 cups, or as needed | 2 cups, or as needed |

1. Position the rack and preheat the oven as indicated for your altitude in the chart above. Prepare the cookie sheets as directed.

2. In a large bowl, using a sturdy spoon, or in the bowl of an electric mixer, preferably with a paddle attachment, beat the butter until creamy and smooth. Gradually beat in the flour, sifted confectioners' sugar, salt, nuts, and extracts.

3. With lightly floured fingers, pinch off small lumps of dough and roll them between your palms into balls about 1 inch in diameter, then set them on the prepared cookie sheet about 1 inch apart.

4. Bake the cookies for the time indicated for your altitude in the chart above, or just until the tops are a pale golden color; don't let them get too brown.

5. While the cookies bake, measure about 2 cups sifted confectioners' sugar into a medium bowl. Place a sheet of wax paper on a tray nearby.

6. When the cookies come out of the oven, set the pan on a wire rack to cool for about 4 or 5 minutes, then, while they are still warm but not too hot to touch, roll each cookie in the sifted sugar to coat it well, and set on the wax paper to cool completely. Store the cooled cookies in an airtight container, layered with additional sifted confectioners' sugar.

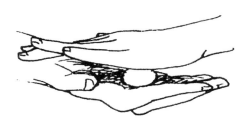

# Highland Shortbread

THIS CRISP Scottish cookie has a classic melt-in-your-mouth crumb and a pure buttery flavor. A dream recipe that uses just four ingredients and takes perhaps five minutes to mix up, shortbread gives rewards out of all proportion to the effort. The only trick is knowing how to cut it. Shortbread must be cut while still warm from the oven because it crisps as it cools (and the higher the altitude, the more quickly it cools); it shatters if cut when cold. For perfect cuts, mark the slices before baking, then recut them as soon as the shortbread is out of the oven. If you forgot the marking and your shortbread cools, put it back in the oven for 2 or 3 minutes—it will cut easily when warm.

Moira Sakren, a Scottish friend who is a fine baker as well as folksinger and drum maker, keeps us supplied with her famous shortbread at holidays and whenever she thinks we need a bit of comfort. To lift and soothe my spirits with a "quintessential Robert Burns experience," she recently gave me a doily-lined tin of her buttery bars, with instructions: "Munch the contents while availing yourself of a bottle of the finest claret, sitting in a comfy chair pulled up to your computer. Listen to Robert Burns's 'Now Westlin Winds' sung by folksinger Alison McMorland on The Tradition Bearers website: www.thetraditionbearers.com/htmfiles/welcome.htm." I can report that this experience (which I urge you to try) worked like a Scottish charm right down to the last note and the final crumb.

I love Moira's basic shortbread, but the recipe lends itself easily to flavor variations. For Lemon or Orange Shortbread, add 1½ teaspoons pure lemon or orange extract and about 2 teaspoons grated lemon or orange zest to the butter. For Half-and-Half Shortbread, dip the end of each bar or wedge into melted semisweet chocolate and sprinkle with finely chopped cashews, pecans, or walnuts; set on wax paper to cool. One of my Denver testers, Melissa Hornung, received raves for her Strawberry Shortbread, topping cookie wedges with berries and whipped cream.

**General High Altitude Notes:** Shortbread ingredients do not change with increases in altitude, but there are variations in the oven rack positions, baking temperatures, and times, all intended to regulate the amount of heat needed to bake the shortbread to an even, barely golden degree of crispness.

**Special Equipment:** Sifter; cookie sheet (not insulated); baking parchment or Silpat or other nonstick mat (optional); flat paddle attachment for electric mixer (optional); rolling pin (optional); ruler; sharp knife

**Pan Preparation:** If you wish, line the pan with baking parchment or a nonstick mat; it is not necessary to grease the pan.

**Makes** 27 bars (1 × 3 inches) or 8 large or 16 small wedges

**High Notes**

*At 7,000 feet and above,* preheat the oven to 350°F, then reduce the heat to 325°F as soon as you put in the cookies.

| Ingredients | Sea Level | 3,000 feet | 5,000 feet | 7,000 feet | 10,000 feet |
| --- | --- | --- | --- | --- | --- |
| **Oven rack position, temperature, and baking time** | Rack in center; bake at 325°F for 25 to 30 minutes | Rack in lower third of oven; bake at 325°F for 20 to 23 minutes | Rack in center; bake at 325°F for 20 to 25 minutes | Rack in center; *preheat* oven to 350°F; *bake* at 325°F for 25 to 30 minutes | Rack in lower third of oven; *preheat* oven to 350°F; *bake* at 325°F for 20 to 23 minutes |
| **Unsalted butter, at room temperature** | ½ pound (2 sticks) | ½ pound (2 sticks) | ½ pound (2 sticks) | ½ pound (2 sticks) | ½ pound (2 sticks) |
| **Sifted confectioners' sugar** | ½ cup | ½ cup | ½ cup | ½ cup | ½ cup |
| **Sifted all-purpose flour** | 2 cups | 2 cups | 2 cups | 2 cups | 2 cups |
| **Salt** | ½ teaspoon | ½ teaspoon | ½ teaspoon | ½ teaspoon | Generous ½ teaspoon |

**1.** Position the rack and preheat the oven as indicated for your altitude in the chart above.

**2.** In a large bowl, with a sturdy spoon, or in the bowl of an electric mixer, preferably with a paddle attachment, beat together the butter and sifted confectioners' sugar until very creamy and smooth. Sift on the flour and salt and beat just until the dough forms large clumps.

**3.** Turn the dough out onto a counter (not floured) and use your lightly floured hands to squeeze the dough into a ball. The warmth of your hands will soften the butter enough to bind the dough; to keep the shortbread tender, handle it lightly and use a minimum of extra flour. In very hot weather, if the dough feels too soft to shape without adding much more flour, first refrigerate it until firm.

**4.** Place the dough ball in the middle of the cookie sheet.

*To shape bars*, pat or roll the dough into a 9-inch square ¼-inch thick (sketch a). With a long-bladed sharp knife, divide the square crosswise into three 3-inch sections and lengthwise into nine 1-inch sections; cut along the marked lines to make 27 bars but do not separate the pieces now.

*To shape wedges*, use a lightly floured rolling pin to roll the dough into a circle about 8 inches in diameter and ¾-inch thick. With the tines of a table fork dipped in flour, prick lines dividing the disk into quarters, then divide each quarter in half, making 8 large wedges (b). If desired, divide each eighth in half, making 16 narrow wedges. Leave the marked wedges in place.

**5.** Bake for the time directed for your altitude in the chart above, or until the top of the shortbread is dry to the touch and a pale golden color and the edges are just beginning to turn a slightly darker golden color. Leave the shortbread on the cookie sheet and set it on a wire rack. The dough spreads slightly as it bakes, so, while it is still very warm, trim the edges of the square by cutting off a very scant ⅛ inch all around (this is the baker's reward). Now neatly recut the bars or wedges along the previously marked lines. Cool completely.

**6.** When the cookies are cool, store in an airtight container, plain or coated with a light sifting of confectioners' sugar.

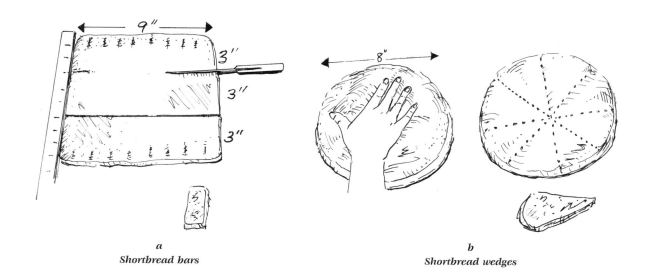

*a*
**Shortbread bars**

*b*
**Shortbread wedges**

# Double Chocolate–Pecan Biscotti

I N   M Y opinion, biscotti, rather than madeleines, are the most evocative of all pastries. One crunchy bite can call to mind similar flavors tasted long ago, nostalgic memories of special people and places. This isn't so surprising when you realize that biscotti were made for socializing—for dipping into sweet dessert wine or cappuccino, pastimes that invite intimate conversation and create lasting impressions. I'll never forget tasting fragrant lavender-honey-rosemary biscotti in a hillside café in Provence, toasted pine nut–chocolate biscotti and cappuccino-nut biscotti created by a friend in Santa Fe (see the variations below), and apricot-saffron-pistachio biscotti at the elegantly rustic Savory Inn and Cooking School in Vail, Colorado. When I visited innkeeper Nancy Hassett, her then-executive chef, Deanna Scimio, served me a biscotti sampler along with afternoon tea (altitude 8,150 feet) that also included lemon–white chocolate macadamia nut and cornmeal-cardamom biscotti.

Typically, biscotti (literally, "twice-baked") are baked once as a log of dough, then sliced and baked again until crisp. Chef Deanna devised a different method: After the first bake, she sliced the biscotti and set them on a wire rack to crisp in the quick-drying mountain air of her lofty elevation; she found that at high altitude this produced a less jaw-breaking texture than the double-bake.

You can substitute any type of nuts, dried fruit, or flavoring extract in the following master recipe. I toast the nuts to enhance their flavor, but if you are in a hurry, you can omit this step, as the second bake exposes the sliced nuts to extra heat, giving them a little more flavor (though not as much as toasting).

**General High Altitude Notes:** Biscotti have a traditional appearance—a long diagonal slice—that risks being misshapen if the dough overspreads when baked at high altitudes. To keep the proper shape and avoid spreading, raise the oven temperature 25 degrees, add a little more flour and an egg, and reduce the leavening as the elevation increases. At high altitude, biscotti dry out very quickly. At high, dry elevations, be sure to wrap them airtight as soon as they are completely cool.

**Special Equipment:** One or two cookie sheets (not insulated); baking parchment or Silpat or other nonstick baking mat (optional); flat paddle attachment for electric mixer (optional); sifter; ruler; broad spatula; wooden skewer or cake tester; serrated knife; cutting board

**Pan Preparation:** Line one cookie sheet with baking parchment or a nonstick mat or lightly coat with butter-flavor nonstick vegetable spray.

**Makes** 36 to 42 biscotti (½-inch thick)

**High Notes**

*At 3,000 feet and above,* reduce leavening, and increase flour.

*At 5,000 feet and above,* increase the extracts.

*At 10,000,* further strengthen the batter by reducing the butter and sugar.

| Ingredients | Sea Level | 3,000 feet | 5,000 feet | 7,000 feet | 10,000 feet |
|---|---|---|---|---|---|
| **Oven rack position, temperature, and baking time** | Rack in center; bake at 325°F for 30 minutes, then at 275°F for 15 to 20 minutes | Rack in lower third of oven; bake at 350°F for 20 to 22 minutes, then at 325°F for 15 to 18 minutes | Rack in lower third of oven; bake at 350°F for 20 to 25 minutes, then at 325°F for 15 to 18 minutes | Rack in lower third of oven; bake at 350°F for 20 to 25 minutes, then at 325°F for 15 to 18 minutes | Rack in lower third of oven; bake at 350°F for 25 to 27 minutes, then at 325°F for 15 minutes |
| **Pecans, hazelnuts, walnuts, or almonds** | ½ cup (2 ounces) | ½ cup (2 ounces) | ½ cup (2 ounces) | ½ cup (2 ounces) | ½ cup (2 ounces) |
| **Sifted all-purpose flour** | 2½ cups, or as needed | 2½ cups plus 1 tablespoon, or as needed | 2½ cups plus 1 tablespoon, or as needed | 2½ cups plus 2 tablespoons, or as needed | 2½ cups, or as needed |
| **Baking powder** | 1½ teaspoons | 1¼ teaspoons | 1¼ teaspoons | 1 teaspoon | ¾ teaspoon |
| **Salt** | ½ teaspoon | ½ teaspoon | ½ teaspoon | ½ teaspoon | ½ teaspoon |
| **Unsifted Dutch-process, or natural cocoa such as Hershey's regular** | ¼ cup | ¼ cup | ¼ cup | ¼ cup | ¼ cup |

(continued)

| Ingredients | Sea Level | 3,000 feet | 5,000 feet | 7,000 feet | 10,000 feet |
|---|---|---|---|---|---|
| **Unsalted butter, at room temperature** | 3 tablespoons | 3 tablespoons | 3 tablespoons | 3 tablespoons | 2 tablespoons |
| **Granulated sugar** | 1 cup | 1 cup | 1 cup | 1 cup | ⅔ cup |
| **Large eggs, at room temperature** | 3 | 3 | 3 | 3 | 3 |
| **Vanilla extract** | 1 teaspoon | 1 teaspoon | 2 teaspoons | 2 teaspoons | 2 teaspoons |
| **Almond or hazelnut extract** | 1½ teaspoons | 1½ teaspoons | 1½ teaspoons | 2 teaspoons | 2 teaspoons |
| **Semisweet chocolate chips** | ⅓ cup (2 ounces) | ⅓ cup (2 ounces) | ⅓ cup (2 ounces) | ⅓ cup (2 ounces) | ⅓ cup (2 ounces) |
| **White chocolate chips** | ¼ cup (1½ ounces) | ¼ cup (1½ ounces) | ¼ cup (1½ ounces) | ¼ cup (1½ ounces) | ¼ cup (1½ ounces) |

**1.** Position the rack as indicated for your altitude in the chart above and preheat the oven to 350°F. Prepare the cookie sheet as directed.

**2.** To toast the nuts, spread them in a shallow baking pan and bake for 8 to 10 minutes, tossing occasionally, until aromatic and golden. To remove the skins from hazelnuts, wrap the still-warm nuts in a towel and rub off the skins. Let cool. If at sea level, reduce the oven temperature to 325°F.

**3.** In a medium bowl, whisk together the flour, baking powder, salt, and cocoa. Put the nuts in a food processor, add about 2 tablespoons of the flour-cocoa mixture, and coarsely chop them. Set the nuts aside.

**4.** In a large bowl of an electric mixer, preferably with a paddle attachment, cream the butter and sugar until well blended. Beat in the eggs and extracts, then scrape down the bowl and beater. Dump the flour-cocoa mixture into the bowl, turn the mixer on to its lowest speed, and slowly mix everything together. Scrape down the bowl and beater, then beat in the chopped nuts and all the chips (with any remaining flour-cocoa mixture).

**5.** Gather the dough into a ball and turn out onto a lightly floured counter. If the dough feels very sticky, work in more flour one tablespoon at a time, up to 3 tablespoons maximum. In extremely hot weather, you may need to chill the dough until firm; do not add any more flour. Divide the dough ball in half.

Shape each half into a log about 13 inches long, 1 inch high, and 1½ inches wide. Place the logs about 2 inches apart on the prepared cookie sheet. With your fingers, gently flatten the top of each log until it is slightly domed and 13½ to 14 inches long, ¾ inch high, and 1¾ inches wide, as shown in sketch a, page 248.

**6.** Bake the logs for the first baking time indicated for your altitude in the chart above, or until they are dry on top and firm to the touch;

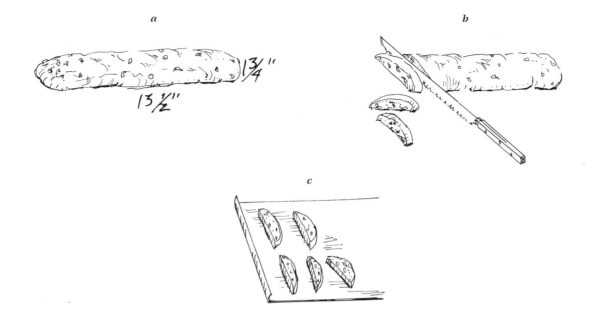

*a*

*b*

*c*

a cake tester inserted in the center should come out clean or show just a speck of chocolate. Remove the pan from the oven and set it on a heatproof surface. Turn down the oven temperature as indicated in the chart. With a broad spatula, carefully transfer each dough log to a cutting board and allow to cool for about 5 minutes.

**7.** With a serrated knife, cutting in a sawing motion, slice the still-warm logs on the diagonal into ½-inch-thick pieces, as shown (b). Place the slices cut side down on the original baking sheet (c, don't regrease); you may need to use a second pan. Bake for the time indicated in the chart, or until the slices feel dry and crisp; they will crisp more as they cool. The longer they bake this time, the harder they will be. Cool the biscotti on a rack. Store, once cooled in an airtight container.

## Toasted Pine Nut–Chocolate Biscotti

Prepare the recipe as above, but omit the white chocolate chips and replace the chopped nuts with ½ cup (2½ ounces) toasted pine nuts. To toast pine nuts, spread them in a frying pan and toss over medium heat for about 5 minutes, or until they are aromatic and beginning to turn golden brown. Cool them completely before adding them to the dough.

## Lavender-Honey-Rosemary Biscotti

The recipe is dedicated to Marilyn Abraham, the "godmother" of this book, owner (with her husband, Sandy MacGregor) of the glorious Santa Fe garden where I picked the lavender and rosemary to re-create these memorable Provençal biscotti. The flavor is delicate and well balanced, not too sweet, with a hint of fragrant perfume. Serve these with lemon sorbet or crème brûlée. Be sure to use fresh, not dried, lavender flowers and rosemary leaves.

Prepare the recipe as above, with the following changes: Omit the cocoa, nuts, chocolate chips, and almond or hazelnut extract. Increase the flour by 2 to 4 tablespoons (up to a total of 2¾ cups), depending on how sticky the dough feels.

Whisk together the flour (add 2 tablespoons to start), baking powder, and salt. Cream together the butter and sugar, then beat in ½ cup honey and the eggs. Scrape down the bowl and beater. Add the vanilla extract, plus 2 tablespoons whole or crumbled fresh lavender flowers, 2 teaspoons crumbled or finely chopped fresh rosemary leaves, and 1 tablespoon fresh lemon juice. Beat well, then mix in a little more flour if needed during shaping. Shape and bake as directed.

## Buckaroo Ball Cappuccino Biscotti

These biscotti were created by Stacy Pearl, my tester and executive chef of Santa Fe's Walter Burke Catering, for the 2004 Buckaroo Ball. At this annual gala to benefit children's charities, a thousand guests gathered to dine and dance at Bonanza Ranch. In addition to serving a fabulous dinner, Stacy and her staff gave each guest a personal beribboned gift packet containing three biscotti. The behind-the-scenes production for this glamorous event was a formidable feat. Just to provide the 3,000 biscotti needed, they made this recipe 65 times (6 batches a day for 11 days). The biscotti were stored in airtight tins, the dry atmosphere of Santa Fe kept them fresh, and they were the hit of the party.

Prepare the recipe as above, but with the following changes: Start with 2½ cups flour and omit the almond extract. Along with the eggs in Step 4, add 1 tablespoon plus 1 teaspoon espresso coffee powder (or 2 tablespoons regular instant coffee powder) plus 1 teaspoon ground cinnamon. Add 1 or 2 tablespoons more flour during shaping only if the dough feels too sticky. Shape and bake as directed.

# Independence Pass Brownies

GOOEY, CHEWY, and dense with chocolate, these brownies are meltingly rich but not too sweet. The secret: cocoa plus chocolate chips. Meditate on a mouthful with a glass of milk in hand and you'll feel like a ten-year-old; add a scoop of vanilla ice cream, warm chocolate sauce, and a dab of whipped cream with, say, an emerald ring encircling a candle on top, and you'll be glad you are a grown-up celebrating a special birthday.

This is my adaptation of a recipe from my friend chef/restaurateur Steve Keneipp of Noblesville, Indiana, who sometimes bakes the batter in mini–muffin pans (for 20 minutes) and calls them Two-Bite Brownies.

The recipe commemorates my solo crossing of Colorado's infamous Independence Pass (elevation 12,095 feet), a harrowing, white-knuckle drive. I was returning to Breckenridge from a visit with friends Marianne O'Carroll and Timm Fautsko in Glenwood Springs, where we had shared recipes, relaxation, and some amazing tourism (see page 22). In one unforgettable afternoon, Marianne and I took a breath-taking tram ride up Iron Mountain to the mouth of the Fairy Caves, then made a dizzying descent into a world of fabulous stalactites and stalagmites. For an encore, we watched the sunset while soaking in the famed hot springs pool next to Teddy Roosevelt's Hotel Colorado. The next day after lunch in Aspen, I had to get back to my baking, but it was hard to leave. Convinced that I was an intrepid traveler, they urged me to take a shortcut home through Hunter–Frying Pan Wilderness across the treacherous seasonal pass. The weather was clear and the drive was a breeze until I literally reached the point of no return. I rounded a bend and disappeared into a vaporous white cloud—zero visibility, 100 percent panic—then out again into blinding sunlight, a steep rock wall brushing one side of my car and a stomach-lurching dropoff to infinity on the other. A van of campers roared by sporting a bumper sticker that read "Real Women Don't Need Guard Rails." That caught my attention for a split second, but it's hard to laugh out loud when you're holding your breath. Distractions and second thoughts were not an option, but these endorphin-releasing brownies were. A comforting test batch sat beside me on the car seat and kept me going as I promised myself I could have one more bite if I lived through one more hairpin turn or survived yet another crazed Jaguar passing me at the speed of light.

**General High Altitude Notes:** Take care not to overbake the brownies, or they will be dry. At 3,000 feet and above, strengthen the batter by adding a little flour and cutting back on the sugar. Add another egg and (except at 10,000 feet) a little more melted butter to increase liquid and improve the texture. Bolster the flavor with a little more salt.

**Special Equipment:** An 8 × 1½-inch square baking pan (a 9-inch pan makes a too-thin layer); wooden skewer or cake tester

**Pan Preparation:** Coat the pan with butter or butter-flavor nonstick vegetable spray.

**Makes** 16 brownies (2-inch square)

**High Notes**

*At 3,000 feet and above,* raise the oven temperature 50 degrees. Add an egg, increase the butter, and cut down the sugar.

*At 10,000 feet,* use the original amount of butter.

| Ingredients | Sea Level | 3,000 feet | 5,000 feet | 7,000 feet | 10,000 feet |
|---|---|---|---|---|---|
| **Oven rack position, temperature, and baking time** | Rack in center; bake at 325°F for 30 to 35 minutes | Rack in center; bake at 375°F for 18 to 20 minutes | Rack in center; bake at 375°F for 20 to 27 minutes | Rack in center; bake at 375°F for 22 to 25 minutes | Rack in center; bake at 375°F for 20 to 22 minutes |
| **Dutch-process cocoa** | ½ cup | ½ cup | ½ cup | ½ cup | ½ cup |
| **All-purpose flour** | ½ cup | ½ cup plus 1 tablespoon | ½ cup plus 1 tablespoon | ½ cup plus 2 tablespoons | ½ cup plus 2 tablespoons |
| **Granulated sugar** | 1 cup | 1 cup minus 1 tablespoon | 1 cup minus 1 tablespoon | 1 cup minus 1 tablespoon | 1 cup minus 1 tablespoon |
| **Salt** | ⅛ teaspoon | ¼ teaspoon | ¼ teaspoon | ¼ teaspoon | ¼ teaspoon |

(*continued*)

| Ingredients | Sea Level | 3,000 feet | 5,000 feet | 7,000 feet | 10,000 feet |
|---|---|---|---|---|---|
| **Large eggs, at room temperature** | 2 | 3 | 3 | 3 | 3 |
| **Vanilla extract** | 1 teaspoon | 1 teaspoon | 1 teaspoon | 1 teaspoon | 1 teaspoon |
| **Unsalted butter, melted and cooled** | 6 tablespoons (¾ stick) | 8 tablespoons (1 stick) | 8 tablespoons (1 stick) | 8 tablespoons (1 stick) | 6 tablespoons (¾ stick) |
| **Semisweet chocolate chips or coarsely chopped chocolate** | 1 cup (6 ounces) | 1 cup (6 ounces) | 1 cup (6 ounces) | 1 cup (6 ounces) | 1 cup (6 ounces) |
| **Chopped walnuts, or white chocolate chips (3 ounces)** | ½ cup nuts (2 ounces) | ½ cup nuts (2 ounces) | ½ cup nuts (2 ounces) | ½ cup nuts (2 ounces) | ½ cup nuts (2 ounces) |

**1.** Position the rack and preheat the oven as indicated for your altitude in the chart above. Prepare the pan as directed.

**2.** In a large bowl, whisk together the cocoa, flour, sugar, and salt. Make a well in the center and add the eggs, vanilla, and the melted and cooled butter.

**3.** Whisk the wet ingredients to blend, then work in the flour-cocoa mixture, the chocolate chips, and the nuts or white chocolate chips, if using. Beat hard until everything is incorporated. The batter will feel quite thick.

**4.** Scoop the batter into the prepared pan. Bake for the time indicated for your altitude in the chart above, or until the brownies look dry on top and are just beginning to pull away from the pan sides. Don't overbake. A cake tester inserted in the center should have a few moist crumbs attached.

**5.** Cool the brownies in the pan on a wire rack, then cut into squares and serve from the pan.

# Rugelach

RUGELACH ARE tender, bite-sized rolled pastries that may include a variety of fillings, such as poppy seeds or cinnamon-sugar and nuts. Instead of the fillings given below, you can use a commercially prepared poppy seed paste or nut butter (see Sources, page 329) to coat the pastry before rolling up. Each filling in the recipe below is enough for half the dough; if you want to make only one type, double the filling quantities.

---

**General High Altitude Notes:** The ingredients in this recipe do not change with elevation, but the position of the oven rack, oven temperature, and baking time do.

**Special Equipment:** Cookie sheets (not insulated); baking parchment or Silpats or other nonstick baking mats (optional); flat paddle if using electric mixer (optional), or food processor; sifter; rolling pin; ruler; wax paper; sharp heavy knife or pizza cutter; pastry brush

**Pan Preparation:** Line the cookie sheets with baking parchment or nonstick mats or lightly coat with nonstick vegetable spray.

**Makes** about 64 bite-sized cookies or 48 large crescents

**High Notes**
*At 7,000 feet and above,* use a whole egg glaze for better browning because egg white glaze looks too pale.

| Ingredients | Sea Level | 3,000 feet | 5,000 feet | 7,000 feet | 10,000 feet |
|---|---|---|---|---|---|
| **Oven rack position, temperature, and baking time** | Rack in center; bake at 375°F for 15 to 20 minutes | Rack in center; bake at 350°F for 18 to 22 minutes | Rack in center; bake at 350°F for 20 to 22 minutes | Rack in lower third of oven; bake at 375°F for 15 to 20 minutes | Rack in lower third of oven; bake at 350°F for 22 to 25 minutes |

*(continued)*

| Ingredients | Sea Level | 3,000 feet | 5,000 feet | 7,000 feet | 10,000 feet |
|---|---|---|---|---|---|
| **CREAM-CHEESE PASTRY** | | | | | |
| **Philadelphia regular cream cheese (not low-fat)** | One 8-ounce package | One 8-ounce package | One 8-ounce package | One 8-ounce package | One 8-ounce package |
| **Unsalted butter, at room temperature** | ½ pound (2 sticks) | ½ pound (2 sticks) | ½ pound (2 sticks) | ½ pound (2 sticks) | ½ pound (2 sticks) |
| **All-purpose flour** | 2 cups, or as needed | 2 cups, or as needed | 2 cups, or as needed | 2 cups, or as needed | 2 cups, or as needed |
| **Salt** | ¼ teaspoon | ¼ teaspoon | ¼ teaspoon | ¼ teaspoon | ¼ teaspoon |
| **POPPY SEED FILLING (FOR *HALF* THE DOUGH)** | | | | | |
| **Poppy seeds** | ⅓ cup | ⅓ cup | ⅓ cup | ⅓ cup | ⅓ cup |
| **Brown sugar** | 2 tablespoons | 2 tablespoons | 2 tablespoons | 2 tablespoons | 2 tablespoons |
| **Granulated sugar** | 3 tablespoons | 3 tablespoons | 3 tablespoons | 3 tablespoons | 3 tablespoons |
| **CINNAMON-NUT FILLING (FOR *HALF* THE DOUGH)** | | | | | |
| **Finely chopped walnuts or almonds** | ½ cup (2 ounces) | ½ cup (2 ounces) | ½ cup (2 ounces) | ½ cup (2 ounces) | ½ cup (2 ounces) |
| **Granulated sugar** | ¼ cup | ¼ cup | ¼ cup | ¼ cup | ¼ cup |
| **Ground cinnamon** | ½ teaspoon | ½ teaspoon | ½ teaspoon | ½ teaspoon | ½ teaspoon |
| **Ground nutmeg** | ½ teaspoon | ½ teaspoon | ½ teaspoon | ½ teaspoon | ½ teaspoon |
| **GLAZE** | | | | | |
| **Large egg (white or whole)** | 1 | 1 | 1 | 1 | 1 |
| **Water** | 1 tablespoon | 1 tablespoon | 1 tablespoon | 1 tablespoon | 1 tablespoon |
| **TOPPING** | | | | | |
| **Granulated sugar** | ¼ cup | ¼ cup | ¼ cup | ¼ cup | ¼ cup |

**1.** Position the rack and preheat the oven as indicated for your altitude in the chart above. Prepare the cookie sheets as directed.

**2.** Prepare the pastry: In the large bowl of an electric mixer, preferably with a paddle attachment, or in the bowl of a food processor, beat or process the cream cheese and butter until very smooth. Add the flour and salt and beat or pulse just to combine; don't overwork, or the dough will be tough. Turn the dough out onto a lightly floured piece of wax paper or plastic wrap and pat it into a flat disk about 8 inches in diameter. Refrigerate for at least 20 minutes, or overnight. In very hot weather, you may need to refrigerate longer, or add up to 2 tablespoons more flour as the dough is shaped.

**3.** While the dough chills, prepare the fillings: Toss together the ingredients for each one in a small bowl (or prepare a double recipe of one filling).

Divide the dough into quarters. Work with one piece at a time, keeping the rest refrigerated.

**4.** On a lightly floured counter, roll the dough into a 9-inch circle about 1/8-inch thick. Use a chef's knife or pizza cutter dipped in flour to cut

the dough. To make 16 bite-sized crescents, cut the circle into quarters, then cut each wedge into 4 equal pieces. To make bigger crescents, cut the circle into only 8 equal wedges. To make straight roll-ups, shape the dough into an elongated rectangle, then cut out 4 1/2-inch-long, slightly tapered strips, about 1 1/2 inches at the wider end.

**5.** Brush some egg glaze all over each piece dough. Spread the dough with filling—cover the surface using about 3/4 teaspoon per small wedge, a little more for larger pieces. Roll each piece up as shown below, starting at the wide end, and place seam side down on a prepared cookie sheet. Brush the tops with more glaze and sprinkle with 1 tablespoon of the topping sugar. Repeat with the remaining dough and filling.

**6.** Bake for the time indicated for your altitude in the chart above, or until the pastry is golden brown. Cool the rugelach on a wire rack. If the rugelach were baked on parchment or a nonstick mat, simply slide it off the cookie sheet onto the wire rack to cool.

**7.** When the rugelach are completely cool, store in an airtight container, separated by layers of wax paper or plastic wrap.

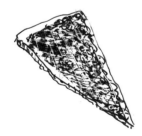   

*Shaping crescents*

*Shaping rolls*

# Twin Peaks Profiteroles with Ultimate Chocolate Sauce

PROFITEROLES ARE crisp pastry shells filled with ice cream and topped with warm chocolate sauce. Just five ingredients are used to make the classic dough called *pâte à choux* (pastry cabbages in French, *Windbeuteln*, or windbags, in German) that magically puffs up in the oven, baking into lovely crisp golden shells of light eggy pastry. They can be filled with whipped cream or pastry cream (for cream puffs or éclairs) or savory creams (for appetizers or hors d'oeuvres). The shells are closely related to popovers, which also depend on eggs for leavening.

The dough, easy to prepare once you understand the technique, is made in two stages: First, water, butter, and salt are brought to a boil in saucepan, the flour is added, and the mixture is beaten hard by hand, then cooled. Second, eggs are beaten in, with an electric mixer (hand-held or stand) or a food processor (my favorite method).

To bake the dough, two different temperatures are used in order to achieve a perfectly crisp result. The rise is achieved first in a very hot oven (look after the first 5 minutes to be sure the dough is not overbrowning), then the shells are dried out in a cooler oven.

Changes in altitude cause only minor alterations in ingredients, but mixing and baking techniques require careful attention.

---

**General High Altitude Notes:** There are two secrets to success at high altitudes: One is to remove the boiling liquid (in Step 3) from the heat *just as soon as* it begins to really bubble up; boiling too long allows too much liquid to evaporate, seriously altering the consistency at higher elevations, where excess evaporation is always a problem. As soon as the flour is beaten into the boiling liquid, it's easiest and most efficient to scoop it all into the bowl of the food processor or a mixing bowl, *let it cool* a little (it should be warm, not hot), and then pulse or beat in the eggs one at a time. If too many eggs go at once into very hot paste, the finished dough will be too soft and will collapse as it bakes.

The second secret is to determine the exact

quantity of egg to use, which can vary (see Step 5)—and a little more egg is usually needed at higher elevations, where the air, and flour, are dry and evaporation is severe. Bread flour has a higher gluten content than all-purpose flour and therefore provides elasticity and best rise, but you can substitute all-purpose. Add flour at 10,000 feet. At 3,000 feet and above, the bottoms of the puffs may overbrown before they are totally dried out; to prevent this, halfway through the baking time you can slip a second (unlined) cookie sheet under each pan to insulate it from the heat if a baking mat doesn't do the trick.

**Special Equipment:** 2 cookie sheets (not insulated); baking parchment or 2 Silpats or other nonstick mats (optional); 1½-to 2-quart heavy-bottomed saucepan; 2 teaspoons or a 16- to 18-inch pastry bag fitted with ½-inch plain tip; pastry brush; paring knife or skewer

**Pan Preparation:** Line the cookie sheets with baking parchment or nonstick baking mats or lightly coat with nonstick vegetable spray. If using parchment, put a dab of butter under each corner to hold the sheet in place.

**Makes** 26 to 30 puffs (2- to 2 ½-inch diameter)

| Ingredients | Sea Level | 3,000 feet | 5,000 feet | 7,000 feet | 10,000 feet |
|---|---|---|---|---|---|
| **Oven rack position, temperature, and baking time** | Divide oven in thirds; bake at 450°F for 15 minutes, then at 325°F for 20 minutes | Divide oven in thirds; bake at 450°F for 13 to 15 minutes, then at 325°F for 20 minutes | Divide oven in thirds; bake at 450°F for 13 to 15 minutes, then at 325°F for 13 to 16 minutes | Divide oven in thirds; bake at 450°F for 8 to 9 minutes, then at 325°F for 12 to 15 minutes | Divide oven in thirds; bake at 450°F for 15 minutes, then at 325°F for 15 to 20 minutes |
| **Eggs, at room temperature** | 4 | 4 | 4 | 4 | 4 |
| **Bread flour** | 1 cup | 1 cup | 1 cup | 1 cup | 1 cup plus 2 tablespoons |
| **Water** | ½ cup | ½ cup | ½ cup | ½ cup | ½ cup |
| **Unsalted butter, cut into small pieces and softened** | 8 tablespoons (1 stick) | 8 tablespoons (1 stick) | 8 tablespoons (1 stick) | 8 tablespoons (1 stick) | 8 tablespoons (1 stick) |
| **Salt** | ⅛ teaspoon | ⅛ teaspoon | ⅛ teaspoon | ⅛ teaspoon | ⅛ teaspoon |
| GLAZE (OPTIONAL) | | | | | |
| **Large egg** | 1 | 1 | 1 | 1 | 1 |
| **Water** | 1 teaspoon | 1 teaspoon | 1 teaspoon | 1 teaspoon | 1 teaspoon |

*(continued)*

| Ingredients | Sea Level | 3,000 feet | 5,000 feet | 7,000 feet | 10,000 feet |
|---|---|---|---|---|---|
| **FILLING AND TOPPING** | | | | | |
| **Ice cream (any flavor)** | 1 quart | 1 quart | 1 quart | 1 quart | 1 quart |
| **ULTIMATE CHOCOLATE SAUCE (RECIPE FOLLOWS)** | | | | | |

**1.** Position the racks and preheat the oven as indicated for your altitude in the chart above. Prepare the cookie sheets as directed.

**2.** In a small bowl, whisk 1 of the eggs; set it aside.

**3.** Place the measured flour and a wooden spoon near the stove. Add the water to a 1½- to 2-quart heavy saucepan, then add the butter and salt. Set over medium-high heat and stir to melt the butter and dissolve the salt; this should happen quickly, especially at high altitudes, so you lose a minimum of water to evaporation. *As soon as* the mixture boils with visible bubbles, remove pan from heat, dump in all the flour at once, turn the heat to low, and replace pan. Beat hard with the wooden spoon for several minutes, so the starch swells and absorbs the liquid. The dough will look smooth and silky and form a ball that pulls away from the pan sides; this takes about 1 or 2 minutes at sea level, a minute or two longer at 5,000 feet and above.

**4.** Cool the dough for 5 to 6 minutes, or until it is about 120°F on an instant-read thermometer. To speed the cooling, scoop the dough from the hot pan into a mixing bowl and stir or refrigerate a few minutes. Then scrape all the dough out into the bowl of a food processor or into a mixing bowl.

**5.** Add the 3 eggs *one at a time* to the processor or mixing bowl, and pulse or beat for 30 to 45 seconds after each addition, until the glossy shine is gone and the egg is well incorporated; scrape down the bowl each time. After

the eggs are added, scoop up a teaspoon of dough and check its consistency. When a teaspoon is held vertically, the dough should slide just a little and droop into an elongated teardrop shape as shown below. It should be slightly sticky yet firm enough to pipe or spoon and hold a shape. If the dough looks too stiff, add a little of the reserved beaten egg—you may need 1 to 2 tablespoons, or almost all of it, but add it 1 tablespoon at a time and don't let the batter get too limp or soft.

**6.** *To spoon out the dough into irregularly shaped puffs*, use two teaspoons. Scoop up a heaping teaspoon of dough and use the second spoon to push it off onto a prepared baking sheet, making mounds about 1¼ inches in diameter and about 1½ inches apart.

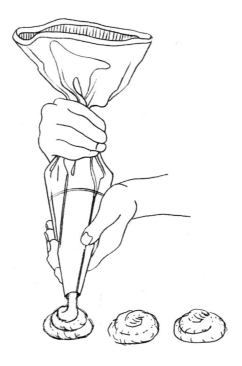

*To pipe the dough into uniformly rounded puffs,* scoop it into a pastry bag fitted with a ½-inch plain tip. Hold the tip of the pastry bag perpendicular to the baking sheet (as above), and squeeze out a snail-like shape about 1¼ inches in diameter. To finish, quickly release the pressure and lift the tip up toward the ceiling in a quick twist of your wrist; if the dough sticks, just cut it free with the tip of a knife. Continue making puffs, spacing them about 1½ inches apart, then smooth over the peak on top of each one by touching it with the tip of your finger dipped in cold water.

**7.** Use a pastry brush to paint a little egg glaze on top of each puff, if you wish. Place the sheets in the oven and bake for the first time indicated for your altitude in the chart above, or until the puffs are rounded, well-raised, and golden brown. Reduce the oven temperature to 325°F and transfer the cookie sheets to a heat-proof surface. With a fork, skewer, or knife tip, prick a small hole in the side of each puff to allow steam to escape, then return them to the oven to dry out for the time indicated. When the puffs are crisp, cool them completely on a wire rack. To store unfilled puffs, place in a crush-proof box, wrap airtight, and freeze for up to 1 month.

**8.** To fill the profiteroles with ice cream, use a serrated knife to slice the puffs in half. Scoop small balls of ice cream into each puff and cover with the top half. Set on a foil-covered tray and place in the freezer until solid. To store, put the frozen profiteroles in an airtight plastic bag.

**9.** To serve, let the ice cream–filled profiteroles sit at room temperature for 20 to 30 minutes. Warm the chocolate sauce. Serve with a dollop of sauce on top of each profiterole, and pass extra sauce in a pitcher.

## Ultimate Chocolate Sauce

**Special Equipment:** Double boiler (optional)

**Makes** about 1¼ cups

8 ounces semisweet chocolate (or 4 ounces
  bittersweet—not unsweetened—plus 4
  ounces semisweet chocolate), chopped
½ cup heavy cream
Optional flavorings: 1 teaspoon vanilla,
  orange, or peppermint extract or 1 to 2
  tablespoons dark rum or liqueur (such as
  Grand Marnier, Chambord, or Frangelico);
  or, for Mexican hot chocolate, a pinch of
  cayenne pepper

Combine the chopped chocolate and cream in the top of a double boiler set over simmering (at sea level to 4,500 feet) or gently boiling (at 5,000 feet and above) water and heat, stirring occasionally, until smooth. (At 5,000 feet and above, you can also melt the chocolate with the cream over direct medium heat, as long as you stir it constantly; at high altitudes, this will be faster than the double boiler.) Remove the chocolate sauce from the heat and stir in any flavoring. Cool slightly and serve warm. If the sauce thickens too much as it cools, stir in a little more cream.

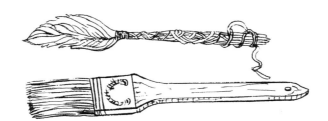

# Kristin's Trail Bars

WHEN I was testing recipes in Breckenridge, Colorado, my Boston friend Kristin Eycleshymer came out for a working holiday. A professional pastry chef, massage therapist, and avid hiker, Kris knew this visit would tap all her talents. After several days of troubleshooting recipes at 10,000 feet, she was ready to explore the mountains, and she looked through the recipes in my cookie chapter for a trail bar snack. When she didn't find one, she made up this recipe, rightly suggesting it was an essential for mountain-bound baker-hikers. The bars are packed with delicious fruits, nuts, and seeds that you can vary, as long as you keep the 6-cup total; the recipe does not change with altitude, and it requires no baking, just melting the syrup on the stovetop. We taste tested our way through many variations: Some were too hard, some were too soft, but this one was . . . just right (see page 21)!

**General High Altitude Notes:** The recipe contains melted marshmallows, an ingredient that may not be first on your "health food" purity list but is a concession to the high altitude challenge. We needed to find a way to bind the ingredients and harden the bars so they could be cut and hold their shape. Boiling sugar syrups to soft- or hard-crack temperatures presented too many difficulties at high altitudes, dry meringue powder didn't work, and peanut butter bars melted in my pocket on a hot day, so we returned to marshmallows, the simplest and most effective solution. Although dried fruits, nuts, and seeds are available in supermarkets, the best-quality items are often found in natural foods stores. Cut or chop fruit or nuts before measuring, weights are approximate.

**Special Equipment:** Frying pan (optional); 5- or 6-quart mixing bowl; 5- or 6-quart Dutch oven or other pot; long-handled sturdy spoon; 9 × 13 × 2-inch baking pan; plastic wrap

**Pan Preparation:** Butter the pan.

**Makes** 16 bars (2 × 3 × 1½-inch)

### Fruit-seed-nut mixture (about 6 cups)

¾ cup (2 ounces) old-fashioned rolled oats

½ cup (3 ounces) packed moist-style dried apricots, cut into ¼- to ½-inch bits

½ cup (3 ounces) packed raisins

½ cup (3¼ ounces) packed dried figs, stemmed and chopped

½ cup (3½ ounces) packed chopped pitted dates

¾ cup (3 ounces) packed dried cranberries or Craisins

3 tablespoons sesame seeds

½ cup (2½ ounces) sunflower seeds or pine nuts

1 cup (4 ounces) chopped walnuts or pecans

1 cup puffed millet or granola or light crisp cereal

### Syrup

4 tablespoons (½ stick) unsalted butter

¼ cup honey, optional

1 teaspoon ground cinnamon

1 teaspoon ground nutmeg

½ teaspoon salt

One 10-ounce package marshmallows (about 40) or 4 cups mini-marshmallows

**1.** To toast the oats, if desired, toss them in a frying pan over medium heat for 3 to 5 minutes, shaking and stirring occasionally, until lightly golden.

**2.** In a very large bowl, toss together the oats with all the fruits, seeds, nuts, and cereals. Use your fingers to separate any large clumps of sticky fruit.

**3.** In a Dutch oven or other large pot, combine the butter, honey, if using, spices, and salt. Set over medium heat and stir until the butter is melted. Add the marshmallows and, with a long-handled spoon, stir over medium-low heat for 3 to 4 minutes (slightly longer at 5,000 feet and above), until the marshmallows are completely melted and the syrup is liquefied and gooey. Toss in the fruit mixture and stir with a sturdy spoon to coat all the pieces.

**4.** Scoop the mixture into the buttered pan. Wet your hands (or cover the mixture with plastic wrap), and press the mixture into a flat layer. Refrigerate or set aside until cooled and set.

**5.** Cut into bars and wrap each one in a piece of plastic wrap. Store in an airtight container at room temperature for up to 3 days, or put the wrapped bars in a sealed plastic bag and freeze.

# Pies

## Baking Pies at High Altitudes

It is certainly not a piece of cake to bake cakes at high altitudes, but it is absolutely as easy as pie to bake pies, because they have comparatively few problems.

The altitude does influence certain aspects of pie baking. For example, when I began to travel in Colorado, I discovered that the higher in altitude I went, the lower, or flatter, the pies. The closer I got to 10,000 feet, the more obvious the trend. In restaurants, cafés, and bakeries, I saw flat crumb or streusel pies, lattice pies, and open-faced tarts, and only rarely the dome-shaped double-crust pie you would find closer to sea level. When I finally discovered a dramatically domed double-crust apple pie in a restaurant at 10,000 feet, I immediately asked about it, only to be told it was "imported from the lowlands" of Denver (5,000 feet), where it was more practical for their baker to work.

I talked about the flat versus fat phenomenon with home cooks and professional bakers, and I got the picture very clearly: It's hard to bake a tall pile of fruit on a mountaintop. As the altitude increases, the boiling point of water decreases, and it takes longer for foods to reach an internal temperature high enough to cook them through. The time required to bake a high-piled mound of sliced hard Granny Smith apples, for example, is about the same time needed to burn the top crust. What can the baker do? There are a couple of easy solutions: The best is to select softer eating (not hard baking) apples (Golden Delicious, for example) that bake more quickly; they will soften before the crust burns. It is up to the baker to carefully gauge the type and hardness of the fruit, and to monitor the oven temperature and baking time. Many high altitude bakers avoid the problem altogether by precooking and flavoring the fruit, particularly apples, on the stovetop before adding it to a pie shell. This works best with hard varieties of apples, like Greening and Granny Smith, which can stand up to being cooked twice. In my tests, though, I found that the stove-softened apple slices were excellent in low-mounded or flat pies but would not hold their shape when I tried to mound and bake them into a high-rise pie.

Very juicy fruit and berry pies are another story: They often need longer baking times because their juices, like water, boil at a lower temperature at high altitudes than at sea level; this lower temperature will take longer to heat and gelatinize the starch that thickens the pies.

Letty Flatt, executive pastry chef at Deer Park Resorts in Utah, taught me about her solution to another well-known pie phenomenon. To avoid soggy-bottomed pies, Letty always prebakes her pastry shells, even if they are to be baked again with filling. Since it is difficult to attach a raw top crust to a crisply baked lower shell, she is more inclined to top a pie with crumbs.

Piecrusts present only one problem for the high altitude baker: as elevation increases, they may need more moisture. As the elevation increases, the dry mountain air makes flour drier and evaporation rates are faster, often leaving crusts without sufficient moisture to hold the starch together. The recipes in this book note the addition of extra liquid where necessary, but sometimes the exact amount is left to the baker's discretion. Care must be taken not to add too much liquid, because that may necessitate adding extra flour, leading, in turn, to a tough crust. I find it helpful to use a heatproof glass (Pyrex) pie plate so I can see the color of the bottom crust and know that it is properly baked and golden in color. As insurance against overbrowning when baking times are long, it is helpful to place a piece of aluminum foil, or a foil frame (see page 33) on the pie top to deflect the heat from the crust during the last stages of baking.

Bakers everywhere, not just at high altitudes, should take preventive measures to keep their bottom crusts golden brown and crisp, avoiding the dreaded soggy bottoms that can occur when custards and fruit fillings release moisture that soaks into the dough. My own solution is to bake any type of pie at high heat (425°F) in the lower third of the oven for the first 12 to 15 minutes, then reduce the heat to bake the fruit. The high heat used at first creates steam to push up flakes of dough quickly, setting the proteins and starches before the fat melts, mixes with the liquid, and glues the crust together. In addition, to prevent fruit juices from seeping into the crust, I moistureproof the bottom crust with an egg glaze or fruit preserves before adding the fruit.

Like Letty, I also prebake pie shells, especially before adding a custard filling (pecan and pumpkin custard pies), then bake the filled pies at a reduced heat so the egg proteins can coagulate slowly and maintain the custard's smooth consistency. With the pumpkin pie, the pumpkin mixed with egg prevents too-rapid shrinking of egg proteins, so the pie can support a slightly higher temperature than a plain egg custard.

You can prepare pie pastry a day or two in advance, wrap, and refrigerate it; or doublewrap it so it is airtight and freeze for a month or so. Thaw the frozen dough overnight in the refrigerator and roll it out while it is still cold.

# Pike's Peak Apple Pie with Flaky Pastry

C LOSE YOUR eyes, and imagine the sight and scent of a just-baked cinnamon-apple pie, its flaky butter crust richly golden brown and sugar-glazed. Smell good? What does your fantasy pie look like? If you are living between sea level and an altitude of, say, 6,500 feet, your dream pie might resemble mine . . . a mountain-high pile of sweetly spiced apples beneath a dramatically tall, dome-shaped crust. But if you live at 7,000 feet or above, you probably have never baked such a pie, or even seen one (unless it was brought up from the "lowlands"). At high elevations, the norm, for very good reason (see below), is likely to be a flat-topped apple pie, with either a crust or a crumb topping. Flat is just as delicious and equally aromatic, though a tad less glamorous. If you are at a high altitude, this recipe will give you sweeter dreams.

**General High Altitude Notes:** Apple pie recipes usually call for hard cooking apples, such as Greenings or Granny Smiths, which, when sliced and packed into a mound, take a lot of heat and a long time to bake through. Since water boils at a lower temperature as the altitude increases, foods take much longer to reach a high internal temperature.

The secret to a (literally) high pie is first, to select the right type of apples. From sea level to about 7,000 feet, use a blend of crisp cooking apples: Granny Smith, Jonathan, and Rome, for example. At 7,000 feet and above, use Golden Delicious, McIntosh, or other softer eating apples. These are usually considered too soft for sea-level pies but they are a perfect choice at high altitudes because they bake more quickly; they can also be piled high and still bake through. Another solution, favored by many high altitude pastry chefs, is to precook harder apples on the stovetop before baking them in the pastry. This is easy enough to do, but I found it unnecessary once I chose the right type of apples.

The second trick is to add enough moisture to the piecrust; at higher elevations, the dry mountain air and fast evaporation mean doughs usually need a little extra liquid to remain pliable. And the third trick is to cover a partially baked pie with an aluminum foil tent to prevent overbrowning.

**Special Equipment:** A 9-inch pie plate, preferably Pyrex; rolling pin; bench scraper or broad spatula; pastry brush; aluminum foil "frame" (see page 33)

**Makes** one 9-inch pie; serves 8 to 10

| Ingredients | Sea Level | 3,000 feet | 5,000 feet | 7,000 feet | 10,000 feet |
|---|---|---|---|---|---|
| **Oven rack position, temperature, and baking time** | Rack in lower third of oven; bake at 425°F for 15 minutes, then at 350°F for 40 to 45 minutes | Rack in lower third of oven; bake at 425°F for 15 minutes, then at 350°F for 40 to 45 minutes | Rack in lower third of oven; bake at 425°F for 15 minutes, then at 350°F for 40 to 45 minutes | Rack in lower third of oven; bake at 425°F for 15 minutes, then at 350°F for 40 to 45 minutes | Rack in lower third of oven; bake at 425°F for 15 minutes, then at 350°F for 40 to 45 minutes |
| **FLAKY PASTRY** | | | | | |
| **All-purpose flour** | 3 cups | 3 cups | 3 cups | 3 cups | 3 cups |
| **Granulated sugar** | 2 tablespoons | 2 tablespoons | 2 tablespoons | 2 tablespoons | 2 tablespoons |
| **Salt** | ¾ teaspoon | ¾ teaspoon | ¾ teaspoon | ¾ teaspoon | 1 teaspoon |
| **Unsalted butter, cold or frozen, cut up** | 12 tablespoons (1½ sticks) | 12 tablespoons (1½ sticks) | 12 tablespoons (1½ sticks) | 12 tablespoons (1½ sticks) | 12 tablespoons (1½ sticks) |
| **Solid vegetable shortening, chilled** | 6 tablespoons | 6 tablespoons | 6 tablespoons | 6 tablespoons | 6 tablespoons |
| **Large egg yolk, at room temperature** | 1 | 1 | 1 | 1 | 1 |
| **Fresh lemon juice or white vinegar** | 2 tablespoons | 2 tablespoons | 2 tablespoons | 2 tablespoons | 2 tablespoons |
| **Ice water** | 3 to 4 tablespoons | 3 to 4 tablespoons | 3 to 4 tablespoons | 5 to 6 tablespoons | 5 to 8 tablespoons |
| **GLAZE** | | | | | |
| **Large egg** | 1 | 1 | 1 | 1 | 1 |
| **Water** | 1 teaspoon | 1 teaspoon | 1 teaspoon | 1 teaspoon | 1 teaspoon |

(continued)

| Ingredients | Sea Level | 3,000 feet | 5,000 feet | 7,000 feet | 10,000 feet |
|---|---|---|---|---|---|
| **FILLING** | | | | | |
| **8 to 9 large apples (see headnote above), peeled, cored, and sliced ⅛ to ¼ inch thick** | 8 to 9 cups of slices (blend of Granny Smith, Jonathan, and Rome) | 8 to 9 cups of slices (blend of Granny Smith, Jonathan, and Rome) | 8 to 9 cups of slices (blend of Granny Smith, Jonathan, and Rome) | 8 to 9 cups of slices (Golden Delicious or other eating apples) | 8 to 9 cups of slices (Golden Delicious or other eating apples) |
| **Light or dark brown sugar, packed** | ⅓ to ½ cup (depending on sweetness of apples) | ⅓ to ½ cup (depending on sweetness of apples) | ⅓ to ½ cup (depending on sweetness of apples) | ⅓ to ½ cup (depending on sweetness of apples) | ⅓ to ½ cup (depending on sweetness of apples) |
| **Fresh lemon juice** | 3 to 4 tablespoons | 3 to 4 tablespoons | 3 to 4 tablespoons | 3 to 4 tablespoons | 3 to 4 tablespoons |
| **All-purpose flour** | 3½ tablespoons | 3½ tablespoons | 3½ tablespoons | 3½ tablespoons | 3½ tablespoons |
| **Ground cinnamon** | 1 teaspoon | 1 teaspoon | 1 teaspoon | 1 teaspoon | 1 teaspoon |
| **Ground nutmeg** | ½ teaspoon | ½ teaspoon | ½ teaspoon | ½ teaspoon | ½ teaspoon |
| **Graham or plain cracker crumbs, or crushed cornflakes** | 2 tablespoons | 2 tablespoons | 2 tablespoons | 2 tablespoons | 2 tablespoons |
| **TOPPING** | | | | | |
| **Granulated sugar** | 1 to 2 tablespoons | 1 to 2 tablespoons | 1 to 2 tablespoons | 1 to 2 tablespoons | 1 to 2 tablespoons |

**1.** Prepare the pastry: In a food processor, pulse together the flour, sugar, and salt to blend. Add the cold butter and shortening and pulse 8 or 9 times, just until the mixture resembles coarse meal, with some butter pieces the size of small peas. Add the egg yolk, lemon juice or vinegar, and 1 to 2 tablespoons ice water through the feed tube and pulse a few times. The dough should just be beginning to get clumpy. If it is too dry, add more water 1 tablespoon at a time, pulse again, and check the consistency. The dough is ready when it holds its shape when squeezed between your fingers; it should be neither wet nor sandy dry. Never allow a dough ball to form on the blade. At altitudes over 5,000 feet, especially in high mountains where the air is very dry, you may need to add a little more ice water than at lower elevations. (Alternatively,

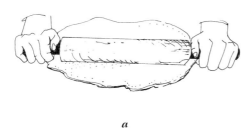

*a*

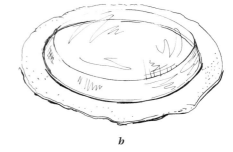

*b*

*c*

*d*

you can mix the piecrust ingredients together in a bowl, using a wire pastry blender, large fork, or your fingertips.)

**2.** When the dough is clumpy, turn it out onto a piece of wax paper or plastic wrap, gather it into a ball, and press it into a flat disk. If the dough doesn't feel too warm or soft, you can roll it out without chilling. Otherwise, wrap it and refrigerate it for about 30 minutes, or as long as overnight.

**3.** Position a rack in the lower third of the oven and preheat it to 425°F.

**4.** Divide the dough ball in half, and refrigerate one piece. Roll out the other portion of dough on a lightly floured surface with a floured rolling pin (sketch a) to a circle at least 2 inches larger diameter than the pie plate edge (turn it upside down in the center of the dough to measure it; b). Use a bench scraper to ease up and loosen the dough edges, then fold the dough into quarters and fit it into the pie plate with the point in the center (c). Unfold the

dough and gently fit into the pan, without stretching it; drape the edges of the dough over the plate rim. If there are any breaks, just press the dough together again with your fingertips; it is fine to mold the dough in the pie plate. If the dough cracks, add a drop of egg glaze to the spot and pinch/press it back together. If you have time, refrigerate until the dough feels firm.

**5.** In a large bowl, toss the sliced apples with the sugar, lemon juice, flour, and spices. To prevent the apple juices from softening the bottom crust, use a pastry brush to paint a coating of egg glaze over the entire pastry shell. Sprinkle on the crumbs or crushed cereal, to absorb excess juice. Pile in the apple slices, using the palms of your hands to mold and pack them into a high dome centered in the pastry shell.

**6.** Roll out the remaining dough to a circle about 2 inches larger all around than the pie plate. Fold the pastry into quarters as before and place it over the mound of fruit, centering the point. Unfold the pastry, draping it evenly over the apples and onto the rim of the plate. Trim the dough to a ¾-inch overhang; reserve the scraps. Fold the edge of the top crust under the bottom one and pinch them together to seal. Pinch up a raised pastry rim all around, then pinch it into points or scallops with your fingers. With a knife tip, cut 5 slits and a center hole in the crust for steam vents (d).

**7.** Brush the pie with the egg glaze and sprinkle with the topping sugar. If you'd like, after glazing but before sugaring, you can decorate the pie top with pastry shapes: Roll out the leftover dough scraps and, with a paring knife or small cookie cutter, cut out leaf shapes. Press veins into the leaves with the back of the knife blade (see sketch below). Position the leaves on the egg-glazed pastry; they can be partially raised, or gracefully curled, to look more realistic. Brush egg glaze on the leaves, then sprinkle the topping sugar all over the pastry. If you have time, refrigerate the pie until the crust feels firm; chilling now will prevent shrinkage or warping of the crust, especially the fluting.

**8.** Bake the pie for 15 minutes, then reduce the heat to 350°F and bake for 40 to 45 minutes, or until the pastry is a rich golden brown and the fruit is tender when pierced with the tip of a knife through a vent hole. When you reduce the oven heat, set a timer for about 20 minutes. Check the pie color at that time, and if the edges are beginning to overbrown, set a foil frame over the pie edges to protect them. Then, once the pie is baked, remove the foil to brown the top a few minutes longer if necessary.

**9.** Cool the pie on a wire rack and serve it warm, topped by a slice of sharp Cheddar cheese or a scoop of vanilla ice cream.

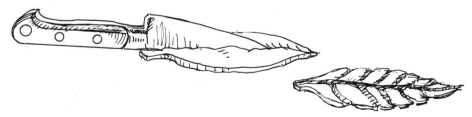

*Pressing leaf veins in dough cut-outs*

# Red Door Pecan Pie with Nut Pastry

THIS CLASSIC pecan pie had always been delicious, and perfectly reliable, until I took it to the ear-popping elevation of 10,000 feet in Breckenridge, Colorado, where it suddenly became the subject of high drama.

I was delivering some apple and plum test pies to friends at the Red Door, a Breckenridge shelter run by Father Ron Griffin of St. John's Episcopal Church, when I got to chatting about pies with his son Nathan, the personable young manager. When I told him I was going home to bake a pecan pie, he looked very alarmed. "You should really talk to my mom first. She loves to bake, but her pecan pie exploded when she made it at this altitude!"

As soon as I got home, I phoned Charlotte Griffin and made the serendipitous discovery that we were literally next-door neighbors (see page 20). That afternoon, she came for tea, bringing with her a cautionary tale. "A few years ago, when we first moved here from Tennessee," she told me, "I invited the whole family to lunch on Easter Sunday. I wanted everything to be perfect. I baked my mother's Kentucky pecan pie that morning and, moments before the guests were due to arrive, I began to smell smoke. I ran to the oven just in time to see the pie turning into a volcano!" She described her panic as she watched a geyser of brown sugar lava erupting from the pecans, spewing all over the oven, and burning quickly to black sticky cinders that smoked demonically. The smoke detector went off with a piercing screech at the same time the doorbell rang. Charlotte greeted her guests with one hand, and dialed the fire department with the other.

Of course, I believed Charlotte's story, but I had to try the process myself before I could even think of solving the problem. The next morning, I lined my oven with foil, got out a fire extinguisher, and prepared my basic sea-level recipe. I popped it into the oven and pulled up a chair. With mounting horror, I watched through the glass oven door as the predicted eruption began. Smoke began to billow from my oven. The screech of the smoke detector accompanied my call to Charlotte saying she was right, the recipe needed help, and so did I.

All that week I talked to local bakers and friends. Some people told me pecan pie could just not be baked there, period. Charlotte found a recipe from a Colorado friend who suggested cooking the filling separately in a saucepan. I tinkered with a variety of adjustments and stovetop techniques and we compared notes. But it was a talk with food scientist Shirley Corriher that finally set us straight. She explained that since liquids evaporate so quickly at 10,000 feet, there was too much sugar in the three-egg pie once the liquid evaporated out. At a certain point, the over-concentrated sugar simply boiled over, or up and out, once it found an escape hole in the crusty pecan topping.

Variations follow for Bourbon Pecan, Cranberry Pecan, Black Walnut, and Hawaiian Macadamia Nut Pie.

**General High Altitude Notes:** The solution to baking the 10K pecan filling was simple. I cooked the syrup first on top of the stove to control the evaporation as the syrup boiled down and thickened. Then I cut some fat and added a little cornstarch for extra thickening and stability (the starch helps prevent the eggs from curdling). By the time I baked the filling in the pastry shell, it was stable, well behaved, and as delicious as ever.

**Note:** To easily measure corn syrup and molasses, first coat the measuring cup with nonstick spray or butter.

**Special Equipment:** Food processor; cookie sheet; 9-inch pie plate (preferably Pyrex); wax paper; rolling pin; pastry brush; aluminum foil; pie weights, rice, or dried beans

**Makes** one 9-inch pie; serves 8 to 10

**High Notes**

*At 5,000 feet,* bake the pie at 375°F and reduce the baking time slightly.

*At 7,000 feet,* bake the pie at 350°F.

*At 10,000 feet,* reduce the fat, add cornstarch and vanilla. Prebake the piecrust longer than at lower elevations. Use a totally different procedure for the filling (Step 8), and bake the pie at 325°F.

| Ingredients | Sea Level | 3,000 feet | 5,000 feet | 7,000 feet | 10,000 feet |
|---|---|---|---|---|---|
| **Oven rack position, temperature, and baking time** | Rack in lower third of oven; partially prebake crust at 425°F for 15 to 17 minutes; reduce heat to 350°F, move rack to center, and bake filled pie for 30 to 35 minutes | Rack in lower third of oven; partially prebake crust at 425°F for 15 to 17 minutes; reduce heat to 350°F, move rack to center, and bake filled pie for 30 to 35 minutes | Rack in lower third of oven; partially prebake crust at 425°F for 15 to 17 minutes; reduce heat to 375°F, move rack to center, and bake filled pie for 20 to 25 minutes | Rack in lower third of oven; partially prebake crust at 425°F for 15 to 17 minutes; reduce heat to 350°F, move rack to center, and bake filled pie for 30 to 35 minutes | Rack in lower third of oven; partially prebake crust at 425°F for 15 to 20 minutes; reduce heat to 325°F, move rack to center, and bake filled pie for 30 to 35 minutes |

**NUT PASTRY**

| Ingredients | Sea Level | 3,000 feet | 5,000 feet | 7,000 feet | 10,000 feet |
|---|---|---|---|---|---|
| **All-purpose flour** | 1½ cups | 1½ cups | 1½ cups | 1½ cups | 1½ cups |
| **Granulated sugar** | 1 tablespoon | 1 tablespoon | 1 tablespoon | 1 tablespoon | 1 tablespoon |
| **Salt** | ½ teaspoon | ½ teaspoon | ½ teaspoon | ½ teaspoon | ½ teaspoon |
| **Walnuts or pecans** | ½ cup (2 ounces) | ½ cup (2 ounces) | ½ cup (2 ounces) | ½ cup (2 ounces) | ½ cup (2 ounces) |
| **Unsalted butter, cut up, chilled** | 6 tablespoons (¾ stick) | 6 tablespoons (¾ stick) | 6 tablespoons (¾ stick) | 6 tablespoons (¾ stick) | 6 tablespoons (¾ stick) |
| **Solid vegetable shortening, chilled** | 3 tablespoons | 3 tablespoons | 3 tablespoons | 3 tablespoons | 3 tablespoons |
| **Large egg yolk, at room temperature** | 1 | 1 | 1 | 1 | 1 |
| **Fresh lemon juice or white vinegar** | 1 tablespoon | 1 tablespoon | 1 tablespoon | 1 tablespoon | 1 tablespoon |
| **Ice water** | 3 to 5 tablespoons | 3 to 5 tablespoons | 3 to 5 tablespoons | 3 to 5 tablespoons | 3 to 5 tablespoons |

**FILLING**

| Ingredients | Sea Level | 3,000 feet | 5,000 feet | 7,000 feet | 10,000 feet |
|---|---|---|---|---|---|
| **Dark brown sugar, packed** | ¾ cup | ¾ cup | ¾ cup | ¾ cup | ¾ cup |

(continued)

| Ingredients | Sea Level | 3,000 feet | 5,000 feet | 7,000 feet | 10,000 feet |
|---|---|---|---|---|---|
| **Large eggs, at room temperature** | 3 | 3 | 3 | 3 | 3 |
| **Unsalted butter, melted** | 6 tablespoons | 6 tablespoons | 6 tablespoons | 6 tablespoons | 4 tablespoons (see Step 8) |
| **Dark corn syrup** | ²/₃ cup | ²/₃ cup | ²/₃ cup | ²/₃ cup | ²/₃ cup |
| **Molasses, unsulfured** | 1 tablespoon | 1 tablespoon | 1 tablespoon | 1 tablespoon | 1 tablespoon |
| **Salt** | ¹/₄ teaspoon | ¹/₄ teaspoon | ¹/₄ teaspoon | ¹/₄ teaspoon | ¹/₄ teaspoon |
| **Fresh lemon juice** | 1 teaspoon | 1 teaspoon | 1 teaspoon | 1 teaspoon | 1 teaspoon |
| **Vanilla extract** | 1 teaspoon | 1 teaspoon | 1 teaspoon | 1 teaspoon | 2 teaspoons |
| **Cornstarch** | None | None | None | None | 2 teaspoons |
| **Pecan halves or pieces** | 1¹/₄ cups (5 ounces) | 1¹/₄ cups (5 ounces) | 1¹/₄ cups (5 ounces) | 1¹/₄ cups (5 ounces) | 1¹/₄ cups (5 ounces) |

**1.** Position a rack in the lower third of the oven and set a cookie sheet on the rack to get hot. Preheat the oven to 425°F.

**2.** Prepare the pastry: In the bowl of a food processor, pulse together the flour, sugar, salt, and nuts until the nuts are finely chopped. Add the cold butter and shortening and pulse 8 or 9 times, just until the mixture resembles coarse meal.

**3.** Add the egg yolk, lemon juice or vinegar, and 1 to 2 tablespoons ice water through the feed tube and pulse a few times. The dough should just be beginning to get clumpy. If it is too dry, add another tablespoon of water and pulse a few more times. The dough is ready when it holds its shape when squeezed between your fingers; it should be neither wet nor sandy dry. Never allow a dough ball to form on the blade. At altitudes over 5,000 feet, especially in high mountains where the air is very dry, you may need to add a little more ice water than at lower elevations. (Alternatively, you can mix the piecrust ingredients together in a bowl with a wire pastry blender, fork, or your fingertips.)

**4.** When the dough is clumpy, turn it out onto a piece of plastic wrap or wax paper, gather it into a ball, and press it into a flat disk. If the dough doesn't feel too warm or soft, you can roll it out without chilling. Otherwise, wrap it and refrigerate it for about 30 minutes, or as long as overnight.

**5.** Roll out the dough on a lightly floured surface with a floured rolling pin to a circle at least 2 inches larger in diameter than the pie plate edge (turn it upside down in the center of the dough to measure it; page 268, sketch b). Use a bench scraper to ease up and loosen the dough edges, then fold the dough into quarters and fit it into the pie plate, with the point in the center

(above). Unfold the dough and gently drape it over the pan; do not stretch it. If there are any breaks, just press the dough together again with your fingertips; it is fine to mold the dough in the pie plate. Trim the excess dough to ¾ to 1 inch, and reserve. Fold under the overhanging dough and pinch the edge up into points or scallops around the rim (below). If the dough cracks, add a drop of water to the spot and pinch/press it back together. If you have time, refrigerate until the dough feels firm.

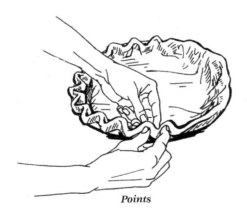

*Points*

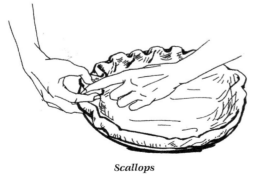

*Scallops*

**6.** Place a cookie sheet on the lower oven rack. Cut a 12-inch square of foil, spread a little butter or nonstick vegetable spray on the shiny side, and set it greased side down in the pastry-lined pie plate. Fill with pie weights (above) and place on the hot cookie sheet in the oven (for ease in handling). Bake the pastry shell for 15 to 17 minutes, until no longer translucent but still pale (at 10,000 feet, bake a little longer, until the crust is a light golden color). Remove the cookie sheet with the pie plate on it, gather up the edges of the foil with all the pie weights inside, and lift it out. Inspect the pastry shell, and if you see any cracks or holes, patch them by brushing on a little water, then gently pressing on bits of the reserved raw dough. (The patches will bake along with the filling.) Set the pie shell aside. Reduce the oven temperature as indicated for your altitude in the chart above, and move the oven rack to the center.

**7.** To prepare the filling and bake the pie at sea level to just below 10,000 feet (for 10,000 feet and above, see Step 8): In the bowl of an electric mixer, or in a large bowl, using a whisk, beat together the brown sugar and eggs. Mix in all the remaining ingredients except the nuts. Pour the filling into the partially baked pastry shell and arrange the nuts on top.

Bake the pie for the time indicated for your altitude in the chart above, or until a table knife stuck into the center comes out clean or coated with a clear syrup.

**8.** To prepare the filling and bake the pie at 10,000 feet and above (see the introductory notes): Melt the 4 tablespoons butter in a medium saucepan, then stir in the brown sugar, corn syrup, molasses, and salt. In a cup, combine the lemon juice and 1 teaspoon of the vanilla and stir in the cornstarch until dissolved, then stir this into the pan. Bring to a full, bubbling boil over medium-high heat, stirring constantly with a wooden spoon, about 3 minutes. Stir down the bubbles, then remove from the heat. Stir in the final teaspoon of vanilla.

Whisk the eggs in a mixing bowl. While continuing to whisk, add a few tablespoons of the hot syrup to the eggs to warm them, then whisk all the eggs into the hot syrup, beating well as you do it so the eggs blend in rather than poaching (strain the mixture if it looks at all lumpy). Pour the hot filling into the prepared pastry shell and arrange the nuts on top.

Bake for about 30 minutes, or until a knife inserted in the center comes out clean or coated with clear syrup. As the pie bakes, you may see the top bubbling and frothing, but it will settle down and bake without overflowing.

**9.** Cool the pie on a wire rack. Serve at room temperature.

# Bourbon Pecan Pie

Prepare the filling as above, but omit the lemon juice and add 1 tablespoon bourbon; at 10,000 feet, stir the bourbon in along with the beaten eggs.

# Cranberry Pecan Pie

Prepare the filling as above, but add ¾ cup coarsely chopped fresh or frozen cranberries and use only ¾ cup (3 ounces) pecans.

# Black Walnut Pie

Prepare the filling as above, but replace the pecans with 1 cup (4 ounces) black walnuts, coarsely chopped, and use light corn syrup instead of dark.

# Hawaiian Macadamia Nut Pie

Prepare the filling as above, but replace the pecans with 1 cup (4 ounces) unsalted macadamia nuts, coarsely chopped.

# Santa Fe Roadhouse
# Nectarine-Plum-Apricot Cobbler

COBBLER IS an old-fashioned, deep-dish "spoon dessert," homey and inviting comfort food at its best. Quick and easy to make, it consists of the ripest fruit in season (plums and apricots, or peaches or nectarines mixed with raspberries, blackberries, or blueberries, for example) topped with a biscuit dough and baked in the oven or cooked on top of the stove.

One of the best versions I have ever had, and I'm glad to say I have had it many times, was the peach cobbler served at Harry's Roadhouse on Old Pecos Trail just outside Santa Fe, New Mexico. One sunny August morning, I had coffee with with Peyton Young, who owns Harry's (with her husband, Harry Shapiro) and is their primary baker. The secret to the cobbler, she said, starts with extra-sweet ripe peaches, which are mixed with a little brown sugar, orange zest, and orange juice. Their cobbler dough, which reminded me of my scone recipe because it contains butter, eggs, and buttermilk, was baked in the oven on top of the intensely flavored peaches. Sounds simple. But the heady perfume of that overflowing bowl of warm juicy fruit topped by a tender biscuit coated with crunchy sugar crystals was pure heaven, breakfast, lunch, or late at night. Its special magic, of course, also had something to do with the colorful, casual ambiance of Harry's place, the tree-shaded back garden, the gaily painted tables, the colorful friendly locals. I ate my way through the menu from brunch, with my lovely neighbor, Virginia Grey, to late-night snacks with my tango-dancing cousin, Bessy Berman, a Santa Fe photographer, but I always saved room for the cobbler. The peaches were sometimes replaced by blackberries and blueberries, but, the magic held, maybe in part because I was a long way from home and it was perfect comfort food.

**General High Altitude Notes:** Stovetop cooking of the fruit takes a little longer above sea level. At 10,000 feet, the cobbler dough needs strengthening with flour, and it will rise too high unless the leavening is reduced. Add extra liquid to counter the rapid evaporation at this elevation.

**Special Equipment:** A 2- to 4-quart Dutch oven or ovenproof skillet (for stovetop cooking, you need a tight-fitting lid), or a 10- to 12-inch deep-dish baking pan (such as a 10 × 2-inch Pyrex pie plate); aluminum foil; wooden skewer or cake tester

**High Notes**

*At 3,000 feet and above,* bake in the lower third of the oven to expose the cobbler to more heat, and bake for a slightly longer time. Stovetop cooking will take longer than at sea level.

*At 10,000 feet and above,* add flour and buttermilk, and reduce baking powder. Preheat the oven to 25 degrees above the actual baking temperature, then reduce the heat when you put the cobbler in the oven.

**Makes** one 10-inch cobbler; serves 6

| Ingredients | Sea Level | 3,000 feet | 5,000 feet | 7,000 feet | 10,000 feet |
|---|---|---|---|---|---|
| **Oven rack position, temperature, and baking time** | Rack in center; bake at 425°F for 20 to 25 minutes (or cook on stovetop) | Rack in lower third of oven; bake at 425°F for 25 to 27 minutes (or cook on stovetop) | Rack in lower third of oven; bake at 425°F for 25 to 30 minutes (or cook on stovetop) | Rack in lower third of oven; bake at 425°F for 25 to 35 minutes (or cook on stovetop) | Rack in lower third of oven; *preheat* oven to 400°F; *bake* at 375°F for 30 minutes (or cook on stovetop) |
| **DOUGH** | | | | | |
| **All-purpose flour** | 1½ cups | 1½ cups | 1½ cups | 1½ cups | 1½ cups plus 1 tablespoon |
| **Baking powder** | 1½ teaspoons | 1½ teaspoons | 1½ teaspoons | 1½ teaspoons | 1¼ teaspoons |
| **Salt** | ¼ teaspoon | ¼ teaspoon | ¼ teaspoon | ¼ teaspoon | ¼ teaspoon |
| **Granulated sugar** | 2 tablespoons | 2 tablespoons | 2 tablespoons | 2 tablespoons | 2 tablespoons |
| **Ground nutmeg** | Generous pinch | Generous pinch | Generous pinch | Generous pinch | Generous pinch |
| **Unsalted butter, cut up, at room temperature** | 4 tablespoons (½ stick) | 4 tablespoons (½ stick) | 4 tablespoons (½ stick) | 4 tablespoons (½ stick) | 4 tablespoons (½ stick) |
| **Buttermilk** | ⅔ cup | ⅔ cup | ⅔ cup | ⅔ cup | ⅔ cup plus 1 tablespoon |

*(continued)*

| Ingredients | Sea Level | 3,000 feet | 5,000 feet | 7,000 feet | 10,000 feet |
|---|---|---|---|---|---|
| **Large egg, at room temperature** | 1 | 1 | 1 | 1 | 1 |
| **FRUIT** | | | | | |
| **Apple or orange juice** | ¾ to 1⅓ cups (depending on juiciness of fruit) | ¾ to 1⅓ cups (depending on juiciness of fruit) | ¾ to 1⅓ cups (depending on juiciness of fruit) | ¾ to 1⅓ cups (depending on juiciness of fruit) | ¾ to 1⅓ cups (depending on juiciness of fruit) |
| **Cornstarch** | 1½ tablespoons | 1½ tablespoons | 1½ tablespoons | 1½ tablespoons | 1½ tablespoons |
| **Granulated sugar or packed light brown sugar** | ⅓ to ¾ cup (depending on sweetness of fruit) | ⅓ to ¾ cup (depending on sweetness of fruit) | ⅓ to ¾ cup (depending on sweetness of fruit) | ⅓ to ¾ cup (depending on sweetness of fruit) | ⅓ to ¾ cup (depending on sweetness of fruit) |
| **Fresh lemon juice—omit if fruit is very tart** | 2 tablespoons | 2 tablespoons | 2 tablespoons | 2 tablespoons | 2 tablespoons |
| **Grated orange zest** | 2 teaspoons | 2 teaspoons | 2 teaspoons | 2 teaspoons | 2 teaspoons |
| **Ground cinnamon** | Generous pinch, plus extra for topping if cooked on stovetop | Generous pinch, plus extra for topping if cooked on stovetop | Generous pinch, plus extra for topping if cooked on stovetop | Generous pinch, plus extra for topping if cooked on stovetop | Generous pinch, plus extra for topping if cooked on stovetop |
| **Ripe plums (Italian prune, Santa Rosa, or any type), pitted and thickly sliced** | 3 generous cups sliced | 3 generous cups sliced | 3 generous cups sliced | 3 generous cups sliced | 3 generous cups sliced |
| **Ripe apricots and nectarines, pitted and thickly sliced** | 3 cups sliced, mixed | 3 cups sliced, mixed | 3 cups sliced, mixed | 3 cups sliced, mixed | 3 cups sliced, mixed |
| **SUGAR TOPPING** | | | | | |
| **Granulated or coarse sugar** | 2 tablespoons | 2 tablespoons | 2 tablespoons | 2 tablespoons | 2 tablespoons |

1. Prepare the dough in a food processor or in a bowl using a wire pastry blender or a fork: Pulse or whisk together the flour, baking powder, salt, sugar, and nutmeg. Add the butter and pulse or cut it into the flour until the mixture is crumbly. Add the buttermilk and egg and pulse or stir just until the ingredients are completely blended; to keep the dough tender, don't overwork it. Set the dough aside.

2. If you will be baking the cobbler, position the oven rack and preheat to the temperature indicated for your altitude in the chart above; otherwise, you can cook the cobbler on top of the stove.

3. Prepare the fruit: In a Dutch oven or large skillet (ovenproof if you will be baking the cobbler), whisk together the juice and cornstarch, then stir in the sugar, lemon juice, orange zest, and cinnamon. Add the fruit, set over medium heat, and cover the pot. Bring to a boil, then reduce the heat and simmer for about 10 minutes (a little longer at 10,000 feet), until the fruit is tender enough to be easily pierced with the tip of a paring knife. If using a deep-dish pie plate or other baking pan, transfer the fruit to it now.

4. As soon as the fruit is cooked through, while it is still piping hot (especially important at altitudes over 5,000 feet), scoop up table-spoons of the dough and set them in a single layer on top of the hot fruit. Sprinkle the topping sugar over the dough.

5. *To bake the cobbler in the oven,* leave it uncovered. If using a deep-dish pie plate, put a sheet of foil beneath it to catch any dripping juice. Bake for the time indicated for your altitude in the chart above, or until the dough is puffed up and golden brown, and a cake tester inserted in the topping (not the fruit) comes out clean; taste a corner of one biscuit to be sure it is baked through and no longer pasty.

*To cook the cobbler on the stovetop,* cover the pot of dough-topped fruit and bring the mixture back to a full boil over medium heat (high heat at altitudes above 7,000 feet). Reduce the heat and simmer (gently boil at higher altitudes) for 12 to 15 minutes, without lifting the lid. Peek inside: The dough should be puffed up, dry inside, and white. Taste a corner of a biscuit, and if it is not completely baked through, cover and cook a bit longer (the higher the altitude, the longer the cooking time). Sprinkle a little cinnamon on top of these pale stovetop-white biscuits to give them some color.

6. To serve, spoon the warm cobbler—biscuit, fruit, and juice—into serving bowls. For a special treat, add a scoop of vanilla ice cream or pass a pitcher of heavy cream to pour on top.

# Plum Good Crumb Pie

THIS IS the pie for all bakers—beginner or expert—all seasons, and all altitudes. Nothing could be easier than tossing together some cut-up ripe fruit and baking it in between two layers of buttery cinnamon-nut crumbs. You can personalize the recipe by selecting your favorite fruit (you need 4 cups total of sliced peaches, nectarines, pears, or berries), substituting whole-wheat flour for white in the crumbs, and varying the type of nuts—or leaving them out altogether. This is a homey, casual dessert that resists neat slicing and should be served in shallow bowls with spoons, preferably warm from the oven and topped by vanilla ice cream or creamy yogurt.

**General High Altitude Notes:** In this recipe, the ingredients and temperature notes do not change as the altitude increases, but you need to watch the oven and determine the correct timing depending upon your ingredients. At higher elevations, you may need to increase the baking time to get the desired coloring in the topping and to bake the fruit through; timing varies depending on the moisture content and ripeness of the fruit. To avoid overbrowning the top crumbs if you need a longer bake for the fruit, cover the top loosely with a piece of aluminum foil for the last 10 minutes of baking time. I like to bake this pie in a Pyrex pie plate so I can see that the bottom crumbs are well browned.

**Special Equipment:** A 9-inch Pyrex pie plate; aluminum foil

**Makes** one 9-inch pie; serves 8 to 10

| Ingredients | Sea Level | 3,000 feet | 5,000 feet | 7,000 feet | 10,000 feet |
|---|---|---|---|---|---|
| **Oven rack position, temperature, and baking time** | Rack in lower third of oven; bake at 400°F for 35 to 40 minutes | Rack in lower third of oven; bake at 400°F for 35 to 40 minutes | Rack in lower third of oven; bake at 400°F for 35 to 40 minutes | Rack in lower third of oven; bake at 400°F for 40 to 45 minutes | Rack in lower third of oven; bake at 400°F for 40 to 45 minutes |

(continued)

| Ingredients | Sea Level | 3,000 feet | 5,000 feet | 7,000 feet | 10,000 feet |
|---|---|---|---|---|---|
| **FRUIT** | | | | | |
| About 1¾ pounds plums (any type, such as Santa Rosa, Damson, or Italian prune), pitted and sliced | 4 cups sliced | 4 cups sliced | 4 cups sliced | 4 cups sliced | 4 cups sliced |
| Granulated sugar or packed light brown sugar | ½ cup | ½ cup | ½ cup | ½ cup | ½ cup |
| Cornstarch | 2 tablespoons | 2 tablespoons | 2 tablespoons | 2 tablespoons | 2 tablespoons |
| Fresh lemon juice | 2 tablespoons | 2 tablespoons | 2 tablespoons | 2 tablespoons | 2 tablespoons |
| Ground cinnamon or nutmeg | ½ teaspoon | ½ teaspoon | ½ teaspoon | ½ teaspoon | ½ teaspoon |
| **CRUMBS** | | | | | |
| All-purpose flour | 1 cup | 1 cup | 1 cup | 1 cup | 1 cup |
| Granulated sugar | ½ cup | ½ cup | ½ cup | ½ cup | ½ cup |
| Salt | ¼ teaspoon | ¼ teaspoon | ¼ teaspoon | ¼ teaspoon | ¼ teaspoon |
| Ground cinnamon | ½ teaspoon | ½ teaspoon | ½ teaspoon | ½ teaspoon | ½ teaspoon |
| Unsalted butter, at room temperature | 8 tablespoons (1 stick) | 8 tablespoons (1 stick) | 8 tablespoons (1 stick) | 8 tablespoons (1 stick) | 8 tablespoons (1 stick) |
| Walnuts or pecans, chopped | ½ cup (2 ounces) | ½ cup (2 ounces) | ½ cup (2 ounces) | ½ cup (2 ounces) | ½ cup (2 ounces) |

**1.** Position the rack in the lower third of the oven and preheat the oven to 400°F. Turn up the edges of a 12-inch square of aluminum foil and set it shiny side up on the oven rack to catch any fruit juice spills.

**2.** In a large bowl, toss the sliced plums with the sugar, cornstarch, lemon juice, and cinnamon or nutmeg.

**3.** In another bowl, or in the bowl of a food processor, toss or pulse the flour, sugar, salt, and cinnamon with the butter until the mixture makes small crumbs. Add the chopped nuts and stir or pulse a couple of times just to mix.

**4.** Scoop 1½ cups of the crumbs into the pie plate and pat them flat with your hand or the bottom of a measuring cup. Spread the fruit and all its juices over the crumbs, then sprinkle on the remaining crumbs.

**5.** Bake for the time indicated for your altitude in the chart, or until the fruit is tender when pierced with the tip of a knife, crumbs (top and bottom) are a rich golden brown, and the fruit juices are beginning to bubble at the pan edges. Cool the pie on a wire rack.

**6.** Serve warm or at room temperature, scooped from the pan with a spoon.

# Peach-Ginger Crisp

CONSIDER THIS old-fashioned country crisp a master recipe for whatever fruit is in season, from peaches and nectarines to pears, plums, apricots, berries, or apples, or a blend of these. I like to flavor peaches with ginger, but you can substitute cinnamon and/or nutmeg. Ginger lovers can also add a teaspoon or more of grated fresh ginger. With the exception of apples and peaches, other fruits do not have to be peeled. For a luscious variation, see Sour Cream–Peach or Apple Crisp.

**General High Altitude Notes:** The ingredients do not change with elevation, but at higher altitudes you may need to increase the baking time, depending on the firmness of the fruit (softer fruit cooks more quickly). To avoid over-browning the top crumbs if you need a longer bake for the fruit, cover the top loosely with a piece of aluminum foil for the last 10 minutes of the baking time. Then remove the foil for the last few minutes to be sure the crumbs are well browned.

**Special Equipment:** A 10-inch deep-dish pie plate, preferably Pyrex, or ovenproof casserole

**Pan Preparation:** Butter the pie plate or ovenproof casserole.

**Makes** one 10-inch deep-dish pie; serves 8 to 10

| Ingredients | Sea Level | 3,000 feet | 5,000 feet | 7,000 feet | 10,000 feet |
|---|---|---|---|---|---|
| **Oven rack position, temperature, and baking time** | Rack in center; bake at 350°F for 45 to 50 minutes | Rack in center; bake at 350°F for 45 to 50 minutes | Rack in center; bake at 350°F for 45 to 50 minutes | Rack in center; bake at 350°F for 45 to 50 minutes | Rack in center; bake at 350°F for 45 to 50 minutes |
| FRUIT | | | | | |
| **7 to 9 ripe peaches, peeled (See note), pitted, and thickly sliced** | 6 cups sliced | 6 cups sliced | 6 cups sliced | 6 cups sliced | 6 cups sliced |

*(continued)*

| Ingredients | Sea Level | 3,000 feet | 5,000 feet | 7,000 feet | 10,000 feet |
|---|---|---|---|---|---|
| **Light or dark brown sugar, packed** | ¼ cup | ¼ cup | ¼ cup | ¼ cup | ¼ cup |
| **Ground cinnamon** | ½ teaspoon | ½ teaspoon | ½ teaspoon | ½ teaspoon | ½ teaspoon |
| **Ground ginger** | ½ teaspoon, or to taste | ½ teaspoon, or to taste | ½ teaspoon, or to taste | ½ teaspoon, or to taste | ½ teaspoon, or to taste |
| **Fresh lemon juice** | 2 tablespoons | 2 tablespoons | 2 tablespoons | 2 tablespoons | 2 tablespoons |
| OAT CRUMBS | | | | | |
| **All-purpose flour** | ¾ cup | ¾ cup | ¾ cup | ¾ cup | ¾ cup |
| **Light or dark brown sugar, packed** | ¾ cup | ¾ cup | ¾ cup | ¾ cup | ¾ cup |
| **Old-fashioned rolled oats** | ½ cup | ½ cup | ½ cup | ½ cup | ½ cup |
| **Chopped or walnuts pecans** | ½ cup (2 ounces) | ½ cup (2 ounces) | ½ cup (2 ounces) | ½ cup (2 ounces) | ½ cup (2 ounces) |
| **Salt** | Pinch | Pinch | Pinch | Pinch | Pinch |
| **Ground cinnamon** | ½ teaspoon | ½ teaspoon | ½ teaspoon | ½ teaspoon | ½ teaspoon |
| **Unsalted butter, at room temperature, cut up** | 8 tablespoons (1 stick) | 8 tablespoons (1 stick) | 8 tablespoons (1 stick) | 8 tablespoons (1 stick) | 8 tablespoons (1 stick) |

**Note:** To peel peaches, use a slotted spoon to gently lower them into a pot of boiling water for about 2 minutes. Remove them to a bowl of cold water to cool, then drain. The peach skins will slip off easily.

**1.** Position the rack in the center of the oven and preheat the oven to 350°F. Prepare the baking dish as directed.

**2.** In a large bowl, toss the peaches with the brown sugar, cinnamon, ginger, and lemon juice, and spread in the baking dish.

**3.** In a medium bowl, combine all the crumb ingredients and pinch them together with your fingertips or mix with a fork to make crumbs. Spread them over the fruit.

**4.** Bake for 45 to 50 minutes, or until the fruit is tender when pierced with the tip of a sharp knife and the crumbs are golden brown. Cool slightly on a wire rack.

**5.** Serve the crisp warm, spooning it from the pan.

# Sour Cream–Peach or Apple Crisp

*(ingredients are the same at all altitudes, but see General High Altitude Notes above)*

### Sour Cream Filling

1 large egg

1 cup sour cream

1 teaspoon vanilla extract

¼ cup granulated sugar

2 tablespoons all-purpose flour

¼ teaspoon salt

Prepare the recipe as above but with 4 cups sliced peeled peaches, or substitute 4 to 5 Golden Delicious apples, peeled, cored, and thinly sliced (⅛-inch thick; 4 cups of slices). Omit the lemon juice, but add the sugar and spices to the fruit as directed, and prepare the crumb mixture. Add the sliced fruit to the buttered baking dish.

In a medium bowl, whisk together all the filling ingredients and pour onto the fruit, then top with the crumbs. Bake for 45 to 50 minutes, or until the filling is puffed up, the crumbs are golden brown, and a sharp paring knife easily pierces the fruit slices. Serve warm, spooning the crisp from the pan.

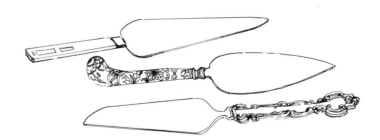

# Pumpkin Custard Pie with Ginger Whipped Cream

**P**ERFECT FOR a Thanksgiving buffet, this easy-to-prepare pie will start a new tradition in your family, joining the most-requested holiday desserts list. Forget bland store-bought pumpkin pies, this is the real thing: robust flavorful spices well balanced in a rich, creamy custard, set off perfectly by the crisp, nutty taste of a whole-wheat crust. Serve it with the Ginger Whipped Cream or a scoop of vanilla ice cream. In a pinch, use a store-bought pie shell (but prebake it yourself).

Custard pies present a challenge. The crust needs to be partially prebaked at a high temperature to keep it crisp and able to withstand the moisture of the soft filling, but the custard needs a more moderate heat so the egg proteins can bond gently, keeping a silken texture. The solution is to prebake the pastry shell at a high temperature in the lower third of the oven, where the heat is more intense, then brush it with a moisture-proofing egg glaze, add the filling, and bake at a reduced temperature.

A whole egg is added to the crust to strengthen it and help prevent absorption of moisture from the custard, but the pastry will still be tender. If you don't have whole-wheat flour, you can replace it with all-purpose. Be sure to select canned plain unsweetened pumpkin puree, not flavored pumpkin pie filling. You can replace the canned puree with cooked and mashed fresh sugar pumpkin, but it will have an unpredictable quantity of moisture, which will affect texture and baking time at 7,000 feet and above. Use either milk or cream; the heavier the cream, the richer the pie—my personal preference is half milk, half cream.

**General High Altitude Notes:** As elevation increases, changes are required for the pastry, filling, and baking time and temperature. You may need to add a few drops more liquid to the pastry dough to make it pliable. To heighten the flavor of the filling, add more spices. To maintain a creamy custard texture at 3,000 feet and above, bake the pie in the center of the oven and reduce the oven temperature. At 7,000 feet and above, reduce the heat an additional 25 degrees.

At 10,000 feet, add one more egg to the filling. To keep the texture creamy, bake it at a moderate (350°F) temperature for about 40 minutes longer than at sea level; it takes more time for the internal temperature to heat up enough to coagulate and set the egg protein. In my tests, I found that I could keep the creamy texture but speed the final bake of the custard at 10,000 feet elevation if I warmed the filling first, so it didn't start out cold. To do this, whisk together the pumpkin, sugar, milk, melted butter, salt, and spices in a large nonreactive saucepan. Beat the eggs in a bowl. When the pumpkin mixture is quite warm, whisk a little of it into the eggs to heat them, then whisk all

the eggs into the pumpkin, whisking hard to blend (rather than poach) the eggs. Scoop the warm mixture into the partially prebaked, glazed pie shell and bake as directed. Watch for the visual doneness signs; the timing will be shorter than with the cold filling.

**Special Equipment:** A food processor (optional); cookie sheet; rolling pin; 10-inch pie plate, preferably Pyrex; bench scraper; aluminum foil; pie weights, rice, or dried beans; pastry brush

**Makes** one 10-inch pie; serves 10 to 12

### High Notes

*At 3,000 to 5,000 feet,* Lower the baking temperature for the filled pie by 25 degrees.

*At 7,000 feet and above,* add extra spices and lower the baking temperature for the filled pie by 25 degrees.

*At 10,000 feet,* add one extra egg. Bake at 350°F for 80 to 90 minutes (see General High Altitude Notes to reduce the baking time somewhat).

| Ingredients | Sea Level | 3,000 feet | 5,000 feet | 7,000 feet | 10,000 feet |
|---|---|---|---|---|---|
| **Oven rack position, temperature, and baking time** | Rack in lower third of oven; bake pastry at 425°F for 17 to 18 minutes; bake filled pie at 400°F for 40 to 50 minutes | Rack in lower third of oven; bake pastry at 425°F for 17 to 18 minutes; then rack in center to bake filled pie at 375°F for 40 to 50 minutes | Rack in lower third of oven; bake pastry at 425°F for 17 to 18 minutes; then rack in center to bake filled pie at 375°F for 40 to 50 minutes | Rack in lower third of oven; bake pastry at 425°F for 17 to 18 minutes; then rack in center to bake filled pie at 350°F for 40 to 50 minutes | Rack in lower third of oven; bake pastry at 425°F for 17 to 18 minutes; then rack in center to bake filled pie at 350°F for 80 to 90 minutes |
| **WHOLE-WHEAT PASTRY** | | | | | |
| **All-purpose flour** | ¾ cup | ¾ cup | ¾ cup | ¾ cup | ¾ cup |

*(continued)*

| Ingredients | Sea Level | 3,000 feet | 5,000 feet | 7,000 feet | 10,000 feet |
|---|---|---|---|---|---|
| **Whole-wheat flour** | ³/₄ cup | ³/₄ cup | ³/₄ cup | ³/₄ cup | ³/₄ cup |
| **Granulated sugar** | 1¹/₂ tablespoons | 1¹/₂ tablespoons | 1¹/₂ tablespoons | 1¹/₂ tablespoons | 1¹/₂ tablespoons |
| **Salt** | ¹/₂ teaspoon | ¹/₂ teaspoon | ¹/₂ teaspoon | ¹/₂ teaspoon | ¹/₂ teaspoon |
| **Unsalted butter, cold, cut up** | 6 tablespoons (³/₄ stick) | 6 tablespoons (³/₄ stick) | 6 tablespoons (³/₄ stick) | 6 tablespoons (³/₄ stick) | 6 tablespoons (³/₄ stick) |
| **Solid vegetable shortening, chilled** | 3 tablespoons | 3 tablespoons | 3 tablespoons | 3 tablespoons | 3 tablespoons |
| **Large egg, lightly beaten** | 1 | 1 | 1 | 1 | 1 |
| **Fresh lemon juice or white vinegar** | 2 teaspoons | 2 teaspoons | 2 teaspoons | 2 teaspoons | 2 teaspoons |
| **Ice water** | 1 to 2 tablespoons, or as needed | 1 to 2 tablespoons, or as needed | 2 to 3 tablespoons, or as needed | 2 to 4 tablespoons, or as needed | 2 to 4 tablespoons, or as needed |
| **GLAZE** | | | | | |
| **Large egg** | 1 | 1 | 1 | 1 | 1 |
| **Water** | 1 teaspoon | 1 teaspoon | 1 teaspoon | 1 teaspoon | 1 teaspoon |
| **FILLING** | | | | | |
| **Large eggs, at room temperature** | 2 | 2 | 2 | 2 | 3 |
| **Large egg yolk, at room temperature** | 1 | 1 | 1 | 1 | 1 |
| **Canned unsweetened pumpkin puree** | 2 cups | 2 cups | 2 cups | 2 cups | 2 cups |
| **Granulated sugar** | ¹/₂ cup plus 2 tablespoons | ¹/₂ cup plus 2 tablespoons | ¹/₂ cup plus 2 tablespoons | ¹/₂ cup plus 2 tablespoons | ¹/₂ cup plus 2 tablespoons |
| **Milk or heavy cream** | 1¹/₂ cups | 1¹/₂ cups | 1¹/₂ cups | 1¹/₂ cups | 1¹/₂ cups |

(continued)

| Ingredients | Sea Level | 3,000 feet | 5,000 feet | 7,000 feet | 10,000 feet |
|---|---|---|---|---|---|
| **Unsalted butter, melted and cooled** | 2 tablespoons | 2 tablespoons | 2 tablespoons | 2 tablespoons | 2 tablespoons |
| **Salt** | ½ teaspoon | ½ teaspoon | ½ teaspoon | ½ teaspoon | ½ teaspoon |
| **Ground cinnamon** | ¾ teaspoon | ¾ teaspoon | ¾ teaspoon | ¾ teaspoon | 1 teaspoon |
| **Ground nutmeg** | ½ teaspoon | ½ teaspoon | ½ teaspoon | ¾ teaspoon | 1 teaspoon |
| **Ground ginger** | ½ teaspoon | ½ teaspoon | ½ teaspoon | ¾ teaspoon | 1 teaspoon |
| **Ground cloves** | ⅛ teaspoon | ⅛ teaspoon | ⅛ teaspoon | ⅛ teaspoon | ¼ teaspoon |

**1.** Prepare the pastry. In a food processor, pulse together the flours, sugar, and salt to blend. Add the cold butter and shortening and pulse 8 or 9 times, just until the mixture resembles coarse meal. Add the lightly beaten egg, lemon juice or vinegar, and 1 tablespoon ice water through the feed tube and pulse a few times. The dough should just be starting to get clumpy. If it is too dry, add water 1 tablespoon at a time, pulsing, and check the consistency. The dough is ready when it holds its shape when squeezed between your fingers; it should be neither wet nor sandy dry. Never allow a dough ball to form on the blade. At altitudes over 5,000 feet, you may need to add a little more ice water to make the dough pliable. (Alternatively, you can mix the piecrust ingredients together in a bowl with a wire pastry blender, fork, or your fingertips.)

**2.** When the dough looks clumpy, turn it out onto a piece of wax paper or plastic wrap, gather it into a ball, and press it into a flat disk. If the dough feels warm or sticky, refrigerate it for about 30 minutes, or as long as overnight. If the dough doesn't feel too warm or soft, you can roll it out without chilling.

**3.** Position a rack in the lower third of the oven and preheat the oven to 425°F. Set a cookie sheet on the rack to get hot.

**4.** Roll out the dough on a lightly floured counter with a floured rolling pin to a circle at least 2 inches larger in diameter edge than the pie plate (turn it upside down in the center of the dough to measure it; below, a). Use a bench scraper to ease up and loosen the dough edges, then fold the dough into quarters and fit it into the pie plate with the point in the center (b). Unfold the dough and gently fit it into the pan without stretching it; drape the edges of the dough over the plate rim. If there are any

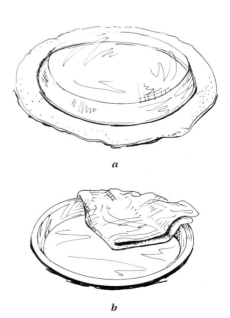

*a*

*b*

*c*

breaks, just press the dough together again with your fingertips; it is fine to mold the dough in the pie plate. Trim the excess dough to ¾ to 1 inch, and reserve. Fold under the overhanging dough and pinch the edge up into a high-standing fluted design as shown. If the dough cracks, add a drop of the egg glaze or water to the spot and pinch/press it back together. If you have time, refrigerate until the dough feels firm.

**5.** Cut a 12-inch square of foil, spread a little butter or nonstick vegetable spray on the shiny side, and set it greased side down in the pastry-lined pie plate. Fill with weights (above, c) and place on the hot cookie sheet in the oven (for ease in handling). Bake the pastry shell for 12 to 13 minutes. Remove the cookie sheet with the pie plate on it, gather up the edges of the foil with all the pie weights inside, and lift it out. Inspect the pastry shell, and if you see any cracks or holes, patch them by brushing on a little egg glaze, then gently pressing on bits of the reserved raw dough. Return the pastry shell to the oven to bake for about 5 minutes longer, or until the dough is a very pale golden color and almost but not totally baked. Remove the pastry shell from the oven, brush it with egg

glaze, and set it aside. Reduce the oven heat to the temperature indicated for your altitude in the chart above, and move the rack to the center if indicated. Return the cookie sheet to the oven to stay hot.

**6.** In the bowl of an electric mixer or in a medium bowl, using a whisk, beat together the eggs and yolk. Beat in the pumpkin and sugar, then the milk or cream, melted butter, salt, and spices. Scoop the filling into the prebaked pastry shell and set it in the oven on the heated cookie sheet. Bake for the time indicated for your altitude in the grid above, or until the top of the pie is golden brown and a table knife inserted into the custard 1 inch from the edge comes out clean. Place the pie on a wire rack to cool to room temperature.

**7.** Serve with the whipped cream. Refrigerate any leftovers.

## Ginger Whipped Cream
*(recipe is the same at all altitudes)*

**Makes** 2 cups
1 cup heavy cream (36 to 40% butterfat), chilled
½ teaspoon ground ginger
2 tablespoons sifted confectioners' sugar
1 to 2 tablespoons finely minced candied ginger, to taste, optional

In a chilled bowl, using a chilled beater, whip the cream until it forms very soft peaks. Add the ground ginger and sugar and whip until nearly stiff. Taste and adjust the flavoring if necessary. Fold in the candied ginger, if using.

# Holiday Cran-Apple Crostata

A CROSTATA (a freeform tart, or fruit pizza, known as a *galette* in French), is basically a pie without the pie plate. It couldn't be easier to prepare or more appealing to serve—its presentation makes a party. In fact, I took one to a backstage cast party at the Lake Dillon Theater, in Dillon, Colorado, where it was rated just after the play itself as the hit of the evening! During my recipe testing visit to Colorado, I had the good fortune to meet the delightful actress-producer Suzanne Pedersen, who welcomed me warmly and invited me to the Dillon performance, as well as to her home, for a high altitude dessert-tasting party starring six of my latest recipes and many of her friends. The desserts were well received, and the evening was a special treat for me as guests reminisced about life's pressing issues: theater, family, and the ups and downs of baking at extreme elevations.

Suzanne generously loaned me a copy of a treasured, string-bound cookbook to which she had contributed several recipes. *The Upper Crust*, by the Reformed Friends of the Summit County Library (Frisco, Colorado, 1976), was compiled to share recipes that worked reliably at 9,000 feet and above. They include Cranberry-Nut Pie, with a crumb topping, and an unusual Paper-Bag Apple Pie (an unbaked pastry shell filled with sugared apples topped with crumbs, set in a brown bag fastened with a straight pin, and baked on a cookie sheet at 425°F for an hour).

**General High Altitude Notes:** Be sure to select Golden Delicious or other soft eating apples, not hard cooking apples, which take too long to bake through at high altitudes. The ingredients measurements do not change with altitude, but you need to add enough moisture to the pie dough to make it pliable; at higher elevations, dry air and faster evaporation contribute to dry flour. Partway through the baking time, cover the crostata with an aluminum foil tent to prevent overbrowning.

**Special Equipment:** A rolling pin; ruler; toothpick; 18-inch square of heavy-duty aluminum foil (fold two narrower pieces together to make the correct width if necessary); pastry brush

**Makes** one 12-inch crostata; serves 10 to 12

**High Notes**

*At 10,000 feet,* be sure to cover the crostata loosely with a foil tent after 15 minutes at 350°F to prevent overbrowning.

| Ingredients | Sea Level | 3,000 feet | 5,000 feet | 7,000 feet | 10,000 feet |
|---|---|---|---|---|---|
| **Oven rack position, temperature, and baking time** | Rack in lower third of oven; bake at 425°F for 15 minutes, then at 350°F for 25 to 35 minutes | Rack in lower third of oven; bake at 425°F for 15 minutes, then at 350°F for 25 to 35 minutes | Rack in lower third of oven; bake at 425°F for 15 minutes, then at 350°F for 25 to 35 minutes | Rack in lower third of oven; bake at 425°F for 15 minutes, then at 350°F for 25 to 35 minutes | Rack in lower third of oven; bake at 425°F for 15 minutes, then at 350°F for 45 minutes |
| **FLAKY PASTRY** (pages 266 to 268, Steps 1–2) | | | | | |
| **FILLING** | | | | | |
| **Fresh cranberries, picked over, rinsed, and blotted dry, or frozen cranberries, unthawed** | One 12-ounce bag (3 cups) | One 12-ounce bag (3 cups) | One 12-ounce bag (3 cups) | One 12-ounce bag (3 cups) | One 12-ounce bag (3 cups) |
| **1 or 2 Golden Delicious apples, peeled, cored, and thinly sliced (⅛-inch)** | 1½ to 2 cups sliced | 1½ to 2 cups sliced | 1½ to 2 cups sliced | 1½ to 2 cups sliced | 1½ to 2 cups sliced |
| **Golden raisins** | ½ cup (3 ounces) | ½ cup (3 ounces) | ½ cup (3 ounces) | ½ cup (3 ounces) | ½ cup (3 ounces) |
| **Grated orange zest** | 1 tablespoon | 1 tablespoon | 1 tablespoon | 1 tablespoon | 1 tablespoon |

*(continued)*

| Ingredients | Sea Level | 3,000 feet | 5,000 feet | 7,000 feet | 10,000 feet |
|---|---|---|---|---|---|
| Granulated white or packed light brown sugar | 1 cup | 1 cup | 1 cup | 1 cup | 1 cup |
| Ground cinnamon | ½ teaspoon | ½ teaspoon | ½ teaspoon | ½ teaspoon | ½ teaspoon |
| Ground nutmeg | ½ teaspoon | ½ teaspoon | ½ teaspoon | ½ teaspoon | ½ teaspoon |
| Chopped walnuts or pecans | ½ cup (2 ounces) | ½ cup (2 ounces) | ½ cup (2 ounces) | ½ cup (2 ounces) | ½ cup (2 ounces) |
| Orange marmalade | ½ cup | ½ cup | ½ cup | ½ cup | ½ cup |
| Cornstarch | 2½ tablespoons | 2½ tablespoons | 2½ tablespoons | 2½ tablespoons | 2½ tablespoons |
| Fresh orange juice | ⅓ cup | ⅓ cup | ⅓ cup | ⅓ cup | ⅓ cup |
| **EGG GLAZE AND CRUMBS** | | | | | |
| Large egg | 1 | 1 | 1 | 1 | 1 |
| Water | 1 teaspoon | 1 teaspoon | 1 teaspoon | 1 teaspoon | 1 teaspoon |
| Graham or plain cracker crumbs | 2 tablespoons | 2 tablespoons | 2 tablespoons | 2 tablespoons | 2 tablespoons |
| **TOPPING AND JAM GLAZE** | | | | | |
| Granulated or coarse sugar | 1 tablespoon | 1 tablespoon | 1 tablespoon | 1 tablespoon | 1 tablespoon |
| Seedless raspberry jam | ½ cup | ½ cup | ½ cup | ½ cup | ½ cup |

**1.** Position the rack in the lower third of the oven and preheat the oven to 425°F.

Prepare the pastry, then chill it while you prepare the filling.

**2.** In a large bowl, toss together all the filling ingredients except the cornstarch and orange juice. Stir the cornstarch and juice together in a small cup until the cornstarch dissolves, then stir the mixture into the fruit.

**3.** Turn an 18-inch square of aluminum foil shiny side down on the counter. With your fingernail or a toothpick, draw a 17- to 18-inch circle on the foil as a guide for rolling out the dough. Spread a little butter or solid shortening (not vegetable spray) in an 8-inch circle right in the middle, then sprinkle the ungreased area around it with a little flour. (Greasing helps the release of the baked pastry when serving, and

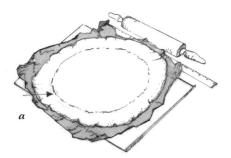

*Mark dough border*

the flour helps in shaping the pastry edge.)

Press the dough into a flat disk, set it on the center of the foil, and roll it out to the edge of the marked circle using a lightly floured rolling pin. Roll from the center of the dough toward the outer edges to keep the shape round until the dough fills the marked circle and has ragged edges extending just beyond it. If the dough sticks in very hot weather, cover it with plastic wrap while rolling it out.

**4.** Slide the foil holding the dough onto a baking sheet. With your fingernail or a toothpick, lightly mark a 2-inch border (above, a) inside the edge of the dough; the border will later be folded over to enclose the fruit filling.

Whisk the egg-water glaze, then brush this moisture-proof coating all over the dough. Sprinkle the cracker crumbs in the marked circle, to absorb excess fruit juices. Stir the fruit mixture, then turn it out, with all its juices, onto the middle of the dough. Pat it out with the palm of your hand until it reaches the marked border.

**5.** To make the edge, put your hand under one edge of the foil and use it to gently flip the dough edges over onto the fruit. Move your hand around the circle, lifting the foil and flipping over the dough edge (the flour under it will help its release), letting the dough fall into pleats or folds as it forms the round shape (below, b).

Brush off any extra flour visible on the overturned dough edge. If you see any cracks in the dough, especially near the bottom, brush them with egg glaze, then pinch them together to seal. Brush the egg glaze over all the pastry edging, then sprinkle with the topping sugar.

**6.** Pinch up a lip about ½-inch high all around the edge of the foil holding the crostata to trap any dripping fruit juices (page 295, sketch c) and set the baking sheet in the oven. Bake for 15 minutes, then reduce the heat to 350°F and bake for the additional time indicated for your altitude in the chart above, or until the pastry is a rich golden brown and you can pierce the fruit easily with the tip of a paring

*Fold over dough edge*

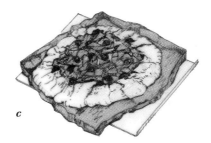

*c*

**Fold up foil edge**

knife. Peek in the oven after about 15 minutes at 350°F and, if the pastry is browning too quickly or the berries look too dark, loosely cover the crostata with a piece of foil.

**7.** When it is baked, carefully slide the foil holding the crostata onto a wire rack. Stir the jam in a small saucepan over medium heat to liquefy it, then brush it over the warm fruit fill-ing to give it a bright shine. The jam glaze will set as it cools.

**8.** Serve at room temperature or slightly warm. Slide the foil with the crostata onto a flat round tray or serving plate and peel away any foil that shows around the edges of the pastry; leave the remaining foil under the crostata. Cut into wedges.

# Mile-High Lemon Meringue Pie

You WILL love the gorgeous cloud of meringue, the tangy lemon filling, and the crunch of the coconut-crumb crust in this old-fashioned favorite. At high altitudes, the recipe reaches celestial heights with specially developed techniques that guarantee a stable meringue.

This recipe presented me with one of the biggest surprises of the whole book. The meringue was perfectly reliable from sea level to just under 10,000 feet, but once I hit the peaks, I was in for a real shock. It took me eight tests (that's a lot of egg whites!) to believe what inevitably happened. Each pie looked perfect at first—high-piled meringue, glossy and glamorous—until it was browned in the oven, when it would suddenly collapse into a runny liquefied mess. (After the first few failures, I learned to use a "dummy" filling and crust.) Friends told me it was impossible to make a meringue topping at that elevation, it just couldn't be done—but professional local bakers knew the secret: whites will never stabilize enough at that altitude using the traditional method; they must be cooked like a seven-minute icing, whipped until stiff in a double boiler, in order to hold their shape.

I have added coconut to the crust because I like the tropical flavor blend of lemon with coconut, but if you prefer, you can omit the coconut and make the crust entirely with graham cracker crumbs.

———————

**General High Altitude Notes:** The meringue is stabilized with a little cooked cornstarch gel (except at 10,000 feet) to ensure a smooth foam that doesn't weep. The filling is made with four eggs yolks, but in order to have a high meringue, I use two additional whites except at 10,000 feet, where the whites are prepared in a different way and four whites are sufficient. The yolks are cooked for four minutes in order to sufficiently heat and kill the enzymes in them that could break down the filling and make it runny.

Don't be tempted to make the filling in a double boiler at 7,000 feet and above—the heat is not sufficient to get maximum gelatization of the cornstarch needed for it to set. For the meringue, the whites are whipped *nearly* to stiff peaks between sea level and almost 10,000 feet.

**Special Equipment:** A 9-inch pie plate, preferably Pyrex; 1½- to 2-quart heavy-bottomed saucepan; hand-held electric mixer and double boiler (at 10,000 feet and above); instant-read thermometer (essential at 10,000 feet)

**Makes** one 9-inch pie; serves 6 to 8

**High Notes**

*At 10,000 feet and above,* the technique for whipping the whites is different. Before browning the meringue, the oven is preheated to 375°F, then the heat is reduced by 25 degrees when the pie is put into the oven.

| Ingredients | Sea Level | 3,000 feet | 5,000 feet | 7,000 feet | 10,000 feet |
|---|---|---|---|---|---|
| **Oven rack position, temperature, and baking time** | Rack in center; bake crust at 350°F for 7 to 8 minutes; brown meringue for 15 to 18 minutes | Rack in center; bake crust at 350°F for 7 to 8 minutes; brown meringue for 15 to 18 minutes | Rack in center; bake crust at 350°F for 7 to 8 minutes; brown meringue for 18 to 23 minutes | Rack in center; bake crust at 350°F for 7 to 8 minutes; brown meringue for 15 to 18 minutes | Rack in center; bake crust at 350°F for 7 to 8 minutes; *heat* oven to 375°F, then *reduce* heat to 350°F to brown meringue for 15 to 16 minutes |
| **COCONUT-CRUMB CRUST** | | | | | |
| **Graham cracker or vanilla wafer cookie crumbs** | 1⅓ cups | 1⅓ cups | 1⅓ cups | 1⅓ cups | 1⅓ cups |
| **Granulated sugar** | 2 tablespoons | 2 tablespoons | 2 tablespoons | 2 tablespoons | 2 tablespoons |
| **Shredded sweetened coconut (or replace with ½ cup more crumbs)** | ½ cup | ½ cup | ½ cup | ½ cup | ½ cup |
| **Unsalted butter, melted** | 5½ tablespoons | 5½ tablespoons | 5½ tablespoons | 5½ tablespoons | 5½ tablespoons |
| **FILLING** | | | | | |
| **Granulated sugar** | 1 cup | 1 cup | 1 cup | 1 cup | 1 cup |
| **Cornstarch** | ⅓ cup | ⅓ cup | ⅓ cup | ⅓ cup | ⅓ cup |
| **Salt** | ¼ teaspoon | ¼ teaspoon | ¼ teaspoon | ¼ teaspoon | ¼ teaspoon |
| **Water** | 1½ cups | 1½ cups | 1½ cups | 1½ cups | 1½ cups |

*(continued)*

| Ingredients | Sea Level | 3,000 feet | 5,000 feet | 7,000 feet | 10,000 feet |
|---|---|---|---|---|---|
| **Large egg yolks, at room temperature** | 4 | 4 | 4 | 4 | 4 |
| **Unsalted butter, at room temperature** | 2 tablespoons | 2 tablespoons | 2 tablespoons | 2 tablespoons | 2 tablespoons |
| **Grated lemon zest** | 1½ tablespoons | 1½ tablespoons | 1½ tablespoons | 1½ tablespoons | 1½ tablespoons |
| **Fresh lemon juice** | ½ cup | ½ cup | ½ cup | ½ cup | ½ cup |
| **Graham or plain cracker crumbs** | 3 tablespoons | 3 tablespoons | 3 tablespoons | 3 tablespoons | 3 tablespoons |
| **MERINGUE TOPPING** | | | | | |
| **Granulated sugar, divided** | 2 tablespoons plus ¾ cup | 2 tablespoons plus ¾ cup | 2 tablespoons plus ¾ cup | 2 tablespoons plus ¾ cup | ¾ cup |
| **Cornstarch** | 1 tablespoon | 1 tablespoon | 1 tablespoon | 1 tablespoon | None |
| **Water** | ½ cup | ½ cup | ½ cup | ½ cup | None |
| **Large egg whites, at room temperature** | 6 | 6 | 6 | 6 | 4 |
| **Salt** | ⅛ teaspoon | ⅛ teaspoon | ⅛ teaspoon | ⅛ teaspoon | ⅛ teaspoon |
| **Cream of tartar** | ½ teaspoon | ½ teaspoon | ½ teaspoon | ½ teaspoon | ¾ teaspoon |
| **Vanilla extract** | ½ teaspoon | ½ teaspoon | ½ teaspoon | ½ teaspoon | 1 teaspoon |

**1.** Position the rack in the center of the oven and preheat the oven to 350°F.

**2.** Prepare the crumb crust: Toss together the crumbs, sugar, coconut, and melted butter in a medium bowl. Turn the crumbs out into the pie plate and press them into a solid layer on the pan bottom and sides, using the back of a large spoon. Or cover the crumbs with a sheet of plastic wrap, then press firmly with your hand.

**3.** Bake the shell for 7 to 8 minutes, until slightly darkened in color. Cool the crust on a wire rack. Turn off the oven, then reheat it shortly before browning the meringue topping.

**4.** Prepare the filling: In a heavy-bottomed 1½- to 2-quart saucepan, whisk together the sugar, cornstarch, and salt. Whisk in the water, scraping the whisk into the corners of the pan to incorporate all the dry ingredients. Set the pan over medium-high heat and stir until it reaches a full, hard-bubbling boil. Then whisk constantly for 1 full minute (count slowly to 60), until the filling thickens, looks clear, and generously coats the back of a spoon. This can take a total of about 5 minutes at sea level, 7 to 8 minutes at 7,000 feet, and longer at higher elevations. Remove the pan from the heat.

**5.** In a medium bowl, whisk the yolks, then whisk in about ½ cup of the hot lemon mixture to warm them. Scrape the warmed yolks back into the pan, whisking hard to blend the mixture before the yolks scramble. Return the pan to the stovetop over medium heat (medium-high heat at 5,000 feet and above), and stir continuously while bringing the mixture to a full, bubbling boil (with bubbles breaking on the surface), then boil, stirring, for a full 4 minutes (set a timer) to cook the yolks so they will remain stable and not break down into a runny filling. Remove the pan from the heat and stir in the butter until it melts, then stir in the lemon zest and juice. Set the filling aside to cool to room temperature.

**6.** *To prepare the meringue at sea level to nearly 10,000 feet* (for 10,000 feet and above, see Step 7), first make a stabilizer gel: In a small saucepan, stir together 2 tablespoons of the sugar, the cornstarch, and water until the cornstarch dissolves. Set over high heat and whisk for 2 to 3 minutes (slightly longer at 5,000 feet and above) until the mixture bubbles up into a full bubbling boil, starts to thicken, and looks almost clear. (*Note:* At high altitudes, evaporation occurs quickly; don't overcook the gel or too much water will evaporate, making it too thick.) Remove from the heat and transfer the gel to a small bowl.

Preheat the oven to 350°F.

To whip the egg whites, place them in the large bowl of an electric mixer, and check to make sure the whites no longer feel cold. Add the salt and cream of tartar and whip on medium-high speed just until foamy. Gradually whip in the remaining ¾ cup sugar, increasing the mixer speed to high, but watch closely: As soon as you start to see beater tracks on top of the whites, stop the machine. Stir the gel to be sure it is still soft. While slowly whipping the whites, add the vanilla and, little by little, scrape in the cooled cornstarch stabilizer (if it is too hot, it will collapse the meringue). Watch the whites carefully, observing the stiffness of the foam. You want *almost* stiff peaks with a tip that just begins to falls over slightly when the beater is lifted. The whites should be thick, glossy, and smooth.

**7.** *To prepare the meringue at 10,000 feet, omit the cornstarch stabilizer.* Preheat the oven to 375°F.

In the top of a double boiler, whisk together the 4 (not 6) egg whites, salt, cream of tartar and ¾ cup sugar. Set over slowly boiling water and whisk until the sugar is melted (about 115°F on an instant-read thermometer). With a hand-held electric mixer on high speed, whip the whites until very stiff peaks form and they reach a temperature of 160°F on an instant-read thermometer. This will take about 5 to 7 minutes, or longer—don't stop until they reach the proper temperature and are smooth, glossy, and very stiff. Whip in the vanilla. You should have approximately 5½ to 6 cups whites.

**8.** At all altitudes, once the meringue is prepared, set it aside for a minute and return the pot of lemon filling to the stove. Stir it over very low heat just until it is *almost* too hot to touch; it needs to be hot to poach the bottom of the meringue that will cover it. When it is hot, spoon it into the prepared crumb crust, smooth the top, and sprinkle on the 3 tablespoons crumbs, to absorb any excess moisture from the meringue. Add about half the meringue and spread it out onto the edges of the crust to seal it and prevent shrinking. Pile on the remaining meringue and shape swirls with the back of a spoon.

**9.** Bake the pie at 350°F for the time indicated for your altitude in the chart above, or until the meringue looks a rich golden brown color. Cool the pie on a wire rack and serve at room temperature or chilled. Refrigerate any leftovers.

# Chimayó Mocha Mousse Angel Pie with Toasted Pine Nuts

ANGEL PIES are heavenly. They are easy to prepare, with whipped, sugared egg whites slowly baked into a crisp white pillow to cradle any filling you can imagine. My favorite is this dark, rich mousse, created after a memorable lunch with my friend Lorraine Schechter on the terrace of the Spanish-style Restaurante Rancho de Chimayó (New Mexico), where we overindulged in goblets of toasted *piñon*-mocha mousse while I photographed our young waitress, Megan. She was even more dazzling than our dessert, with shining black hair pulled into a taut bun, shoulders bare above a gaily embroidered white blouse, and a megawatt (but modest) smile. When she hoisted a salsa-laden tray to her shoulder, started to descend the adobe staircase, and turned back to look up at our table, I snapped the shutter. She stopped and blushed, looking down quickly. "You want *my* picture? You make me feel pretty for the first time in my life!"

Flavorful New Mexican *piñon* are locally grown and sold in burlap sacks along the roadside and at market stands during the fall harvest season. The mousse makes a perfect pie filling—the rich chocolate-coffee cream contrasts with the nutty flavor of toasted pine nuts and the crunch of a sweet meringue pie shell. The mousse is made with uncooked eggs; it needs to chill for at least 1 hour (or up to 3) to set enough to slice neatly.

Make the meringue shell when the weather is dry, and prepare it a few hours or even the day before making the filling. The secret to keeping the shell white or pale ivory as it bakes is to use very low heat for about 30 minutes, then let it dry out for several hours, or overnight, in the oven with the heat off. But don't worry if the shell tans slightly, because the filling will cover the bottom.

This recipe calls for superfine sugar (also called bar sugar, see page 38), because it dissolves in the egg whites more quickly than regular granulated sugar. You can make it yourself by whirling granulated sugar in the food processor until it is fine.

For another type of filling, try a Strawberry Fool: 1 pint of ripe strawberries, rinsed, hulled, and mashed, folded into ¾ cup heavy cream that has been whipped to soft peaks and sweetened with a little sugar.

———ɯɯ———

**General High Altitude Notes:** As the altitude increases, the stability of the meringue is enhanced by adding a little more cream of tartar and (at 10,000 feet) sugar. Since the meringue is not used as a leavening, you can beat the egg whites until stiff (rather than soft) at high altitudes.

**Special Equipment:** A 9-inch pie plate, preferably Pyrex; electric mixer

**Pan Preparation:** Coat the pie plate with butter or butter-flavor nonstick vegetable spray.

**Makes** one 9-inch pie; serves 6 to 8

**High Notes**

*At 3,000 feet and above,* add a little more cream of tartar to increase the stability of the meringue.

*At 10,000 feet and above,* increase the cream of tartar and sugar for a more stable meringue. Bake the shell in the lower third of the oven for slightly more heat, and leave it in the oven overnight (heat off) to dry completely.

| Ingredients | Sea Level | 3,000 feet | 5,000 feet | 7,000 feet | 10,000 feet |
|---|---|---|---|---|---|
| **Oven rack position, temperature, and baking time** | Rack in center of oven; bake shell at 275°F for 1½ hours; *or* bake for 30 minutes, then turn off heat and leave shell in oven to dry | Rack in center of oven; bake shell at 275°F for 1½ hours; *or* bake for 30 minutes, then turn off heat and leave shell in oven to dry | Rack in center of oven; bake shell at 275°F for 1½ hours; *or* bake for 30 minutes, then turn off heat and leave shell in oven to dry | Rack in center of oven; bake shell at 275°F for 1½ hours; *or* bake for 30 minutes, then turn off heat and leave shell in oven to dry | Rack in lower third of oven; bake shell at 275°F for 20 to 30 minutes, then turn off heat and leave shell in oven to dry |
| **ANGEL PIE SHELL** | | | | | |
| **Large egg whites, at room temperature** | 3 | 3 | 3 | 3 | 3 |
| **Cream of tartar** | ¼ teaspoon | ½ teaspoon | ½ teaspoon | ½ teaspoon | ¾ teaspoon |
| **Salt** | ⅛ teaspoon | ⅛ teaspoon | ⅛ teaspoon | ⅛ teaspoon | ⅛ teaspoon |
| **Superfine sugar** | ¾ cup | ¾ cup | ¾ cup | ¾ cup | 1 cup |
| **Vanilla extract** | 1 teaspoon | 1 teaspoon | 1 teaspoon | 1 teaspoon | 1 teaspoon |
| **CHIMAYÓ MOCHA MOUSSE (RECIPE FOLLOWS)** | | | | | |

1. Position the rack and preheat the oven as indicated for your altitude in the chart above. Prepare the pan as directed.

2. Place the egg whites in the large bowl of an electric mixer, and test them to make sure they are no longer cold. Add the cream of tartar and salt and whip on medium-high speed just until foamy. Gradually whip in the sugar and vanilla, increasing the mixer speed, but watch closely. As soon as you see beater tracks on top of the whites, stop the machine, lift the beater, and check the stiffness of the foam: At all altitudes, you need stiffly beaten whites that stand up in stiff peaks when the beater is lifted (see sketch, page 303). If the whites look too soft, continue beating for just a few more seconds and check again; do not overbeat. The whites should be glossy and smooth.

3. Scoop the whipped whites into the prepared pie plate and use the back of a spoon to spread them in an even layer over the bottom and up the sides of the plate; make an indentation in the meringue to give it the shape of the pie plate and make room for the filling; build up a swirled or peaked design along the rim. Alternatively, you can pipe the meringue through a pastry bag fitted with a ½-inch star tip, covering the bottom and sides and also making decorative rosettes around the rim.

4. Bake the shell for the time indicated for your altitude in the chart above. Peek occasionally to be sure the meringue is not browning; it should stay white or ivory. If you see that it is turning beige, lower the heat, or turn it off and leave the shell in the oven for several hours, or overnight. The baked shell should be completely crisp. Store it in an airtight container.

5. Scoop the mousse into the shell. Refrigerate for at least 1 hour, and up to 3 hours, and garnish with the reserved nuts from the mousse before serving. Refrigerate any leftovers.

# Chimayó Mocha Mousse with Toasted Pine Nuts
*(recipe is the same at all altitudes)*

Shelled pine nuts (*piñon*, *pignoli*, or Indian nuts) are sold in some supermarkets and in natural food stores and by mail (see Sources, page 329); or omit if unavailable.

**Makes** 4 cups, enough to fill a 9-inch pie shell

¾ cup (3.75 ounces) pine nuts
6 ounces semisweet or bittersweet (not unsweetened) chocolate, chopped (1 cup)
6 tablespoons (¾ stick) unsalted butter, cut up
3 large egg yolks
2 teaspoons instant espresso powder
4 large egg whites, at room temperature
Pinch of salt
2 tablespoons superfine or granulated sugar
¾ cup chilled heavy cream (36 to 40% butterfat)

The flavor of pine nuts is greatly enhanced if they are toasted: Place them in a frying pan and shake or stir them over medium heat, watching constantly, until they are aromatic and a golden color (about 5 minutes at sea level to 7,000 feet, slightly longer at higher elevations). Set aside to cool.

Melt the chopped chocolate with the butter in the top of a double boiler set over simmering (sea level to 5,000 feet) or gently boiling water (5,000 feet and above); or melt in the microwave (see page 35). Stir until smooth, remove from the heat, and set aside to cool until comfortable to the touch.

When the chocolate mixture is cool, whisk in the egg yolks and espresso powder, blending well. Set aside.

Place the egg whites in the large bowl of an

electric mixer, and check them to make sure they are no longer cold. Add the salt and whip on medium-high speed just until foamy. Gradually whip in the sugar, increasing the mixer speed to high, and beat until the whites just form stiff peaks that stand up when the beater is lifted. The whites should be glossy and smooth; do not overbeat. Scoop the whites into another bowl so you can reuse the bowl and beater for the cream, without washing.

Whip the chilled cream just until soft peaks form. Set aside.

Test the temperature of the melted chocolate: it should be comfortable to the touch, slightly cooler than body temperature (75° to 80°F on an instant-read thermometer), to blend smoothly with the egg whites and cream. If it is still too hot, refrigerate for a few minutes.

Fold some of the whipped whites into the chocolate to lighten it, then use a flexible spatula to fold the remaining chocolate into the whites, and then the whipped cream. Finally, fold in ½ cup of the toasted pine nuts, reserving the rest to garnish the top.

*Egg whites whipped to stiff peaks*

On a culinary tour in Oaxaca, Mexico (5,000 feet), I was asked, at the very last minute, to contribute a recipe to a dinner. I decided to make chocolate rice pudding, a [sea-level] recipe I learned growing up in Asturias, Spain. It is usually easy: the rice, milk, and cinnamon are cooked together until the rice is done, and then chopped chocolate is stirred in at the end. But this time it easily took twice as long to cook and needed lots more milk. I was caught by surprise. I didn't expect cooking at this altitude would be so different. I was glad I was alone in the kitchen and not teaching the recipe in front of a group.

—**Elaine Gonzales, chocolate expert, cooking teacher,**

**and author, *The Art of Chocolate***

# Fresh Fig Tart with
# Mascarpone-Honey Cream

THIS MARVELOUS tart makes a lovely presentation and offers refreshing, sophisticated flavors. The pastry is crisp and flaky, the honey-mascarpone cream rich and delectable, the currant jelly–balsamic vinegar–glazed sweet figs succulent. The fruit is garnished with fresh thyme leaves, but fresh lavender leaves or flowers or lemon mint could be substituted. The combination of flavors was inspired by recipes I found in very early Mediterranean cookbooks. You can use this as a master recipe, topping the cream with any ripe seasonal berries or sliced fruits; to glaze the top, simply melt the currant jelly alone, without honey or vinegar, and brush it over the fruit. Or, prepare the variation, Fresh Berry Tart with Lemonade Cream Filling and Cream Cheese Pastry, that follows.

If you are one of the many who love pie but hate making crust, this recipe will change your life. You get to toss away your rolling pin and simply mix the ingredients, then press them into the baking pan with your fingertips. As a bonus, this recipe has a fraction of the saturated fat of a basic flaky butter crust.

**General High Altitude Notes:** As the altitude increases, you will need to add a little more milk and/or a few drops of ice water to prevent the dough from feeling dry as you mix and mold it. At the highest altitudes, add 1 or 2 tablespoons more flour, along with a few drops of liquid, to give the pastry a better texture and a little more strength.

**Special Equipment:** An 11-inch tart pan with removable bottom or 10-inch pie plate; aluminum foil; pie weights, rice, or dried beans; small saucepan; pastry brush

**Pan Preparation:** Spray the tart pan or pie plate with butter-flavor nonstick vegetable spray or coat with butter.

**Makes** one 11-inch tart or 10-inch pie; serves 8 to 12

| Ingredients | Sea Level | 3,000 feet | 5,000 feet | 7,000 feet | 10,000 feet |
|---|---|---|---|---|---|
| **Oven rack position, temperature, and baking time** | Rack in lower third of oven; bake shell at 425°F for 12 minutes, then at 350°F for 12 to 14 minutes | Rack in lower third of oven; bake shell at 425°F for 12 minutes, then at 350°F for 12 to 14 minutes | Rack in lower third of oven; bake shell at 425°F for 12 minutes, then at 350°F for 12 to 14 minutes | Rack in lower third of oven; bake shell at 425°F for 15 to 17 minutes, then at 350°F for 12 to 14 minutes | Rack in lower third of oven; bake shell at 425°F for 15 to 18 minutes, then at 350°F for 12 to 14 minutes |
| **All-purpose flour** | 2 cups | 2 cups | 2 cups | 2¼ cups | 2¼ cups plus 1 tablespoon |
| **Granulated sugar** | 1 teaspoon | 1 teaspoon | 1 teaspoon | 1 teaspoon | 1 teaspoon |
| **Salt** | 1 teaspoon | 1 teaspoon | 1 teaspoon | 1 teaspoon | 1 teaspoon |
| **Canola oil** | ⅔ cup | ⅔ cup | ⅔ cup | ⅔ cup | ⅔ cup |
| **Nonfat or whole milk** | 3 tablespoons, or as needed | 3 tablespoons, or as needed | 3 tablespoons, or as needed | 3 to 4 tablespoons, or as needed | 3 to 6 tablespoons, or as needed |
| **Ice water** | None | None | None | None | 1 tablespoon, or as needed |

**MASCARPONE-HONEY CREAM FILLING AND GLAZED FIGS (RECIPE FOLLOWS)**

**1.** Position the rack in the lower third of the oven and preheat the oven to 425°F. Prepare the pan as directed.

**2.** Prepare the pastry: In a medium bowl (if using a tart pan), or in the pie plate, toss together the flour, sugar, and salt. Add the oil and milk (and ice water at 10,000 feet) and stir with a fork or your fingertips until the dough clumps together easily. Sprinkle on a few more drops of milk or ice water if the dough feels too dry.

**3.** Press the dough into an even layer over the bottom and up the sides of the tart pan or pie plate. If using a pie plate, press the pastry into a thick edge on the rim, then pinch into points or scallops. If the dough sticks to your fingers, cover it with a piece of plastic wrap and press on top of that; remove the wrap.

**4.** Cut a 12-inch square of foil, spread a little butter or nonstick vegetable spray on the shiny side, and set it greased side down in the pastry-lined pan. Fill with pie weights (see page 290, sketch c) and bake for the time indicated for your altitude in the chart above, reducing the temperature when indicated, until the pastry is a rich golden brown color. After the first 15 minutes of baking, remove the foil and weights and check the color. Bake longer if necessary. At 10,000 feet, it can take a little longer to bake. Cool on a wire rack; the shell must be thoroughly cooled before adding the cream filling.

## Mascarpone-Honey Cream Filling and Glazed Figs
*(recipe is the same at all altitudes)*

**Makes** 2 cups filling, for one 11-inch tart or 10-inch pie

Mascarpone is a rich double-cream cheese traditionally made from cow's milk in Italy's Lombardy region. The best flavor comes from imported brands, but cream cheese can be substituted. For the glaze, select a balsamic vinegar with a richly sweet or mellow flavor, rather than one that is sour or sharp. Choose the ripest, sweetest fresh figs available—there are many varieties and it makes no difference whether they are black/purple or green.

**Cream and Figs**
   **2 cups mascarpone cheese**
   **¼ cup honey**
   **1 tablespoon fresh lemon juice**
   **2 pounds ripe figs**

**Glaze**
   **2 tablespoons honey**
   **⅔ cup currant jelly**
   **1 tablespoon balsamic vinegar**

**Garnish: Fresh thyme leaves**

Beat together the mascarpone, honey, and lemon juice in a bowl, with a spoon or an electric mixer, until smooth. Spread in an even layer in the cooled pastry shell.

Rinse the figs and gently pat dry with paper towels. Cut a cross in the pointed top of each one to open it up. Set the figs on top of the cream filling.

Stir the honey and currant jelly in a small pan over low heat until liquefied and smooth.

Stir in the balsamic vinegar and drizzle over the figs. Refrigerate until ready to serve. Scatter fresh thyme leaves on top just before serving.

## Fresh Berry Tart with Lemonade Cream Filling

Prepare pastry above or use Cream Cheese Pastry (pages 254 to 255). Roll out the dough and line a buttered 11-inch tart pan with a removable bottom. Completely prebake the shell following Step 4 above. Completely cool.

Add the filling (below). Cover the filling with 4 cups ripe berries and grapes (picked over, rinsed, and dried on paper towels) or sliced peeled fruit. To glaze the fruit, brush with melted currant jelly as above (omitting the honey and vinegar), and refrigerate until ready to serve. (Melted and strained apricot jam can be substituted for the currant jelly.)

## Lemonade Cream Filling
*(recipe is the same at all altitudes)*

**Makes** 1½ cups, enough to fill an 11-inch tart shell

   12 ounces (1½ eight-ounce packages) Philadelphia regular cream cheese (not low-fat)
   3 to 4 tablespoons granulated sugar
   1 tablespoon grated lemon or orange zest, optional
   1½ tablespoons frozen lemonade concentrate, thawed (or frozen margarita mix, tangerine juice, or limeade concentrate), not diluted
   2 tablespoons orange-flavored liqueur, or rum, optional

In a food processor or in a bowl with an electric mixer, blend all the ingredients together until creamy and smooth.

# Soufflés

## Baking Soufflés at High Altitudes

If there ever were a marriage made in heaven, soufflés and high altitudes are it! The higher you climb in elevation, the higher the soufflé rises . . . in theory. And in practice . . . up to a point. The sky's (practically) the limit if you beat the egg whites correctly. The first time I baked my chocolate soufflé at 10,000 feet, it rose right through the oven rack above it! However, if you overbeat the egg whites, they will fall as fast as they rose.

There are two tricks to high altitude soufflé baking: knowing how much to whip the whites and getting the knack of folding them into the flavor base. Both the orange and chocolate soufflés in this book appear in two versions. The first (master) recipes have an egg yolk–rich pastry cream base. One variation is almost fat-free (but high in flavor), the other is fat- and cholesterol-free. You can serve either one without apology to your guests, as both are delicious, though the richer version does taste more silken and creamy.

Eggs can be separated most easily when cold, but whites whip to their fullest volume when at room temperature. If your eggs are still cold when you are ready to bake, put the whites in a metal bowl, set it in a second bowl of hot water, and stir until they lose their chill. Whites will not whip properly if there is a trace of fat on the bowl or beater; be sure your equipment is absolutely clean and grease free (for insurance, wipe the bowl and beaters with a towel dampened with white vinegar). Place the room-temperature whites in the large bowl of the electric mixer, add the cream of tartar and/or salt, if called for, and whip on medium-high speed just until foamy. Gradually whip in the sugar, increasing the mixer speed to high, but watch closely: As soon as you see beater tracks on top of the whites, stop the machine, lift the beater, and check the stiffness of the foam. At sea level, you want stiffly beaten whites that stand up in stiff peaks, but at 2,500 and above, you only want soft, droopy peaks (see page 312). If the whites look too soft, continue beating for just a few more seconds and check again; do not overbeat. You want to leave room so the air cells can expand (like little balloons) during baking. At high altitudes, overwhipped whites blow up so fast that if they have no room for expansion, they burst, causing the soufflé to collapse.

When the whites are ready, set them aside for a moment and check the temperature of the base—it should be comfortable to the touch, neither hot nor cold. With a flexible spatula, fold/stir about one cup of the whipped whites into the base to lighten and soften it, then add generous scoops of the lightened base to the whipped whites in several additions. Fold with a very light touch, cutting through the center of the whites and down to the bottom of the bowl, then bringing the spatula up again toward you while giving the bowl a quarter turn. Repeat the folding action until all the base is incorporated, but don't worry if there are a few white streaks remaining.

To maintain their silken texture, soufflés are baked in a water bath (at high altitude be sure this water is boiling) that gives a gentle, steady heat. The steamy atmosphere also helps prevent crusting over of the top, allowing a good rise.

One time I was making a raspberry soufflé in Bogotá, Columbia (8,000 feet), and it shot up, then deflated. I didn't know why. Since then, I've cooked in many high altitude places and once you know about high altitude, you adjust. When I bake a genoise cake at the Food & Wine Classic in Aspen (7,800 feet), I change my sea level recipe from six whole eggs to four whole eggs plus two yolks, for a heavier and stronger mixture that won't collapse. And when I make a soufflé, I always slightly underbeat the egg whites, so they will have a high rise and not fall too quickly.

—Jacques Pépin, chef, cookbook author, *The Apprentice*

# Summit Orange Soufflé with Grand Marnier Sauce

A DRAMATIC finale after a heavy meal, this soufflé is not too sweet and has a bold, refreshing citrus flavor achieved by using oranges four ways—juice, grated zest, extract, and marmalade. (Select the best-quality "sweet," rather than "bitter orange," marmalade.) When perfectly baked, the soufflé center should be slightly creamy and the top golden brown. Serve with a light dusting of confectioners' sugar and a spoonful of the Grand Marnier Sauce, or Apricot-Orange Sauce (page 207). This master recipe is rich and velvety because it is made with an egg-yolk pastry cream. The fat-free variation following is made without milk or yolks, but it is equally high rising and flavorful, lacking only the fat and cholesterol. To maintain a silken texture, the soufflé is baked in a water bath.

Superfine sugar, also called bar sugar, is used in this recipe because it dissolves more quickly than regular granulated (which can be substituted), or you can make your own by whirling granulated sugar in the food processor until it is fine.

**General High Altitude Notes:** The higher you climb in elevation, the more the soufflé wants to rise. Above 2,500 feet, the trick is to underbeat the whites, whipping just until they form soft, slightly droopy peaks. At this stage there is still room in them to expand when baked. If overbeaten, to stiff peaks, the air cells, and the soufflé, will collapse on cooling. The oven temperature must be carefully monitored, because you need just enough heat to allow the whites to expand sufficiently and to set the starch and protein supporting the air cell structure before the soufflé overbrowns. To get the strongest, most stable orange base, the starch and liquid are cooked together so the starch swells to the maximum before the acidic juices are added. At 5,000 feet and above, to get a higher, more stable rise add a little more cream of tartar, cornstarch, and sugar. To enhance the flavor as the altitude increases, add more extract, but reduce the soufflé weight by cutting back on the marmalade.

**Special Equipment:** A 2-quart straight-sided soufflé mold; roasting pan large enough to hold the soufflé mold; instant-read thermometer (optional)

**Pan Preparation:** Butter the inside of the soufflé mold or spray it with butter-flavor nonstick vegetable spray, then coat with granulated sugar (see Step 3).

**Makes** 2-quart soufflé; serves 6 to 8

**High Notes**

**At 5,000 feet and above,** add cornstarch, cream of tartar, sugar, extra zest, and orange extract. Reduce the marmalade. For the best rise, preheat the oven to 400°F, then lower the temperature by 25 degrees when you put the soufflé in the oven.

**At 10,000 feet,** add one egg white and additional cream of tartar.

| Ingredients | Sea Level | 3,000 feet | 5,000 feet | 7,000 feet | 10,000 feet |
|---|---|---|---|---|---|
| **Oven rack position, temperature, and baking time** | Rack in lower third of oven; bake at 350°F for 35 to 40 minutes | Rack in lower third of oven; bake at 350°F for 35 to 40 minutes | Rack in lower third of oven; *preheat* oven to 400°F; *bake* at 375°F for 30 to 32 minutes | Rack in lower third of oven; *preheat* oven to 400°F; *bake* at 375°F for 30 to 32 minutes | Rack in lower third of oven; *preheat* oven to 400°F; *bake* at 375°F for 30 to 32 minutes |
| **ORANGE FLAVOR BASE** | | | | | |
| **Granulated sugar** | ¼ cup, plus 2 tablespoons for the mold | ¼ cup, plus 2 tablespoons for the mold | ¼ cup, plus 2 tablespoons for the mold | ¼ cup, plus 2 tablespoons for the mold | ¼ cup, plus 2 tablespoons for the mold |
| **Cornstarch** | 2 tablespoons | 2 tablespoons | 3 tablespoons | 3½ tablespoons | ¼ cup |
| **Whole milk** | ¾ cup | ¾ cup | ¾ cup | ¾ cup | ¾ cup |
| **Large egg yolks, at room temperature** | 4 | 4 | 4 | 4 | 4 |
| **Frozen orange juice concentrate, thawed** | ¼ cup | ¼ cup | ¼ cup | ¼ cup | ¼ cup |
| **Orange extract** | 1 teaspoon | 1 teaspoon | 1½ teaspoons | 1½ teaspoons | 1½ teaspoons |
| **Vanilla extract** | ½ teaspoon | ½ teaspoon | ½ teaspoon | ½ teaspoon | ½ teaspoon |
| **Grated orange zest** | 2 teaspoons | 2 teaspoons | 1 tablespoon | 1 tablespoon | 1 tablespoon |
| **Orange marmalade** | 3 tablespoons | 3 tablespoons | 2 tablespoons | 2 tablespoons | 2 tablespoons |
| **Unsalted butter, in one chunk, cold** | About 2 tablespoons | About 2 tablespoons | About 2 tablespoons | About 2 tablespoons | About 2 tablespoons |

*(continued)*

| Ingredients | Sea Level | 3,000 feet | 5,000 feet | 7,000 feet | 10,000 feet |
|---|---|---|---|---|---|
| **WHIPPED WHITES** | | | | | |
| **Large egg whites, at room temperature** | 8 | 8 | 8 | 8 | 9 |
| **Cream of tartar** | ¼ teaspoon | ¼ teaspoon | ¾ teaspoon | ¾ teaspoon | 1 teaspoon |
| **Salt** | Pinch | Pinch | Pinch | Pinch | Pinch |
| **Superfine sugar** | ½ cup | ½ cup | ¾ cup | ¾ cup | ¾ cup |
| **TOPPING (OPTIONAL)** | | | | | |
| **Confectioners' sugar** | About 1 tablespoon | About 1 tablespoon | About 1 tablespoon | About 1 tablespoon | About 1 tablespoon |
| **GRAND MARNIER SAUCE (RECIPE FOLLOWS)** | | | | | |

**1.** Prepare the orange base (this can be made a day in advance, covered, and refrigerated; bring to room temperature before proceeding): In a heavy-bottomed nonreactive saucepan, whisk together the ¼ cup granulated sugar, the cornstarch, and milk. Set over medium heat and whisk constantly for 5 to 7 minutes (a little longer at 10,000 feet), until it reaches a bubbling boil. Raise the heat slightly and boil hard for 1 full minute (count to 60), whisking or stirring constantly—be sure to cover the entire pan bottom and reach into the corners. The mixture should become thick, almost gluey, and generously coat the back of a spoon. Remove from the heat. Vigorously whisk in the egg yolks, then the orange juice concentrate, extracts, grated zest, and marmalade, until smooth. Transfer to a bowl.

**2.** Holding the chunk of butter so it just touches the top of the orange base, dab it all over; the melted butter will prevent a skin from forming (save the extra butter for another use). Cool the orange base to room temperature.

**3.** Position the rack and preheat the oven as indicated for your altitude in the chart above (remove the rack immediately above the soufflé so it doesn't bump into it as it rises). Grease the mold as described above, toss the remaining 2 tablespoons sugar into the mold, and tip it back and forth until the sugar clings all over the inside; tap out any excess sugar. Set a kettle of water on the stove and bring to a boil so it will be ready to add to the water bath when the soufflé goes into the oven. Pour ½ to ¾ inch of very hot water in the roasting pan and place it in the oven on the baking rack to continue to heat while you prepare the soufflé.

**4.** Place the egg whites in the large bowl of an electric mixer, and check them to make sure they are no longer cold. Add the cream of tartar and salt and whip on medium-high speed just until foamy. Gradually whip in the superfine sugar, increasing the mixer speed to high, but watch closely: As soon as you see beater tracks on top of the whites, stop the machine, lift the beater, and check the stiffness of the foam. At sea level, you want whites that are medium-stiff but not dry, but at 2,500 feet and above, you only want soft, slightly droopy peaks (see below). If the whites look too soft, continue beating for just a few more seconds and check again; do not overbeat. The whites should be glossy and smooth.

**5.** Be sure the orange base is cooled to room temperature. Stir it well until soft and smooth. Add about 1 cup of the whipped whites and whisk to lighten and soften the orange base. Fold the softened orange mixture into the remaining whites. Fold with a very light touch, cutting through the center of the whites and down to the bowl bottom, then bringing the spatula up again toward you while giving the bowl a quarter turn.

**6.** Scoop the batter into the prepared mold and smooth the top. Carefully set the mold into the roasting pan of water in the oven, then slowly pour a little more boiling water into one corner of the roasting pan; the water should come about one-third of the way up the sides of the mold. Bake the soufflé until it is well risen, golden brown, and firm on top when lightly jiggled with your hand; an instant-read thermometer placed in the center should read 155°F to 160°F.

**7.** Remove the soufflé from the oven, lift it out of the water, and sift on a bit of confectioners' sugar, if desired. Serve immediately, with the sauce.

# Fat-Free Orange Soufflé

The orange base for this soufflé omits the milk and yolks of the original, thus eliminating fat and cholesterol. Prepare the recipe as above, with the following changes: In Step 1, make the orange base with water instead of milk. Cook it as directed, then remove it from the heat and whisk in the orange juice concentrate, extracts, grated zest, and marmalade; omit the yolks. Proceed as directed.

# Grand Marnier Sauce
*(recipe is the same at all altitudes)*

Serve this sauce warm for maximum flavor. It is perfect with the soufflé and is equally good over sponge or chiffon cake. This sauce is both fat and cholesterol free.

**Makes** about 1 cup; serves 6 to 8

½ cup orange marmalade
¼ cup orange juice
3 to 4 tablespoons Grand Marnier or other orange-flavored liqueur

Stir the marmalade with the orange juice in a small saucepan set over medium heat until melted and smooth. Remove from the heat and stir in the liqueur. Serve warm, or let cool, then refrigerate until needed and rewarm over low heat before serving.

*Whipped Egg Whites*

*droopy peaks*

*stiff peaks*

# Paradise Peak Chocolate Soufflé

THIS INTENSELY chocolate, lusciously creamy soufflé rises dramatically (2½ to 3½ inches above the dish at 10,000 feet) as it bakes. The first time I baked it in Breckenridge (10,000 feet), I was trying to show off to some friends. We all gathered in front of the oven to take a peek. When we opened the door, we discovered that the soufflé had risen through the bars of the oven rack sitting above it! If you are smarter, and remove the upper rack in the oven, you will have a dessert you can really be proud of.

This soufflé is rich and silken on the tongue because it is made with an egg-yolk pastry cream base. The low-fat variation following is made with skim mik and no yolks but is equally high rising and flavorful, lacking only most of the fat and cholesterol of the original.

Superfine sugar, also called bar sugar, is used in this recipe because it dissolves more quickly than regular granulated (which can be substituted here, see page 38). The cocoa provides a strong chocolate flavor and also acts as a starch to help stabilize the soufflé; the grated chocolate adds depth of flavor. To grate chocolate, use the medium holes on a box grater, or use a Microplane (see page 32). To maintain its silken texture, the soufflé is baked in a water bath. The soufflé is elegant served by itself, but reaches superlative heights accompanied by Raspberry Sauce (page 149) or Champagne Sabayon Sauce (page 201).

**General High Altitude Notes:** Above 2,500 feet, the trick with a soufflé is to underbeat the whites, whipping just until they form soft, slightly droopy peaks. At this stage there is still room in them to expand when baked. If overbeaten, to stiff peaks, the air cells, and the soufflé, will collapse on cooling. The oven temperature must be carefully monitored, because you need just enough heat to allow the whites to expand sufficiently and to set the starch and protein supporting the air cell structure before the soufflé overbrowns.

**Special Equipment:** A 2-quart straight-sided soufflé mold; roasting pan large enough to hold the soufflé mold; instant-read thermometer (optional)

**Pan Preparation:** Butter the inside of the soufflé dish or spray it with butter-flavor nonstick vegetable spray, then coat the inside with granulated sugar (see Step 3).

**Makes** 2-quart soufflé; serves 6 to 8

### High Notes

*Between 3,000 and 7,000 feet,* raise the oven heat by 25 degrees.

*At 7,000 feet,* bake at 350°F (as for sea level), and bake for the same time as for sea level but slightly longer than at 3,000 to 7,000 feet.

*At 10,000 feet,* preheat the oven to 400°F, then reduce it by 25 degrees when you put the soufflé into the oven.

| Ingredients | Sea Level | 3,000 feet | 5,000 feet | 7,000 feet | 10,000 feet |
|---|---|---|---|---|---|
| **Oven rack position, temperature, and baking time** | Rack in lower third of oven; bake at 350°F for 35 to 40 minutes | Rack in lower third of oven; bake at 375°F for 30 to 35 minutes | Rack in lower third of oven; bake at 375°F for 30 to 35 minutes | Rack in lower third of oven; bake at 350°F for 35 to 40 minutes | Rack in lower third of oven; *preheat* oven to 400°F; *bake* at 375°F for 30 to 32 minutes |
| **Unsweetened natural cocoa such as Hershey's regular** | ⅔ cup | ⅔ cup | ⅔ cup | ⅔ cup | ⅔ cup |
| **Granulated sugar** | ¼ cup, plus 2 tablespoons for the mold | ¼ cup, plus 2 tablespoons for the mold | ¼ cup, plus 2 tablespoons for the mold | ¼ cup, plus 2 tablespoons for the mold | ¼ cup, plus 2 tablespoons for the mold |
| **Cornstarch** | 1 tablespoon plus 1 teaspoon | 1 tablespoon plus 1 teaspoon | 1 tablespoon plus 1 teaspoon | 1 tablespoon plus 1 teaspoon | 1 tablespoon plus 1 teaspoon |
| **Ground cinnamon** | Pinch | Pinch | Pinch | Pinch | Pinch |
| **Milk** | 1 cup | 1 cup | 1 cup | 1 cup | 1 cup plus 1 tablespoon |
| **Large egg yolks, at room temperature** | 4 | 4 | 4 | 4 | 4 |
| **Vanilla extract** | 2 teaspoons | 2 teaspoons | 2 teaspoons | 2 teaspoons | 2 teaspoons |
| **Unsalted butter, in one chunk, cold** | About 2 tablespoons | About 2 tablespoons | About 2 tablespoons | About 2 tablespoons | About 2 tablespoons |

*(continued)*

| Ingredients | Sea Level | 3,000 feet | 5,000 feet | 7,000 feet | 10,000 feet |
|---|---|---|---|---|---|
| **WHIPPED WHITES** | | | | | |
| **Large egg whites, at room temperature** | 7 | 7 | 7 | 7 | 7 |
| **Cream of tartar** | ¼ teaspoon | ¼ teaspoon | ¼ teaspoon | ¼ teaspoon | ½ teaspoon |
| **Salt** | Pinch | Pinch | Pinch | Pinch | Pinch |
| **Superfine or granulated sugar** | ½ cup | ½ cup | ½ cup | ½ cup | ½ cup |
| **Unsweetened chocolate, grated** | ½ ounce | ½ ounce | ½ ounce | ½ ounce | ½ ounce |
| **TOPPING (OPTIONAL)** | | | | | |
| **Confectioners' sugar** | ½ tablespoon | ½ tablespoon | ½ tablespoon | ½ tablespoon | ½ tablespoon |

**1.** Prepare the chocolate base (this can be made a day in advance, covered, and refrigerated; bring to room temperature before proceeding): In a heavy-bottomed nonreactive saucepan, whisk together the cocoa, the ¼ cup granulated sugar, the cornstarch, and cinnamon. Whisk in the milk, set over medium heat, and whisk constantly for 5 to 7 minutes (a little longer at 10,000 feet) until it reaches a bubbling boil. Raise the heat slightly and boil hard for 1 full minute (count to 60), whisking or stirring constantly—be sure to cover the entire pan bottom and reach into the corners. The mixture should become as thick as chocolate pudding and generously coat the back of a spoon. Remove from the heat. Vigorously whisk in the egg yolks and vanilla until smooth. Transfer to a bowl.

**2.** Holding the chunk of butter so it just touches the top of the hot chocolate mixture, dab it over the surface to prevent a skin from forming (save the extra butter for another use). Cool the base to room temperature.

**3.** Position the rack and preheat the oven as indicated for your altitude in the chart above (remove the rack above the soufflé so it doesn't bump into it as it rises). Grease the mold as described above, toss the remaining 2 tablespoons sugar into the mold, and tip it back and forth until the sugar clings all over the inside; tap out any excess sugar. Set a kettle of water on the stove and bring to a boil so it will be ready to add to the water bath when the soufflé goes into the oven. Pour ½ to ¾ inch very hot water in the roasting pan and place it in the oven on the baking rack to continue to heat while you prepare the soufflé.

**4.** Place the egg whites in the large bowl of an electric mixer, and check them to make sure they are no longer cold. Add the cream of tartar and salt and whip on medium-high speed just until foamy. Gradually whip in the superfine sugar, increasing the mixer speed to high, but watch closely. As soon as you see beater tracks on top of the whites, stop the machine, lift the beater, and check the stiffness of the foam: At sea level, you want whites that are medium-stiff but not dry, but at 2,500 feet and above you only want soft, slightly droopy peaks (see below). If the whites look too soft, continue beating for just a few more seconds and check again; do not overbeat. The whites should be glossy and smooth.

**5.** Be sure the chocolate base is cooled to room temperature. Stir it well, until soft and smooth. Add about 1 cup of the whipped whites and whisk to lighten and soften the chocolate base. Then sprinkle in the grated chocolate. Fold the softened chocolate mixture into the remaining whites. Fold with a very light touch, cutting through the center of the whites and down to the bowl bottom, then bringing the spatula up again toward you while giving the bowl a quarter turn.

**6.** Scoop the batter into the prepared mold and smooth the top. Carefully set the mold into the roasting pan of water in the oven, then reach in and slowly pour a little more boiling water into one corner of the roasting pan to come about one-third of the way up the sides of the mold. Bake the soufflé until it is well risen and firm on top when lightly jiggled with your hand; an instant-read thermometer placed in the center should read 155° to 160°F.

**7.** Remove the soufflé from the oven, lift it out of the water, and sift on the confectioners' sugar, if desired. Serve immediately.

## Low-Fat Chocolate Soufflé

The chocolate base for this soufflé uses skim milk and omits yolks, thus eliminating most of the fat and cholesterol. Prepare the recipe as above, with the following changes: In Step 1, make the chocolate base with water instead of milk. Cook it as directed, then remove it from the heat and whisk in the vanilla; omit the yolks. Proceed as directed.

*Whipped Egg Whites*

*droopy peaks*

*stiff peaks*

# Appendix

## About Cake Mixes

I was lying back in the dentist's chair one morning, my mouth full of fingers and tools, when my dentist, Dr. Steven Reiss, told me that his daughter, Rachel, living in Vail, Colorado (8,500 feet), had called home to say she was baking brownies from a mix and it didn't work. Her mother, Elsa, knew I was coming into the office, so they decided to ask my advice.

I felt as if I was in a dream, on a high-stakes quiz show, bursting with a win-the-jackpot response but not able to talk. I immediately began gesticulating wildly and mumbling through the cotton. Steve laughed and removed the paraphernalia, and I blurted out my diagnosis: "Follow the box high altitude directions but add 3 tablespoons flour and 2 tablespoons water. Bake again, and call me in the morning." She did, and it worked.

Anyone who has ever used a boxed mix has seen (with a magnifying glass) the "high altitude" directions in fine print at the bottom of the recipe. But unless you live at high altitude, the importance of these instructions may have escaped your scrutiny.

When I began to test recipes at high altitudes, I decided to include boxed mixes because they are so widely used. I knew my from-scratch recipes would involve hard work and repeated tests, but I thought testing the mixes would be easy since food manufacturers have high altitude testing laboratories (General Mills's lab is in Albuquerque, at 5,000 feet). My expectation was that these products would rise properly, release smoothly from the pans, and have a typically soft, tender crumb. What did I find? Mixed results.

I tested Duncan Hines Moist Deluxe cake mixes, Betty Crocker Super Moist cake mixes, and Pillsbury Brownie Classics at 3,000, 5,000, 7,000, and 10,000 feet. Results were good between 3,000 and 5,000 feet (though cakes at the latter altitude had a little problem sticking to the pan). At 7,000 feet, there was some room for improvement, but at 8,000 feet and above, results ranged from poor to pitiful. Buyer beware, you say? Actually, there is no way to tell from the packaging exactly how high in altitude they would work. The Duncan Hines cake mix boxes read simply "High altitude directions over 3,500 feet"; Pillsbury mixes, "Above 3,500 feet"; and Betty Crocker mixes, "High Altitude 3,500–6,500 feet." I found no mixes that mentioned elevations above 6,500 feet. When I phoned the consumer lines for the three companies, I was told that their high altitude adjustments "were tested and they work at every elevation" (Duncan Hines), or were "designed for use only to about 6,000 feet because there's not a big enough market above that" (General Mills). Their bottom line: market size. The bottom line for us: You are on your own above

6,500 feet! Luckily, the problems are not hard to fix.

My testing method was to prepare each mix several times. As with scratch cakes, the necessary adjustments varied from one type of cake to another—there was no all-purpose answer, but there were many similarities. In each case, my first test followed the manufacturer's high altitude directions exactly, which usually called for the addition of a little flour and water, occasionally a little oil, and sometimes an increase in baking temperature and/or time. I used shiny metal cake pans and followed their instructions to grease (or grease and flour) the pans (none used paper liners).

I baked the cakes on the center rack of the oven unless otherwise directed, and I followed the temperature and time recommendations for two 9-inch round cake pans. I cooled the layers on a wire rack for about 10 minutes, then ran a knife between the cake and pan sides to loosen it and inverted the layers onto aluminum foil–covered cardboard cake disks. After the layers cooled, I photographed the results, and I deemed them acceptable if the layer was flat or slightly domed on top, released easily from the pan, and had a tender crumb.

- At 3,000 feet, they rose well and released easily.
- At 5,000 feet, they rose properly but occasionally stuck to the pans (for the solution, see A, right).
- At 7,000 feet, they rose properly, but many stuck to the pans (see A, right).
- From 8,500 feet to 10,000 feet and above, forget it. All products stuck, all had serious sinkholes (or craters) in the center when they cooled, and many had a sticky, coarse texture (see A through E, right).

My second (or third or fourth) tests tried to overcome the problems of sticking, sinking, or coarse texture. My conclusions: you should follow the high altitude adjustments given on the box AND ALSO do the following:

**A** **To prevent sticking to the pan,** grease the pans, line with wax paper or baking parchment, and grease and flour the paper; tap out the excess flour.

**B** **To prevent sinking or cratering,** add between 1 tablespoon and ¼ cup more flour to strengthen the batter so it can hold itself up once risen; at 10,000 feet, it is essential to add 2 to 4 more tablespoons flour.

**C** **To overcome loss of liquid by evaporation,** add 1 to 3 tablespoons water.

**D** **To increase or improve flavor** (which weakens at high altitudes), add 1 teaspoon vanilla or other appropriate flavoring.

**E** **To get a better rise or more even bake,** at 7,000 feet and above, place the rack in the lower third of the oven so the cake will receive a little more intense heat or bake the layers in the center of the oven for more moderate heat but increase the baking time by 2 to 4 minutes.

Mix cakes are usually sweeter and have a softer, more "disappearing," or cottony, crumb than scratch cakes. What is in a cake mix? Boxed mixes are made with commercial ingredients. For example, the flour is usually bleached (with chlorine gas—not necessarily bad, but it does cause changes), which, among other things, inhibits its gluten development and helps the flour tolerate more sugar and fat than unbleached flour. Special emulsifiers like mono- and diglycerides are added to the vegetable shortening (partially hydrogenated soybean or other oil) so it can absorb and retain more liquid. Emulsifiers also help the air cells hold their size while the cakes rise. Vitamins and artificial flavoring and coloring are also added, along with preservatives and chemicals that extend shelf life and help keep the texture smooth. I counted twenty ingredients listed on the label for Duncan Hines

Moist Deluxe Butter Recipe Fudge Cake, most unavailable in your home pantry.

## Into Thin Air: The Science Behind High Altitude Baking

Recipes developed for baking at sea level react differently when prepared at high altitudes. What happens and what causes the changes? I wrote this book to answer these questions, repeatedly baking and testing a group of my favorite sea-level recipes at different altitudes, until I understood what was going on and why.

Baking results depend on many factors: food chemistry, atmospheric pressure, humidity, and climatic conditions, in addition to elevation. When I began working at different elevations, I tried adding a pinch of this and taking out a pinch of that. At first I baked by touch, feel, and the look of things. I learned, however, that there was no straight linear progression from one adjustment to the next, no magic wand to wave, no single calculation that would transform a sea-level recipe into a perfect 5,000-foot recipe. I found that high altitude baking is an art, not a science, involving a world of technical complexities and infinite variables, only a few of which I could control.

The first thing you notice as you climb in altitude is that the higher you go, the thinner the air—the lower the atmospheric pressure. My testing experiences showed me that this reduced air pressure starts to affect the food preparation, and especially baking, at between 2,000 and 3,000 feet above sea level. The effects grow more serious with gains in elevation and are particularly noticeable in baking, where results are sensitive to carefully balanced formulas and temperature/time calibrations.

As the elevation rises, three major factors may cause a recipe to need adjustment in ingredients, cooking times, and/or temperatures. The higher in elevation you go:

1. The lower the boiling point of water

2. The faster liquids (and moisture in general) evaporate

3. The more quickly leavening gases (air, carbon dioxide, water vapor) expand

What is the boiling point? When water is heated in a pan on the stove, its molecules absorb energy and begin to move faster and faster, forming bubbles, or pockets of water vapor. When the bubbles absorb enough energy to be equal to or overcome the combined weight of the water plus the atmosphere pressing down on them, they rise to the surface and pop. The temperature at which liquid water changes to water vapor is the "boiling point"—water can get no hotter. At high altitudes, where there is less pressure on the surface of the water, it takes less heat energy for the bubbles to rise and break; in other words, the water has a lower, or cooler, boiling point. Baking requires a specific amount of heat; for many baked goods, the maximum internal temperature is about the same as the boiling point of water.

Each 500-foot increase in altitude causes the boiling point of water to drop about 1°F (see the table on page 322), so if you live on a hill or in a valley, you can count on just a very slight variation from the figures in the table. Under standard atmospheric conditions, water boils at 212°F at sea level, 203.2°F at 5,000 feet, and 194.7°F at 10,000 feet. At a given altitude, the boiling point also varies slightly as the weather changes the atmospheric pressure.

At high elevations, where water boils at a lower temperature, it takes longer to cook foods in or over that liquid: custards take longer to set and a double boiler often does not provide enough heat to gelatinize the starch that thickens a pudding. While the moisture inside a dough or batter takes a shorter time to reach the point of boiling or steaming, the point will be at a lower temperature than 212°F. Therefore, a dense, moist cake batter, for example, will often crust over on top before the interior gets hot enough to bake through; a piecrust will overbrown before the apples underneath it get soft. A cake that bakes in 30 minutes at sea level can take 40 minutes to bake at 10,000 feet. Baking times and temperatures often need to be adjusted at high altitudes.

Also, when water boils at a lower temperature at a given oven temperature, it will evaporate from a batter or dough more quickly than at sea level, changing the ratio of liquid to solids in a batter or dough and causing serious changes in the baked result. The evaporating liquid leaves high concentrations of sugar and fat in a cake batter, which weaken the batter's cell structure and can cause the cake to fall during baking or cooling. Extra-high concentrations of sugar can also cause the cake's structure to set too slowly or result in a dry or coarse baked texture.

Atmospheric pressure has a great effect upon leavening gases in baked goods. Each 1,000-foot increase in altitude causes a decrease of about half a pound of atmospheric pressure per square inch of surface. At sea level, the weight of the atmosphere pressing on one square inch of surface is 14.7 pounds; at 5,000 feet above sea level, it is 12.2 pounds; and at 10,000 feet, it is 10.1 pounds (see the table on page 322).

Why does atmospheric pressure affect baking? The less weight (air pressure) there is pushing down on the surface of something, the easier it is for it to rise up (think of pushing your hand down on a helium-filled balloon). In practical terms, the volume of gas produced by the leavening *increases* as the atmospheric pressure *decreases*: more altitude (less air pressure)

= more leavening effect. The higher a helium balloon goes, the more it swells up, because the pressure decreases with increasing altitude. For the baker, the change in pressure means it is necessary to make adjustments and improvise certain techniques to replicate the results expected at sea level.

When leavening gases (including those produced by baking powder, baking soda, or the air in whipped whole eggs or whites) expand too quickly, a cake, meringue, or soufflé can rise with such unbridled enthusiasm that it pops up and then collapses. When the carbon dioxide gas produced by yeast in bread dough expands too quickly, bread can overproof or rise up too fast, losing flavor and texture ordinarily developed through long, slow rising. Overproofed bread can also droop or even fall flat during or after baking.

Atmospheric pressure and altitude have obvious effects on food preparation, but there is a third factor to consider: humidity. It gave me trouble now and then at every altitude I tested, and I never found a systematic method to adjust for it. Humidity is a baker's wild card. You may already accommodate to it instinctively. Most people know, for example, that you shouldn't try to bake meringue shells on a rainy day. And most bakers will admit that, occasionally, their always-reliable recipes fail suddenly and without apparent explanation. Maybe it is due to the weather!

Two things influence the evaporation rate of exposed food surfaces: atmospheric pressure and humidity. The higher you climb above sea level, the fewer air molecules there are to carry or impart energy (the thinner the air). The air feels, and is, drier and colder. Average air temperature drops about 12°F (6.5°C) for every 3,281 feet (1,000 meters). Just as your body cools off quickly, so does the surface temperature of food: Baked goods dry out, and your hot coffee or soup gets cold surprisingly fast. The moisture in baked goods (at any given humidity, say 38 percent) in your 5,000-foot kitchen will evaporate about 15 percent faster than at sea level, while at the same humidity in an 8,000-foot kitchen the moisture will evaporate 29 percent faster than at sea level.

Drier high altitude air can also mean drier flour, so your recipes may need a little more liquid. However, the most important factor governing liquid the flour absorbs is the flour's protein content: At any altitude and in any weather, high-protein bread flour can absorb more liquid than all-purpose, which absorbs more than cake or pastry flour.

The amount of humidity in the air also affects surface evaporation. When the air is dry, it can literally suck moisture from exposed surfaces (uncovered meringues stay crisp, unwrapped cakes dry out). On the other hand, when air contains a lot of water vapor (very high humidity), it can reach a point where it can't hold any more. Surfaces exposed to the air then will retain their own moisture or absorb some from the air (meringues get soft and soggy, cakes stay moist longer). In rainy weather or in a humid climate, flour may contain slightly more moisture than usual, so you may need to use either a little more flour or a little less liquid (but again, the need for added liquid depends more on the protein content of the flour itself than the weather; see above).

According to food scientist Shirley Corriher, the reason you want to add extra humidity to an oven when baking bread is because the warm, moist air, unlike hot, dry air, slows down evaporation from the dough's surface, keeping it supple and flexible (rather than crisp) longer—so it can rise higher before its structure sets from the heat.

To see the direct relationship between changes in altitude, boiling point of water, and atmospheric pressure, see the table on page 322. Refer to this table when you want to know the *approximate* boiling point of water at different altitudes. (Since the boiling point values are averages, rather than precise figures for each elevation, you may find slightly different values if you compare this table with others.) My values are based on the Standard Atmosphere table created by the international scientific community to give, among other data, the values of atmospheric pressure in relation to altitude.

Changes in atmospheric pressure are measured by a barometer (one common type is a vacuum-sealed glass tube containing mercury that rises or falls on a scale calibrated in inches). The table shows how the boiling point of water becomes lower as the barometric pressure decreases when altitude increases. The barometric figures in the table are actual, not adjusted, measurements. (When barometric pressure is reported by a local weather service or in the media, the numbers used will have been adjusted to a sea-level equivalent for that particular locale, so they cannot be used as an indication of the boiling point of water there.)

How much do changes in barometric pressure actually affect the boiling point of water? Just a little. The extremes of barometric pressure tracked over a period of years in a specific location varied no more than plus or minus one inch of mercury, or about 2 degrees Fahrenheit, with the average at $\frac{1}{4}$ to $\frac{1}{2}$ inch, or about one-half to one degree Fahrenheit.

How can you determine your elevation? Elevation statistics may vary greatly. If you can pinpoint your location on a U.S. Department of the Interior Geological Survey Topographic Map (see Sources, page 329), however, you can be precise.

## Approximate Boiling Point of Water and Atmospheric Pressure at Various Altitudes Based on U.S. Standard Atmosphere

| Elevation<br>Feet (Meters) | Boiling Point<br>Fahrenheit: °F<br>(Celsius: °C) | Atmospheric Pressure<br>in Pounds per<br>Square Inch: psi<br>(millibars: mb) | Barometric Pressure<br>in Inches of Mercury<br>shown on a Barometer<br>(Note: Figures not<br>adjusted to sea level) |
|---|---|---|---|
| 0 feet (0 meters) | 212.0°F (100°C) | 14.69 psi (1013 mb) | 29.92 inches |
| 500 (152.4) | 211.1 (99.50) | 14.43 (995) | 29.38 |
| 1,000 (304.8) | 210.2 (99.00) | 14.17 (977) | 28.85 |
| 1,500 (457.2) | 209.3 (98.50) | 13.91 (959) | 28.32 |
| 2,000 (609.6) | 208.5 (98.06) | 13.66 (942) | 27.82 |
| 2,500 (762.0) | 207.6 (97.56) | 13.42 (925) | 27.32 |
| 3,000 (914.4) | 206.7 (97.06) | 13.17 (908) | 26.81 |
| 3,500 (1,067) | 205.8 (96.56) | 12.92 (891) | 26.31 |
| 4,000 (1,219) | 204.9 (96.06) | 12.69 (875) | 25.84 |
| 4,500 (1,372) | 204.1 (95.61) | 12.46 (859) | 25.37 |
| 5,000 (1,524) | 203.2 (95.11) | 12.23 (843) | 24.89 |
| 5,500 (1,676) | 202.4 (94.67) | 11.99 (827) | 24.42 |
| 6,000 (1,829) | 201.5 (94.17) | 11.78 (812) | 23.98 |
| 6,500 (1,981) | 200.6 (93.67) | 11.56 (797) | 23.54 |
| 7,000 (2,134) | 199.8 (93.22) | 11.34 (782) | 23.09 |
| 7,500 (2,286) | 198.9 (92.72) | 11.12 (767) | 22.65 |
| 8,000 (2,438) | 198.1 (92.27) | 10.91 (752) | 22.22 |
| 8,500 (2,591) | 197.2 (91.78) | 10.70 (738) | 21.79 |
| 9,000 (2,743) | 196.4 (91.33) | 10.50 (724) | 21.38 |
| 9,500 (2,895) | 195.5 (90.83) | 10.30 (710) | 20.76 |
| 10,000 (3,048) | 194.7 (90.39) | 10.11 (697) | 20.58 |
| 15,000 (4,572) | 185.0 (85.00) | 8.30 (572) | 16.89 |

Data compiled from National Oceanic and Atmospheric Administration/National Weather Service, New Mexico State University, and others

# High Altitude Recipe Adjustment Guide

The table below is a generalized adjustment guide, a place to start when making trial-and-error changes to your own sea-level recipes that don't work at high altitudes. To start, it will help to find a similar recipe in this book and bake it once according to the formula I developed for your altitude. To understand the theoretical background for any changes, you will find it helpful to read the introductory section at the beginning of each chapter. When embarking on a new recipe, I advise you to follow it once as written, taking notes on the results. If they are less than wonderful, try it again referring to the table below; start with smaller adjustments and work up to the larger ones if necessary.

I developed and tested all the recipes in this book in my home kitchen, at 540 feet above sea level (basically sea level), and in home kitchens at 2,750 and 3,500 feet in North Carolina and Virginia; 5,000 and 5,015 feet in Denver; 5,023 feet in McCall, Idaho; 7,000 feet in Santa Fe; and 10,000 feet in Breckenridge, Colorado. The recipes listed at 3,000 feet will work from 2,000 to 3,500 feet; those listed for 5,000 feet will work from 3,500 to 6,500 feet; those listed for 7,000 feet will work from 6,500 to 8,500 feet; and those listed for 10,000 feet will work from 8,500 to 11,500 feet.

## Recipe Adjustment Guide

| ADJUSTMENTS | ALTITUDES | | | |
|---|---|---|---|---|
| | **3,000 feet** | **5,000 feet** | **7,000 feet** | **10,000 feet** |
| Flour<br>*Increase* each cup by | 0 to 1 tablespoon | 0 to 2 tablespoons | 3 to 4 tablespoons | 2 to 4 tablespoons |
| Baking powder or baking soda<br>*Decrease* each teaspoon by | 0 to ⅛ teaspoon | ⅛ to ¼ teaspoon | ¼ to ½ teaspoon | ½ to ⅔ teaspoon |
| Sugar<br>*Decrease* each cup by | 0 to 1 tablespoon | 0 to 2 tablespoons | 2 to 4 tablespoons | 3 to 4 tablespoons |
| Liquid<br>*Increase* each cup by | 0 to 2 tablespoons | 2 to 4 tablespoons | 3 to 4 tablespoons | 3 to 4 tablespoons |
| Fats (may not be necessary)<br>*Decrease* each cup by | 0 | 0 | 0 | 1 to 2 tablespoons in very high-fat cakes and some cookies |

# Useful Weights and Measurements and Ingredients

To convert ounces (oz.) to grams (g), multiply ounces by 28.35. One ounce = 28.35 grams, which rounds off to 30 g.

To convert pounds (lbs.) to kilograms (kg), multiply pounds by 0.45.

To convert fluid ounces to milliliters (ml), multiply fluid ounces by 30.

Values below have been rounded off. To measure dry ingredients, note: *Unsifted flour* is whisked to lighten, then spooned into a measuring cup and leveled off; *sifted flour, cocoa, or confectioners' sugar* is sifted first, then spooned into a measuring cup and leveled off.

| Ingredients | Volume Measure | Ounces/ pounds | Grams (g)/ kilograms (kg) (1 kg = 1000 g = 2.2 lbs) | Canadian metric/ Milliliters (ml)/liters (l) (1 liter = 4⅓ cups) |
|---|---|---|---|---|
| | | *(fluid ounces)* | *(solids/weight)* | *(liquids)* |
| | 1 teaspoon | ⅛ ounce | 9 g | 5 ml |
| | 1 tablespoon = 3 teaspoons | ½ ounce | 15 g | 15 ml |
| | 2 tablespoons = ⅛ cup | 1 ounce | 28 g | 29.5 ml |
| | 3½ tablespoons | 1¾ ounces | 50 g | 51.75 ml |
| | ¼ cup = 4 tablespoons | 2 ounces | 60 g | 59 ml |
| | ⅓ cup = 5⅓ tablespoon | 2¾ ounces | 78 g | 81 ml |
| | 7 tablespoons | 3½ ounces | 100 g | 104 ml |
| | ½ cup = 8 tablespoons | 4 ounces | 113 g | 120 ml |
| | 1 cup = 16 tablespoons | 8 ounces = ½ pint | 227 g | 250 ml |
| | 2 cups | 16 ounces = 1 pint | 454 g | 473 ml |
| | 4 cups | 32 ounces = 1 quart | 900 g | 1 l |

*(continued)*

| Ingredients | Volume Measure | Ounces/ pounds | Grams (g)/ kilograms (kg) (1 kg = 1000 g = 2.2 lbs) | Canadian metric/ Milliliters (ml)/liters (l) (1 liter = 4⅓ cups) |
|---|---|---|---|---|
| All-purpose flour, unsifted | 1 tablespoon<br>1 cup | ⅓ ounce<br>5 ounces | 10 g<br>140 g | |
| All-purpose flour, sifted | 1 tablespoon<br>1 cup | ⅕ ounce<br>4½ ounces | 5 g<br>120 g | |
| Unbleached bread flour, unsifted (King Arthur) | 1 cup | 4½ ounces | 125 g | |
| Cake flour, sifted | 1 tablespoon<br>1 cup | ¼ ounce<br>3½ ounces | 7.5 g<br>100 g | |
| Whole wheat flour, unsifted | 1 cup | 5 ounces | 140 g | |
| Cocoa, sifted | 1 cup | 2.6 ounces | 75 g | |
| Cornstarch | 1 tablespoon | ¼ ounce | 8 g | |
| Potato starch, sifted | 1 cup | 6 ounces | 170 g | |
| Confectioners' sugar, sifted | 1 cup | 3½ ounces | 100 g | |
| Dark brown sugar, packed | 1 cup | 9 ounces | 255 g | |
| Light brown sugar, packed | 1 cup | 7½ ounces | 213 g | |
| Butter | 1 tablespoon<br>4 tablespoons (½ stick) = ¼ cup<br>8 tablespoons (1 stick) = ½ cup<br>12 tablespoons (1½ sticks) = ¾ cup<br>16 tablespoons (2 sticks) = 1 cup<br>4 sticks = 2 cups | ½ ounce<br>2 ounces<br>4 ounces<br>6 ounces<br>8 ounces<br>16 ounces = 1 pound | 15 g<br>60 g<br>113 g<br>170 g<br>227 g<br>454 g | |
| Granulated sugar | 1 tablespoon<br>1 cup | ⅓ ounce<br>7 ounces | 10 g<br>200 g | |

*(continued)*

| Ingredients | Volume Measure | Ounces/ pounds | Grams (g)/ kilograms (kg) (1 kg = 1000 g = 2.2 lbs) | Canadian metric/ Milliliters (ml)/liters (l) (1 liter = 4⅓ cups) |
| --- | --- | --- | --- | --- |
| Milk or buttermilk | 1 cup | 8.5 ounces | 242 g | 250 ml |
| Sour cream | 1 cup | 8 ounces | 242 g | 250 ml |
| Egg | 1 large (out of shell) | 1.75 ounces | 50 g | |
| | Large yolk | 0.65 ounces | 18 g | |
| | Large white | 1.06 ounces | 30 g | |
| Raisins, packed | 1 cup | 6 ounces | 170 g | |
| Currants, packed | 1 cup | 3½ ounces | 100 g | |
| Dried apricot halves, packed | 1 cup | 6 ounces | 170 g | |
| Cranberries, fresh | 1 cup | 3¾ ounces | 105 g | |
| Cranberries, dried | ½ cup | 2 ounces | 60 g | |
| Pine nuts | ½ cup | 2½ ounces | 75 g | |
| Walnuts or pecans, chopped | 1 cup | 4 ounces | 110 g | |
| Almonds, blanched, or hazelnuts, skinned, chopped | 1 cup | 5 ounces | 140 g | |
| Chocolate chips | 1 cup | 6 ounces | 170 g | |

# Frequently Used Measurements

INCHES (in)/CENTIMETERS (cm)

(inches × 2.5 = centimeters)

1 inch = 2.54 cm; ¾ inch = 2 cm; ½ inch = 1 cm

0.4 in = 1 cm

FEET (ft)/METERS (m)

(feet ÷ 3.28 = meters)

1 foot = 0.305 m

3 feet = 0.914 m

1000 feet = 304.9 m

3.28 ft. = 1 m

## Common Baking Pan Sizes (measured across top from rim to rim)

| Pans | Inches | Centimeters |
|------|--------|-------------|
| Round | 7 | 17.8 |
| | 8 | 20 |
| | 9 | 23 |
| | 10 | 25.5 |
| | 11 | 28 |
| | 12 | 30.5 |
| Square | 8 | 20 × 20 |
| | 9 | 23 × 23 |
| Cookies sheets | 14 × 17 | 35.5 × 43 |
| Rectangular (sheet pan) | 9 × 13 | 22.9 × 33 |
| Jelly roll pan | 15½ × 10½ × 1 | 39 × 27 × 2.5 |
| Tube, ring, or Bundt | 9 | 23 |
| | 10 | 25.5 |
| Loaf | 9 × 5 × 3 | 23 × 12.5 × 7.5 |
| | 8½ × 4½ × 2¾ | 22 × 11 × 7 |
| | 5½ × 3 × 2⅛ | 14 × 8 × 5 |
| Soufflé mold, round | 8¼ (8-cup capacity) | 20 |

# Oven Temperature Chart

To convert Fahrenheit to Celsius, subtract 32 from °F, multiply by 5, and divide by 9.
To convert Celsius to Fahrenheit, multiply °C by 9; divide by 5, and add 32.

| °F (Fahrenheit) | °C (Celsius) | Gas Mark |
| --- | --- | --- |
| 32 | 0 | |
| 212 (boiling at sea level) | 100 | |
| 300 (slow oven) | 149 | 2 |
| 325 | 163 | 3 |
| 350 (moderate oven) | 175 | 4 |
| 375 | 190 | 5 |
| 400 (hot oven) | 204 | 6 |
| 425 | 220 | 7 |
| 450 | 230 | 8 |
| 475 | 246 | 9 |
| 500 | 260 | 10 |

# Sources

American Almond Products Company, Inc.
103 Walworth Street
Brooklyn, NY 11205
(800) 825-6663; (718) 875-8310
*www.americanalmond.com*
    Nut pastes and pastry fillings, especially:
roasted hazelnut praline, almond paste,
marzipan, pistachio paste, poppy seed filling,
and prune lekvar. (These products are also
available from King Arthur Flour Baker's
Catalogue; see below)

Broadway Panhandler
477 Broome Street
New York, NY 10013
(866) COOKWARE; (212) 966-3434
*www.broadwaypanhandler.com*
    A wide variety of cake-, pie-, and pastry-
baking equipment; cake decorating utensils

La Carreta
Sylvia Vergara
P.O. Box 70
Dixon, NM 87527
info@lacarretanewmexico.com
(505) 579-4358
*www.lacarretanewmexico.com*
    Organic New Mexican fruit preserves (with
and without chiles), especially: wild cherry
chile jam, green chile-lemon marmalade, wild
mint lemon jelly; also herbal vinegar and tea

Dean & DeLuca
560 Broadway
New York, NY 10012
(800) 221-7714; (212) 226-6800
*www.deandeluca.com*
    A wide variety of baking equipment and
utensils; dark and white chocolate, cocoa,
dried fruits and berries, nuts, many types of
flour, flavoring extracts

King Arthur Flour Baker's Catalogue
58 Billings Farm Road
White River Junction, VT 05001
(800) 827-6836
*www.bakerscatalogue.com*
    A wide variety of pie-, pastry-, and cake-
baking equipment and utensils, including
Silpat baking mats, baking parchment,
instant-read thermometers, rotary nut mills;
many types of chocolate and cocoa, pure extracts, coarse crystal and pearl sugar, fruit
oils, dried buttermilk powder, nuts, many
types of organic seeds, dried berries and
fruits, chocolate-coated raisins, grains, and
flours

New York Cake and Baking Distributors
56 West 22nd Street
New York, NY 10010
(800) 942-2539; (212) 675-2253
*www.nycake.com*

A wide variety of pastry-, pie-, and cake-baking and decorating equipment and utensils, including cardboard cake disks; many types of chocolate, decorating sugar

Penzeys Spices
19300 W. Janacek Court
P.O. Box 924
Brookfield, WI 53045-0924
(800) 741-7787; (262) 785-7677
*www.penzeys.com*
A wide variety of herbs and spices (including high-quality ground cinnamon, nutmeg, and ginger), cream of tartar, some extracts, cocoa, Mexican and Madagascan vanilla beans, dried and powdered lemon and orange peel

Simpson & Vail
P.O. Box 765, 3 Quarry Road
Brookfield, CT 06804
(800) 282-8327; (203) 775-0240
*www.svtea.com*
A wide variety of flavored citrus oils, El Rey white and dark chocolate, hazelnut and walnut oil, honey, unrefined, castor, and amber crystal sugar

Sweet Celebrations
7009 Washington Avenue South
Edina, MN 55439
(800) 328-6722; (952) 943-1508
*www.sweetc.com*
Cake-baking and decorating equipment and utensils, including cardboard cake disks, Silpat baking mats, pastry bags and tips; pie-baking equipment; dark and white chocolate, large crystal sugar, extracts

USGS Information Services
Box 25286
Denver, CO 80225
(888) ASK-USGS
*www.usgs.gov*
To order topographic maps indicating elevation, ask for customer service, and give your town and state (credit cards accepted)

Williams-Sonoma, Inc.
Mail Order Department
P.O. Box 379900
Las Vegas, NV 89137-9900
(800) 541-2233
*wws.williams-sonoma.com*
A wide variety of baking equipment and utensils, instant-read thermometers, Silpat baking mats, baking parchment, pie and pastry tools, some baking ingredients

Wilton Industries
2240 West 75th Street
Woodridge, IL 60517
(800) 794-5866; (630) 963-7100
*www.wilton.com*
Meringue powder, full line of cake-decorating products and utensils

Vanns Spices Ltd.
6105 Oakleaf Avenue
Baltimore, MD 21215
(800) 583-1693; (410) 358-3007
*www.vannsspices.com*
Exceptional spices (especially cinnamon), a wide variety of extracts

# Index

orange *(cont.)*

four-layer, sponge cake with tangerine mousse filling, 174–78

Grand Marnier sauce, 312

reduced-fat, tube cake with blueberry honey sauce, 211–14

shortbread, Highland, 242–44

Summit, soufflé with Grand Marnier sauce, 309–12

oven racks and thermometers, 34–35

oven temperatures, 24, 27, 34–35, 109–10, 328

Paradise Peak chocolate soufflé, 313–16

Parsons, Russ, 48

Passover mocha sponge cake, 187–90

Patent, Greg, 214

Payette pound cake with raspberry sauce, 146–50

peach(es):

-ginger crisp, 283–85

peeling of, 284

sour cream crisp, 285

peanut butter–butter cookies, Sun Valley, 225–27

Pearl, Stacy, 15, 138, 249

pecan(s):

in apricot upside-down cake with cardamom-honey sauce, 142–45

in black-and-white chocolate chip cookies, 236–38

bourbon pie, 275

cranberry pie, 275

cranberry streusel muffins, 47–50

-double chocolate biscotti, 245–48

in El Dorado cheesecake with glazed mango topping, 161–65

pie with nut pastry, Red Door, 270–75

Pedersen, Suzanne, 22, 291

Pépin, Jacques, 308

Perseo, Maureen, 10

piecrusts, pastry:

angel (meringue) pie shell, Chimayó mousse, with toasted pine nuts, 300–3

coconut crumb, mile-high lemon meringue pie with, 296–99

cream cheese, for rugelach, 253–55

crumb, for plum good crumb pie, 280–82

flaky butter, Pike's Peak apple pie with, 265–69

high-altitude baking of, 25, 264, 286

no-rolling-pin, for fresh fig tart with mascarpone-honey cream, 304–6

nut, Red Door pecan pie with, 270–75

whole-wheat, for pumpkin custard pie with ginger whipped cream, 286–90

pies (and cobblers, crisps, tarts), 263–306

black walnut, 275

bourbon pecan, 275

Chimayó mocha mousse angel, with toasted pine nuts, 300–3

cranberry pecan, 275

fresh berry tart with lemonade cream filling, 306

fresh fig tart with mascarpone-honey cream, 304–6

Hawaiian macadamia nut, 275

high-altitude baking of, 263–64

holiday cran-apple crostata, 291–95

mile-high lemon meringue, 296–99

peach-ginger crisp, 283–85

Pike's Peak apple, with flaky pastry, 265–69

plum good crumb, 280–82

pumpkin custard, with ginger whipped cream, 286–90

Red Door pecan, with nut pastry, 270–75

Santa Fe Roadhouse nectarine-plum-apricot cobbler, 276–79

sour cream peach or apple crisp, 285

Pike's Peak apple pie with flaky pastry, 265–69

pine nuts:

Chimayó mocha mousse angel pie with toasted, 300–3

-chocolate biscotti, 248

toasting of, 248

plum(s):

good plumb pie, 280–82

-nectarine-apricot cobbler, 276–79

popovers:

Durango, 81–83

high-altitude baking of, 59–60

poppy seeds:

for celestial challah, 92–96

filling, for rugelach, 253–55

-lemon loaf, Vail, 69–71

Porterfield, Sandy and Skip, 18, 22, 157

Porterfield pumpkin Bundt with snow white glaze, 154–56

potato starch and flour, 37, 187

in Passover mocha sponge cake, 187–90

pound cake, Payette, with raspberry sauce, 146–50

profiteroles, Twin Peaks, with ultimate chocolate sauce, 256–60

pumpkin:

Bundt with snow white glaze, Porterfield, 154–56

custard pie with ginger whipped cream, 286–90

raisin(s):

in Ann's Irish soda bread, 60–62

in applesauce cake with icing glaze, 134–37

in Aspen apple cake, 128–30

-cinnamon bread, 91

or currant scones, Highland, 72–74

in holiday cran-apple crostata, 292–95

in Kristin's trail bars, 261–62

-oatmeal cookies, Trout Dale, 234–35

Smoky Mountain, bran muffins, 54–57

in whole-wheat apple-oat muffins, 51–53

raspberry mousse, 177–78